19 Urban Questions
Teaching in the City
SECOND EDITION

EDITED BY Shirley R. Steinberg

FOREWORD BY Antonia Darder

PETER LANG
New York • Washington, D.C./Baltimore • Bern
Frankfurt am Main • Berlin • Brussels • Vienna • Oxford

The Library of Congress has catalogued the first edition as follows:

Steinberg, Shirley R.
Nineteen urban questions: teaching in the city—second edition /
edited by Shirley R. Steinberg.
p. cm. — (Counterpoints; vol. 215)
Includes bibliographical references and index.
1. Education, Urban—United States. 2. Critical pedagogy—United States.
I. Kincheloe, Joe L. II. Steinberg, Shirley R.
III. Series: Counterpoints (New York, N.Y.); v. 215.
LC5131.N56 2004   370'.9173'2—dc22   2003026733
ISBN 978-0-8204-5772-7 (first edition)
ISBN 978-1-4331-0886-0 (second edition)
ISSN 1058-1634

Bibliographic information published by **Die Deutsche Bibliothek**.
Die Deutsche Bibliothek lists this publication in the "Deutsche
Nationalbibliografie"; detailed bibliographic data is available
on the Internet at http://dnb.ddb.de/.

Cover design by Clear Point Designs
The paper in this book meets the guidelines for permanence and durability
of the Committee on Production Guidelines for Book Longevity
of the Council of Library Resources.

© 2010 Peter Lang Publishing, Inc., New York
29 Broadway, 18th Floor, New York, NY 10006
www.peterlang.com

Printed in the United States of America

for joe

Table of Contents

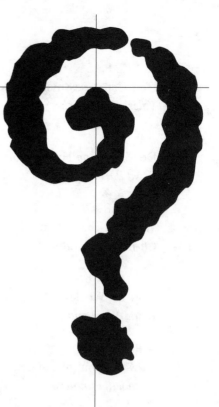

Shirley R. Steinberg

In Praise of Urban Educators and Urban Kids

 Creating a subculture of education called urban education has not been all that easy. Creating anything that wasn't prescribed by the forefathers (whomever they were) is never easy. North American education is traditional, and we aren't supposed to mess with the traditional. However, in the past two decades new voices have scratched and scraped the concept of urban education into the dominant educational discourse and convinced many that, indeed, urban education is different than suburban or rural education. Included in this revelation is the tacit embedding of race, class, and ethnicity. In fact, the word urban has become a thinly veiled descriptor for the dangerous, the bad neighborhoods, the non-white, and the poor. Along with that redefinition of urban is the feeling by many educators that teaching in the city is the worst job possible. Different programs have half-heartedly attempted to draw teachers into urban areas with scholarships, additional pay (sort of like battle pay), and forgiven college loans. When I taught pre-service teachers in Brooklyn, I heard the groans every semester when students were placed in Bed/Sty or Flatbush, and the jealous flashes when others were placed in Park Slope. In the city there are good neighborhoods and bad neighborhoods...urban education is in the bad neighborhoods.

When Joe Kincheloe and I conceptualized this book in 2004, we knew that the conversation in education needed to address the needs of urban schools, teachers, students, and parents. We felt the best way to start this engagement was through questions. The first edition was a resounding success, and this second edition echoes the first volume but has replaced some questions and added to others. And, in the end, we ended up with even more questions. The contributors to this new volume have taken into account the previous conversations and attempted to expand and enhance this new urban discourse. In doing so, we all are committed to the celebration of the urban: the kids, the teachers, the schools, the cities, and the communities. While realizing that it can be hard to teach in the city, we also contend it can be the most rewarding place to be: for a teacher or a student. The city calls, and good urban educators answer.

Images of urban kids and teachers have been splashed through television and film for decades. Teachers downtrodden by gangs, students' refusal to engage, dark crevices and corners in which danger lurks…drugs, rape, shootings, the list goes on. Hollywood answers urban school problems by enlisting the principal *Lean on Me* or *The Substitute* to make sure the kids get straightened out. Depictions of white savior teachers who come (with risk to life and limb) to teach these wild city beings and their *Dangerous Minds,* are frequent, and viewers assume that urban schools are dangerous and hopeless. These media representations have contributed to a cultural consciousness that creates a fear of urban schools.

This book does not address urban education as a deficit model. We do not believe that one is punished when assigned to an urban school, and we do not believe that students will fail because they are in an urban school. We believe that those who teach in urban schools should be prepared to be the cream of the educational crop. Instead of the deskilled rubric-chanting teachers slumped behind their broken-down desks, handing out worksheets and looking through the kids, we call for urban educators to be the best-informed, research-oriented, engaged teachers with the highest expectations. In order to nurture urban intellectuals, we have prepared this book, which will support and inform those who want to prepare urban kids to be successful in and out of school. Our work is grounded in a critical pedagogy, which recognizes that educators work with students within their own cultural context. One of the most important aspects in hip hop is the notion of respect: where musicians, DJs, poets, writers, dancers and audiences engage in the urban discourse of respect. Instead of touting the worn-out notion of 'loving one's neighbor,' one should look to respect and to be respected. Our concepts of critical urban pedagogy begin with respect and the intrinsic need to be respected. Urban educators who respect students, community, and the city are able to access needs and create meaningful environments for education to take place.

My deepest thanks to those who have contributed to this volume; I respect each of you and am privileged to have your work here. I also want to thank my students, you have informed and challenged me, and you have my deepest respect and admiration. And finally, I want to acknowledge Joe Kincheloe, my partner in every conceivable way; his death has left a void in my heart, and I honor him and miss him. Joe was the Tennessee hillbilly who was as at home in the heart of Manhattan as he was in his Blue Ridge Mountains. Joe co-created the Urban Education Program at the CUNY Graduate Program and left a legacy in the scores of students who passed through doors once closed to kids from bad neighborhoods.

Antonia Darder

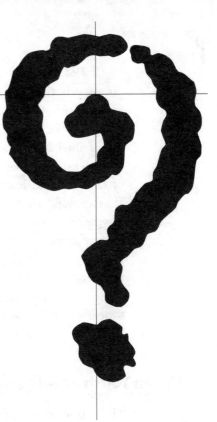

Schooling Bodies
Critical Pedagogy and Urban Youth

The body is our medium for having a world.

— *Maurice Merleau-Ponty*

[T]he body is also directly involved in a political field; power relations have an immediate hold upon it; they invest it, mark it, train it, torture it, force it to carry out tasks to perform ceremonies, to emit signs.

— *Michel Foucault*

Estranged labor . . . estranges humanity from its own body, as it does the external, natural world, as it does . . . [our] mental existence . . . [our] human existence.

— *Karl Marx*

The human body constitutes primacy in all material relationships. Without the materiality of the body, all notions of teaching and learning are reduced to mere abstractions that attempt to situate the mind as an independent agent, absent of both individual and collective emotions, sensations, yearnings, fears and joys. It is the body that provides the medium for our existence as subjects of history and politically empowered agents of change, but, as Peter McLaren (1999) reminds us, "bodies are also the primary means by which capitalism does its job" (xiii). We are molded and shaped by the structures, policies and practices of domination and exclusion that violently insert our bodies into the alienating morass of an intensified global division of labor.

In *Pedagogy and the Politics of the Body,* Sherry Shapiro (1999) contends that "any approach committed to human liberation must seriously address the body as a site for both oppression and liberation" (18). Yet, seldom are the significance and place of the body made central to discussions of emancipatory pedagogy. As a consequence, educational efforts to reinvent the social and material conditions within classrooms do closely consider the significance of the flesh in the process of teaching and learning. That is, unless the discussion turns to "classroom management"—a convenient euphemism for both the covert and overt control of youth's corporeality. Meanwhile, many classrooms and community settings exist as arenas where knowledge is objectified and abstracted from its concrete reality. Youth are then expected to acquiesce to an alienating function, which artificially severs their body from its role in the construction of knowledge. Hence, the production of knowledge is neither engaged nor presented as a historical and collective process, occurring within the flesh and all its sensual capacities for experiencing and responding to the world.

Urban Youth as Integral Beings[1]

The notion of engaging urban youth as embodied and integral human beings has received limited attention. Instead psychosocial discussions tend to over-emphasize the role of subjectivity or over-psychologized notions of the self at the expense of critical development and collective consciousness. This inadvertently sidelines affective and relational needs of the body that must endure, resist, and struggle to become free from the ideological and corporal entanglements that domesticate youth. Yet, as educators and cultural workers, we cannot deny that the body is enormously significant to the development of critical capacities in youth. Often missing in discussions of pedagogy is a more complex understanding of our humanity, in which the body is central to critical formation. Paulo Freire, particularly in his later works, attested firmly to this significance of the body in the act of knowing. "I know with my entire body, with feelings, with passion and also with reason" (1995, 30). "It is my entire body that socially knows. I cannot, in the name of exactness and rigor, negate my body, my emotions and my feelings" (1993, 105).

Unfortunately, however, the rubrics of traditional pedagogy assume that teaching and learning are solely cognitive acts. As such, educators and cultural workers need not concern themselves with the affective responses of youth, unless they are deemed as "inappropriate," at which time the psychologist or social worker is summoned to evaluate the "problem" youth. Nevertheless, it cannot be denied that learning, as well as teaching, can be very exciting, painful, frustrating, and joyful. Freire (1998) often referred to these very human responses when he considered the process of studying. "Studying is a demanding occupation, in the process of which we will encounter pain, pleasure, victory, defeat, doubt and happiness" (78)—all, affective and physical responses of the body.

Thus, to become *full subjects of history* requires that educators grapple with the fact that intellect is but one aspect of our humanity, which evolves from the body's collective interactions with the world. And as such, this requires our willingness to engage with youth bodies more substantively in our efforts to forge a revolutionary practice of education. It is not enough then to teach and learn solely as an abstract cognitive process, where the analysis of words and texts is considered paramount to the construction of knowledge. Such an educational process of estrangement functions to alienate youth from "nature . . . the inorganic body of humanity" (Marx, 1844). As such, they become alienated from their own bodies and that of others. Hence, educators must create the conditions for urban youth to labor in the flesh, investing themselves materially, in the construction of meaning and in the struggle to reinvent their world. This is vital to a critical pedagogy of the body, given that "we learn things about the world by acting and changing the world around us. It is [through] this process of change, of transforming the material world from which we emerged, [where] creation of the cultural and historical world takes place. This transformation of the world [is] done by us while it makes and remakes us" (Freire, 1993, 108).

Teaching in the Flesh

In our efforts to understand the dynamics of the classroom, teaching and learning have to be acknowledged as human labor that takes place within our bodies as we strive to make sense of the material conditions and social relations of power that shape our particular histories. Only through such an approach can educators begin to build an emancipatory practice of education where youth are not expected to confront themselves, and one another, as strangers but rather as fully embodied human beings from the moment they enter the classroom. This is to say that a pedagogy of the body seeks to contend in the flesh with the embodied histories and knowledge of the disenfranchised as well as the social and material forces that shape the conditions in which we teach and learn. This requires that educators acknowledge with legitimacy the manner in which youth read their world, without denying their own visceral responses—whether these include fear, confusion, doubt or anger. Instead, educators can create meaningful opportunities to grapple with the tensions that differences in worldview create. In this way, our bodies remain central to the construction of knowledge.

Again, Freire (1993) speaks to the undeniable centrality of the body in the act of knowing:

> The importance of the body is indisputable; the body moves, acts, rememorizes, the struggle for its liberation; the body in sum, desires, points out, announces, protests, curves itself, rises, designs and remakes the world . . . and its importance has to do with a certain sensualism . . . contained by the body, even in connection with cognitive ability . . . it's absurd to separate the rigorous acts of knowing the world from the [body's] passionate ability to know. (87)

But it is exactly this sensualism with its revolutionary potential to nurture self-determination and the empowerment of youth as both individuals and social beings that is systematically stripped away from the educational process of public schools and community programs. Conservative ideologies of social control historically linked to Puritanical notions of the body as evil, sensual pleasure as sinful, and passions as corrupting to the sanctity of the spirit continue to be reflected in the rule-based pedagogical policies and practices of schooling today. The sensuality of the body is discouraged in schools through the prominent practice of containing and immobilizing youth bodies within hard chairs and desks that restrict their contact with each other and the environment around them. In the classical tradition, the sensual body is quickly subordinated to the mind, while ideas are privileged over the senses (Seidel, 1964). As a consequence, urban youth, who come from the working class or cultural communities where the senses and the body are given greater primacy in the act of knowing and being, are often coerced into sacrificing their knowledge of the body's sensuality, creativity and vitality, in favor of an atomized, deadened, and analytical logic of existence. This may help to explain the propensity for white educators to diagnose African American boys as hyperactive or Chicano boys as suffering from "attention deficit disorder."

Sexuality is also strongly repressed and denied within the four walls of the classroom, despite the fact that it is an ever-present human phenomenon. This is the case even at puberty, when bodies are particularly sensitive to often heightened and confusing sensations. Many educators who are not particularly comfortable with their bodies fail to critically engage questions of sexuality beyond the often-repeated cliché of "raging hormones" to refer to teenage sexuality. Consequently, youth are not only pedagogically abandoned but also left at the mercy of the media and corporate pirates[2] that very deliberately and systematically prey upon the field of powerful bodily sensations, emotions and stirrings of youth.

> In the slick world of advertising, teenage bodies are sought after for the exchange value they generate in marketing an adolescent sexuality that offers a marginal exoticism and ample pleasures for the largely male consumer. Commodification reifies and fixates the complexity of youth and the range of possible identities they might assume while simultaneously exploiting them as fodder for the logic of the market (Giroux, 1998).

Frightened by their ambivalence and fear of youth bodies, public schooling and even community policies and practices coerce educators into silence, rigidly limiting any discussion of one of the most significant aspects of our humanity. The message is clear; everyone, especially youth, is expected to check their sexuality (along with all other aspects of their lived histories) at the door prior to entering. Yet despite the difficulties and hardships that such silence creates for many youth—isolation and increasing rates of suicide among many gay and lesbian youth, for instance—schools, much like churches, act as moral leaders, monitoring and repressing the body's participation.

Missing is both the school and community's willingness to bring together the sexuality and intellectuality of youth in the process of their social and academic formation. This functions to sever the body's desires and sensations from the construction of knowledge and consciousness. In turn, this also interferes dramatically with the capacity of urban youth to know themselves, one another, and their world. Similarly, such practices negatively impact their knowledge of "the other," rendering youth alienated and estranged from any human suffering that exists outside of the particular and limited scope of their identities, whether linked to gender, ethnicity, sexuality, or skin color (Soelle, 1975; Shapiro, 1999).

Hence, it should be no surprise to learn that domesticating policies and practices of urban education (i.e., high-stakes testing, teaching-to-the-test, tracking, etc.) which abstract, fragment, and decontextualize theories of teaching and learning, seldom function in the interest of oppressed populations. Instead, youth are objectified, alienated and domesticated into passive roles that not only debilitate but also sabotage their capacity for social agency. In so doing, the existing physical needs of urban youth are generally ignored or rendered insignificant in an overriding effort to obtain their obedience and conformity to the oppressive policies and practices of public schooling.

Yet in spite of major institutional efforts to control the body's desires, pleasures, and mobility, youth seldom surrender their bodies completely or readily acquiesce to authoritarian practices—practices which in themselves provide the impetus for resistance, especially in those youth whose dynamic histories are excluded within mainstream life (Shapiro, 1999). Instead, many of them engage in the construction of their own cultural forms of resistance that may or may not always function in their best interest. More often than not these expressions of youth resistance are enacted through their bodies—be it with clothing, hairstyle, postures, manner of walking, way of speaking, and the piercing and tattooing of the body. These represent not only acts of resistance but alternative ways of knowing and being in the world, generally perceived by officials as both transgressive and disruptive to the social order of schools. Moreover, such views of youth are exacerbated by what Henry Giroux (1998) contends is a "new form of representational politics [that] has emerged in media culture fueled by degrading visual depictions of youth as criminal, sexually decadent, drug crazed, and illiterate. In short, youth are viewed as a growing threat to the public order."

Educators, whose bodies are similarly restricted, alienated, and domesticated by their school districts, are under enormous pressure to follow strict district policies and procedures for classroom conduct. This includes dispensing prepackaged curricula, instead of employing more creative and critical approaches, grounded in the actual needs of youth. Given the impact of disembodied practices, urban educators often experience uphill battles in meeting the standardized mandates, which systematically extricate youth's bodies from their learning. Nowhere is this more apparent than in low-income schools across the nation, where teaching-to-the-test has become the curriculum of choice.

As a consequence, many educators, consciously or unconsciously, reproduce a variety of authoritarian practices—in the name of classroom or group management—in efforts to maintain physical control. Those who struggle in these repressive contexts to implement more liberating strategies are often forced to become masters of deception—saying what the school principal wishes to hear, while doing behind closed doors what they believe is in concert with a more democratic vision of education. Unfortunately, the hidden physical stress of such duplicity can drive some of the most effective educators away from their chosen vocation, irrespective of their political commitment. The alienation that this engenders often becomes intolerable. Others, who begin to feel defeated and frustrated, adopt more authoritarian approaches to manipulate and coerce *cooperation,* while justifying the means in the name of helping urban youth succeed socially, academically, or as good workers. What cannot be overlooked here is the manner in which authoritarian practices are designed not only to "blindfold youth and lead them to a domesticated future" (Freire, 1970, 79) but also to alienate and estrange educators and cultural workers from their labor. Concerned with the need to restore greater freedom, joy and creativity in their pedagogy, Freire (1998) urged educators to:

> critically reject their domesticating role; in so doing, they affirm themselves . . . as educators and cultural workers by demythologizing the authoritarianism of teaching packages [or prescribed youth programs] and their administration in the intimacy of their world, which is also the world of [the youth with whom they labor]. In classrooms, with the doors closed, it is difficult to have the world unveiled (9).

A critical pedagogy of the body is also salient to rethinking university education, where there seems to be little pedagogical tolerance for the emotional needs of young adults. "Somewhere in the intellectual history of the West there developed the wrongheaded idea that mind and heart are antagonists, that scholarship must be divested of emotion, that spiritual journeys must avoid intellectual concerns" (Lifton, 1990, 29). This tradition sets an expectation, for example, that professors and students compartmentalize themselves within the classroom, without any serious concern for the manner in which the very essence of university education is often tied to major moments of life transitions. That is to say that it is a time when students are being asked to make major commitments and material investments related to the direction of their very uncertain futures. Simultaneously, students are expected to engage their studies and research as objective, impartial observers, even when the object of their study is intimately linked to conditions of human suffering.

Freire (1993) argues that traditional academic expectations of the university affirm "that feelings corrupt research and its findings, the fear of intuition, the categorical negation of emotion and passion, the belief in technicism [which] all ends in convincing many that the more neutral we are in our actions, the more objective and efficient we will be" (106). Hence, college youth are slowly but surely socialized to labor as uncritical, descriptive, "neutral" scholars, dispassionate and removed from their intellectual constructions of the world. This results in scholarship conceived through a deeply alienated way of knowing, where "values are restricted to a scientific definition" and knowledge becomes the property of something separated from human emotions, feeling, and connection" (Shapiro, 1999, 40). The sad and unfortunate consequence here is that such knowledge seldom leads urban youth to grapple with moral questions that might fundamentally challenge the social and material relations that sustain human suffering in their communities. Hence, as Shapiro (1999) argues, such "abstraction and exclusion break down relational understanding and bleed history dry, leaving the scars of separation" (39).

A Critical Pedagogy of the Body

As our consciousness becomes more and more abstracted, we become more and more detached from our bodies. One could say that a hidden function of public schooling is, indeed, to initiate and incorporate poor, working-class youth and youth of color into social and material conditions of labor that normalize their alienation and detachment from the body. This function is absolutely necessary for social control and the extraction of surplus labor, given that the body is the medium through which we wage political struggle and through which we transform our historical conditions as individuals and social beings.

Hence, the perception of youth as integral human beings is paramount to both questions of ethics and the development of critical consciousness. All aspects of our humanity, with their particular pedagogical needs, are present and active at all times—that is to say, that all aspects of our humanity are integral to the process of teaching and learning. Hence, to perceive students in terms of only their minds and to subscribe to only one way of knowing can translate into an objectifying and debilitating experience for urban youth despite the intellectual and cultural strengths they might possess. Instead, they must be acknowledged as entering any context as whole persons and should be respected and treated as such. The degree to which this is possible, however, is directly linked to how willing and able educators are to be fully present as well as to their capacity to enter into intimate and meaningful relationships with urban youth, their parents, and their communities.

For educators who aspire to a critical pedagogy of the body, the willingness to enter into relationships with urban youth that are respectfully personal and intimate is paramount. Such horizontal relationships go hand in hand with obliterating the debilitating myth that an impersonal and emotionally distant approach to engaging youth is more "professional or appropriate." Similarly, the notion of being "professional" is also often tied to the belief that our academic relationships with urban youth in the classroom are not really part of the "real world." Yet, Freire adamantly countered this view of teaching. Instead, he argues that,

> What we do in the classroom is not an isolated moment separate from the "real world." It is entirely connected to the real world and it is the real world, which places both powers and limits on any critical course. Because the world is in the classroom, whatever transformation we provoke has a conditioning effect outside our small space. But the outside has a conditioning effect on the space also, interfering with our ability to build a critical culture separate from the dominant mass culture (Shor and Freire, 1987, 26)

For this reason, enacting a critical pedagogy of the body within the classroom demands that educators be cognizant of the social, political, and economic conditions that shape urban communities and the youth who share their classrooms. To do this requires the integration of critical principles that can support urban youth in their struggle to name their own world and to consider ways in which to transform conditions or inequalities that reproduce their marginalization. In brief, this calls for an educational approach that encompasses the following principles of practice associated with the incorporation of the body into the process of teaching and learning:

- Educators engage the emotional and physical responses and experiences of urban youth as meaningful indicators of strengths and limitations that they face in the process of their academic, social, and political formation.
- Knowledge is understood as a historical and collective process, emanating from the body's relationship to the world. The body is seen as primary in efforts by urban youth to construct knowledge and develop moral thought.
- The mind and its cognitive capacities are understood as only one medium for the construction of knowledge. With this in mind, urban youth are seen as integral human beings, whose minds, bodies, hearts and spirits are all implicated in the process of teaching and learning. This also speaks to the manner in which our educational practices must reach youth in their innermost emotional and psychic centers.
- Cultural knowledge derived from the body's collective interactions with the world constitutes a significant resource of human survival. Classroom and community relationships, materials, and activities must reflect this knowledge with both respect for difference and cultural accuracy.
- Teaching and learning are understood as a process of human labor that is intricately tied to the material conditions and social relations of power that shape classroom life. Hence the question of power and the uses of authority must be interrogated consistently in academic relationships with urban youth.
- Knowledge construction is a collective, historical phenomenon which occurs continuously both in and outside of the school environment. To privilege school knowledge and ignore the lived experience of urban youth limit their capacities to participate effectively in the construction of knowledge.
- Educators are committed to creating meaningful interactions and activities within classrooms that support urban youth as they grapple honestly with

tensions of inequality they encounter daily, whether these are associated with race, class, gender, sexuality, or other forms of difference.

- Educators' knowledge of their own bodies, including their sexuality, is an important teaching competency and understood as significant to their ability to interact effectively with urban youth.

- Acts of resistance by urban youth tied to their bodies (i.e., clothes, piercings, tattoos, etc.) can signal meaningful and alternative ways of knowing and relating to the world. Opportunities are created for youth to reflect, affirm, and challenge the meaning of these acts of resistance in their lives.

- Space is consistently created within classrooms to permit urban youth to control the aesthetic and physical conditions, including the definition and execution of their knowledge, politics, fashion, voice, and participation.

- Decolonizing the body from educational and social constraints that limit and repress the development of social agency is a major intent within a critical pedagogy of the body. Educators work together with urban youth to challenge those conditions of their labor within schools that render them passive and domesticate their dreams.

Forging an Emancipatory Vision

Forging an emancipatory educational practice, then, is about bringing us all back home to our bodies in a world where every aspect of our daily life—birth, death, marriage, family, school, work, leisure, parenthood, spirituality, and even entertainment—is monitored and controlled.[3] Under such a regime of power our bodies are left numb; alienated and fragmented, urban youth are left defenseless and at the mercy of capital. The consequence is a deep sense of personal and collective dissatisfaction generated by a marketplace that cannot satisfy the human needs of the body—needs that can only be met through relationships that break the alienation and isolation so prevalent in the classroom life of urban youth today (Brosio, 1994). Through integrating principles that sustain a critical pedagogy of the body, educators in concert with youth can create a space in which such relationships can be established and nourished within the process of teaching and learning.

As such, it is absolutely imperative that in constructing principles for a critical pedagogy, we acknowledge that the origin of emancipatory possibility and human solidarity resides squarely in the body (Eagleton (2003). It is through the collective interactions of integral bodies within the classroom that the possibility of moral thought can be awakened. And it is such moral thought that places our collective bodies back into history and into the political discourse. Moreover, it is the absence of a truly democratic moral language and practice of the body that stifles our capacity for social struggle today. For example, many educators across the country bemoan, justifiably so, the conditions created by high-stakes testing and other accountability measures that negatively impact their lives as educators and the lives of their students. Yet there has been a failure among educators to communicate a clear and coherent emancipatory moral message to challenge the shallow moralism of the current administration's educational panacea—No Child Left Behind.[4] In response, there are those that would argue that this is a direct result of educators' alienated complicity with the structure of educational inequalities and the contradictions inherent in their lack of politics within a highly charged political arena.

However, what I argue here is that life within schools and society requires the development of a moral political language that can safeguard the dignity and integrity of all human differences intrinsic to a pluralistic nation. This is impossible to achieve without an educational approach anchored in the needs of the body. For without a critical pedagogy of the body to enact an emancipatory vision, the rhetoric of democratic education or democratic society is rendered meaningless. Genuine democracy requires the body's interaction with the social and material world in ways that nurture meaningful and transformative participation. It must exist as a practice in which human beings interact individually and collectively as equally empowered subjects.

Because we produce our lives collectively, any critical praxis of the body must engage oppression as "the starting point for the explanation of human history. This then becomes a materialist liberation, where explanations cannot be limited to any one oppression, or leave untouched any part of reality, any domain of knowledge, any aspect of the world" (Shapiro, 1999, 65). For all forms of social and material oppression block, disrupt, and corrupt the fluid participation of oppressed bodies within the world, reifying exclusionary human relations in the interest of economic imperatives without regard for the destruction to bodies left behind. When human needs such as food, shelter, meaningful livelihood, healthcare, education, and the intimacy of a community are not met, bodies are violated. Violated bodies easily gravitate to whatever can provide a quick fix to ease the pain and isolation of an alienated existence. As such, a critical pedagogy of the body must seek to create the social and material conditions that can give rise to the organic expression of our humanity and the practice of *teaching as an act of love* (Darder, 2002; Freire 1997, 1998).

Love as an emancipatory and revolutionary principle compels us to become part of a new, decolonizing and embodied culture that cultivates human connection, intimacy, trust and honesty, from the body out into the world. "With love we affirm and are affirmed. In the sociopolitical struggle against death from hunger, disease, exploitation, war, destruction of the earth, and against hopelessness, there is a great and growing need for out capacity to become 'body-full' with love" (Shapiro, 1999, 99). Love herein functions as an ethical principle which motivates the struggle to create mutually life-enhancing opportunities for all students. It is for this reason that Freire repeatedly argued that ethics is a significant place of departure for both our private and public lives.[5] Here, ethics constitutes a political question, which in the final analysis is also a moral one.

In times of uncertainty and economic instabilities, as are currently at work in urban settings, great moral courage is required to voice our dissent against public policies and practices that betray urban youth and their communities, systematically rendering them expendable and disposable. To transform such conditions within classrooms and society, we need a critical pedagogy solidly committed to the body's liberation as a sensual, thinking, knowing, and feeling subject of history. This entails rewriting the body into our understanding of teaching, through calling forth the establishment of new conditions for both thinking and acting within urban schools. *19 Urban Questions: Teaching in the City* asks questions which need to be asked. The answers given in these chapters open a dialogue, which addresses integral needs of urban students. Of course, the book also leaves us with more questions; one hopes that we will continue creating more questions, more conversation about the needs of urban children and youth. Classroom conditions that begin with the primacy of the body carry radical possibilities for reconnecting urban youth more deeply to their development as fully integral human beings. Most importantly, the body "is the material foundation upon which the desire for human liberation and social transformation rest" (Shapiro, 1999, 100). And in so being, the body constitutes an essential dimension in the development of a critical pedagogy for the schooling of urban youth today.

NOTES

1. I expand here on the idea of "students as integral beings" first presented in Chapter 3 of Darder, A. (2004). *Reinventing Paulo Freire: A Pedagogy of Love.*

2. See the *Frontline* production of *Merchants of Cool* by Douglas Rushkoff, an incisive report on the creators and marketers of popular culture for teenagers.

3. See Henri Lefebvre (1971). *Everyday Life in the Modern World.*

4. See Stan Karp's article "Equity Claims for NCLB Don't Pass the Test" in *Rethinking Schools* (Spring 2003). The article provides a great explanation about the shortcomings of the act. You can find the article and more information about Rethinking Schools online at: www.rethinkingschools.org

5. See Paulo Freire's writings: *Pedagogy of the City*; *Pedagogy of Hope*; and *Teachers as Cultural Workers: Letters to Those Who Dare Teach.*

REFERENCES

Brosio, R. (1994). *A Radical Democratic Critique of Capitalist Education.* New York: Peter Lang.

Darder, A. (2002). *Reinventing Paulo Freire: A Pedagogy of Love.* Boulder, CO: Westview.

Eagleton, T. (2003). *After Theory.* New York: Basic Books.

Foucault, M. (1995). *Discipline and Punish: The Birth of the Prison.* New York: Vintage.

Freire, P. (1970). *Pedagogy of the Oppressed.* New York: Seabury.

——.(1993). *Pedagogy of the City.* New York: Continuum.

——.(1995). *Pedagogy of Hope.* New York: Continuum.

——. (1997). *Pedagogy of the Heart.* New York: Continuum.

——(1998) *Teachers as Cultural Workers: Letters to Those Who Dare Teach.* Boulder, CO: Westview.

Giroux, H. (1998). *Teenage Sexuality, Body Politics and the Pedagogy of Display.* in Jon Epstein and Simon Prosser, eds. *Youth, Youth Culture, and Identity.* Malden, MA: Basil Blackwell, pp. 24–55. Article available at: http://www.gseis.ucla.edu/courses/ed253a/Giroux/Giroux3.html

Lefebvre, H. (1971). *Everyday Life in the Modern World.* London: Penguin.

Lifton, R. (1990). "The Genocidal Mentality." *Tikkun,* 5(3), 29–32 and 97–98.

Marx, K. (1844) *The Alienation of Labor. Economic and Philosophic Manuscripts of 1844.* See <www.wsu.edu:8080/~dee/MODERN/ALIEN.HTM#NT2>

McLaren, P. (1999). Foreword for S. Shapiro *Pedagogy and the Politics of the Body.* New York: Garland.

Merleau-Ponty, M. (2002). *The Phenomenology of Perception.* New York:Routledge.

Seidel, G. (1964). *Martin Heidegger and the Pre-Socratics: An Introduction to His Thought.* Lincoln: University of Nebraska Press.

Shapiro, S. (1999). *Pedagogy and the Politics of the Body: A Critical Praxis.* New York: Garland.

Shor, I. and P. Freire (1987*). A Pedagogy for Liberation.* South Hadley, MA: Bergin and Garvey.

Soelle, D. (1975). *Suffering.* Philadelphia: Fortress.

CHAPTER ONE

Joe L. Kincheloe

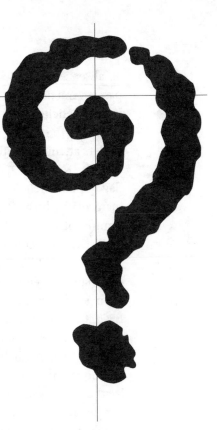

Why a Book
on Urban Education?

 Why a book on urban education? Because in the early twenty-first century one of the most compelling concerns involves the question of what to do about our neglected urban schools. Thirty-one percent of U.S. elementary and secondary students go to school in 226 large urban districts. There are nearly 16,000 school districts in the United States, and almost one-third of all students attend 1.5 percent of them (Fuhrman, 2002). As Philip Anderson and Judith Summerfield write in their chapter in this volume, another important reason for focusing attention on urban education involves the fact that in the urban context one finds "the emergent American culture." Indeed, they conclude, the ways in which urban educators shape the urban pedagogy in the coming years are central to the way Americans reinvent the nation. With this in mind, the United States faces an uncertain future because in these 226 urban districts, observers have found a wide diversity of problems and successes.

The Perpetual Crisis of Urban Education

Urban education is always in crisis—yesterday, today, and certainly in the near future. Teacher shortages force many urban school administrators to scramble madly during the first weeks of school to fill classroom vacancies. Inadequate funds cause cutbacks in essential services in the middle of the school year. In contemporary U.S. society, the use of the term *urban* itself has become in many quarters a signifier for poverty, nonwhite violence, narcotics, bad neighborhoods, an absence of family values, crumbling housing, and failing schools. Over the past several decades educational researchers have been producing data confirming the deficits of urban youth, while sensationalizing media produce images of urban youth running wild and out of control. In this context many urban school leaders attempt to hide the problems undermining education at their particular schools (Kozleski, 2002; Ciani, 2002; NWREL, 1999). Many schools, under the flag of public relations, mask their dropout rates. The critical problems besiege many of us who work in urban systems, and we have come to realize that without significant structural changes, even increased funding will only prop up pathological systems and provide little help for students and teachers.

In the middle of the eye of the perpetual crisis, teachers keep on teaching and many students keep on learning. Indeed, there are urban teachers who perform good work in a context in which impediments are many and resources few. Even if resources were provided, if equal funding of urban school systems were mandated, there would still be inadequate monies. Poor urban schools are so in need of financial help that equal funding would have to be supplemented by additional infusions of resources just to get to where they might be able to visualize the equality of resources on the distant horizon. Overwhelmed by these disparities and the crisis atmosphere surrounding them, urban policymakers have sought to replace huge, bureaucratic systems overseen by boards of education with new smaller, locally operated organizations.

Chicago experimented with such a plan in the late 1980s, establishing local school councils that attempted to put communities in contact with their schools. Results have been mixed and their successes open to diverse interpretations (Halford, 1996). In New York City in 2002–2003, political and educational leaders debated the role of boards of education as Mayor Michael Bloomberg sought an alternative framework for governing the city's schools. The crisis atmosphere and the uncertainty of the continuity of urban educational governance structures make it difficult for urban school administrators and teachers to focus on long-term projects. Teachers learn quickly that numerous classroom interruptions are the norm and that they have precious little time for lesson planning and pedagogical reflection on their practice (Lewis & Smith, 1996). Crisis management and survival until the end of the school day too often become the modi operandi of urban education.

Gangsta Paradise: Representations of Urban Education

It has become obvious to many scholars and educators that something has changed in the contemporary era. Over the last several decades, new structures of cultural space and time generated by the bombardment of electronic images have colonized our consciousness, shaping the way we see ourselves and the world. Electronic transmissions from radio, TV, popular music, movies, video, e-mail, and the Internet have saturated us with information about the world around us. Some refer to this new world as hyperreality—a place with so much input that we have difficulty processing all the data we encounter. In hyperreality the information that is electronically produced often takes on a realism that trumps our everyday lived experiences. The world we view on TV often shapes our perspectives more profoundly than what we directly observe in the society around us (Kincheloe, 2001; Kincheloe, 2002). In this context, consider media representations of urban education. Portrayed in film and TV as a danger zone, inner-city schools are seen as homogeneous locales of peril where no one should ever venture.

In the 90s, Hollywood films about urban education moved from the feminine missionary of Michelle Pfeiffer's Lou Anne Johnson in *Dangerous Minds* to Tom Berenger's macho special forces operative Shale in *The Substitute*. Whereas *Dangerous Minds* promotes Pfeiffer as a white savior of the uncivilized African American and Latino students of the 'hood, Berenger's Shale represents the end of hope. Shale's final solution is to kill them all as he "terminates" the cocaine ring-leading black principal (Ernie Hudson) and many of his students of color in full gangsta regalia, representing public education's Battle of Armageddon. The audience knows that tax-supported city schooling is a failure and that society must find a new way—prison—to deal with these "urban animals." *The Substitute* resonated with so many viewers that it spawned two appropriately named sequels—*The Substitute 2: School's Out* and *The Substitute 3: Winner Takes All*.

While there are many other films in this genre, such as *187*, suffice it to say that these films, combined with literally millions of TV news images of inner cities, city youth of color, and urban schools in poor neighborhoods, help inscribe particular affective and cognitive impressions with political/ideological consequences. Indeed, many Americans from suburban and rural areas know more about urban youth and city-dwelling African Americans, Latinos, Asian Americans, and Arab Americans from media images than from face-to-face contact. Thus, a sociocultural chasm has been produced between middle-class teacher education students and the students they will teach if they do their student teaching or obtain positions in urban schools in poor communities. Also, these representations, as they filter into the racial common sense and the folk psychologies of the larger society, present real obstacles to urban students attempting to succeed in schools. In this context such students have to deal with negative stereotyping in relation to their scholastic aptitude and their character.

Such representations even affect scholarly fields. In adolescent psychology, for example, it is interesting that so little research has been produced about factors of race and socioeconomic class as they relate to the identity development of young people. In many educational circles, inquiry into the representations of urban schools and students in media productions is still viewed as a frivolous form of research, with little to contribute to the study of teaching and learning (Henke, 2000). It is amazing that in the first decade of the twenty-first century, so little research has been produced in relation to urban education and urban students (Fuhrman, 2002). Indeed, most research on child and adolescent development involves middle-class whites. The lack of information on low-socioeconomic-class nonwhite urban youth is in itself a form of institutional racism (IUYL, 1996). A critical urban education that understands the complexity of the intersection of race, class, gender, sexual, religious, and ability-related dynamics as they relate to education seeks to address these racism-produced deficiencies.

The Blurred Boundaries of Urban Education

There is nothing simple about urban education. Just when we think that we've made a definitive statement about the uniqueness of the category, up pops a contradiction that subverts our confident pronouncement. What passes as urban education involves a wide range of circumstances (Willard-Holt, 2000). Sometimes the boundaries between suburban, rural, and urban schooling are more blurred than we initially realized. As Anderson and Summerfield point out in their chapter here, analysts need to be very careful when they proclaim, for example, that urban schools are more dangerous than suburban schools. Violent crime statistics indicate that the difference in violence between urban and suburban schools is minimal.

Researchers confirm that nowhere are the obstacles to success and the existential needs of students as great as in urban areas. Yet at the same time it has to be said that urban locales also contain some of the most helpful resources for young people and their families. We return to our dialectic of challenges and opportunities. Educators, researchers, and school leaders must view every school as a self-contained entity that might be similar to or different from the urban schools around it. Thus, we must rid ourselves of assumptions and study each school on its own merit. This means that we must focus attention on the sociocultural context of each urban school, examine student backgrounds, the positions of empowerment and disempowerment from which they operate, the knowledges they bring to the classroom, the languages they speak, and the ways in which all of these dynamics shape learning and teaching (Wang & Kovach, 1996; Willard-Holt, 2000).

What Are the Unique Features of Urban Education?

Keeping in mind the complexity and contradictions of the category, it is important to ask whether there are features of urban education that are unique. After careful study of the question, I believe that the following characteristics apply.

- *Urban schools operate in areas with high population density.* Technical definitions of urban areas typically maintain that they are characterized by plots of land on which population density is at least 1,000 individuals per square mile. In addition, many urban scholars contend that such areas average at least one building per two acres of land.

- *Urban schools are bigger, and urban school districts serve more students.* Simply put, urban schools and their districts have larger enrollments than rural or suburban ones. These large urban educational institutions are more likely than their suburban and rural counterparts to serve large numbers of students of low socioeconomic class. In these densely populated urban areas and large schools, students are more likely to be ignored or overlooked in the crowds. In such a context it is difficult for urban students to experience a sense of community, and this alienation all too often leads to low academic performance and high dropout rates.

- *Urban schools function in areas marked by profound economic disparity.* Even though numerous poor people can be found in rural areas, urban venues are characterized by high concentrations of poverty existing in close proximity to affluence. Over 80 percent of high-density poverty areas in the United States are located in the nation's 100 largest cities. A disproportionate percentage of minority students and their families are plagued by this concentrated urban poverty, which hampers their quest for academic success on many levels. In urban schools located in these areas, it is not uncommon to find an appalling lack of resources. Financial inequalities mar these schools and school districts, undermining efforts to repair dilapidated buildings, supply textbooks for all students, and provide teachers with instructional materials and equipment. Even when such schools get equipment such as computers, they may sit unused for months or even years because schools have no money for the wiring and phone lines necessary for their use. It is not surprising, therefore, that urban students in poor areas have less access to computers and the Internet than their rural and suburban counterparts. All teachers, no matter in what area they pursue their practice, face the challenges of teaching students from low socioeconomic backgrounds. There is a compelling difference in teaching a class in which 2 students out of 20 are poor and teaching one in which 36 out of 37 come from a low socioeconomic background.

- *Urban areas and urban schools have a higher rate of ethnic, racial, and religious diversity.* In densely populated urban locales, people coming from different ethnic, racial, and religious backgrounds, to say nothing of different economic, social, and linguistic arenas, live in close proximity to one another. Nearly two-thirds of urban students do not fit the categories of white or middle class, and within these populations high percentages of students receive free or reduced-price lunches. Achievement rates for poor minority students consistently fall below those of white and higher-socioeconomic-class students. Surveys of teachers and staff in these highly diverse and poor urban schools consistently indicate that they often feel overwhelmed by the problems that undermine lower-socioeconomic-class minority students' quest to succeed in schools. The frustration of such teachers and staff members is exacerbated by the perception that few care about the well-being and the success of these students.

- *Urban schools experience factionalized infighting on school boards over issues concerning resources and influence.* In almost all urban contexts, school boards have fought over salaries for particular school employees, personnel hiring and firing, school assignments for particular students, and the micro-dynamics of school construction. In densely populated, diverse, and poor areas, such disputes have erupted as local school boards find themselves as the major dispensers of jobs in the area. Because of the important role they play in areas with few resources and opportunities for employment, urban school boards have focused more and more on day-to-day school operations and less and less on policy-level deliberations concerned with improving student success.

- *Urban school systems are undermined by ineffective business operations.* Urban schools in poor areas have more trouble obtaining the basic resources needed to operate schools than do their rural and suburban counterparts. School buildings are often run-down and in dangerous states of disrepair; substitutes are frequently used to cover classes for months at a time, and business staff at the district level often have obtained their jobs through political patronage and longevity rather than expertise. Promotions in the central offices, contracts for school services and supplies, and even curricular decisions with accompanying contracts for purchasing instructional materials are often made on the basis of political favors and influence, much to the detriment of educational quality.

- *Poor urban students are more likely to experience health problems.* In many urban schools, the effort to construct a high-quality learning environment is, in the immediacy of everyday needs, less important than addressing issues of student health and safety. For example, school administrators are often more concerned with providing a warm building on a cold day or fixing unsanitary and disease-producing bathrooms than with more long-term academic concerns. When compared with rural and suburban students, urban students are less likely to have access to regular medical care. Concurrently, such urban students are more likely to develop cases of measles and tuberculosis and suffer the effects of lead poisoning. As Leah Henry-Beauchamp and Tina Siedler report in their chapter in this volume, the number of urban students with asthma has reached epidemic proportions and is growing. Far too many of these urban children with asthmatic conditions do not receive medical attention.

- *Urban schools experience higher student, teacher, and administrator mobility.* In poor urban schools, researchers find that frequent moving between schools undermines student achievement. Some analysts have noted that the poorer the student, the more moves he or she is likely to make. The same schools experience higher teacher turnover—one out of every two teachers in urban schools leaves in five years. Poor inner-city schools find it difficult to retain teachers when school systems in surrounding suburban areas can offer teachers more lucrative salaries, better-maintained schools, a higher-achieving student body, and less demanding work conditions. In addition, studies illustrate that urban teachers are treated with less respect and participate less in decision-making that affects their working lives. Thus, students in poor urban schools who are most in need of experienced teachers, are often taught by the least experienced teachers. In addition to high student and teacher turnover, urban administrators do not serve in their positions as long as their suburban and rural counterparts. Superintendents in urban systems stay for an average of three years—an insufficient period for their policy changes to have an effect.

- *Urban schools serve higher immigrant populations.* In the twenty-first century, not unlike the nineteenth and twentieth centuries, urban schools educate a large number of students who are immigrants or whose parents are immigrants. Many of these families came to the United States to escape political harassment and/or financial despair. Along with these voluntary immigrants, urban schools serve students whose ancestors were involuntary immigrants (African Americans, for example) who share a history of discrimination and injustice. Each of these groups experiences problems unique to its background, and urban educators need to understand and know how to address these concerns.

- *Urban schools are characterized by linguistic diversity.* Because of their large immigrant populations, urban schools have more students speaking different languages than their suburban and rural counterparts. In New York City, for example, more than 200 languages and dialects are spoken in the school system. Because our teachers and educational leaders are generally white and middle class, they usually do not have the heritage or educational background to make positive use of such linguistic diversity, which tends to be seen as a problem rather than a unique opportunity.

- *Urban schools experience unique transportation problems.* When urban students are asked why they are late to school, one reason that particularly stands out involves their dependence on public transportation—subways and buses in particular. Such public transportation is not designed for school schedules and can often be unreliable. Subways sometimes are too crowded to get on in order to get to school on time. Schedules are sometimes changed abruptly and the subway train may skip stations. I have engaged in numerous conversations with urban students who pick up a subway or bus at one station and have to transfer two or three times in order to get to school. Each transfer, of course, increases the chance that they will experience a delay or cancellation. Urban teachers who do not understand these dynamics will often punish students for tardiness. Such teachers assume that the students made no effort to get to school on time.

- *Teachers working in poor urban schools are less likely to live in the communities surrounding the schools than teachers in suburban and rural systems.* In this context teachers become socially, culturally, and economically isolated from their students and the parents. In their isolation, teachers do not understand their students' ways of seeing school as an institution and the world around them. Teachers who find themselves in such a situation are cut off from the helpful information that parents can give about their children and the communities in which they live. Without such valuable knowledge, teachers often make judgments about particular students without having more than one perspective to explain why these students perform as they do (Bamburg, 1994; Lewis & Smith, 1996; Halford, 1996; NWREL, 1999; Weiner, 1999; Kozleski, 2002; Fuhrman, 2002; Westview Partnership, 2002; Ng, 2003; Mezzacappa, 2003).

Keeping Hope Alive: Possibility, Change, and Resilience

Often in the literature of urban education, wide-angle views of the field project a depressing picture of inner-city schools. More specific studies and analysis often uncover success stories that play out daily among dedicated and knowledgeable teachers, visionary administrators, and brilliant students. It is very important that as we paint a macroportrait of the problems of urban education, we do not forget the heroic efforts of these individuals. This is the case especially in relation to the children and young people who attend poor urban schools. Despite the poverty, racial and class discrimination, intelligence and achievement tests that distort their abilities (Kincheloe, Steinberg, & Hinchey, 1999; Kincheloe, Steinberg, &Villaverde, 1999), the linguistic differences, and the many other problems of inner-city life, many students still succeed. No educator should ever forget this. The editors and authors of *19 Urban Questions* keep this knowledge in mind every day that we walk into urban schools and work with students and teachers. In this context we fervently believe that positive change is possible.

While refusing to ignore the problems, we continue to struggle to help more urban students succeed in their academic pursuits and their quest for socioeconomic mobility. In this context we walk a tightrope between pointing out the problems (while avoiding cynicism) and calling attention to the successes (while avoiding rose-colored perspectives). We advocate a curriculum that draws on the strengths of urban students, rather than relying on indicators that point out only their weaknesses. In the domain of linguistic diversity, for example, instead of framing this reality as a problem, we might view it as a dynamic asset in planning one's vocational life. In a globalized world, Americans in a variety of occupations need bi- or multilingual skills, and employers will pay to find such individuals (Halford, 1996; IUYL, 1996; NWREL, 1999).

This critical reframing of urban education in terms of possibility is no easy task in the first decade of the twenty-first century—but it is necessary. Jonathan Kozol (2000) is helpful in this reframing effort in his book *Ordinary Resurrections,* which examines urban life and education through the eyes of children in a poor neighborhood in the South Bronx. Documenting the difference between teaching in 1960s Boston, in the hopeful atmosphere that racism and poverty would soon be eliminated, and teaching in the more cynical South Bronx of the 1990s, Kozol uses the phrase "ordinary resurrections" to signify that in the worst of times educational victories can be won. In a sociopolitical atmosphere in which the public and even the educational conversation about promoting racial justice is not commonly overheard and when precious few political leaders speak of making urban schools less separate and more equal, some urban teachers and educators become very discouraged. Other teachers and even educational leaders, so caught up in the right-wing discourse of urban minority-student incompetence, lose faith in their students' abilities and the possibility of teaching them rigorous academic material (Bamburg, 1994).

In such an atmosphere, diatribes against urban teachers and their "criminal students" become the order of the day (Willard-Holt, 2000). As a teacher-educator in New York City during the Rudolph Giuliani administration, I was amazed at the mayor's verbal attacks on the alleged across-the-board incompetence of the city's teachers. On numerous occasions Giuliani attempted to humiliate teachers to punish them for their "failures." Students going into urban education need to understand the harsh and unfair representations of urban teachers that circulate in the twenty-first century pedagogical zeitgeist.

In this hostile context, many urban educational researchers and scholars are using the term *resilience* to describe the amazing perseverance of poor urban students. Never ignoring for a second the problems that exist, this emphasis on resilience focuses our attention for a while on the ways that savvy students make use of urban resources. The popular stereotype of minority-group urban students is that they don't try in school and have no inclination to succeed in academic affairs. In an interview with *Education World* (2001), Jonathan Kozol maintained: "No matter how we treat them, no matter how many times we knock them down, no matter how we shortchange them, no matter how we isolate them, no matter how we try to hide them from the rest of society, they keep getting up again, and they refuse to die."

In this context of hope, it is probably time to move from a rhetoric of "at risk" to one of resilience. Instead of constructing services to overcome their deficits, it might be better to formulate programs that cultivate the strengths of urban students. Even in the worst situations, brilliant teachers can change students' lives. Setting high expectations for students deemed to have low academic ability by positivistic assessments can pay high educational dividends for such individuals. Engaging marginalized students in everyday classroom decisions, bringing their interests into lessons, and granting them the right to express their opinions can contribute to miraculous transformations. In addition to these relatively simple steps, urban teachers can work to connect students to unique urban resources such as museums, the arts, urban architecture, and developments in science and industry that are found in cities. Taking advantage of such learning resources can change the lives of poor urban students (NWREL, 1999; Wang & Kovach, 1996; FAUSSR, 1998).

It is essential that urban educators keep hope alive by working to reframe the ways that many people view urban schooling and urban students. A critical urban education views education as an effort not merely to prepare students for jobs but to develop new forms of consciousness that help urban students conceptualize ways of inventing *new* jobs that change the status quo. Such a vision of urban education addresses marginalized students' social and personal needs, recognizes their too often overlooked cognitive abilities, and taps into the forces that motivate them. Such a pedagogy helps urban teachers succeed with students, and it is important to note that urban teachers in low-income schools need to see students succeed. Just as physicians need to see their patients return to health, teachers need to see students learn (Lewis & Smith, 1996). It is not surprising that teachers who don't see their students learning are less likely to stay in the profession. Teachers need to keep hope alive, not only for their students but for themselves as well.

Teacher Education in the Urban Context

Another answer to the question of why write a book on urban education involves the fact that there is simply not enough compelling information about the subject for teachers and other professionals. The information that exists often fails to develop a deep understanding of educational purpose vis-à-vis the complexity of "teachin' in the city" and the nature and needs of urban students. Although I am a critic of colleges and schools of education in their urban and other forms, I am also critical of the arts-and-sciences dimensions of higher education that are just as much responsible for the failings of teacher education as are colleges and schools of education. With that caveat, it is important to improve urban teacher education and to produce literature that helps us understand the larger purposes and contexts of urban education as well as scholarly work which grants insight into working in the everyday world of urban schools and other educational locales.

Producing literature and research on urban education in the contemporary sociopolitical climate is difficult in that it has to address the dominant representations of the urban poor and poor urban students as "the undeserving poor." Such individuals are often seen as the sole makers of their own fate. They are poor because they are lazy, dumb, immoral, and/or incompetent. Producers of literature on urban education must help teacher education students, teachers, and other professionals understand the politics of the construction of such fabrications while concurrently facilitating their efforts to gain a more trustworthy perspective on the urban poor (Henke, 2000). Such fallacious but widely accepted images of urban students from lower socioeconomic classes keep tens of thousands of talented students from entering the field of urban education.

Unfortunately, such representations sometimes negatively influence urban teachers and school leaders in their perceptions of students. I have heard educational leaders at the highest levels echo these prejudices as they express the belief that such students "can't learn even if they try." This is why it's so important to get teacher education students into poor urban schools and communities. Such experiences grant them a far more balanced viewpoint, and studies indicate that when this is combined with teaching experience in professional development schools, teachers come to know far more about the unique needs of urban students and how to deal with them. Moreover, such teachers are more likely to spend more years teaching in urban schools. They tend to feel better both about themselves as professionals and about the quality of their pedagogical work (Kozleski, 2002).

Teacher educators must understand and confront the notion that urban schools are thorny and complicated places for teachers because of the unique characteristics previously listed. Many new teachers experience culture shock during the first few weeks and months in their new positions. Too often these teachers leave the profession without ever learning diverse ways of working with and motivating urban students. As we know, many times these young urban teachers come from socioeconomic levels very different from those of their lower-socioeconomic-class students. These are the teachers who are sometimes the most vulnerable to the social representations of urban poverty and poor urban students. Living lives so culturally distant from their students, these teachers and teacher education students need to understand both the communities in which poor urban students live and the nature of their daily lives. They need to have field experiences during their teacher education in urban schools so they won't experience culture shock when they assume teaching positions. These are also teachers and teacher education students who—moving to the other end of the spectrum—sometimes develop an unhealthy desire to "save" or "rescue" poor Latino or African American students. In this mode such teachers see the cultural capital of white middle-class lifestyles as the antidote to "urbanness." These rescuers are missionaries who bring salvation through "proper ways of being."

Urban teacher education must work to help teachers avoid the prejudiced view of poor urban students as dangerous criminals incapable of learning or, at the other extreme, as communicants who may be reformed by the gospel of white culture as pedagogy. This is one of many reasons that teachers must develop a strong notion both of self and of the forces that have shaped them. In other works, I have referred to this knowledge as the ontological dimension of teacher knowledge, i.e., the philosophy of *being* itself—what it means to *be* human, to *be* an urban teacher. Too infrequently are teachers in university, student teaching, or in-service professional education encouraged to confront why they think as they do about themselves as teachers, especially in relation to the social, cultural, political, economic, and historical world around them. Mainstream teacher education provides little insight into the forces that shape identity and consciousness. Becoming educated as a critical practitioner necessitates personal transformation.

With such dynamics in mind, a critical urban education asks teachers to confront their relationship with some long-term historical trends rarely discussed in the contemporary public conversation and in urban teacher education. Critical teacher educators maintain that these trends hold profound implications for both the cultivation of professional awareness and the development of a teacher persona vitally needed in urban education. Indeed, everyone in the contemporary United States is shaped by this knowledge in some way, whether or not we are conscious of it. We cannot erase the fact that European colonialism dominated the world from the late fifteenth century until the twentieth century, when it mutated into a neocolonialism grounded in economic and cultural dynamics led primarily by the United States. By the middle of the twentieth century, anticolonial activity had developed in India, Indochina, Africa, Latin America, and other places around the world seeking self-determination for colonized peoples. It was this movement that provided the spark for the Civil Rights movement, the anti-Vietnam War movement, the women's movement, gay rights, and other liberation movements in the United States.

While anticolonial activity continues into the twenty-first century, such discontent achieved its apex in the United States in the 1960s and early 1970s. By the mid-1970s a conservative counterreaction was taking shape with the goals of "recovering" what was perceived to be lost in these movements. Thus, the politics, cultural wars, and educational debates, policies, and practices of the last three decades cannot be understood outside of these efforts to "recover" white supremacy, patriarchy, class privilege, heterosexual "normality," Christian dominance, and the European intellectual canon. We all must decide where we stand in relation to such profound yet blurred historical processes. We cannot conceptualize our teacher persona outside of them. They are the defining macroconcerns of our time, as every topic is refracted through their lenses. Any view of the purpose of urban education, any curriculum development, any professional education conceived outside of their framework ends up becoming a form of ideological mystification.

In this ideological context, urban teacher education students from white backgrounds must understand the power of whiteness in shaping their perspectives toward urban schools and urban students. How does their racial identity position them in relation to educational purpose and the lives of their poor and nonwhite students? How does their relation to whiteness shape their sense of privilege and their understanding of the forces shaping urban students' lives? These are questions that a critical urban teacher education must raise with its students. While such questions elicit difficult and often contentious responses, they are necessary in twenty-first-century urban education. Numerous curricular experiences can help students gain more insight into the race, class, gender, and sexual dimensions of their identities and the impact of these dynamics on their teaching.

As urban teachers, we are invested in the ontological knowledge of teacher selfhood, the knowledge of what it means to be a teacher in the culturally different settings that many white upper-middle-class urban teacher education students must confront before they enter the profession. Contemporary studies show that about 59 percent of beginning urban teachers feel unprepared to work with students who are having academic trouble (Kozleski, 2002). Also many new urban teachers feel estranged from both schools as social units and the urban communities in which the schools are located. Knowing the context in which students live, gaining experience in urban communities from preservice field placements, and developing a strong sense of the construction of one's consciousness along race, class, gender, and religious lines are all profoundly important aspects of urban teacher education.

The knowledges of teacher education coming from both colleges of education and colleges of liberal arts and sciences are too often based on an acceptance of the status quo in urban education. Urban students from diverse backgrounds are often treated as though their knowledges, values, and ways of living are not important. Schools are here to provide them with the correct ways of being, the proper ways of seeing that come from dominant white upper-middle-class culture. Such insights force us to rethink knowledge production, curriculum development, and the core of urban educational practice. In this context we begin to see urban education not as a means of socially controlling the poor and nonwhite but as a means of liberating and cultivating the intellect while providing the tools for socioeconomic mobility.

Understanding the Importance of the Context in Which Urban Education Takes Place

Urban education teachers and educators need a rigorous, inter/multidisciplinary understanding of urban education. They need to draw on a number of disciplines and transdisciplines such as history, cognitive studies, sociology, anthropology, cultural studies, philosophy, political science, economics, geography, and others to help them understand the complex context in which urban education takes place. In this way teachers and educators gain unique and powerful insights into research on educational policy, pedagogy, and the lives of children living in densely populated urban settings. Understanding this wide range of disciplinary and interdisciplinary knowledges about the urban context, teachers are much better equipped to understand the interrelationships that shape their professional practice. Too often in university arts and sciences and professional education courses, professors fail to help students make connections between the issues confronting urban schools and the historical and sociological contexts in which both cities and educational systems have developed. Schools mirror and refract these historical and sociological dynamics. Teachers operate at a distinct disadvantage if they don't recognize these interrelationships (Slaughter-Defoe, 2002; FAUSSR, 1998).

Indeed, the role of context in understanding and engaging in good work in urban education cannot be exaggerated. When teachers understand the historical, cultural, and political context of urban education, they develop a frame of reference, a big picture that not only helps them appreciate why some things work as they do but facilitates their construction of a sense of purpose. Such contextual understandings help them answer the questions about *why* they do what they do. It helps them develop a vision of what they want to accomplish in their professional activities. In contemporary education, this sense of purpose is too often lacking. Educational leaders and teachers must appreciate the ecological embeddedness of teaching and learning. While a school is a local institution, it is inscribed by the macro- and microstructures that surround it. While individual schools and individual teachers can succeed despite the problems of the contexts in which they are embedded, long-lasting educational reform must include changing the inequitable and problematic social and cultural dynamics surrounding schools. Schools are part of a larger public democratic space. When the public democratic space is unhealthy, the schools are negatively affected. Given that the world is becoming more and more urban, educators around the world will have to deal with similar contextual factors as they begin their efforts to improve urban education in the twenty-first century.

When teachers in urban schools discern that students are not ready for learning, they often can connect such problems to the context in which students operate. What is often referred to as the "achievement gap" in urban schools simply cannot be understood as a problem of individual students in particular urban schools. When such a problem is reduced to an individual issue, researchers and educators often mistake an ecologically contextualized problem for a failure of particular individuals. The field of psychometrics often makes this very mistake by insisting that the so-called achievement gap is a manifestation of the intellectual inferiority of poor and nonwhite urban students. In a politicoeconomic context, the decline of urban schools and student achievement has paralleled the decline of the manufacturing and tax base of U.S. cities.

The poorer and more hopeless the residents in the inner cities of the country become, the more likely their children are to have trouble in school. In the 1950s urban schools in the United States tended to be largely white and middle class and boasted some of the wealthiest tax bases in the country. With the white, middle-class flight to the suburbs and the migration of industry to other regions and nations, urban schools now draw for financial support upon an area of continuously shrinking economic production. Knowing these contextual problems, educational leaders must promote a metropolitan outlook that views the economic problems of urban schools as more than a local issue. City residents in higher socioeconomic neighborhoods and suburbanites must help support poor urban schools. Without such help, the crisis of urban education will be exacerbated.

Urban teachers have no choice—they must work with what they have. Until more well-to-do citizens assume their civic responsibility to help the fiscal condition of inner cities, urban teachers in poor schools will have to operate in a hostile socioeconomic environment. The popularity of massive tax cuts in the political climate of the first decade of the twenty-first century does not bode well for the future of urban schooling. Observing the shift from an industrial to a service-based economy (Kincheloe, 1999) over the last few decades, urban economists maintain that most of the newly created jobs in cities either are highly specialized or fail to pay subsistence wages. Economically isolated, poor urban residents also find themselves politically marginalized by the electoral power of their more economically solvent suburban counterparts (USSR, 1998; Wang & Kovach, 1996; Halford, 1996; Ng, 2003).

Urban teachers, of course, need to be students of the microcontexts in which their schools operate, namely, the communities surrounding them and the network of families with children in the school. Knowledge of these communities, families, and parents can change the lives of urban educators, as they are able to make connections that lead to indispensable modes of educational involvement of these groups and individuals in the emotional, social, and intellectual life of the school. Some of the urban teachers with whom I work in New York City have developed interactive bonds with local communities and families that have not only helped students from lower socioeconomic backgrounds negotiate the minefield of school but have helped their parents as well. As they interacted with the teachers and the local school their children attended, such parents came to understand the educational landscape in a way that empowered them to go back to school to get their general equivalency diplomas and even begin college. Thus, they not only gained the ability to better help their children academically but changed their own lives in the process.

Connectedness is a central dimension of a critical vision of urban educational and social change. There is no limit to what can happen when urban teachers possess the intellectual and interpersonal savvy to forge relationships based on a vision of educational purpose, dignity, respect, political solidarity, and cooperation with the local community. In order to lower the urban dropout rate, teachers must address contextual issues within communities and families. Schools should not be locked up when school is not in session but should be used as recreational, academic tutoring, health, mental health, and social support centers for the residents of the communities surrounding them. In this way, students and families gain the ability to forge unique connections with schools toward which they presently harbor a debilitating sense of alienation.

Understanding context, thus, is essential, but a caveat concerning the application of such an understanding in urban pedagogy is important at this juncture. Much of my work in education has involved researching the context in which education takes place and theorizing the effects of contextual forces on the pedagogical process (Kincheloe, 1993, 1999, 2002; Kincheloe & Steinberg, 1993, 1997). Understanding the effects of such forces, however, must not lapse into a deterministic view of how such contextual forces inexorably shape the schooling process and student performance. Understanding the impact of the political and economic factors and the cultural mismatches between home and school culture referenced in this chapter does not mean that students, teachers, and parents *cannot* overcome these contextual impediments.

Indeed, the better we understand these factors, the more empowered we are to mitigate their influence—a position that undermines any lingering determinism in the act of contextualization. A critical urban pedagogy studies the context of education for the purpose of enhancing human agency—the capacity to act in transformative ways—not to minimize it. Such a pedagogy fervently believes that brilliant and committed urban teachers can make a positive difference in the lives of students and communities, no matter how bad the situation may be. Honestly, I would love to witness a sociopolitical revolution based on equity and social justice before I leave this earth—but I don't think it's going to happen at least in the next few months. Until the revolution comes, I will continue to work to make good things happen in individual school systems, schools, classrooms, and nontraditional educational venues.

In postformal cognitive theory (Kincheloe & Steinberg, 1993, Kincheloe, 1995), the ability to contextualize is viewed as a central dimension of higher-order thinking. Contrary to the pronouncements of the types of cognitive theory taught in mainstream psychology courses, lower-socioeconomic-class minority-group urban students are as capable of learning as students from higher socioeconomic and majority-group backgrounds. Our rigorous understanding of the context in which urban schooling takes place informs our cognitive assertion. There is no reason that urban students themselves can't understand such contextual insights. I have argued in numerous works (Kincheloe, 1995; Kincheloe, Steinberg, & Villaverde, 1999) that a central aspect of a curriculum for marginalized students involves analysis of the social, cultural, political, economic, epistemological, and historical forces and contexts that limit their chances for success. Such analysis becomes a central feature of a critical urban pedagogy.

Cognition and Urban Education

A key dimension of urban education that is too often left unexamined is the role of cognition and cognitive theory. One of the most important problems plaguing urban education involves prevalent beliefs about the nature of intelligence and how human beings learn. Intelligence in the mainstream psychometric formulation is defined simply as how one scores on an IQ test. It doesn't matter where we come from, the educational attainment of our parents, the valuing of education in our peer group, our expectations for translating hard academic work into vocational reward, or the language we speak in our homes. None of these factors matters in the psychometrics used in most urban schools. Test scores are all the evidence needed to determine students' intelligence and academic ability. Humans are culturally embedded entities wracked by the unpredictability of both rationality and irrationality and operating spontaneously in response to the complex machinations of everyday life. Psychometrics and the pedagogies it spawns do not view urban students, or anybody else for that matter, in those contexts in which they exhibit profoundly intricate forms of thinking. Their intelligence is measured by their performance on one decontextualized activity—taking a written test.

With these ideas in mind, urban education can no longer afford to organize curriculum and instruction around cognitive assessments that are used to undermine the success of children who come from lower-socioeconomic-class and nonwhite backgrounds. Such theories and practices have harmed such children in irreparable ways. These ways of assessing intelligence and academic ability have provided "scientific" validation to those inclined to believe that poor urban students can't perform as the academic equals of more privileged students. This allows urban educators to exclude these marginalized students from specific curricular experiences, particular forms of knowledge, and the benefits of great expectations. This exclusion is grounded by a sorting system based on standardized test scores. Critical urban educators throw a monkey wrench into the sorting machine as they expose the ways that such technologies operate to reproduce racial and class-based power relations (Bamburg, 1994; USSR, 1998; Halford, 1996; FAUSSR, 1998).

Many poor and/or minority-group students clearly understand that they are not viewed as intelligent in urban schools that assume the validity of psychometric data. Why stay, many of these students understandably ask, when they think we're stupid? Why be subjected to the classifying and sorting that goes on in the name of helping us? It is said that once a child has been labeled as a weak student, there's little that can be done to change the perception. These savvy students realize that the psychometric paradigm creates sorting systems and special-needs categories requiring that students be removed from regular classrooms and assigned to specialist teachers. While good things may happen when highly proficient and dedicated teachers work with students in urban contexts, student performance is undermined by the low expectations that accompany the categorization of special needs. A multitude of studies over the last three decades have reported that expectations play a profound role in shaping the quality of a student's school experience (Bamburg, 1994). As long as norm-referenced tests are misused as reliable measures of a student's academic ability, these low expectations will continue to subvert the efforts of poor and nonwhite students to make positive use of schools.

Many urban school leaders in the United States continue to believe—especially with the influence of the psychometrically driven No Child Left Behind legislation of the G. W. Bush administration—that the key factor in shaping student performance is *ability*. One would think that after Vygotsky's delineation of the importance of the context in which a learner operates that the centrality of ability might be questioned. Indeed, numerous cognitive and sociocognitive theorists in the contemporary academy question the idea that we can even isolate an individual's intellectual ability as a discrete entity. Such an emphasis on ability assumes an acceptance of a mechanistic worldview that is caught in a socially decontextualized cause-and-effect, hypothetical/deductive system of reasoning.

Such a way of viewing intelligence is unconcerned with questions of social-cultural-linguistic context and power relations and the way they structure human identity and the nature of our interactions with institutions such as school. Coming from a family that valued education as a child, I had a very different relationship to school and learning than did some of my peers from very poor and often illiterate families in the mountains of eastern Tennessee. I walked into school with a body of knowledges and dispositions that allowed me to succeed academically. They walked into school not knowing what to expect and not sure that anything going on there was relevant to their lives. These orientations at the very least had as much to do with school success as the abstract notion of ability. When they were deemed to have low IQs—a.k.a. low abilities—they were *predestined* by the existing cognitive paradigm to do poorly in their studies.

In other works, Shirley Steinberg and I have delineated a cognitive theory, postformalism, that asserts that most students who don't suffer from brain disorders or severe emotional problems can (and do) engage in higher-order thinking. Such students engage in sophisticated forms of cognition outside of school in everyday life but are sometimes perplexed by the unfamiliar tasks and ways of thinking demanded of them in school. Their inability to successfully negotiate such assignments has less to do with ability and more to do with their lack of familiarity with the culturally and class-inscribed ways of communicating (discursive practices) of school. Poor urban students of color are often baffled by the culture of school. It is unlike anything they have previously experienced. Middle- and upper-middle-class children from white backgrounds typically see little that is unusual in the cultural dimensions of schooling. They know what teachers are talking about and see their requests of them as logical and reasonable. It is important that teachers and school leaders appreciate these dynamics and understand the harm caused by the myth that poor urban students have low ability.

To overcome these designations of low ability, every teacher must know every student in order to develop curricula specifically designed for their interests and needs. Only with this type of individualized pedagogical work can the stigma of inability be exposed and countered in urban schools. Children's cognitive abilities often exhibit themselves in situations in which teachers can't see them. The cognitive theory embraced here contends that teachers identify these abilities and use them as a framework on which to build a variety of academic skills. Again, these students are capable of higher-order thinking; teachers need to understand how to tap into such cognitive abilities.

What other reasons move us to write a book on urban education? One of the most important answers to such a question involves delineating and discussing the construction of a rigorous and just urban pedagogy. Such a discussion is extremely important in the first decade of the twenty-first century because of the prevalence of test-driven, standardized curricula in urban school systems. The teaching that results from these standardized curricula, proponents claim, is rigorous, fair, and equitable. These advocates do not take into account the unique situations and needs of particular urban students. When a curriculum is standardized, the students suffering from the effects of poverty, racial discrimination, and other problems are less likely to receive the specific pedagogical help they need to overcome the effects of such impediments. Please do not confuse the argument being made here—I am not asserting that these students are not able to deal with the academic requirements. The point is that they have very special orientations, which teachers must have the curricular freedom to address. For example, the decision to introduce reading instruction to students from socio-economically, ethnically, and linguistically diverse backgrounds may involve factors that differ profoundly from normalized criteria. Different pedagogical actions and interventions are needed in diverse circumstances.

The paradigmatic basis on which technical standards and their standardized curricula are grounded assumes a positivistic notion that learning takes place in a linear way and the context in which the learner operates is irrelevant. First one teaches certain basic skills, and then once these are mastered through repetition, more advanced skills can be taught. With particular learners, especially those who fall outside the category of white/upper middle class/English speaking, such a "logical" pedagogy may not work at all. Indeed, the first lesson such students might need to set them on a rigorous learning path could involve the valuing of the type of knowledge and skills one confronts in school or learning to feel comfortable in the culture of the school. Also, when the decontextualized linear basic skills curriculum is taught to many poor nonwhite urban students, researchers uncover particular problems. Emphasis on drill and repetition of the so-called basics tends to exclude experiences involving higher-order academic skills such as higher-order reasoning, reading grounded in the making of meaning, and particular forms of writing exercises (FAUSSR, 1998; Bamburg, 1994).In the positivistic linear model promoted by technical standards, what often ends up happening is that drilling for the standardized tests consumes the entire school day. No real learning takes place, and students who learn the fragmented content of the drills soon forget it. It has no meaning in their lives beyond its use on the tests. Watching this mindless drill for standardized evaluations, many brilliant teachers refuse to seek positions in the schools.

Often months of the academic high school year are wasted in preparation for the standards tests. Urban students often, I think understandably, resist such low-level, pedagogically deformed curricula. This pedagogy of low expectations fragments curricular knowledge, in the process removing learning from the lived worlds of students. It relegates motivation to the trash heap of education, as it avoids thinking about learning activities designed to get students interested in becoming scholars. A critical complex urban pedagogy uses students' fervent desires to make their communities better places as a motivational basis for learning. It is important to prepare lessons in which students can easily discern the ways such learning can be applied to the world around them. A pedagogy of low expectations treats urban students as if they were produced by a cookie cutter. It assumes that all humans learn in the same way; thus, one pedagogy fits all of their needs. Such a deficit pedagogy refuses to question the knowledge taught to these "inferior" learners. The curriculum is presented simply as "the truth," as it is assumed that such students do not have the ability to evaluate the information they are provided.

We grapple with many of the same issues raised by concerns over a rigorous and just urban education vis-à-vis a pedagogy of low expectations. Represented as a deficit pedagogy that keeps students who speak other languages from speaking English, bilingual programs that have existed over the last couple of decades have been undermined by right-wing policymakers (Lamb, 2002). As Anderson and Summerfield frame it in their chapter here: "Bilingualism is treated as a problem to be eradicated in U.S. schools." Bilingual education escapes its deficit status as a remedial program to become a program that holds compelling benefits for all students, even those from mainstream backgrounds. Research indicates that bilingual students possess "greater communicative sensitivity than monolingual speakers . . . an increased sensitivity to the social nature and communicative functions of language." Bilingual education doesn't undermine the learning of English, as it takes advantage of the cognitive abilities many urban students bring to school and contributes to the rigor of their education.

As we pursue a rigorous and just urban pedagogy, we are informed by the insights of Vanessa Domine in her chapter on technology and urban education. Domine argues that unless those who would integrate technology into urban education are aware of larger educational purposes and the scourge of the fragmented education of low expectations, technology can be virtually irrelevant in the urban school. Of course, she argues, students should be proficient in the use of various technologies, but unless these abilities are integrated into an understanding of the larger context in which urban education takes place, they are of minimal value. Technology provides no educational panacea and can be harmful when it diverts attention from the political, economic, and social forces that shape urban education. Domine is specific in delineating her disgust with many of the government officials who promote technology as a cure for urban educational ills. Those political leaders who passed the No Child Left Behind Act in 2002, for example, required that all pupils be technologically literate by the time they reach the eighth grade, while they themselves concurrently cut funds to programs designed to teach technological literacy. Such showmanship and cynicism about truly facilitating the work of urban educators can be psychologically distressing for those of us committed to the well-being of urban students.

As we stress throughout *19 Urban Questions,* urban educators face numerous obstacles in the first decade of the twenty-first century and must work extra hard to develop educational and political strategies to counter the landmines placed in our path. In the name of social justice and racial and class equity, urban educators must devise and teach a rigorous curriculum that takes into account the needs of different learners with diverse backgrounds. If we want to talk about standards, then we must move beyond defining high standards in terms of students' memorizing fragmented information represented as final truths. We must engage the profession, political leaders, and the public in a conversation about what constitutes a rigorous education. In addition, we must make one of the most important standards the realization of high academic achievement by students from diverse socioeconomic, racial, and linguistic backgrounds. A large failure rate, contrary to the pronouncements of some, is not a manifestation of high standards.

One of the most important dimensions of developing a rigorous and just urban education is expecting even more from our teachers and our teacher educators. Obviously, so many urban teachers are dedicated professionals who give so much to their students, their schools, and their communities. At the same time, some of the most brilliant scholars I have ever observed in higher education have been teacher education scholars. We need more, however. Teachers must become researchers and curriculum developers who take the lead in shaping the scholarly atmosphere of urban schools. Teacher educators, especially those in the arts and sciences, must help preservice and in-service teachers become researchers and more adept knowledge workers, as well as psychologists and sociologists who understand the contextual forces that shape student learning. There is absolutely no reason to believe that teachers are not capable of such work. I wince when I hear colleagues in teacher education or in the arts and sciences argue that teacher education students are inferior to the "other students." Such biases must be confronted directly.

The teacher-scholars emerging from these invigorated and rigorous teacher education programs will help transform urban schools into learning organizations, "postformal workplaces," as I refer to them in *Toil and Trouble* (Kincheloe, 1995). In such schools, educational purpose is discussed in relation to the social context in which schools exist. Questions that address the needs of the community and the special needs of particular students help teachers develop curricula that embrace the challenges of their classrooms. Teachers who are effective in these schools approach subject matter as a historical artifact, analyzing the discursive practices that shaped it, the epistemologies assumed within it, the knowledges that compete with it, and what is important for their particular urban students to know about it. In other work, I refer to this rigorous pedagogy in an era of standards as "standards of complexity" (Horn & Kincheloe, 2001; Kincheloe and Weil, 2001). In this book, Winthrop Holder describes the rigorous pedagogy he pursued at Walton High School in the Bronx. At Walton, students with Holder's guidance published a literary journal of their work (*Crossing Swords*) that was widely read and touted. It is a treat to watch Holder work his pedagogical magic with these accomplished students. We can help produce thousands of Winthrop Holders who can capture the imagination of urban students from all backgrounds.

Developing a Vision of a Rigorous Urban Education

A key purpose of writing a book on urban education at this period of history involves helping to develop a sense of purpose for urban educators. We can discuss collaborative school cultures and reflective practice all we want, but such concepts mean very little outside of a rigorous, informed discussion of the purpose of education in general and urban education in a specific setting in particular. Many urban educational leaders and school boards are crippled by the absence of informed discussion about educational purpose. Without this grounding, their conversations about urban schooling go around in circles, with little direction and less imagination. As Susan Fuhrman (2002) argues, in the contemporary era there are endless attempts at urban school reform with little improvement to show for the efforts. She is correct, and one of the most important reasons for these failures at reform involves the lack of a sense of educational purpose. Without this key ingredient, most educational reforms amount to little more benefit than taking an aspirin to ease the pain of a kidney stone. The urban education promoted here demands a fundamental rethinking, a deep reconceptualization of what human beings are capable of achieving; the role of the social, cultural, and political in shaping human identity; the relationship between community and schooling, and ways that power operates to create purposes for schooling that are not necessarily in the best interests of the children who attend them.

A complex vision of urban education, grounded as it is in social, cultural, cognitive, economic, and political contexts, understands schooling as part of a larger set of human services and community development. Any viable vision of urban education has to be grounded in larger social and cognitive visions. In this context urban educators deal with questions not only of schooling, curriculum, and educational policy, but also of social justice and human possibility. Understanding these dynamics, critical urban educators devise new modes of making connections between school and its context as well as catalyzing community resources to help facilitate quality education. With this larger vision in mind and knowledge of these different contexts, urban educators are empowered to identify the insidious forces that subvert the success of particular urban students. This ability is not typically found in urban educational practice. Without it, educators and school leaders experience great difficulty in determining what is important knowledge in the field of urban education. Such individuals cannot determine why some policies and pedagogies work to accomplish certain goals, while others do not (Peterson, 1994; Bamburg, 1994; Wang & Kovach, 1996; MDRC, 2002).

An educational reform promoted by many—especially in New York City—is the "small-schools movement." I agree with the basic principles of the movement as they are generally articulated. But when small schools are promoted without a complex view of educational purpose, they are simply another wasted aspirin. We can build 500 new small schools in New York City, but without the type of vision promoted here, we may find 500 principals and thousands of teachers asking, "Now what?" Reform proposals are a dime a dozen; an informed, contextualized, rigorous vision of what urban schools can become is priceless. When we examine the history of urban education, we find that too often urban schools served as impediments for students of color and those from lower socioeconomic classes. A critical vision of urban education takes this historical knowledge seriously and works to avoid the same mistakes. As Deborah Meier (as quoted in NWREL, 1999) asks: "How could the children at the bottom of America's social ladder use their schools to develop rather than stunt their intellectual potential?"

This stunting of potential takes place in the pedagogy of low expectations, where concern with disciplining the incompetent poor to create a more ordered and efficient society takes the place of a democratic social vision. Historical accounts of urban schools designed for these purposes alert us to the dangers of such educational structures. Such schools in the past and unfortunately in the present have served to categorize, punish, restrict, and restrain those students who failed to fit the proper demographic.

Our critical, complex, democratic vision of urban education enables us to see education in a systemic context, in which we gain an appreciation of the importance of the relationship between education and other social dynamics (FAUSSR, 1998). These interactions are complex, as all social, political, economic, cultural, and educational decisions are interrelated. With such an understanding, we can begin to reshape these relationships and the decisions we make in relation to them in new and previously unexplored ways.

What this means in concrete terms is that teachers can begin to develop distinct practices to help particular students flourish in urban schools located in specific communities. Teachers draw upon their larger vision to help them determine what types of human beings they want to graduate from urban schools. Do we want socially regulated workers with the *proper* attitudes for their respective rungs on the workplace ladder? Or do we want empowered, learned, highly skilled democratic citizens who have the confidence and the savvy to improve their own lives and to make their communities more vibrant places to live, work, and play? Such students will confront and change the encoded use of "urban" as menacing alterity—a dangerous place for "good people" to be. If such meanings in the public consciousness are not modified, then the job of urban schooling will continue to involve taming, controlling, and/or rescuing the progeny of the urban jungle. We write a book on urban education to avoid such a dystopian pedagogy.

REFERENCES

Bamburg, Jerry D. (1994). *Raising expectations to improve student learning.* http://www.ncrel.org/ sdrs/ areas/issues/educatrs/leadrshp/le0bam.htm

Ciani, Alfred (2002). *Teacher education issues for urban middle schools.* http://www.nmsa.org/ about/urban_ teachered.pdf

FAUSSR [First Annual Urban Schools Symposium Report] (1998).*Relationship, community, and positive reframing: Addressing the needs of urban school*s. http://www.inclusiveschools.org/ proc_sho.htm

Ferguson, Dianne L. (2000). *On reconceptualizing continuing professional development: A framework for planning.* http://www.edc.org/urban/op_rec.htm

Fuhrman, Susan (2002). *Urban educational challenges: Is reform the answer?* http://www.urbaned-journal.org/ archive/Issue%201/FeatureArticles/article0004.html

Halford, Joan M. (1996). Policies of promise. *Urban Education,* Summer. http://www.ascd.org/ publications/infobrief/issue5.html

Henke, Suellyn M. (2000). *Representations of secondary urban education: Infusing cultural studies into teacher education.* Dissertation, Miami University http://www.units.muohio.edu/ edu-leadership/ DISSERTATIONS/ Henke_dis/ Henke_0_Preliminaries.pdf

Horn, Raymond A., & Kincheloe, Joe L. (Eds.). (2001). *American standards: Quality education in a complex world: The Texas case.* New York: Peter Lang.

Irvine, Jacqueline J. (1999). The education of children whose nightmares come both day and night. *Journal of Negro Education, 68,* 244-253.

IUYL (1996).*Institute for Urban Youth Leadership—summer 1996.* http://www.siena.edu/uyli/ manual1996.htm

Kincheloe, Joe L. (1993). *Toward a critical politics of teacher thinking: Mapping the postmodern.* Westport, CT: Bergin and Garvey.

—— (1995). *Toil and trouble: Good work, smart workers, and the integration of academic and vocational education.* New York: Peter Lang.

—— (1999). *How do we tell the workers? The socioeconomic foundations of work and vocational education.* Boulder, CO: Westview.

—— (2001). *Getting Beyond the Facts: Teaching Social Studies/Social Sciences in the Twenty-First Century.* New York: Peter Lang.

—— (2002). *The sign of the burger: McDonald's and the culture of power.* Philadelphia: Temple University Press.

Kincheloe, Joe L., & Steinberg, Shirley (1993). A tentative description of post-formal thinking: The critical confrontation with cognitive theory. *Harvard Educational Review, 63,* 296-320.

—— (1997). *Changing multiculturalism.* Philadelphia: Open University Press.

Kincheloe, Joe L., & Weil, Danny (2001). *Standards and schooling in the United States: An encyclopedia.* Santa Barbara, CA: ABC-CLIO.

Kincheloe, Joe L., Slattery, Patrick, & Steinberg, Shirley (2000). *Contextualizing teaching.* New York: Addison Wesley Longman.

Kincheloe, Joe L., Steinberg, Shirley, & Hinchey, Patricia H. (Eds.) (1999). *The post-formal reader: Cognition and education.* New York: Falmer.

Kincheloe, Joe L., Steinberg, Shirley, & Villaverde, Leila E. (1999*). Rethinking intelligence: Confronting psychological assumptions about teaching and learning.* New York: Routledge.

Kozleski, Elizabeth (2002). Educating special education teachers for urban schools. *Urban Perspectives Newsletter*, Summer/Fall. http://www.edc.org/collaborative/summer02.txt

Kozol, Jonathan (2000). *Ordinary resurrections: Children in the years of hope.* New York: Crown.

———— *Education World* (2001) "Ordinary resurrections: an e-interview with Jonathan Kozol. http://www.education-world.com/a_issues/issues164.shtml

Lamb, Terry (2002). *Language policy for education in multilingual settings.*http://tntee.umu.se/lisboa/papers/abstract-g.html [Abstract].http://tntee.fceduc.umu.se/0001256b-80000008/g4terrylamb.rtf [authorization required].

Lewis, Karen S., & Smith, BetsAnn (1996). Teacher engagement and real reform in urban schools. In B. Williams (Ed.), *Closing the achievement gap: A vision for changing beliefs and practices.* Alexandria, VA: Association for Supervision and Curriculum Development.

MDRC [Manpower Demonstration Research Corporation] for the Council of the Great City Schools (2002).*Foundations for success: Case studies of how urban school systems improve student achievement.* http://www.cgcs.org/reports/foundations.html

Mezzacappa, Dale (2003). Turmoil in teaching: Teacher attrition sapping urban schools. http://www.philly.com/mld/inquirer/living/education/5369853.htm

Ng, Jennifer (2003).Multicultural education in teacher training programs and its implications on preparedness for effective work in urban settings. In G. Lopez & L. Parker (Eds.), *Interrogating racism in qualitative research methodology.* New York: Peter Lang.

NWREL [North West Regional Educational Laboratory] (1999).*Lessons from the cities, part two: The strengths of city kids.* http://www.nwrel.org/nwedu/winter99/lessons2.html

Peterson, Kent (1994). *Building collaborative cultures: Seeking ways to reshape urban schools.* http://www.ncrel.org/sdrs/areas/issues/educatrs/leadrshp/le0pet.htm

Slaughter-Defoe, Diana (2002). Introduction: The Clayton lectures. http://www.urbanedjournal.org/ archive/Issue%201/HomePage/guest.html

USSR [Urban Schools Symposium Report] (1998). Relationship, community, and positive reframing: Addressing the needs of urban schools. Available at: http://www.inclusiveschools.org/proc_sho.htm. Accessed November 15, 2003.

Wang, Margaret C., & Kovach, John A. (1996). Bridging the achievement gap in urban schools: Reducing educational segregation and advancing resilience-promoting strategies. In B. Williams (Ed.), *Closing the achievement gap: A vision for changing beliefs and practices.* Alexandria, VA: Association for Supervision and Curriculum Development.

Weiner, Lois (1999). *Urban teaching: The essentials.* New York: Teachers College Press.

Welcome to Urban Education Module (2003). http://jewel.morgan.edu/~seus/module.html

Westview Partnership (2002). http://www.edu.yorku.ca/~westview_web/info.html

Willard-Holt, Colleen (2000). Preparing teachers for urban settings: changing teacher education by changing ourselves. *The Qualitative Report, 4.* http://www.nova.edu/ ssss/QR/QR4-3/willard.html

CHAPTER TWO

Kecia Hayes
(with Introduction by Joe Kincheloe)

Why Teach
in Urban Settings?

 Introduction

One of the key questions that should be asked in a book of inquiries about urban education is why one would want to teach in urban schools. If urban education is faced with a perpetual crisis, is represented in the media as a gangsta paradise, characterized by dramatic economic disparity with deteriorating neighborhoods, and destined to limp along without a guiding vision, then why get involved in such a concrete briar patch? The answer to such a question by many prospective teachers is a resounding "It's not for me—see you in the suburbs." But there are many, of course, who take up the challenges. Why do they do it? What do they have to teach individuals pondering a career in urban education?

A key premise of this book is the belief that teacher educators should be brutally honest with those contemplating going into urban teaching. No punches should be pulled, and no harsh reality should be sugarcoated for the uninitiated. Urban teaching is hard work, with some days unavoidably running over 14 or 15 hours, teaching loads characterized by more than 160 students a day, and stacks of papers waiting for responses and grades. And all of this work is for about $15 an hour—the salary of a manager at McDonald's. Urban teachers cannot help but think about this comparison as they eye the Devils Tower of student papers littering their dining room tables. They cannot listen to The Clash's "Should I Stay or Should I Go?" with personal detachment. Of course, few of them go into the field for the money, but personal fulfillment doesn't count for much when one is unable to purchase a middle-class home on an urban teacher's salary.

As if these concerns were not enough, there's the matter of society's blatant lack of respect for teachers in general and urban teachers in particular. "Why are many urban schools so bad?" people ask. Despite having to deal with every possible problem resulting from poverty, racism, and underfunding, poor urban schools fail for simply one reason, TV talking heads and many local politicians frequently tell us: bad teachers. This single-bullet theory of urban education does not play well with exhausted teachers staring at student papers at 11:45 P.M. Remembering the way teacher education students were viewed as the least talented college graduates, urban teachers can hardly imagine what it might mean to work in a respected profession. I remember in my own professional life, after leaving Penn State University to come to Brooklyn College, being surprised when Brooklyn education students asked me: "Why would you leave there to come here?" The question was asked with a sense of incredulity, as in, what kind of fool would make such an ill-advised decision? Over and over again, urban teachers tell researchers that while salaries are bad, they loathe the lack of respect.

While we are depressed about this lack of respect, it is important to mention the new educational reforms of the twenty-first century that have institutionalized this degrading view of teachers. The premise supporting many of the No Child Left Behind reforms involves the belief that the curriculum must be teacher-proof. This means that since teachers are so bad, we must control their classroom practice in every way possible, leaving as little as possible to their own prerogative. Thus, many urban teachers are handed scripts to read to their students and pre-made standardized evaluation procedures with which to grade them. The idea of a brilliant professional diagnosing the needs of particular students in specific situations and constructing a curriculum tailor-made for them is old, stale news in many contemporary reforms.

The central objective of these reforms involves raising published indicators of school success. Thus, raising standardized test scores for public relations purposes becomes an obsession in many urban school systems. Of course, the benefits for students derived from rising test scores may be negligible. Indeed, in many circumstances there may be an inverse relation between rising test scores and student intellectual development. The Texas educational reforms of the 1990s provide an excellent example of the ways such reforms manipulate test scores, dropout rates, and real student achievement (see Ray Horn and Joe Kincheloe's *American Standards: Quality Education in a Complex World: The Texas Case* for an expansion of these themes). In such teacher-proof, deskilled, manipulated contexts, teachers are rewarded for delivering unquestioned data to students for their memorization. Even when teachers are not given scripts to read to students, the notion that school involves handing out factoids to students for their regurgitation on the test is the instructional rule of the day. Have we had enough reality therapy yet? No teacher should walk into an urban school in the first decade of the twenty-first century without exposure to these chilling dynamics.

I am sure that some potential teachers may read this and say, "Urban education is not for me." It is better that they realize that now than when they are in a classroom with students who are depending on them to contribute positively to their lives. Better that they pursue another profession now than join the 50 percent leaving the profession within the first five years. A critical and rigorous teacher education must work to perfect the recipe for advice to potential urban teachers. The reality therapy that involves understanding the hard work, the problems, the frustrations, and the failures involved with urban education must always be balanced by the possibilities, the rewards, the brilliant students and community members, the resilience, and the inspiration that comes with the job. All urban educators walk a tightrope of joy and despair, of pain and pleasure, and of fulfillment and alienation. There is no way around these polarities. And just because there are daunting obstacles does not mean that there is no chance for urban teachers to make a difference in schools, communities, and individual student lives.

Great urban teachers make a difference in these domains every day. Indeed, brilliant students, teacher colleagues, and tough-minded, visionary community leaders make a difference in the lives of urban teachers every day. I am humbled, amazed, and inspired by gifted urban teachers who motivate and support resilient urban students in their efforts to avoid the pitfalls of growing up in urban poverty. They are some of the most heroic figures of our era, working their magic in the most difficult of circumstances.

Of course, a central question of urban education that we all must deal with is why so many teachers leave the profession so quickly. Our reality therapy helps us with this one. Maybe a more important question in this context is why so many stay. What about those teachers who after five years are still plugging away in urban schools? Many of those who stay are those who possess a clear understanding of what urban education entails and are not shocked by the first day of school. Such educators build networks with other teachers, community members, parents, helpful organizations, and professionals in other fields. They respect their students, work to understand what their lives are like, and accordingly struggle to figure out how they can meet their needs. Such teachers never stop researching the answer to the question: Why teach in urban settings?

Kecia Hayes

This question, "Why teach in urban settings?" is an increasingly critical point of reflection for educators as the social challenges that confront urban communities and the schools that are embedded within them continue to mount. It requires that an individual first consider the social context within which urban education occurs, as well as the consequent educational or learning needs of urban youth.

In terms of the current social context, there has been a 3 percent increase, from 48 percent in 2000 to 51 percent in 2005, in the number of children in urban communities who live in low-income families (Douglas-Hall and Chau, 2009). According to the National Center for Children in Poverty, children living in low-income families are disproportionately Black or Latino. More than half of them live with parents who are immigrants, nearly two-thirds live with parents who have only a high school diploma or have not completed high school, more than half have at least one parent who is a full-time, year-round worker, and more than one-third of their parents work in the service industry. Seventeen percent are without health insurance, and 16 percent experience persistent hunger.

Additionally, in some states, urban youth are more likely to be netted by the school-to-prison pipeline, which compounds the negative impacts of their poverty and complicates efforts to engage them in the educational process. The Committee on Education of the New York City Council reports, "Each year, roughly 10,000 New York City children come into contact with the courts. More than 2,000 students are in juvenile detention in the city every day, and each year some 1,200 students return to the city from upstate jails. More than two-thirds of children released from custody never go back to school, where they might learn skills that could help them build a positive future" (Moskowitz, 2005). According to Fagan and Freeman, as cited by Roberts (2002, p. 209), "Children who are incarcerated have virtually no chance of getting a good job when they grow up." Not only are these youth, many of whom hail from urban communities, likely to perpetuate the poverty status in which they were raised, but they also are likely to experience further marginalization of their political (voluntary and involuntary) disenfranchisement and social capital, which has the impact of weakening the viability of their communities. Examining the period of 1973 to 2002, Drucker found that "thirty years of forced removal to prison of 150,000 young males from particular communities of New York represents collective losses similar in scale to the losses due to epidemics, wars, and terrorist attacks—with the potential for comparable effects on the survivors and the social structure of their families and communities" (2002, p. 7).

So, if this is the social context, then what are the educational or learning needs that exist for the young people who exist within these conditions that overwhelmingly shape life in urban communities? Whether or not it is fair or appropriate, urban schools must contend with the fact that a majority of their students will arrive at the schoolhouse doors victimized by the pernicious and persistent consequences of growing up in our nation's poverty tracts. Consequently, those who want to teach in urban settings must understand that urban youth and their communities need the type of educational experiences that will bridge the gaps that exist in their learning and that will enable them to substantively develop their intellectual capital so it can be leveraged in the economic, political, and social domains of society as a catalyst to transform the conditions that have problematically structured their lives. Cultivating their intellectual capital cannot simply revolve around their superficial acquisition of culturally arbitrary curricula, as conceptualized by Bourdieu and Passeron (1990), which frames much of the teaching and learning in our urban schools. It must be fundamentally anchored in the development of cultural competence and critical literacy that allows young people to achieve a personalized understanding of the sociohistorical evolution of their racialized communities within national and international contexts, and to grasp the ever-changing sociopolitical, cultural, and economic dynamics of our hegemonic global society, their positions within it, and how to strategically change those dynamics in the interests of themselves and their communities.

Urban educators must deeply and authentically understand the ways that the arbitrary curriculum which shapes their work with young people, impedes the development of students' cultural competence. According to Bourdieu and Passeron, "All pedagogic action (PA) is, objectively, symbolic violence insofar as it is the imposition of a cultural arbitrary by an arbitrary power" (1990, p. 5). The educational establishment has empowered itself to decide the knowledges and skills in which an individual must achieve proficiency to be considered educated. Unfortunately, most urban youth don't find their own cultural knowledges, ways of knowing, and histories included in what the establishment has deemed as legitimate curricula. The symbolic violence occurs through the inclusion of particular knowledges and the exclusion of others. As students learn that they are culturally absent from the socially constructed and validated core curriculum, they are made to feel othered and disconnected from the value of the pedagogic action of teaching and learning. "Through decisions on which knowledge is acceptable, desirable, and respected, teachers (as the guardians and pawns) of educational structures regulate how the world enters into students as well as how students enter the world. Logically, dominant group educational structures are not overly concerned with empowering the dominated" (Jones, 2001, p. 3). An uncritical and solitary adherence to the arbitrary curriculum results in the inability of students to develop their cultural competence, which could help to place them and their communities as intellectual assets within the society's canon of knowledge, as well as help them to understand the connections between their intellectual assets, educational achievement, and social transformation.

When urban youth, particularly those from our racialized communities, are educated in the absence of any focus on the development of cultural competence, they may not fully understand how to effectively leverage their evolving intellectual capital to not only advance their specific social position but to simultaneously engage in efforts to uplift their racialized community. Consider, for example, W. E. B. Du Bois's reconceptualization of the *Talented Tenth*. Initially, Du Bois thought that the cadre of African Americans who were well educated in the canon of knowledge would be able to counter the prevailing stereotypes of the race and manage the uplift of the masses. "With their talents honed by college and university training, as the vehicle for black uplift and the vanguard to democratize U.S. society, Du Bois's tenth countered the image of black incivility and inhumanity" (James, 1997, p. 19). As this cadre of African Americans was fully immersed in culturally arbitrary curricula devoid of any substantive focus on their or other racialized knowledges, ways of knowing, and histories, however, they were Americanized in ways that disconnected them from the goal of collective uplift for the community. Their efforts were moreover geared towards the achievement of individual social transcendence rather than collective social transformation. "This deradicalization process, according to Du Bois occurs when more privileged African Americans (re)align themselves to function as a middle class interested in individual group gain rather than race leadership for mass development" (James, 1997, p. 24). This problem was not only recognized and conceptualized by Du Bois but also by Paulo Freire, who noted, "The central problem is this: How can the oppressed, as divided, unauthentic beings, participate in developing the pedagogy of their liberation? . . . As long as they live in the duality in which *to be* is *to be like,* and *to be like* is *to be like the oppressor,* this contribution is impossible" (1996, p. 48). As urban educators, you must be actively committed to engaging in the pedagogic work of liberation so that urban youth acquire the tools to not only become well-credentialed within society but also simultaneously be empowered to more strategically develop and use their economic, political, and social capital in service of their communities and themselves.

In addition to assertively focusing on the development of broad-based cultural competence of young people, urban educators must also work for critical literacy. Macedo (1994) conceptualizes the phenomenon of a traditional or instrumentalist approach to literacy versus a critical literacy. He notes:

> The instrumental literacy for the poor, in the form of a competency-based skills-banking approach, and the highest form of instrumental literacy for the rich, acquired through the university in the form of professional specialization, share one common feature: they both prevent the development of the critical thinking that enables one to read the world critically and to understand the reasons and linkages behind the facts. Literacy for the poor is, by and large, characterized by mindless, meaningless drills and exercises given in preparation for multiple-choice exams and writing gobbledygook. . . . This instrumental approach to literacy sets the stage for the anesthetization of the mind, (Macedo, 1994, p. 16)

Within this context, urban youth are intellectually stunted by an overexposure to pedagogical actions that dampen, rather than awaken, their abilities to interrogate, analyze, and respond to the world around them. Furthermore, it has had the impact of not only anesthetizing the minds of our urban youth but also alienating them from learning. Shor (1992) correctly contends that there is a natural and authentic point of entry to the type of pedagogical work that cultivates the development of a critical literacy. It begins with helping students to examine the socioeconomic, political, cultural, and historical contexts of their lives to identify the intersections, contradictions, and gaps and continues by helping them to utilize their analysis to make more productive decisions so that they can be active, rather than passive, agents in the transformation of their lives and their communities.

Urban youth must develop a critical literacy so they can juxtapose the different socioeconomic, political, cultural, and historical contexts that frame the lived experiences of people from different racialized, classed, and gendered communities within the world. This need is made more evident through consideration of Du Bois's concept of *double consciousness,* which "emerges from the unhappy symbiosis between three modes of thinking, being, and seeing. The first is racially particularistic, the second nationalistic in that it derives from the nation state in which the ex-slaves but not-yet-citizens find themselves, rather than from their aspiration towards a nation state of their own. The third is diasporic or hemispheric, sometimes global and occasionally universalist" (Gilroy, 1993, p. 127). Critical literacy can help urban youth make sense of these "three modes of thinking, being, and seeing" that form the basis of who they are—racially marginalized citizens of a nation as well as of a diaspora. Through a more critical read of the world and their place within it, the context of their lives takes on new meanings that are more authentic, nuanced, connected, and relevant. A more critical understanding of this context empowers urban youth to be more strategic social actors.

The failure of urban youth to achieve a critical literacy is evident in the varied ways in which they have been complicit in the negative commodification of their cultural knowledges and artistic forms. Record companies, through their A&R (artists and repertoire) departments, fit artists into best-selling genres, so that as gangsta rap gained market share, artists were steered towards its production. Urban youth, particularly those of color, have demonstrated an inability to scrutinize how their uncritical participation in the production and consumption of negative musical forms like gangsta rap, which promotes hyperessentialized images of them as uneducated, violent, apolitical, and misogynistic thugs who are only concerned with the acquisition of "bling," significantly shapes their social positionality. They fail to comprehend the extent to which these images, scripted in boardrooms outside of their sphere of control and influence, dictate how others perceive and engage them, which consequently influences their life chances. The point herein is that urban youth need a well-designed pedagogy for the cultivation of their critical literacy so they are not only able to problematize how our society's hegemonic dynamics around dimensions of race, class, and gender structure their lives but also able to problematize their own complicit reinforcement of those hegemonic dynamics through some of their naive actions.

While the pedagogical work for critical literacy is a significant task, there are viable points of entry that can be leveraged. As earlier noted, Shor (1992) implores us to utilize natural and authentic points of entry, and one such point can be the musical forms of the subculture of urban youth of color. A critical examination of urban youth's complicity in the problematic dynamics of their musical forms is one frame for this point of entry, but there are others. For instance, Decker contends that within the hip-hop genre, there has been an emergence of a nationalist community of artists who have structured their music to reveal a more critical examination of the different dynamics of the economic, political, and social domains of our society as well as the ways in which different communities are impacted by the dynamics. "While hip hop nationalists are not politicians, they are involved in the production of cultural politics—its creation, its circulation and its interpretation—which is tied to the everyday struggles of working-class blacks and the urban poor . . ." (Decker, 1994, p. 101). This is evident in the work of rappers like KRS-One, such as his track entitled "You Must Learn" (2000), and Dead Prez, including their track entitled "They Schools" (2000). In both instances, the artists provide an essential critique of the ways in which the core curricula of our schools privilege particular knowledges and subjugate others and how this curricular structure cultivates students' alienation and disengagement. KRS-One explicitly makes the point that Black children in the racially segregated schools of urban communities need to learn about their racialized history. They force listeners to question whether the resistance to school demonstrated by urban youth is really a resistance to the reluctance of school culture and curricula to authentically acknowledge them and their heritage.

The discourse of these artists and others within the nationalist community of hip hop culture is reminiscent of Bourdieu and Passeron's (1990) articulation of the symbolic violence inherent in pedagogic actions whereby an arbitrary authority legitimates and imposes a culturally arbitrary set of knowledges, ways of knowing, and histories on individuals. They explicitly articulate the fact that education is a valuable tool for the empowerment and social uplift of the community. However, just as Dewey warned that not all experiences are educative, these artists contend that not all education is equally valuable to the work of individual and collective social uplift for marginalized urban communities. They clarify that urban youth need an education that will not simply prepare them to obtain a job but that will equip them to use their agency to transform the social, political, and economic dynamics that structure their lives and their communities.

Elements of the hip hop cultural form produced by local urban youth as well as by youth of color within the diaspora provide urban educators with one resource that can be leveraged as a viable point of entry to the pedagogy of critical literacy as well as for cultural competence. To be clear, the point herein is not to specifically advocate an uncritical embrace of hip hop or any particular cultural form as a learning tool but to acknowledge that urban educators must capitalize on the instructional value of a critical utilization of content from various cultures, including the subcultures of urban youth. Urban educators must not be outright dismissive of this pedagogical opportunity. They must be willing to accept the cultural representations of their students' indigenous knowledges and ways of knowing as instructional assets upon which to build cultural competence and critical literacy. They must learn to skillfully utilize these assets within the teaching and learning dynamic to help young people identify, analyze, construct, and apply a deep understanding of the intersections and contradictions between and within the knowledges of the curricular canon of schools and the knowledges of students' own cultural understandings and histories. In this way, urban educators are collaborating with students to construct new meanings and learning.

Semali reminds us that "through this constructivist methodology, students can generate an interest and ownership in the subject matter, because it is relevant to the learner and because the subject matter is rooted or based on the students' prior knowledge, history, and culture. It would seem that many opportunities are lost when prior knowledge of indigenous ways of knowing things are ignored by teachers" (1999, p. 106). Unless educators are willing to authentically incorporate students' indigenous knowledges, children are going to be disconnected from learning and continue to resist the knowledge of schools, which seems so irrelevant to their lives. In order to contemplate the question of "Why Teach in Urban Settings?," individuals must decide whether they are willing to commit to all that the task and urban youth requires of them—specifically, a constructivist methodology to frame a pedagogy of critical literacy and for cultural competence. It entails pedagogical efforts that are well beyond a focus on education for credentialing, which tends to preoccupy the current practices of schools. As Du Bois once argued, "when we call for education we mean real education. We believe in work. We ourselves are workers, but work is not necessarily education. Education is the development of power and ideal. We want our children trained as intelligent human beings should be, and we will fight for all time against any proposal to educate black boys and girls simply as servants and underlings, or simply for the use of other people. They have a right to know, to think, to aspire" (Carroll et al., 2000, p. 19). Individuals who want to be urban educators must authentically grapple with how to make manifest a deep commitment to this fundamental ideal.

For me, the understanding and commitment to the ideal and the work required of urban educators resulted from my childhood experiences. I grew up in an urban neighborhood, which at the time, was one of the largest African American communities in the nation and had a significant stock of brownstone houses. It also was hobbled by the crack cocaine epidemic, the prison industrial complex, illegal redlining practices carried out by several financial institutions, inadequate healthcare services, declining educational institutions, poorly maintained public housing, and dwindling social services. The statistics behind these conditions were used to create a dominant narrative for my life as an African American girl from the 'hood. The messages within the public sphere were that I was not likely to graduate from high school or to attend college, I was likely to be a teenage single mother who would become welfare dependent, I was likely to not be competitive within the labor market and would have to accept a low-level position in a service industry, and I would not be able to legally accumulate wealth or property to achieve financial security.

According to this dominant narrative of plight and despair, I would not acquire the education and skills to transcend and transform the conditions that structured my childhood within this socially marginalized urban neighborhood. The narrative's messages were bolstered by media coverage that predominantly focused on stories that reinforced negative and problematic imagery of everyone who existed within the community. Unfortunately, I encountered several teachers throughout my school career who uncritically embraced this narrative. For instance, I had one teacher who, during a parent–teacher conference, told my parents that I was not as smart as they contended and routinely attempted to publicly denigrate my intellectual contributions to class discussions. While some may make the "one rogue teacher" argument to explain this incident, it does not lessen her potential negative impact on my sense of efficacy as a learner. Additionally, the fact is that she was representative of some of my other teachers. For classmates who had few academic achievements and a weak sense of efficacy as a learner, I expect that this teacher's attitude and pedagogical approach were especially damaging. Not once did she show any attempt to critically read the dominant narrative or any interest in helping us to create and live a counternarrative. Rather than accept the norm of negativity projected in the narrative, my classmates and I needed all of our teachers, not just some of them, to imagine what was possible and to collaborate with us to achieve it.

Fortunately, my parents, who had similar educational experiences during their childhoods, diligently worked to help me establish a counternarrative about who I was and to ascribe particular meanings informed by race, class, and gender to education that would empower me to transcend and transform the conditions that structured my urban childhood. While I encountered teachers throughout my schooling who successfully demonstrated an educational philosophy in their pedagogical practices that was similar to my parents, my parents were my first urban educators to engage in this work with a clear and specific intentionality. My parents carefully framed a counternarrative of what it meant to be an African American girl from the 'hood and structured my non-school educational experiences to reinforce it. They used books, museums, television programs, the oral histories of family members, and other resources to expose me and my brothers to the cultural heritage and legacy of the African American community. They engaged us in critical dialogues about the things that we were learning. They expected us to be able to not only describe the importance of different historicultural events but also to be able to take and argue specific positions around events and issues, to articulate our roles within the context of different events—what impact did they have on our lives and how did our current actions impact the subsequent significance of the events?—and to make explicit the ways in which the events and their significance were connected to what we were learning in school. In doing so, they ensured that our education reflected a comprehensive cultural competence as well as a critical literacy.

In a broad sense, my parents, who were high school graduates, were the type of urban educators that Giroux (1988) conceptualizes as *transformative intellectuals* "who develop counterhegemonic pedagogies that not only empower students by giving them the knowledge and social skills they will need to be able to function in the larger society as critical agents, but also educate them for transformative action" (p. xxxiii). They were willing to be intellectually vulnerable so that we were able to learn together through collaborative construction of knowledge and understandings. While there were many things that were non-negotiable in our home, debate of knowledge and ideas was encouraged. My parents embraced the different, sometimes wacky, perspectives that we brought to the table because they represented another point of entry to escalate our learning. They taught us to enjoy and deeply value education, knowledge, and the multiple ways of learning that exist. School was one venue where we were able to become educated, but they showed us that many venues outside of the school were also sites for learning. They acknowledged the problematic exclusivity inherent in the curricula of our school-based education and that they had to supplement our learning in order to fully cultivate our intellectual potential. They were transparent in their intention to use education as the tool to empower us to construct and live a narrative of our racialized and classed selves that allowed us to compellingly counter and disrupt the hegemonic dominant narrative that would have confined us to social irrelevance. These lessons, understandings, and skills have served me well, and are the basis of my commitment to the pedagogical work that I know urban youth deserve and need.

My commitment redoubled when I entered the corporate sector after college and was responsible, in part, for counseling individuals who were unable to effectively compete within the local, much less global, labor markets. According to Rifkin (1995), individuals who have no possibility of contributing to society due to their lack of desirable skills or significant purchasing power are economically irrelevant. I believed that the issue was not only about economic irrelevance but also about a more encompassing social irrelevance wherein people were unable to effectively participate in all of the domains of society, and that education had to play a role in the dynamic. I wondered what had happened in the educational experiences of the people whom I counseled such that they were now experiencing different degrees of social irrelevance. If, as my parents had strongly communicated, education was the key to transformative social empowerment, why was it elusive for others who had acquired the credentials of our school system? Why wasn't the school-based education sufficient to fend off conditions of social irrelevance? As I contemplated these questions, I more clearly understood that in our public discourse, we aggressively promote the rhetoric that education is the great equalizer that empowers individuals to achieve social mobility, but we fail to acknowledge that the type of education in many of our urban schools reproduces paradigms of oppression as well as social inequality and irrelevance.

In response to these reflections, I decided my vocation was in urban education. I headed to 110 Livingston Street, the former headquarters of the New York City Board of Education, where I spent a full eight-hour day and accomplished nothing. When I left the building, I knew that I did not want to become a teacher within that bureaucracy. I was astonished that not one of the many people with whom I had conversations ever asked me about my experiences with children, whether I liked children, why I wanted to be a teacher, or asked me to articulate my educational philosophy. I seriously questioned whether this was a site where I would be able to provide urban young people with an education reflective of the transformative power that was embedded in the messages and efforts of my parents, which I believe is critical for our youth. I consequently explored community-based opportunities to be the type of urban educator that I thought was appropriate and necessary. Soon thereafter, I began working with a grassroots Harlem-based community organization focused on enhancing the social and educational opportunities of urban youth. Through this organization, I was able to collaborate with other urban educators to construct learning activities that provided our students with experiences to expand their critical understanding of historicultural events through thematic curricula and excursions, to critically explore social issues through research and debate, as well as to develop their civic responsibility and capacity in the community. Eventually, we established an education component to help parents develop the necessary skills and understandings to be more effective educational consumers, advocates, and supports for their children. It was a great time, as I had the educational space to be the type of educator that I had experienced in the work of my parents and some of my teachers.

My work with this community-based organization represented a broader conceptualization of how to create and deliver education to urban communities. It acknowledged the need to leverage spaces within urban communities as viable sites and resources for transformative learning. It was an opportunity to create alternative pedagogical models where educators, parents, and students collaborated to construct new understandings that informed everyone's cultural competence and critical literacy. It allowed us to have an intergenerational and multicultural focus through our use of the spaces and members of communities as points of entry to disciplinary and interdisciplinary discussions. It forced us to respect and openly value the indigenous knowledge and skills of our students as they contributed to the teaching and learning dynamic. It required us to abandon our assumptions and to authentically and actively appreciate our parents and students as educational partners who were not people to be educated but people with whom to learn—we worked to co-construct and impart knowledge to each other. It was an experience that humbled and deeply gratified me.

So, why teach in urban settings? If you can embrace the challenge of developing your pedagogical acumen and expertise to engage in this critical work, and are willing to always be critically reflective of your assumptions and pedagogical practices, then you can make significant contributions to the sustainable development of socially marginalized urban communities through the cultivation of the young people's intellectualism. There is joyful satisfaction in fulfilling such a civic responsibility. As you engage urban youth in constructivist pedagogy for cultural competence and critical literacy, you will substantively expand your own intellectualism and ways of knowing. You will begin to more critically reflect upon the world around you as well as the ways in which you engage it and it engages you. Just as you help to expose your urban students to an entirely new world, they will do likewise for you. You will become a much more intentional social actor as a result of the learning that you will experience through your work with urban youth. The experience of being an urban educator is an invaluable gift of self-empowerment anchored in new understandings and ways of knowing that are collaboratively constructed with young people whose perspectives help to challenge and expand your cultural competence and critical literacy. These are the reasons why I am an urban educator.

REFERENCES

Bourdieu, P., & Passeron, J. (1990). *Reproduction in education, society, and culture.* Newbury Park, CA: Sage Publications.

Carroll, A., Torricelli, R., & Goodwin, D. K. (2000). *In our own words: Extraordinary speeches of the American century.* New York: Washington Square Press.

Casella, R. (1998). The theoretical foundations of cultural studies in education. *Philosophy of Education Society Yearbook.* Retrieved September 2003, from http://www.ed.uiuc.edu/EPS/PES.Yearbook/1998/casella.html

Dead Prez. (2000) They schools. *Lets get free.* Loud Records.

Decker, J. L. (1994). The state of rap: Time and place in hip-hop nationalism. In A. Ross and T. Rose (Eds.), *Microphone fiends: Youth music & youth culture* (pp. 99–121). New York: Routledge.

Douglas-Hall, A. and Chau, M., (2009). Basic facts about low-income children: Birth to age 18. National Center for Children in Poverty. Retrieved July 2009, from http://www.nccp.org/publications/pdf/download_281.pdf

Drucker, Ernest. (2002). Population impact of mass incarceration under New York's Rockefeller Drug Laws: An analysis of years of life lost. *Journal of Urban Health: Bulletin of the New York Academy of Medicine, 79*(3), 434–435. Retrieved December 2005, from http://www.prison-sucks.com/scans/rockefeller.pdf

Freire, P. (1996). *Pedagogy of the oppressed.* New York: Continuum.

Gilroy, P. (1993). *The Black Atlantic: Modernity and double consciousness.* Cambridge, MA: Harvard University Press.

Giroux, H. (1988). *Teachers as intellectuals: Toward a critical pedagogy of learning.* Westport, CT: Bergin & Garvey.

James, J. (1997). *Transcending the talented tenth: Black leaders and American intellectuals.* New York: Routledge.

Jones, R. (2001). The liberatory education of the talented tenth: Critical consciousness and the continuing Black Humanization Project. *The Negro Educational Review, 52*(1–2), 3–18.

KRS-One/Boogie Down Productions. (2000). You must learn. *A Retrospective.* Jive Records.

Macedo, D. (1994). *Literacies of power: What Americans are not allowed to know.* Boulder, CO: Westview Press.

Moskowitz, E. (2005). Correcting juvenile injustice: A Bill of Rights for children released from custody.New York City Council Education Committee. Retrieved December 2005, from http://www.nyccouncil.info/pdf_files/reports/04_27_05_childbor.pdf

Rifkin, J. (1995). *The end of work: The decline of the global labor force and the dawn of the postmarket era.* New York: G.P. Putnam's Sons.

Roberts, D. (2002). *Shattered bonds.* New York: Basic Civitas Books.

Semali, L. (1999). Community as classroom: (Re)valuing indigenous literacy. In L. Semali & J. Kincheloe (Eds.), *What is indigenous knowledge? Voices from the academy* (pp. 95–118). New York: Falmer Press.

Shor, I. (1992). *Empowering education: Critical teaching for social change.* Chicago, IL: University of Chicago Press.

CHAPTER THREE

Rochelle Brock

What Does "Good" Urban Teaching Look Like?

What is my philosophy of good urban education? How does it reflect my pedagogical style? How do I understand myself as an urban teacher? The answers to these questions are constantly changing and growing, because the more I learn about myself, the more I learn about my purpose as an urban educator. I am able to ask my students the right questions when I can ask myself the right questions. Although there are always common themes running throughout my philosophy of urban education, it is constantly in flux. The more I learn and experience life, the better able I am to teach my students.

I hold certain beliefs based on my life assumptions. I accept that there are certain facts and truths based on my life experiences. The combination of my beliefs and truths becomes my philosophy and pedagogy. A truth: minority and poor people are always fighting to get through the back doors of educational systems. A truth: in a colonial system, the colonizer has a dual purpose in educating the colonized. The first is socialization into accepting the value system, history, and culture of the dominant society. The second is education for economic productivity. A truth: the oppressed are treated like commodities imbued with skills that are bought and sold on the labor market for the profit of capitalists. These are my truths as an African American woman and an urban educator.

We live in a society that places people based on their race, class, and gender. I believe that students who are poor and/or minority exist under a system that accepts and promotes their failure. I know that in most schools, World History equals Western History; children celebrate Thanksgiving by dressing as Indians with art class feather headbands and are told that Columbus discovered America. I know that students of color are hungry for knowledge about their culture, not tolerance. I know that Black and Brown children are tracked into *special* classes where they typically remain for the entirety of their school career. I know that the ideology under which America exists constructs these children as nothing and ensures through that construction that these children believe they are nothing. All of these things I know, and I cannot accept . . . not when I feel the failure of a large segment of the population. My knowledge and observations contextualize my beliefs.

As an urban teacher, I must teach all of my students, especially my minority and disenfranchised students, to think critically and to deconstruct the world. I must provide them with the tools to analyze their everyday life through the lenses of race, class, and gender oppression. They must think politically and see the connections between what they see on a comedy sitcom, to what they read or don't read in the newspaper. My pedagogy is educating my students for struggle, survival, and the realization of their humanity. I believe I must teach to demystify the injustices of the world by becoming a radical teacher, facilitating students in the understanding of their self-identity and outside constructed identity, the structures working against them, what they must fight, and the form the fight will take—education of self and activism for the community.

How do I go about enacting my truths and my beliefs as they change and I change, although my truths and beliefs manifest themselves differently depending on the needs and identities of my students? What stays constant, and what all my students recognize about me, is that they will leave my class more aware than when they entered.

The following is a fictional constructed conversation with my African goddess Oshun. Using a Black feminist theoretical framework, the reader becomes privy to our conversation on urban education and teaching. Black feminist thought is a useful tool in framing this chapter because, as Patricia Hill Collins (1991) asserts, it furnishes a space for voice by challenging prevailing approaches to studying oppressed groups. These approaches support the notion that the oppressed identify with the powerful and are seen as less human, and therefore less capable of interpreting their own oppression. A feminist perspective allows a language of critique to be developed that questions this assumption. This language of critique is developed through an epistemological framework, which is useful in understanding urban teaching. Collins (1991) delineated a Black feminist epistemology which has the following four characteristics: (1) "concrete experience as a criterion of meaning" (2) "the use of dialogue in assessing knowledge claims" (3) "the ethic of caring" and (4) "the ethic of personal accountability."

Epistemology, the study of how knowledge is constructed, lets us construct the questions to delve more deeply into the realities of the urban family. Moreover, we are better able to understand the answers we receive from those questions.

For the purpose of this chapter the first two characteristics will be used to frame how we look at urban teaching and to help us understand what we ultimately see.

The conversation is based on the group conversation method, which is a culturally relevant qualitative ethnographic strategy. Taking the group conversation method one step further, the constructed conversation is based on the tenets of Black feminist thought and allows a fictional dialogue to personalize the subject by creating a connectedness between the words. A constructed conversation asks us to momentarily suspend reality. The essence of the constructed conversation is the "use of dialogue in assessing knowledge claims," the second characteristic of a Black feminist epistemology (Brock, 2005).

Dialogue implies talk between two subjects, not the speech of subject and object. According to Collins (1991), "a primary epistemological assumption underlying the use of dialogue in assessing knowledge claims is that connectedness rather than separation is an essential component of the knowledge validation process." Collins further states that people become human and empowered only in the context of a community, and only when they "become seekers of the type of connections, interactions, and meetings that lead to harmony." Dialogue allows this to happen.

Dialogue presupposes that we talk with each other not at each other. In addition, dialogue is an important aspect of both African American language and Latino(a) language. It assumes an understanding that language is more than words and cannot be a singular event as in one-sided talk. A feminist epistemology demands discourse. In order for ideas to be tested and validated, everyone in the group must participate. As in the first characteristic, which speaks of the importance of community, as well as knowledge and wisdom, dialogue occurs within a community of individuals.

The use of dialogue in assessing knowledge claims supports the methodology of constructed conversation. The method of constructed conversation is "in tune with" the African American and Latino(a) tradition of dialogue within a community setting. In addition, the constructed conversation methodology allows research to be presented in a more realistic format.

In this context, I address the nuances involved in teaching urban kids of color, specifically Black and Brown students.

OSHUN: Rochelle, tell me about your classroom. How do you enact your philosophy of urban education?

ROCHELLE: I teach through a pedagogy of wholeness which allows me to work with all parts of the student (Brock, 2005). I see and talk to so many students who are struggling to believe in themselves and end up doubting their existence, their right to be. The most important issue to me as a teacher and as a political activist working toward social justice and equity for all students is to bridge that disconnect. I want a conversation about the curriculum or pedagogy needed for urban and minority students. What type of education is needed? What type of education will be empowering? How do I as an instructor foster in my students a commitment toward radical agency?

These are questions I have asked myself and am still struggling to answer. I realize that there are inequalities, poor schools, racist teachers, bad curricula, and children coming into the class ill-prepared to learn. There are countless reform movements aimed at making urban schools better. Some movements blame the teachers; others blame the students, and others are convinced that urban schools are destined to fail. The movements are not successful. Despite the failures in urban school reform and teaching reform movements, we can't give up. Effective teachers of urban students understand the symbiotic relationship between their teaching philosophy and their pedagogy and how both have been influenced by their culture (Bartolome, 2008; Dimitriadis, 2008; Joyce, 2008; Foster, 1994). How can I take my intellectual knowledge and make it work in urban settings? How can I dance with theory in a rhythm which is indigenous to my culture?

OSHUN: Gestalt—understand all the parts of your whole. As a minority in a society that devalues us at every turn, survival is often the main goal. From negative depictions on television to negative depictions in the ideology of America, we are under a constant siege, battling for survival. How do you enact this pedagogy of wholeness in your classroom?

ROCHELLE: Let me use as an example of my pedagogy a class I teach called *The African American Woman.* As a critical teacher, I try to facilitate my students to understand the anger and the pride I feel in my Black identity. I attempt to lead them to an understanding of the *culture of survival* that Black people have historically possessed. In my class, my students and I discuss the insidious ways Black women are constructed in society. We discuss the social, historical, political, and economic realities of an urban environment. I begin the class with a word list scribbled on one half of the bulletin board: "ideology, epistemology, deconstruction, hegemony, devaluation, Other, dichotomy, binary opposition, stereotypes." I then ask the students for adjectives they think of when describing Black women. Of course they begin with politically correct, positive words—strong, beautiful, mother—until I tell them to be honest and tell me the words that most of society uses to describe Black women. At that point a fervor is created, as students hurl words at me faster than I can write them down—slut, ho, matriarch, ugly, sexual, aggressive, demanding, fat, unattractive, teen mothers. Once the board is filled I just let them look at the words, allow them to seep into their consciousness. (We also do this exercise discussing Latina women; many of the descriptors are the same.)

OSHUN: Aren't the words already part of their consciousness?

ROCHELLE: Singularly, maybe, but not together. There is an impact on students when the students see the board dripping with the venomous lexicon.

OSHUN: Kind of a drama queen, aren't you?

ROCHELLE: Whatever it takes. It's important that the students realize from the start that this is not a history class and we are not going to go through a long litany of historical facts on Black women. We analyze the construction of Black womanhood and the etymology of these words through the lenses of ideology, epistemology, the Other, deconstruction, hegemony, devaluation, dichotomy, binary opposition, stereotypes. They learn these concepts, pay close attention to them in their readings; it is through an understanding of these concepts that they will begin to partially open the door in their realization of Black women. Whatever time remains in the class on that first day is spent talking about the meaning of Black feminist thought—its purposes, goal, and benefit to our understanding of Black and Brown women. It is also important to understand that many, many Brown women are included in the categories, situations, and assumptions that are placed on Black women. Given the conditions of slavery and indenture in the Caribbean, South and Central America, and the diaspora which blended Black and Brown together, we are looking at complex racialized groups. For the purpose of this conversation, I relate to Black and Brown women through Black feminist thought.

Borrowing from Patricia Collins (1991), I divided the discussion of African American women, and to a large part, Latina women, into five themes:

- Black Feminist Thought
- Legacy of Struggle
- Representation and Controlling Images
- Search for Voice
- Empowerment in Everyday Life.

Through readings, documentaries, films, and class discussions, the class dissects the life of African American women. This dissection allows the students (Black, Brown, and White—male and female) to understand the various ways ideology has attempted to control and dominate Latina and African American women. In addition, an understanding of Black feminist thought allows the students to see the ways Black and Brown women are not only deconstructing the race, gender, and class oppression of women but also Black and Brown female activism and empowerment.

I am aware of the need to assess the abstract through concrete experience. Although I use *Black feminist thought* to teach students the theory that underlies Black women's lives, I also weave in *We Are Your Sisters: Black Women in the Nineteenth Century,* an anthology of Black women's writings edited by Dorothy Sterling (1984). In this excellent volume, students read firsthand accounts of Black women under enslavement, freedom, the Civil War, and post-World War I through letters, diaries, interviews, and Freedmen's Bureau records. In this way two purposes are served: the first is the women become subjects in their own history and are no longer objectified by present-day scholars. Students are allowed to hear their voices, concerns, and intelligence, and then relate that voice to the tenets of Black feminism. For example, they receive a glimpse of the bewilderment and confusion the concept of freedom caused some enslaved people. Take for example the following passage from Sterling's *We Are Your Sisters* (1984):

> Member de fust Sunday of freedom. We was all sittin' roun' restin' an' tryin' to think what freedom meant an' ev'ybody was quiet an' peaceful. All at once ole Sister Carrie who was near 'out a hundred started in to talkin':
>
> Tain't no mo' sellin today,
> Tain't no mo' hirin' today,
> Tain't no pullin off shirts today,
> Its stomp down freedom today.
> Stomp it down!
> An' when she says Stomp it down, all de slaves commence to shoutin' wid her:
> Stomp down freedom today—Stomp it down! Stomp down Freedom today.

OSHUN: You trouble and layer the realities of knowledge or in some cases what we think we know. Speaking of knowledge I remember once how you used the book to lay a guilt trip on your students.

ROCHELLE: As soon as I realize my class is not doing the assigned reading I recite a passage from *We Are Your Sisters* where various women discussed their struggle to learn to read during enslavement, despite fear of death if discovered. I have to bring it home to the students. Personal accountability (Collins, 1991; Villaverde, 2008) is not just a notion. In my class, students are accountable for their actions and when they aren't . . . I let them know. Tapping into my Black matriarchal self—we have had that guilt trip laid on us since we were babies . . . I like to think of it as more of a reality check.

OSHUN: It's the juxtaposition of accountability within the ethic of caring; both are qualities of effective and affective teaching.

ROCHELLE: In addition, students begin to appreciate that African American women who were enslaved understood their objectification and oppression at the hands of a cruel system and found ways to survive. Either due to a lack of education or miseducation, many students believe that other than Sojourner Truth and Harriet Tubman, slave women were just singing in the fields and accepting their conditions. Black women have always participated in the legacy of resistance and struggle from the social, historical, and political conditions of society. For example, Lewis Hayden, a leader of Boston's Black community in the 1900s, tells of how his mother kept her children from being sold:

My mother often hid us all in the woods, to prevent master selling us. When we wanted water, she sought for it in any hole or puddle formed by falling trees or otherwise. It was often full of tadpoles and insects. She strained it, and gave it round to each of us in the hollow of her hand. For food, she gathered berries in the woods, got potatoes, raw corn & c. After a time, the master would send word to her to come in, promising he would not sell us (Hayden, in Sterling, 1984, p. 58).

It is important for my students to understand the strength that these women possessed despite the hell they were living in. I often remind them of the words and images we wrote on the board the first day of class so that they can see the dichotomy between the reality of Black women and the perception of Black women.

Although I occasionally use the didactic method when there was particular information the students needed, my pedagogy is built around the second characteristic of an African American epistemology, the use of dialogue in assessing knowledge claims. In the African American community, words carry power. An African American epistemology demands discourse and pursues the connectedness of dialogue (Collins, 1991). Connectedness, an important part of African American roots, asserts that the importance of community outweighs the need of the individual in African American thought, which is related to a sense of being human (Asante, 1991; Collins, 1991; Hurtado, 1996; Jocson, 2008). Asante (1991) believes that becoming human or realizing the promise of becoming human is the only task of the person. Likewise, Collins asserts that people become human and empowered only in the context of a community and only when they "become seekers of the type of connections, interactions, and meetings that lead to harmony" (p. 185).

In my class I strive to create a community of learners through dialogue where the talk is simultaneously distinct and collective. I create a safe space where the freedom exists to explain self and others. When a teacher engages a class in personal introspection, they must be prepared to hear the painful questioning of students. In one log entry a Black female student cried, "Me questioning me . . . am I the source of the friction never forgetting or forgiving?" (log entry, July 10, 1997). She went on to say:

I started to question the fact if there was racism, because the people in that circle would never express or better yet have or entertain an ill thought against a black person . . . BULLSHIT! I know that when I have people look at us strange.

I know that when I am with a white guy people stare. I know that my colored skin matters. I know when people see me some tell me I'm pretty *for a Black girl*. I know when I talk to people about State they assume I'm here on scholarship or because of affirmative action. I know that people give me grief because I am an African American. I know that I was scared for my boyfriend every time he drove home. *I know that I know.* Being in that class made me wonder. Made me wonder about reasoning and logic (log entry, July 10, 1997).

OSHUN: Do you think you make learning meaningful for your students?

ROCHELLE: I believe that to make learning a meaningful experience students must become active in the attainment of knowledge. In order for this to happen, it is critical to create a space within the class in which student–teacher and student–student discourse can occur. For this reason, at least 70 percent of class time is spent in discussion, where we critically analyze the class readings in a sociohistorical context. We need to know how we got here, why we got here, and how power worked in creating the current context in urban schools, with Black and Brown students. Each semester, many students enter the class afraid to speak, fearful that their knowledge will not be valued or they will have nothing important to add to the discussion. Students of all colors and classes, though to different degrees, have been silenced through years of schooling in a system that operates on the belief that non-credentialed knowledge is unimportant. Although at first apprehensive to speak, eventually most students begin to use their voice and engage in dialogue where they are using their specialized knowledge to theorize about the taken-for-granted or personal feelings and experiences they hold.

If I become too theoretical, I can lose sight of the subjugated knowledge, which has helped Black people survive in this country since the 1600, as well as Brown people who have entered the U.S. to seek a better life. Finding a method to combine my empirical and experiential way of knowing is paramount to my survival both as a teacher and a Black woman. More importantly, it is paramount that I use my personal dilemma to appreciate the realities of students and better equip my pedagogical philosophy to foster a mental–spiritual decolonization of the mind and spirit.

OSHUN: Simmons (1962) states, "Trying to write beyond the assignment of language to a medium of personal expression. I have been cognizant that writing does not translate a reality outside itself but, more precisely, allows the emergence of a new reality." I think of Moraga and Anzaldúa's questions, "How do we organize ourselves to survive this war? To keep our families, our bodies, our spirits intact?" (Moraga & Anzaldúa, 1981).

In response to both Simmons and Moraga and Anzaldúa, I say we develop a language of critique, but one in our own voice, filled with anger, emotion, and caring.

ROCHELLE: Often in heated class discussions, White students feel under attack because of the emotional mode of expression that some Black and Brown students engage in. Often it is the first time White students have been physically and socially close (as in proximity) to Brown and Black students. As the teacher and facilitator I am left with either the choice of silencing students of color, encouraging them speak in a dry, detached style, or utilizing the teachable moment and opening a discussion on different styles of communication. Of course the discussion is more than a simple talk on different communication styles; instead, it is a view into the historical and social effects on the construction of culture. Safety for all students to tell their truth takes time and patience.

An ethic of caring is developing the capacity for empathy. We share with others when we empathize with them and they with us. For example, an interesting conversation took place among several students when I asked them to discuss the class so that I could use their words for a paper I was writing at the time. The discussion eventually turned to the topic of hate and the question of whether we as a society ever get beyond it. Lisa, an extremely emotional and caring person, sincerely attempts to deal with her Whiteness and understand Black culture.

> **Lisa**: (White female) I want to touch it [the pain of Black people] and make it better . . . I have to watch it and can't do anything about it . . . my White friends don't understand when I talk about the importance of this class and the fact that I have learned so much.

> **Tina**: (North Indian female) I understand your pain and I feel bad for it but Black people have to go through the pain every day of being the Other and as much as I feel for what you are experiencing you will never understand the daily pain that Black people experience.

Tina empathized with Lisa's frustration but also was not going to allow Lisa to become wonderful *in-your-face-with-the-truth* white savior community. The respect and understanding they had for each other were evident when they joked with Lisa about her constant crying and said they were going to make her a stronger person by the end of the semester. In my classroom I attempt to invoke an ethic of caring in my teaching as well as the ways students interact with each other.

The last theme of the class, Empowerment in Everyday Life, attempts to show students how Black and Brown women are redefining and empowering themselves and their community and also how each student has the responsibility to take the learning beyond the class into everyday life. Tell me, Oshun, have you ever given birth?

OSHUN: From my womb I have given birth to a civilization.

ROCHELLE: Yeah, well, I can't lay claim to a civilization, but one night for three hours I felt like I gave birth to the consciousness of 40 students.

OSHUN: Sounds painful.

ROCHELLE: It was. My labor pain lasted four months. But seriously, the birth was actually the fruition of a teaching dream. See, every time I develop a new syllabus for *The African American Woman,* I have the final assessment a major class project—a collective project. A cultural production, with song, dance, and drama. It's very hard to pull it all together. I am usually little scared of tying a large portion of the students' grades into one assignment. It came about as I neared my last semester teaching at State, and I knew I most likely would never get the chance to teach this particular class again.

OSHUN: There are times when life forces us to take action.

ROCHELLE: My pending graduation gave me the freedom to pull together everything I hoped I had taught my students. The development of a pedagogy of wholeness that had consumed me for two years, more or less, coalesced in the final class project. Understand, I didn't want my students to leave with disconnected bits of information. The class, or my pedagogy, wasn't meant to present factoids of information but rather to paint a realistic picture of the African American woman, specifically, and women of color, in general. Earlier I talked about the connection between thought and action being a central part of Black feminist thought. Well, my challenge was how that connection could manifest itself in a semester-length class.

OSHUN: Why a class project?

ROCHELLE: I wanted to see the students bring together and make whole all of the knowledge from the entire semester. I attempted to utilize an alternative mode of assessment to really force the students into new ways of thinking. The celebration as I pictured it would allow students to not only express their individual talents but also concentrate on the specific aspect of the class that had been of greatest significance to their growth. I guess there were two central reasons why I decided on the class project. First, I believe in the importance of public pedagogy—taking what we had learned into the public sphere, beyond the confines of our classroom. I tried to instill in my students the commitment to teach what they had learned throughout the semester. Second, a social justice component had to be part of the project in order for it to be real. Again, it's not just about regurgitating the info back to me but making a difference.

With the project as 40 percent of their grade, I asked the students to design a program celebrating Black women. The only parameters were that it would be held on the last evening of the semester and that it would be open to the campus community. Many times throughout the semester I regretted my decision. Despite my best efforts and pedagogical strategies most students refused to take the project as seriously as I had hoped they would. Their initial lack of commitment left me with two choices—give failing grades or have a serious, open discussion with the class. I love to expose myself in class.

OSHUN: Isn't that against the law?

ROCHELLE: A goddess with a wicked sense of humor—I love it. Maybe the law of a traditional removed pedagogy, but I prefer to create an open, safe

What Does "Good" Urban Teaching Look Like?

environment in my class where we share our feelings, so I had no choice but to choose the latter and spend an entire class period expressing my disappointment. I wanted the students to know that although I cared about their learning I was not going to accept their lack of respect for me as an African American woman. I told them I felt as though they were treating me with less respect, based purely on my race and gender, thereby proving to me that they were not learning anything. I also gave them the alternative assignment in a very long research paper.

OSHUN: Don't try to make light of what happened. I know you were upset with the class and with yourself for not giving them what they needed.

ROCHELLE: You're right. I was upset and I blamed myself for the disaster that the class project had turned into, more than I blamed the students. But I did not hide my hurt and disappointment from the class. Instead I gave the students an honest expression of my feelings and the power to either disappoint the class mandate and me, or make rise to the occasion, do what they were capable of doing and create in me, a happy Black woman.

They did the latter. They pulled it together and held a program for the community celebrating Black women. Not only did they have poetry, African and modern dance, skits, and monologues, but they also raised $200 for the local women's shelter.

Learning is, and should be, messy, confusing, and painful. Although at times I doubted the effectiveness of my pedagogy, in the final analysis it worked. The students ultimately developed a sense of social commitment: they cared about the subject, they took responsibility for their failures, and made the needed changes. They acted as a community. Importantly, they began to understand the connectedness of social forces on the perceptions of Black women because they could see their actions as a manifestation of those forces. Ultimately, the students had empowered themlves and in turn empowered me as a teacher. They joined the pedagogical community.

OSHUN: A synergistic relationship exists between what you as a teacher and they as students receive from each other. As long as both you and the students through your interaction provided the force to keep the synergy alive growth occurs. If either retreated from the interaction the synergistic relationship would cease to exist.

ROCHELLE: I infuse Black feminist thought and critical pedagogy to gain a better understanding of myself, my students, and the ways in which I design my teaching strategies. I use the tenets of Black feminist thought, critical pedagogy, and critical multiculturalism as I try to foster in my students not only a love of knowledge but also a commitment to political activism and dedication to social change in the urban environment. I think I am a good teacher, but often in the midst of my inner turmoil I ask myself whether I am leading them far enough. Am I really giving my students what they need or just disconnected bits of knowledge that will not provide the necessary inner strength? Have I taken my students far enough, to the level of healing necessary to go beyond the Other? This was perhaps the most important question, and I needed to find the answer.

Education should provide students "care for their being," with a pedagogy that teaches love of self and others, inner strength, humanity and humanness, survival and struggle, and hope and knowledge. King (1994) declares that "the potential to exist fully in alignment with one's human spirit is already present in each of us" (p. 270) and a task of education "is to help us learn hopeful principles of human existence" (p. 273). According to King, Afrohumanity is a soul-freeing liberatory education that nourishes well-being in the individual and helps a person reconnect with their humanity. When education does not provide a person with the right tools to tap into their humanity, it is impossible for hope to survive (Bartolome, 2008; Brock, 2005; Hollins, 2008). A freeing legacy in a curriculum of hope and Afrohumanity affords the acceptance of the humanity of everyone without being entangled in the web of proving legitimacy of any individual or group. In contrast to the effects of justifying self, Afrohumanity allows students to see the benefits of engaging with others on an equal basis. As long as North American cities—urban environments—are racially encoded with Black and Brown . . . I believe Black feminist thought and critical liberatory pedagogy are what we need to infuse in the education of new urban teachers.

We see our brothers and sisters as human and we understand the urgency in our "getting it together." Finally, we realize and act on the socioemotional intimacy of sharing in truth seeking and truth speaking amid gender equitableness. One of my students in the class *The African American Woman* gave me the answer when she said:

> I've been given . . . to deal with myself. I now know I have a foundation from which to start to build my own Black consciousness, my own female consciousness and bring them together to where they impact me so that I can then turn around and impact people. The most important thing I got out of this class was that it's so important for me to go back and get them little Black girls. It's so important because a lot of us didn't have that and a lot of the Black girls right now don't have it. It's important for me to get them, you know, while they're young as opposed to older, so they don't go through this. They'll have some more different issues, but at least those will have some balance for them instead of just finding out now. So that's it.

REFERENCES

Asante, M. K. (1991). The Afrocentric idea in education. *The Journal of Negro Education*, 60, 170–179.

Bartolome, L. I. (2008). *Ideologies in education: Unmasking the trap of teacher neutrality.* New York: Peter Lang.

Brock, R. (2005). *Sista Talk: The personal and the pedagogical.* New York: Peter Lang.

Collins, P. H. (1991). *Black feminist thought: Knowledge, consciousness and the politics of empowerment.* New York: Routledge.

Dimitriadis, G. (2008). *Studying urban youth culture primer.* New York: Peter Lang.

Foster, M. (1994). The power to know one thing is never the power to know all things: Methodological notes on two studies of Black American teachers. In A. Gitlin (Ed.), *Power and method: Political activism and education research* (pp. 129–146). New York: Routledge.

Hollins, E. R. (2008). *Culture in school learning: Revealing the deep meaning.* New York: Routledge.

Hurtado, A. (1996). *The color of privilege: Three blasphemies on race and feminism.* Ann Arbor, MI: The University of Michigan Press.

Jocson, K. M. (2008). *Youth poets: Empowering literacies in and out of schools.* New York: Peter Lang.

Joyce, P. A. (2008). *School hazard zone: Beyond the silence/finding a voice.* New York: Peter Lang.

King, J. E. (1994). Being the soul-freeing substance: A legacy of hope and humanity. In M. J. Shujaa (Ed.), *Too much schooling too little education: A paradox of Black life in White societies* (pp. 269–294). Trenton, NJ: Africa World Press.

Moraga, C., & Anzaldúa, G. (Eds.). (1981). *This bridge called my back: Writings by radical women of color.* New York: Kitchen Table Women of Color Press.

Simmons, D. (1962). Possible West African sources for the American Negro dozens. *Journal of American Folklore 75,* 339–340.

Sterling, D. (Ed.). (1984). *We are your sisters: Black women in the nineteenth century.* New York: W. W. Norton.

Steinberg, S. (2009). *Diversity and multiculturalism: A reader.* New York: Peter Lang.

Tatum, B. (2003). *"Why are all the Black kids sitting together in the cafeteria?" and other conversations about race: A psychologist explains the development of racial identity* (revised edition). New York: Basic Books.

Villaverde, L. E. (2008). *Feminist theories and education primer.* New York: Peter Lang.

CHAPTER FOUR

Greg S. Goodman & Adriel A. Hilton

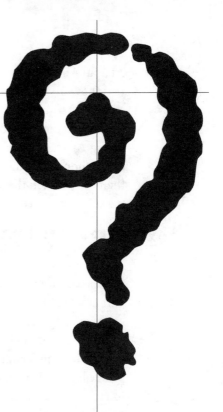

Urban Dropouts:
Why Persist?

 As we are keenly aware, the national educational statistics tell a very troubling and foreboding story about life for students within America's urban classrooms (Banks & Banks, 1989; National Center for Education Statistics, 2006). African American students embody 17 percent of the total U.S. student population, but African American teachers represent only 6 percent of all teachers in the U.S. ("*Leaving Schools,*" 2004). For Hmong and other minority groups, the gap can be even more acute. African American male teachers constitute just 1 percent of America's total teaching force. Underscoring those dismal numbers is the fact that there are no staff of color in 44 percent of the nation's schools (National Center for Education Statistics, 2006). Based upon these demographics and the cultural mismatch they portray, is it any wonder that inner city schools are failing their students and continuing to fall further behind (Beachum & McCray, 2008)? This is failure by design (Duncan-Andrade & Morrell, 2008). Why persist? Indeed.

The Children's Defense Fund reports the alarming fact that one American high school student drops out every nine seconds ("*Leaving Schools,*" 2004). In 2007, that statistic equated to 6.2 million students in the United States between the ages of 16 and 24 dropping out of high school. These data are further substantiated by the Center for Labor Market Studies at Northeastern University and the Alternative Schools Network ("High School," 2009): the demographics represent roughly 16 percent, or one student in eight, of all of the students in the United States who were in that age group. As these data consistently show, most of the students who are dropping out of school are minority youth, specifically

African American and Hispanic (National Center for Education Statistics, 2006), and they are living in our nation's largest urban areas. Seventy-one percent of students nationwide graduate from high school, but less than half of the students of color graduate (Greene & Forster, 2003). These data spotlight the fact that our young African American and Hispanic men are the most prone to drop out of high school. For most urban youth, the question "why persist?" is a metaphor of their dilemma in the struggle for survival.

Why Do Urban Students Fail to Persist in School?

Angela Pascopella (2003) pulls no punches when she states that the schools themselves are to blame for most students dropping out of high school. Why persist when the school is large and alienating, students are confronted with less experienced teachers in their classrooms, schools are given fewer resources and support, and it is clear that the majority White policy-making community is complicit in undermining the education of its urban youth (Duncan-Andrade & Morrell, 2008)? According to Pascopella (2003), even the teachers unions work to support a corrupt system of ineptitude. Teacher contracts can result in the more knowledgeable and skilled teachers being rewarded for their performance by moving from low-performing schools to escape the ghetto. These systems support a vicious cycle of cultural reproduction. Students who lack qualified teachers and pupil personnel services in their schools fall further behind (Bourdieu, 1993; White & Cones III, 1999). Why persist when the scene is set for failure? Research also demonstrates that a significant number of students drop out of urban high schools because their schools are not offering real life opportunities for learning (Duncan-Andrade, 2008). The curriculum is not relevant, and student lives and the experience within the classroom are grossly disconnected. Teachers are presenting materials that are prescribed by central office administrators in a misguided attempt to increase standardized test scores (Goodman & Carey, 2004). When students are exposed to the mandated curriculum within their classrooms, the subject content often has no relevance to the real problems they confront on a daily basis. Schools must be held accountable for what they are teaching and how it translates to the real world of their community, not to the dictates of the Educational Testing Service (ETS) or a central office oligarchy fearful of losing cushy, politically parceled jobs (Carnevale & Desrochers, 2003).

Researchers tie at least part of the problems facing urban schools to their makeup. Although these schools are populated mainly by students of color, educators within these settings are mostly White and female (National Center for Education Statistics, 2006). Hancock (2006) notes,

> The reality that White women are on the front lines of urban education is clear. While we continue to recruit and retain minority teachers, it is critical that we also focus our attention on helping to educate White women teachers about the realities of teaching

students who may hold a different sociopolitical, sociocultural, and socioeconomic perspective (p. 97).

The effect of the cultural mismatch is supported by the work of Malloy and Malloy (1998). These researchers have discovered that many urban teachers consider the culture of the student and the culture of the classroom to be very different. A solid example of this mismatch is found in the debate concerning the use of Ebonics in schools. To teachers supporting White curriculum, the wealth of opportunity that a mix of experiences brings to the classroom is threatening, unappreciated, and devalued (Goldenberg et al., 2003). In urban school districts, as many as 95 percent of the students are minority. Large urban states such as New York report 86 percent of the teachers are White (National Center for Education Statistics, 2006). In rural states such as New Hampshire and Maine, the population of White teachers climbs to 98 and 99 percent, respectively! According to Cross (2003), concerns related to race and culture are of tremendous significance in today's educational environment. Issues of an irrelevant curriculum and the attitudes, color, and disposition of the educators charged with teaching our youth bring additional evidence to support our fundamental question: Why persist? Why persist when you cannot see yourself represented in any of the identifications of your school?

An urban school is so designated, generally, because of its location, rate of poverty, percentage of students of color, and proportion of students who are limited in English proficiency (i.e., Hispanic and other English Language Learner (ELL) students). Most teachers going into urban schools for the first time face unexpected challenges as they confront the everyday problems of inner city classrooms (McKinsey & Company, 2009). For inexperienced and untrained White teachers, the adjustment is even more profound. Season four of the critically acclaimed, award-winning HBO series *The Wire* focuses on the stories and the lived experiences of several young boys in Baltimore City Public School System. The youth featured in this dramatic television series continuously grapple with authentic problems within their homes and the Baltimore ghetto/community. In this fourth season, the writer/producer David Simon focused on an urban middle school in West Baltimore that faced a critical shortage of teachers, especially in the important areas of science and math. *The Wire* provides viewers with a drama accurately representing most urban school districts. The drama exposes the policy of urban school systems that elect to employ teachers who are not certified but are offered alternative methods for certification such as teaching residency programs. The training represented in *The Wire* is positively ludicrous. Teachers are instructed to chant "I am lovable and capable" with their charges. This 1960s pablum nourished hippies, but in this episode of *The Wire* it effectively demonstrates how out of touch trainers and administrators are with the urban classroom of the twenty-first century.

David Simon is acutely aware of both the research and the lived experience of the people existing within the inner city of Baltimore. *The Wire* is set in an urban district that is one of the largest in the nation. Baltimore includes a very highly educated and affluent community, yet it also is home to a significantly large number of undereducated and poor. In 2006, 33 percent of the population aged 25 and older had a college degree, yet conversely, Baltimore had one of the highest rates of people over the age of 25 without a high school diploma (*Greater Baltimore State of the Region Report,* 2006).

Season four of *The Wire* features a suspended police detective who seeks a career change with the goal of impacting the lives of youth. Naively, our protagonist decides to teach math in an urban school district. Driving the drama, this White male with little experience in urban schools has no idea what challenges are ahead. As he begins to struggle with gaining command and order within the classroom, the students are more engaged in creating a brutal and hectic culture reflective of their lives on the street. As one could expect, our protagonist was surprised to learn just how little help was available to teachers or students. The program depicts a system characterized by a lack of intervention and support mechanisms, a system designed to perpetuate failure. Why persist as either teacher or student within this mismatch?

The Wire reveals many of the reasons why urban students drop out of high school. A recurring theme in the show identifies the role of the gangstas and their grip on the young and vulnerable wannabes. To fulfill the need for quick, if not always easy, money to take care of themselves and their loved ones, the gangstas enlist the children of their block to distribute drugs (mules) to drive-through customers. As the show deftly demonstrates, the lure of quick money in real time makes education for a future and distant reward appear meaningless and disconnected. Within a culture of violence, the lure of gangs is clear. Joining can help young people feel and be more protected within the violent inner city neighborhoods where they live. Gangs are a support network that fills the void manifested by society's abandonment of the ghetto's inhabitants. The gang is the family, the court, the administration, and the authority.

Urban school districts, such as Baltimore, are facing major problems, made worse by a very nomadic student and teacher population. Of inner city teachers, 40 percent will transfer within five years of placement. Sara Neufeld (2006), a reporter with the *Baltimore Sun,* stated that only 38.5 percent of Baltimore's high school students graduate four years after entering. Too much of the city's workforce is undereducated and poorly prepared for the economy of today, much less the future. The ripple effect on quality of life issues throughout our nation is apparent—it leads to more crime and a less healthy, less wealthy population. Employment opportunities are few because businesses will not locate in areas where schools are subpar. Further driving the economic and social downturn, businesses choose to relocate away from communities with such issues, meaning fewer jobs, a declining population and, of course, higher taxes for those who stay.

When segregation ended to make way for integration, many dedicated African American teachers and administrators lost their jobs. Black schools were closed and their students were bused to White schools (McCray et al., 2007). Also exacerbating the lack of Black educators for our urban students, young African American college students opted to major in fields of study other than education (Kunjufu, 2002). These shifts left a void of teachers who had traditionally provided quality education to America's Black students. In their place, White educators largely took on the job of educating African American and other urban students. Despite multiple efforts to recruit minority candidates within urban school districts, the teaching force (along with administrators) continues to be predominately White (McCray et al., 2007).

While we live in a more inclusive society than that which existed in pre-Civil Rights America, continuing segregation and inequality have made the hope of living "The American Dream" illusory and an irony for many young Blacks. "The illusion of integration allows for some access, while countless roadblocks persist in critical areas where blacks continue to be discriminated against in often subtle and sometimes not so subtle ways" (Kitwana, 2002, p. 13). White and Cones III (1999) agree that contemporary prejudice exists mainly in the form of institutional racism:

> Institutional racism exists where whites restrict equal access to jobs and promotions, to business and housing loans, and the like. White bankers and mortgage companies can secretly collaborate to redline a neighborhood so that such loans are nearly impossible to obtain. White senior faculty members in predominately white universities (public and private) determine who gets promoted to tenured faculty positions . . . Good-old-boys' clubs in the corporate structure determine who will be mentored and guided through the promotional mine fields (p. 136).

African American youth witness the continuing legacy of segregation and racism and its impact on their lives. They see their schools continuously underfunded, lacking in modern facilities, supplied with inadequate and inappropriate textbooks, and staffed with teachers who are poorly trained and who have low expectations of youth. Why persist when those who need to support you are so conspicuously absent?

Wacquant (2000), a noted sociologist, takes the racism theory several steps further, proposing the notion of hyperghetto to describe African Americans who were steered to certain areas of Northern cities, areas that came to be known as ghettoes. Wacquant created the neologism hyperghetto to identify the environment of urban African Americans from 1968 to the present day. He points out the relationship between hyperghetto and prison in the way African Americans are forced to live. According to Wilson (2009), hyperghettos are characterized by increased crime, illegal drug activity including addiction, economic depravity, police surveillance and brutality, and struggling schools, all of which force businesses to relocate to the suburbs.

The hyperghetto evolved in a post-White flight era when the residential barriers that barred African Americans from moving into White suburbs were relaxed (Wilson, 2009). When Blacks move up and make it to middle or upper class status, they often move out of inner cities and develop amnesia concerning where they come from, neglecting to reach back and uplift their former community. The lack of involvement in their old community, including the schools, can only be described as abandonment. This alienation between middle and upper class Blacks and the hyperghetto exacerbates the recurring problems of inadequate urban school funding, parental detachment from the schools, and the continuing cycle of conditions detrimental to student success. Many scholars and authors have warned of the increasing separation, segregation, and stratification within the African American community (Dyson, 2005; Kitwana, 2002; Kunjufu, 2002; West, 2008). West (2008) elaborates, "Once we lose any sense of a black upper or black middle class or a black upper working-class connecting with the black underclass with a 'we' consciousness or sense of community, it becomes much more difficult to focus on the plight of the poor" (p. 57).

Urban school districts have their share of problems that are not often experienced by suburban schools. Dropout rates of 70 percent or higher are common in many inner city schools (Alexander et al., 1997). The impact of these students' decision to drop out can be felt throughout their communities and into society as a whole. Communities already plagued by high rates of crime and physical and mental challenges often find those problems are exacerbated by high numbers of citizens experiencing disenfranchisement. Dropouts, for example, have been shown to account for half of the nation's prison population (Coley, 1995; Goodman, 2007). One of every three African American males spends time in a penal institution, but only one of ten male high school graduates is enrolled in college (Coley, 1995).

Urban Dropouts: People Make the Difference

The recurring question, why persist? gets a resounding round of reinforcement: it's cool, schools sucks, my teachers hate me, I don't fit, America ain't right, everybody else does. . . . It is the truth that arguments for dropping out too often outweigh the cries for persistence. "The situation in far too many schools is one of despair, poverty, isolation, and distress" (Beachum & Obiakor, 2005, p. 13). As we stated in the first half of this chapter, the student dropout problem is reinforced with obsolete and counterproductive pedagogical practices that extend beyond the individual classrooms into the halls, cafeteria, bathrooms, and the entirety of the culture known as school. Often the result of this complex ecology is a "cultural collision" in which " . . . the culture of educators clashes with that of their students . . ." (Beachum & McCray, 2008, p. 55), and the mismatch is devastating. Jeff Duncan-Andrade and Ernest Morrell (2008) take this argument one step further and make the claim that urban schools are performing exactly as they were designed to function. "If urban schools have been decried for decades as 'factories for failure' (Rist, 1973), then their production of failures means they are in fact successful at producing the results they are designed to produce. To the degree that we continue to misname this problem by calling schools designed to fail 'failing schools' we will continue to chase our tails" (p. 5).

Consequently, for students facing the paradox of successful "factories for failure" (Rist, 1973), what could be the counternarrative to the urban question: why persist? What factors contribute to students' resiliency and school persistence? In this second half of our investigations into the questions of urban middle and high school dropouts, we will explore some of the successful initiatives that have been utilized in building healthy learning communities. The complex ecologies of these learning communities will be explored and deconstructed to reveal the ways in which they work to keep students connected and on track toward graduation. These are not presented as simple panaceas to the huge problem of dropouts. All of these initiatives require hard work, courage, tenacity, intelligence, emotional toughness, and, as Barack Obama observed, audacious hope.

James Comer (1980) has been one of the undisputed leaders in the development of successful learning communities for the past 30 years. Comer was one of the first urban educators to identify the holistic nature and the complex ecology of the learning community. "When satisfactory home and school conditions exist the caretaker and the school staff constitute an alliance and are both able to interact with a child in a series of social and teaching experiences in which the child can gain personal control, motivation for learning, a balance between individuality and cooperation, interpersonal and social skills, and a sense of responsibility for his or her own behavior" (Comer, 1980, p. 33–34). Although Comer's work centered on preschool and elementary school children in New Haven, which is not New York or Los Angeles, his model School Development Program (SDP) was innovative for its attention to all of the ecological factors contributing to student success: the school, the home, and the community. This early work applied social and behavioral science to the operation of the whole school and community environment.

Comer's SDP also has spurred the growth of interest in addressing the myriad elements of each of these complex ecologies. "Our work over the years shows that curriculum and instruction are at the heart of the education enterprise, but that relationships must be such that young people can imitate, identify with, and internalize the attitudes, values, and ways of the meaningful adults around them in order to be motivated to learn academic material and, eventually, to become self-motivated, disciplined, self-directed learners capable of taking advantage of the resources of our society" (Comer, 1980, p. 295). Comer redefined and revitalized the role of psychology and social science within the school.

Unfortunately, attempts to widely reproduce Comer's SDP have proved limited in their possibilities for replication. The reality is that people, not programs, are the change. Within the culture of each school and the community they represent, there are key individuals who are responsible for the myriad factors that contribute to the success or failure of the school organization's complex ecology. Dropouts are the result of the failure to successfully resolve the issues of "cultural collision" (Beachum & McCray, 2008), and each community needs a leader who can interpret both the existing research on urban school reform and translate this into a workable program for their unique community.

California's Clovis East High School is an example of an urban high school that has developed a culture effective in reducing school dropouts and in creating strong and personally meaningful bonds within its community's shareholders. Clovis East High School's 3,000 students, drawn from a mix of diverse socioeconomic and cultural subcommunities located in California's Central Valley, are typically Californian, as exemplified by being mainly minority in racial identification. In addition to the racial diversity of the student body, the academic abilities of the students are wide-ranging. Most students are well below grade level in both reading and math scores.

When the school opened in the fall of 1999, there was a new principal, Jeff Eben, greeting the students as they walked onto the campus. Jeff Eben is a quadriplegic, yet his stature in his Quickie wheelchair resembles that of a professional basketball center. His presence on campus is ubiquitous, and his sensitivity to issues of culture is unparalleled. "On the day we opened, our students brought with them varied experiences in school. When we looked at the test results on the academic records of our first group of students, almost 70 percent couldn't read at grade level. Many of them had never been on teams or part of performing groups. School had not been a friendly place for a large portion of our clientele and our community didn't come in with a great deal of trust in education. . . . We had no credibility, and it felt like we were actually starting at whatever comes before square one" (Eben, 2006, p. 193). The tasks were daunting, but the persistence of this principal and many of the staff caused the culture to form and take hold.

In his autobiography, *How Many Wins Have YOU Had Today?*, Eben (2006), recounts his experiences from the early days of Clovis East High School:

> If we were going to have any academic success, we had to be able to teach our kids how to read, a tough task with teenagers. A struggling reader will have trouble in every discipline, so we had to find instructional practices that were innovative and effective, and we aren't necessarily trained at the secondary level for that type of instruction. Motivation was critical, and I thought our students would try harder if they participated in activities outside of class. We wanted to create opportunities for our young people to participate in sports, the arts, agriculture, and any other programs that would make their school experience more fun. Many of our students had not been part of high profile groups, but they would be here. We even adopted a schedule with eight class periods as opposed to the typical six to force students to take elective classes. Finally, I wanted students to feel safe and was concerned about how well our different cultures would interact with each other. It seemed natural to use our diversity as an on-going tool to teach inclusion, social tolerance and justice, and caring. So we took our Feel the Love motto and defined it with three words "Competence, Connectedness, and Compassion." These words combined our goals of helping students achieve academically, provide them with a sense of belonging, and create an environment where we care about each other. We put these words on a poster and hung them in every room and office in the school. It became who we were and caught on quickly. Two of my colleagues even gave us the name of "The Love Shack" and our marching band still plays the song as a way of celebrating our identity (p. 194).

Eben's work at Clovis East follows a line of thought well accepted and articulated within current critical constructivist pedagogical perspectives. Constructivists subscribe to the belief that the individual must invest of themselves in order to acquire knowledge. Using a combination of external and internal motivations, the individual learner is engaged in learning and meaning-making. Critical constructivists further the championing of an individual's self-efficacy as a learner with an application of social justice education. Social justice education is focused upon the liberation of all individuals from the destructive forces of racism, sexism, poverty, and the oppression of ignorance and hate. Dropping out of school reflects the victory of these destructive forces by being self-perpetuating and contributing to the cultural reproduction of failure (Bourdieu, 1993). More than any other factors, critical constructivist pedagogy can provide a positive intervention for ecological and educational success. "Understanding the problem of high school dropouts requires looking beyond the limited scope of individual student characteristics to include school (read: ecological) factors in student decisions to stay in or leave school" (Knesting, 2008, p. 3).

Eben's culture of caring has replicability. In her research on dropout prevention in high school students, Knesting (2008) lists a caring culture and three other factors as key to promoting student school persistence and dropout resistance. "Four factors emerged as critical for supporting student persistence: (a) listening to students, (b) communicating caring, (c) the school's role in dropout prevention, and (d) the students' role in dropout prevention" (p. 3). The generalizability of caring and compassionate teachers is clear. What is not so obvious is the tremendous effort and persistence that is required of staff. Knesting concludes: "Developing caring, supportive, and mutually respectful relationships with students in a large, comprehensive high school is not an easy task . . ." (p. 9). This is why people, not programs, are the key to success in creating 'wins' with our students.

Another important and successful school reform for improving students' school persistence is found through the creation of charter schools, school within a school, and other alternative ecologies for learning, for example, smaller learning communities (SLC). Transitions from grade to grade and school to school are disrupting and threatening to adolescents. When these transitions from school to school are not supported with the creation of solid bonds to either the new school's culture, individuals such as teachers or counselors, or another emotional and/or social anchor for the student, the risks of dropout loom large. Conversely, the literature is replete with examples of reclaiming youth through the development of alternative educational programming featuring adventure activities, relevant curriculum, and the development of close bonds between students and staff (Goodman, 2007; Brendtro et al., 2002). SLCs have been proven to significantly contribute to student school persistence (Darling-Hammond, 2002).

Very often the failure of students to bond with the new school and its culture results in social frustrations and academic failure (Diller, 1999). Across the nation, the dropout rate for freshmen in urban settings hovers around 40 percent (EPE, 2006). In many schools, students get stuck in ninth grade, and their experience is one of a continuing cycle of repeating because of a failure to win the credit-banking game of high school (Freire, 1970). Patterson et al. (2009) explain:

> For many urban school districts, the response to the dehumanizing condition of the large urban high school has been the creation of smaller learning communities (SLC). The impressive benefits of SLCs have been well-established in the literature, with increasing examples of success across the country (Cotton, 2001; Darling-Hammond, 2002). Hundreds of SLCs have been created in urban areas, including Chicago, Denver, Los Angeles, New York, Philadelphia, Seattle, and Ohio. Small school researchers are careful to assert, however, that shrinking the size of schools is not a panacea; rather, smaller environments make it easier to give kids the things they really need to succeed: collegiality among teachers, personalized teacher-student relationships, and less differentiation of instruction by ability (Cotton, 2001; Gladden, 1998; Raywid, 1999) (p. 128).

Although this process of creating dropout preventions can sound simple as described in these pages, what is not easy is finding instructional and support staff with the strength, courage, conviction, and love of humanity to pull this off. Jeff Duncan-Andrade is a professor who walks the talk. A member of the faculty at San Francisco State University, Jeff was also the teacher of a twelfth-grade English literature class at the Oasis Community High School (now closed), in Oakland, California. Jeff understands and communicates caring as a primary value, but he demonstrates his love (Freire, 1970) for his students by providing them with a rich, culturally relevant curriculum. This curriculum places students' cultural identification and icons at the center of their educational experience. Duncan-Andrade (2008) says,

> A curriculum that draws from youth culture would embrace . . . expanding definitions of literacy by viewing students as producers of and participants in various cultural literacies, such as: image, style, and discursive practices. This more inclusive approach to literacy instruction recognizes students as cultural producers with their own spheres of emerging literacy participation. This pedagogy of articulation and risk (Grossberg, 1994) values and learns from the cultural literacies students bring to the classroom and assists them as they expand those literacies and develop new ones. Teachers should aim to develop young people's critical literacy, but they should also recognize students as producers of literacy and support that production (p. 140).

Duncan-Andrade also trusts his students. He believes in their ability to know the truth and their skills in detecting elements of the popular and school's culture that enhance and scaffold their success. This is the ultimate show of respect and caring. Students don't drop out of Duncan-Andrade's class: they are practically breaking down the doors to get in. Within his classroom, students have the opportunity to learn how to create an activist agency to transform themselves and their community's ecology by applying an authentic social justice and critical pedagogy. Duncan-Andrade has dubbed this process "Doc ur block":

The Doc Ur Block project was a commitment to those principles of humanization by providing young people an education that prepares them to analyze their world critically. It put tools of critical thinking, research, and intellectual production in the hands of young people so that they could counter-narrate pathological stories of their families and communities. Along the way, many students discovered that they too had come to believe the dominant discourse about their community and had lost sight of the countless indicators of hope and strength that are present on their blocks every day (Duncan-Andrade & Morrell, 2008, p. 147).

Conclusions

The examples we have provided are evidence of some of the successes that can be achieved in countering successful factories of failure, of promoting school persistence, and reversing the tsunami of student dropouts. All of these examples are the products of individuals' efforts—the real results of work by teachers and staff who are leading a revolution in education (Ladson-Billings, 1994). These individuals are bucking social and political forces that act to perpetuate the dropouts; and their work is nothing shy of courageous. As we witnessed in *The Wire*, standing in front of a class of urban youth and chanting "I am lovable and capable" is an exercise in pretending to make the changes that real love can bring (Freire, 1970). Perpetuating absurd, trite, trivial, and outdated practices maintains the hegemony of the dominant culture upon a failed community and its main socializing institution: the school.

Resisting hegemony, schools can produce a counternarrative to the forces trying to perpetuate student failure (as success). Although the story was typically Hollywood, the portrayal of Erin Gruwell's struggle to transform her students through her own metamorphosis is absolutely on point (Gruwell, 2006). Many urban sites are centered in 'the war,' and winning these battles begins with the courage to transform one's self into a warrior's character much like heroine Erin Gruwell: to fail and to come back, to risk defeat and to refuse to accept losing, to persist and not to yield! This is the circle of courage required to answer the question: Urban dropouts: Why persist? This is what the pedagogy of love means.

REFERENCES

Alexander, K., Entwisle, D., & Horsey, C. (1997). From first grade forward: Early foundations of high school dropout. *Sociology of Education, 70*(2), 87–107.

Banks, J. A., & Banks, C. A. M. (1989). (Eds.). *Multicultural education: Issues and perspectives.* Boston: Allyn & Bacon.

Beachum, F. D., & McCray, C. (2008). Dealing with cultural collision in urban schools: What pre-service educators should know. In G. Goodman (Ed.), *Educational psychology: An application of critical constructivism.* New York: Peter Lang

Beachum, F. D., & Obiakor, F. E. (2005). Educational leadership in urban schools. In F. E. Obiakor & F. D. Beachum (Eds.), *Urban education for the 21st century: Research, issues, and perspectives* (pp. 83–99). Springfield, IL: Charles C Thomas.

Bourdieu, P. (1993). *The field of cultural production: Essays on art and literature.* New York: Columbia University Press.

Brendtro, L., Brokenleg, M., & Van Bockern, S. (2002). *Reclaiming youth at risk: Our hope for the future.* Bloomington, IN: National Educational Service.

Carnevale, A. P., & Desrochers, D. M. (2003). *Standards for what? The economic roots of K-16 reform.* Princeton, NJ: Educational Testing Service.

Coley, R. (1995). *Dreams deferred: High school dropouts in the United States.* Princeton, NJ: Educational Testing Services.

Comer, J. P. (1980). *School Power: Implications of an intervention project.* New York: The Free Press.

Cotton, K. (2001). *New small learning communities: Findings from recent literature.* Portland, OR: Northwest Regional Educational Laboratory.

Cross, B. E. (2003). Learning or unlearning racism: How urban teachers transfer teacher education curriculum to classroom practices. *Theory into Practice. 42*(3), 203–209.

Darling-Hammond, L. (2002). Redesigning schools: What matters and what works. Stanford, CA: School Redesign Network. Retrieved October 20, 2009 from http://www.schoolredesign.net

Diller, D. (1999). Opening the dialogue: Using culture as a tool in teaching young African American children. *Reading Teacher, 52,* 820–827.

Duncan-Andrade, J. (2008). Your best friend or worst enemy: Youth popular culture, pedagogy, and curriculum in urban classrooms. In G. Goodman (Ed.), *Educational psychology: An application of critical constructivism* (pp. 113–143). New York: Peter Lang.

Duncan-Andrade, J. & Morrell, E. (2008). *The art of critical pedagogy: Possibilities for moving from theory to practice in urban schools.* New York: Peter Lang.

Dyson, M. E. (2005). *Is Bill Cosby right? Or has the Black middle class lost its mind?* New York: Basic Civitas Books.

Eben, J. (2006). *How many wins have YOU had today?* Clovis, CA: Garden of Eben Press.

Educational Projects in Education (EPE). (2006). Ohio graduation report. *Education Week.* Retrieved October 20, 2009 from http://www.edweek.org/ew/toc/2006/06/22/index.html

Freire, P. (1970). *Pedagogy of the oppressed.* New York: Continuum.

Gladden, R. (1998). The small school movement: A review of the literature. In M. Fine & J. Sommerville (Eds.), *Small schools, big imaginations: A creative look at public schools* (pp. 113–133). Chicago: Cross City Campaign for Urban School Reform.

Goldenberg, I. I., Kunz, D., Hamburger, M., & Stevenson, J. M. (2003). Urban education: Connections between research, propaganda & prevailing views of education. *Education, 123*(3), 628–634.

Goodman, G. S. (2007). *Reducing hate crimes and violence among American youth: Creating transformational agency through critical praxis.* New York: Peter Lang.

Goodman, G. S., & Carey, K. T. (2004). *Ubiquitous assessment: Evaluation techniques for the new millennium.* New York: Peter Lang.

Greater Baltimore state of the region report. (2007). Greater Baltimore Committee: Retrieved June 15, 2009 from http://www.gbc.org/reports/GBCSOR2007.pdf

Greene, J., & Forster, G. (2003). *Public high school graduation and college readiness rates in the United States.* New York: Manhattan Institute for Policy Research.

Grossberg, L. (1994). Bringin' it all back home—Pedagogy and cultural studies. In H. Giroux & P. McLaren (eds.), *Between borders: Pedagogy and the politics of Cultural Studies* (p. 335). New York: Routledge.

Urban Dropouts: Why Persist?

Gruwell, E. (2006). *Freedom writers. How a teacher and 150 teens used writing to change themselves and the world around them.* New York: Broadway Books.

Hancock, S. D. (2006). White women's work: On the front lines of urban education. In J. Landsman & C. W. Lewis (Eds.), *White teachers/diverse classrooms: A guide to building inclusive schools, promoting high expectations, and eliminating racism* (pp. 93–109). Sterling, VA: Stylus.

"High school dropout crisis" continues in U.S., study says. (2009). CNN: Retrieved June 18, 2009 from http://www.cnn.com/2009/US/05/05/dropout.rate.study/index.html

Kitwana, B. (2002). *The hip-hop generation: Young blacks and the crisis in African American culture.* New York: Basic Civitas Books.

Knesting, K. (2008). Students at risk for school dropout: Supporting their persistence. *Preventing School Failure, 52* (4). Retrieved June 3, 2009 from ERIC EBSCO.

Kunjufu, J. (2002). *Black students—Middle class teachers.* Chicago: African American Images.

Ladson-Billings, G. (1994). *The dreamkeepers: Successful teachers of African American children.* San Francisco: Jossey-Bass.

Leaving schools behind: When students drop out. (2004). University of Minnesota: Retrieved June 16, 2009 from http://education.umn.edu/research/ResearchWorks/checkconnect.html

Malloy, C. E., & Malloy, W. M. (1998). Issues of culture in mathematics teaching and learning. *The Urban Review, 30,* 245–57.

McCray, C. R., Wright, J. V., & Beachum, F. D. (2007). Social justice in educational leadership: Using Critical Race Theory to unmask African American principal placement. *Journal of Instructional Psychology, 34*(4), 247–255.

McKinsey & Company (2009). *The economic impact of the achievement gap in America's schools.* New York: McKinsey & Company.

National Center for Education Statistics. (2006). *Status and trends in the education of racial and ethnic minorities.* Retrieved July 10, 2009 from http://nces.ed.gov/pubs2007/minoritytrends/

Neufeld, S. (2006). Schools challenge report: Journal says city graduates 38.5 percent of students; Only Detroit fared poorer. *The Baltimore Sun.* June 26, 2006. Retrieved June 12, 2009, from http://www.redorbit.com/news/education/551340/schools_challenge_report_journal_says_city_graduates_385_percent_of/index.html

Pascopella, A. (2003). Drop out. *District Administration, 38*(11), 32–36.

Patterson, N. C., Beltyukova, S. A., Berman, K., & Francis, A. (2007). The making of sophomores: Student, parent, and teacher reactions in the context of systematic urban high school reform. *Urban Education, 42*(2). Retrieved May 24, 2009 from http://uex.sagepub.com

Raywid, M. (1999). *Current literature on small schools.* Retrieved September 20, 2009 from http://www.ael.org/eric/digests/edorc988.htm

Rist, R. (1973). *The urban school: A factory for failure.* Cambridge, MA: MIT Press.

Wacquant, L. (2000). The new "peculiar institution": On the prison as surrogate ghetto. *Theoretical Criminology, 4*(3), 377–389.

West, C. (2008). *Hope on a tightrope: Words and wisdom.* Carlsbad, CA: Hay House, Inc.

White, J. L., & Cones III, J. H. (1999). *Black man emerging: Facing the past and seizing a future in America.* New York: W. H. Freeman & Company.

Wilson, W. J. (2009). *More than just race: Being Black and poor in the inner city.* New York: W. W. Norton & Company.

CHAPTER FIVE

Valerie J. Janesick

How Can Assessment Work in Urban Schools?

Tighter control of the curriculum, the tail of the test wagging the dog of the teacher and the curriculum, more pressure, more reductive accountability plans—all of this may lead to less equitable results, not more. Boredom, alienation, and increased inequalities are not the ideal results of schooling.

—*Michael Apple, 2009*

We should begin a discussion of assessment in urban schools with some information on No Child Left Behind (NCLB) and high stakes testing, since we now have data to show that many children are being left behind as a direct result of the effects of high stakes testing. I will describe in this chapter why I see high stakes testing as a form of child abuse. NCLB refers to the act of that name which requires adequate yearly progress on state standardized tests. Tragically, most states are unable to demonstrate adequate yearly progress. At the local level, schools are graded and there are penalties for low performance, including in some cases the closing of a neighborhood school. High stakes testing refers to standardized or packaged tests administered annually to students, who understand the stakes are high. The stakes may include public announcement of a school's so-called failure, sometimes with dire consequences. I became increasingly concerned about the continuing emphasis on high stakes testing despite what we know of its harmfulness and biases. This inadvertently led me to think about high stakes testing as a form of child abuse. In addition, the systemic and systematic attack on public education that began in the 1980s with the Reagan administration has not abated. In fact, it has intensified as a corporate model of profiteering for test makers and tutors and has replaced an emphasis on learning, despite child development studies and research which clearly show how disadvantaged populations in urban settings in particular have suffered due to high stakes standardized testing. This has created a climate of fear and instability in the urban school setting. No doubt many chapters in this text will reiterate some of these points and refine and present data to illuminate more fully the problems in urban settings. Of course if we assume that schools reflect society, one only has to look around at the politics of the day. It is no wonder that schools are being cast as mini corporations with a one size fits all model of education and testing. I have written earlier (2000, 2006) about authentic assessment as a meaningful, effective alternative to high stakes testing. I will discuss authentic assessment here as well. Authentic assessment works and is actually a viable alternative to high stakes testing in all schools but certainly in urban settings.

I like to think of this chapter as a journey toward a fuller understanding of the contentious space of urban schools and consequently the matters related to assessment and testing. It is written for those who want to learn about the importance and value of authentic assessment as a real opportunity and alternative to high stakes testing in urban schools. In addition, the social context of high stakes testing and current political intrusion into public education will be discussed. In fact, some of the so-called interventions and experiments in urban schools when a school is listed as failing amount to a separate pedagogy for urban schools, which often results in children being left behind no matter that the law says no child will be left behind. For example, one toxic side effect of high stakes testing is consistently higher dropout rates for Hispanic and African American children. These dropout rates are camouflaged with trickery and false reporting. For example, in Chicago the underreporting of dropout rates has been traced to the decision to eliminate counting eight and ninth grade dropouts, giving a very different picture of the percentage of dropouts. Here in Florida, there is also an underreporting of dropouts for political reasons, and the effect is that we often receive information that does not match the reality of the amazingly high dropout rates in the urban setting. Let us begin with the problems facing urban schools in the area of assessment and testing. I wish to discuss these matters through the lens of repositioning. *Repositioning* (Harding, 1991) is a component of cultural theory which basically says that to understand a phenomenon, in this case assessment and testing in urban schools, we should see it from the viewpoint of those who have the least power. In this case it would be the students, educators, and parents of students in urban schools.

Teaching for the Test and Other Complications

One has only to look at Texas for an example of the flaws inherent in the high stakes testing model. McNeil (2000) reported that many of the schools she studied used large amounts of time practicing for tests. Students practiced bubbling in answers and learned to recognize that test makers never have the same letter choice for a correct answer three times in a row. In fact, to help students remember this, a catchy phrase was repeated. They said "Three in a row, no, no, no." What are we to make of this? Furthermore, principals who participated in the study reported using the lion's share of the budget to purchase expensive study materials. Again we return to the question, who benefits from all this? Do children benefit from this or do test makers? What would the state of the art look like if we were to make standards for critical thinking in classrooms? Or alternately, we could at least incorporate a space for emphasizing critical thinking activities such as journal writing, reflective essays, and critical reasoning into testing and into the written standards. What this case shows us is that teaching toward the test alone diminishes the student's ability to practice critical thinking skills. Do we really want to go that route? Do our children deserve this? Can we not do better?

Another group of writers has come together and raised the case of Texas as illustrative of the dismal results of teaching to the test at the expense of the original and actual curriculum. In the text *American Standards,* Horn and Kincheloe (2001) have documented how activist parents have sued the State of Texas for this and other reasons. In fact, Horn and Kincheloe (2001) point out the larger issues that emerged from the Texas case.

They mention the following as problematic:

1. The acceptance of the efficiency, technical or rational model

    This problem is best understood by the turnaround in trying to make teachers good little managers of student workers. With prepackaged teaching recipes or worse, teaching to the test, teachers are no longer public intellectuals in charge of their craft. In addition, key questions about education such as what we teach and how we teach it are outright dismissed. In Texas, when people fell into the techno-rational trap they avoided dealing with the rigor of academic excellence. It is much easier to go for the one-shot typical test, after all. Teachers are erased as reflective agents and masters of their content knowledge when they are reduced to teaching to the test.

2. Fragmentation and reduction of the curriculum

    Teachers operate in a complex world. They know about individual differences and about how children grow, develop, and learn. By reducing the curriculum to excessive reliance on standardized one-shot test scores, a great disservice if not harm is done to children who have special needs, diverse backgrounds, speak English as a second or third language, etc. In fact, in the case against the State of Texas (*GI Forum v. TEA*, 2000), in speaking of the Texas Assessment of Academic Skills exit test (TAAS), the plaintiff's summary included some powerful testimony. It stated that the TAAS exit test wreaks havoc with the educational opportunities of the state's African American and Hispanic students. Basically, the results of the test show that minorities consistently scored lower than whites individually and collectively. They were trying to point out that there was surely something wrong with the test. Unfortunately, the court sided with the State of Texas rather than the coalition suing Texas and ended up upholding states' rights over students' rights. Complexity and ambiguity have no place in Texas, apparently.

3. Dumbing everyone down via standards, tests, etc.

Since testing drives everything in the schools, all other parts of schooling are left out and as a result, the people who end up graduating are either simply good at test taking or naively satisfied with memorizing answers to multiple choice tests. Perhaps the greatest mistake here is that since so much energy goes into testing, the actual rigor of scholarship and content knowledge is overlooked. This gives a false sense of learning to all involved in education. In effect, the curriculum is cast aside.

4. Standards as part of a right wing reeducation project

The power holders in Texas are known as those in control. The control is held by a group of far right ideologues. But instead of admitting it, they claim to be neutral. In a way, the Texas case is a reaction to all the advancement of the Civil Rights Movement, Feminism and the Gay Rights Movement. The religious far right wants to take the education system back to the time when things were neat and of course in their favor. But to deny the diversity in society makes no sense. This approach is called by many writers the "one size fits all" approach. It never worked in the past and certainly does not work in the present. One can easily say instead that one size fits few.

5. Standards as part of the return of White Supremacy

Ray Horn (2004) has studied the Texas case and what the TAAS actually has succeeded in doing is clear. He has exposed the racist nature of the TAAS and the evidence is overwhelming. Not only do minorities fare worse, as multiple studies have shown, but in order to not be labeled as racist, Texas personnel have exempted those students who may continue to do poorly on tests. They have tried to manage the social world in a way that will avoid controversy based on results of the tests. Interestingly enough, Texas has failed to mention the facts that Texas students who drop out of high school prior to the test do not get counted as dropouts and are entirely forgotten in the entire story. In other words, of the many Hispanic and African American dropouts in Texas, most are unreported in the formal rolls. Furthermore, the current lawsuits against the State of Texas Education Agency claim that Texas is single-handedly not providing an equal educational opportunity for minority students. Since the time of Horn's study, Texas has actually changed the name of the Texas test from the TAAS to the TAKS (Texas Assessment of Knowledge and Skills). This was due in part to the amazing amount of negative publicity about the test and its unfairness to Hispanic and African American students. In addition, the number of lawsuits is growing, hanging in mid air waiting for decisions. Lawsuits may drag on for years, but the statements of the parents and educators remain on the record. They may also serve to inspire others in seeking legal redress.

6. The need for a social vision apart from corporate logic and its dismissal of insights from professional educators.

Shamefully, the corporate model has tried to eclipse and erase professional educators from working out a strong vision, philosophy of education, and care for young people of all cultures. What we learn from the Texas case is how rampant racism is in the United States. We also learn that profits trump knowledge in the game of high stakes testing.

Obviously Texas is not the only state with these problems. I am using the Texas case because it has been researched very carefully, and numerous books, web sites, and articles have exposed these problems. My hope is that we can learn from history rather than repeat the mistakes already verified through the Texas case. In the meantime, all the results are not in as many lawsuits against the Texas Education Agency are in progress and may take decades to resolve. In the meanwhile, surely we can call upon our best ideas to solve some of these self-created problems. I use the case of Texas because it is so transparent. But many other states are complicit in the money-making, which is very good for test makers but not good for students and educators. This case offers us a great deal to think about in terms of what is wrong about our system. What is wrong is that many people fall for this without question.

About Authentic Assessment

As a result of dissatisfaction with typical tests, high stakes testing, and an emphasis on rote and repetition in classrooms indicating a misplaced nostalgia for the olden days, many professionals, researchers, and educators began to ask questions in the 1980s and onwards about a better way to assess student work. Consequently, the authentic assessment movement evolved and is alive and well today. Educators and researchers began to concentrate relentlessly on authentic assessment to see whether students could explain, apply, and critique their own responses and justify the answers they provided. In addition, authentic assessment is dynamic and looks at what students should be able to do and continually learn and how students progress through their studies. It is most like the process in the arts, with critique, feedback, redirection and reconstruction. Authentic assessment stands in contrast to typical tests. Typical tests are known by the following traits:

1. usually require one and only one correct response,
2. usually are disconnected from the learner's environment,
3. usually are constructed by a bureaucrat removed from the learner's environment,
4. the test maker may in fact **not be knowledgeable** about the field in which questions are being constructed,

5. usually are simplified for ease in scoring,
6. provide a one-shot, one-time score.

Many educators were dissatisfied with this approach to testing and evaluating students. Thus, a new way of defining and viewing assessment took shape. This new approach is called authentic assessment.

There are numerous books and articles on authentic assessment. Many writers have devoted their lives to examining assessment, offering strong criticism for standardized tests, and suggesting reasonable alternatives to uniform standardized tests. Writers such as Grant Wiggins, Alfie Kohn, Joe Kincheloe, Ray Horn, Mark Goldberg, and Susan Ohanian have written numerous books and articles on the topic; you will find them listed in the references. Wiggins (1998) suggests the following standards for authentic assessment. An assessment task is authentic when:

1. It is realistic. The assessment task should closely follow the ways in which a person's abilities are tested in the real world. For example, as a former dancer, in ballet class I practiced dance exercises such as plies, jetes, turns, etc. But these are merely exercises. A realistic assessment task would be found in the actual performance of the ballet. As a cast member in the *Nutcracker Suite* ballet, I was forced to show what I could do. This is a realistic test, an authentic assessment measure.
2. It requires judgment and innovation. Here, the learner must use knowledge and skills to solve problems.
3. It asks the student to "do" the subject. Going back to the example of the ballet dancer, the dancer must put all the steps together and perform a role in an actual ballet.
4. It replicates or simulates actual tests in the workplace, personal life, and civic life. Since each learner is at a unique stage of growth and development at any given time, you can easily see why authentic assessment is more sensible than contrived standardized tests. One size does not fit all learners. Common sense surely indicates this.
5. It assesses the student's ability and skills to effectively and efficiently use a repertoire of many skills to complete a problem or task. In terms of accessing more than verbal or mathematical skills, authentic assessment relies on all the many intelligences a person can develop.
6. It allows many opportunities to practice, rehearse, consult, get feedback, and refine actual performances and productions. Thus we have performance, feedback, performance revision, feedback, performance, etc. In other words, students must learn something and get better at doing the task at hand. In many ways this is like the artist who is constantly critiqued for improvement. To use dance as an example, after each performance the director of a ballet or performance piece typically reads critique notes at the end of every performance. Thus, built in to the concept of feedback is the assumption that the learner will work to improve performance on the next test.

How Can Assessment Work in Urban Schools?

The reason authentic assessment is important is obvious. Every teacher is forced to assess the achievement and progress of learners. Since teachers deal with assessment issues constantly, educators in every arena want to find a realistic, workable, authentic system of assessment. Likewise, the reader can clearly see the difference between typical tests and authentic assessment as listed above.

Why Authentic Assessment Works

If I had to select one major idea regarding the heart and soul of authentic assessment, it would be this: authentic assessment insures that the learner is not a bystander but an actual participant in the process. It also requires the learner to think critically by using experience-based activities to solve a given problem. As a natural evolution, authentic assessment requires that the learner be able to describe, explain, and justify the understandings surrounding any given problem. Thus the learner cannot and should not be asked to dumb down education by merely reciting or memorizing facts disconnected from a context or from an experience. If we seriously employed authentic assessment performance tasks, we would definitely give up the drill and kill exercises. For example, not long ago I visited an urban third-grade classroom, where students were literally shouting out loud the words "Don't bubble in C—bubble in B." Since they were preparing for the high stakes tests they were to take in the state of Illinois, the teacher was getting them to realize that most standardized tests often have the letter "B" answer as the correct choice. This is irrespective of the fact that all choices could be correct. What the learner ends up learning is how to beat the system, with little or no understanding of what the content of the question contained. In fact, research on the Texas TAAS shows more alarmingly how much time has been taken away from the actual time originally allotted to study of a given content area and sidetracked to test prepping that is similar to the example above. But what are children actually learning here? You be the judge.

Authentic assessment requires what John Dewey (1859–1952) described as habits of mind. Children who have solid habits of mind resonant with authentic assessment techniques would:

1. learn from experience,
2. in a given context,
3. in a given learning community,
4. with a responsibility for improving their own performance,
5. demonstrating through a performance task what the learners can do.
6. This then would lead to understanding a concept, not merely memorizing an isolated fact that a test maker who is not a professional educator deems as a correct answer.

Authentic assessment is a much more rigorous approach to teaching and learning as you can see. Is it any wonder that professional educators have denounced the high stakes testing/bogus model as a bad habit of mind?

Furthermore, authentic assessment is an orientation that relies on empirical evidence of what a student can do. Let's pause to take a look at the word "empirical." In a quick search of the word in online dictionaries, the word *empirical* means capable of being verified by observation or derived from observation and experiment rather than theory. When a learner actually demonstrates in the real world what the learner can do with any performance task, there is a subsequent growth and movement toward knowing something in context. On the other hand, what high stakes testing has achieved, outside of making test makers rich, is an erasure of learning. I do not need to tell you, the reader, of the deep revulsion many if not most students have toward test taking which is enforced and which carries a serious punishment for getting an answer wrong.

Alternatives to High Stakes Testing: Authentic Assessment Practices

The reader may more fully come to know the importance of authentic assessment by looking at the following examples. Here are some of the most common authentic assessment techniques:

1. performances
2. demonstrations
3. simulations
4. oral presentations
5. progress interviews
6. writing samples such as essays
7. formal observations
8. self-assessment
9. evaluations of case studies
10. audio or video recordings of readings or performances
11. journal writing
12. writing folders which chronicle a student's development through a course of study
13. role plays
14. portfolios

For the moment, let us focus on the authentic assessment task of portfolio development. The portfolio is often the most recognized of authentic assessment techniques. Portfolio assessment is widely used to review the progress of a learner's work over time. The learner selects which artifacts go into the portfolio. For example, a learner may include research papers, book reports, reflective writing, journal reflections, group work or projects, videotapes, photographs, drawings, software, slides, holograms, and even test results such as report cards. Most often there is some standard, or learning objective, which guides the learner to select examples of best practices for the portfolio. Again, one can see that this is a technique borrowed from artists and designers, who have always kept portfolios. In

How Can Assessment Work in Urban Schools?

a way, the portfolio is a learner's historical record. It is an information gathering process for the purpose of reflection and growth. Likewise, the portfolio uses multiple indicators and sources of evidence to demonstrate a person's learning. This is a technique generated from the Arts and Humanities which provides educators with a historical documentation of the progress of a learner's understanding of a given subject or knowledge base. It also puts responsibility on the learner to actively select best examples of his or her work. It is meant to be an active process. It is not a one-shot procedure but a work in progress. The portfolio is constantly changing and continually upgraded.

I mention portfolios here to illustrate their value as an authentic task, their accessibility, and the fact that students and educators alike validate the use of portfolios as an authentic performance task. All the techniques listed share the characteristics described earlier: they require a performance and product; they are connected to the learner's world and experience; they are complex; they require multiple tasks and problem solving skills, and they provide feedback on a continual basis. The learner adjusts to the feedback and performance is improved. The reader may be asking, if portfolios are so valuable, how are the contents of the portfolio reviewed and assessed? What rubrics are used in the process? A rubric is a set of categories with a value assigned for each category in order for a teacher to evaluate a student's work. Think of it as a scoring matrix, if you will. For example, here is a rubric I use with some of my classes.

Sample Writing Rubric

Evaluation of your Writing Rubric:

	Exceeds the standard	*Meets the standard*	*Is below standard*
1.	_____	_____	_____

The title captures the meaning of the work and is reflective of a theme. The concepts are clear; major themes are found and explained.

2.	_____	_____	_____

The introduction to the piece adequately captures the meaning, content, and data.

3.	_____	_____	_____

Adequate information is presented and all questions are adequately addressed.

4.	_____	_____	_____

The report contains the purpose of the work, questions raised by the topic, evidence from the literature to support the work, solid conclusions, and recommendations for the future.

5.	_____	_____	_____

The report is submitted typed, double spaced, and in APA style. Appropriate support data such as figures, graphs, illustrations, photos, etc., are included (writer's choice of at least one).

Educators may create any number of rubrics pertinent to the content area of study. Professional educators know their content areas and the processes of learning. Why would anyone want to give up that important activity to bureaucrats and politicians? Rubrics then become part of the various portfolios to ensure authentic assessment is documented. But what about the types of portfolios?

Portfolios in Many Formats

A portfolio has long been a key method for presenting what a student has learned. It is a multifaceted and complex product. It may have a theme and surely will be judged against a set of criteria usually evidenced in a given rubric. The rubric shows the viewer of the portfolio levels of performance. Constructing portfolios and assessing them takes time, effort, and dedication to the task. Many practitioners define portfolios as a historical record of student work. It is more than a collection of papers in a folder. It is evidence of a student's work over time and may include accomplishments, capability records, a history of the student's development, and critiques of the student's work by both the student and the teacher. Of course, the items included can be many; however, whatever is included should be authentic measures of what the student learned. Usually the tasks that the student performs show evidence of learning and may fall in the following major categories:

1. The tasks performed were done in multiple ways for a variety of purposes over time.
2. The tasks provide evidence of learning and growth and sample a wide spectrum of cognitive tasks.
3. The tasks show evidence of work at many levels of understanding.
4. The tasks are tailored to the individual learner and show what the learner knows.

Thus, we can see how the learner is involved in the assessment process. Unlike standardized testing, authentic assessment values the person who is the learner. Why would we give that up to take on a one-shot measure, the standardized test?

There is no single sacred model or type of portfolio. Depending on the discipline of study (e.g., reading, math, physical education, art, or music), the portfolio construction varies. However, in looking over the body of literature on portfolios, there seem to be at least three categories of portfolios: (1) the working portfolio, (2) the record-keeping portfolio, and (3) the showcase portfolio. Note that often parents are involved in looking over the portfolio, giving some feedback on its contents, and even rating the student's work. Let us review what these major types might look like.

The Working Portfolio

This type of portfolio is mostly the work of the student, on a daily basis, and gives evidence of ongoing learning in one or more areas of study. The samples for the portfolio are most often selected by the student, described fully, and critiqued by the student. Teachers and parents, of course, comment as well. However, this type of portfolio offers the learner the opportunity to be self-aware and more articulate about learning and the learner's own growth process. Many schools begin portfolios at the elementary level and carry through to high school. One example of this is the San Diego School District, which has continuously worked on the use of portfolios for its students and provides resources to train teachers in the use of portfolios.

The Record-Keeping Portfolio

This type of portfolio may be used along with or even integrated into the working portfolio or the showcase portfolio. As the name implies, it is a history of records. It may contain samples of report cards, results of tests and other such records. It is also monitored and devised by the learner with input from teachers, parents, or administrators.

The Showcase Portfolio

This is the best known and most often used type of portfolio. Here, the learner constructs a showcase of samples that best describe the learner's progress to date in a given area or multiple areas. It is something like the portfolio a photographer or artist might put together. Usually this includes completed works that are excellent or outstanding. It is meant to be the record of the student's best work. Thus, we see at least three types of portfolios that provide a record of authentic tasks and learning. Many states have encouraged the use of the showcase portfolio; in fact some use the portfolio in electronic format, which is discussed below.

The Electronic Portfolio

Portfolio assessment is well in place in most of the 50 states. In the past decade, with the growth of technology and computers in the classroom, electronic portfolios have become a valuable method of assessment. Electronic portfolios allow for easier storage and retrieval of information and also allow for easier inclusion of parental input and feedback. Any type of portfolio can make use of the electronic delivery system. Portfolios are kept on diskette or CD-ROM. A big bonus of the electronic portfolio is the ability to store material that a traditional notebook portfolio lacks. For example, songs, poetry, video performances, music, and dramatic readings are more easily stored in digital form and more accurately and visually capture the activity. Furthermore, with an electronic portfolio a new dimension may be introduced, that of interactivity. With the elegant software available for electronic portfolios, students can be more creative and use digital means to verify and adjust their portfolio contents. Also, the electronic portfolio works for any format and can be created with just about any software. Why use an electronic portfolio? The benefits are obvious.

1. Work can be stored digitally more efficiently and allows for more student options. In addition, students today take digital records as a given.
2. If students happen to stay in the same district, they will have a true historical record of their work from K-12. If they leave the district, they may more easily carry a digital portfolio reflective of their work over time than any other portfolio format.
3. Students' best examples may be represented more elegantly and often with greater flexibility in a digital format. Here, you can really see what a student can actually do.
4. Most professional organizations have already created models of electronic portfolios for social studies teachers, English teachers, math teachers, etc.
5. Today's learners are often knowledgeable in computer use and continue to refine and develop computer literacy skills with the construction of an individual electronic portfolio.
6. Today's learners spend many hours watching TV and playing video and computer games. Why not harness that creative energy into learning activities that stretch learners' imagination and multiple intelligences through the creation of an electronic portfolio?

Students love electronic portfolios, for they allow students to edit, cut, paste, and play back what they have entered, thus giving students a voice in the projects they create and evaluate. Parents are delighted with the ability to take part in this and learn about computers and their child's work at the same time. The State of California has strongly supported authentic assessment and the use of electronic portfolios, as evidenced by virtue of their Senate Bill 662. This bill actually mandates authentic assessment measures for all students in reading, mathematics, writing, science, and social science. Thus, the prognosis is very good for portfolio assessment and states are getting behind educators to support these endeavors.

While teachers, parents, and students move into the computer age with all that it entails, one can imagine that the transition to electronic portfolios is gradual and not necessarily easy. Yet the benefits of an electronic portfolio can surely be persuasive as teachers move to electronic records. For example, consider the following:

1. Electronic portfolios foster engaged learning, active learning, and student ownership of ideas. Parents also become part of the process.
2. Electronic portfolios are repositories of feedback in a medium familiar to many of today's students.

3. Electronic portfolios are the basis for student discussion of their own progress and a record of their reflections on what they learn.

4. Electronic portfolios are easily accessible, portable, and able to store vast amounts of data and information.

5. Electronic portfolios are set up to cross-reference student work in a way that is remarkably efficient and effective.

6. Electronic portfolios allow the learner to access and display evidence of multiple intelligences.

7. Electronic portfolios can be used to teach many content areas and encourage creative writing.

8. Electronic portfolios can be tools for encouraging dialogue with peers and fostering cross-cultural communication.

9. Electronic portfolios can redirect some of the energy students use on video games toward actual learning and performance-based tasks.

10. Electronic portfolios can develop the multiple intelligences Howard Gardner advocates for a well-rounded education.

11. Electronic portfolios have inspired many to write, to use digital stories to create autobiographies, online journals, and interactive texts and to give feedback to peers.

Obviously, the electronic portfolio is here to stay and is a welcome addition to our understanding of authentic assessment.

Portfolios Advance Learning

Wiggins (1993a, 1993b, 1998) and Janesick (2000) have argued that the student learner is like an apprentice to a craftsperson or a protégé of a master artist. As such, the student would have access to continual feedback, access to multiple ways and models of knowing, and an opportunity to reshape or refashion the performance or performance task. Similarly, earlier in educational history, John Dewey argued relentlessly for clear, public, specific criteria and standards for learning. Authentic assessment is an approach that provides such standards outright. There is no secrecy with authentic assessment. Let us take an example from the arts regarding performance. I was a choreographer earlier in my life; all the dancers in my dance company knew the so-called testing points in a given piece from the first day of rehearsal. They knew when they had to execute a particular formation or individual movement during rehearsal. Each dancer received individual feedback, and the company as a whole received feedback and notes for the next rehearsal and, obviously, for the performance before an audience. Thus we can learn from the apprentice model and the mentor-protégé model in terms of schooling. Performance-based tasks require doing, not watching, immersion in the activity, not spectator behavior. As the great choreographer Twyla Tharp, along with Mark Reiter, (2003), points out in her famous text, *The Creative Habit*, creativity is not a once in a while sort of thing. Being creative is an everyday thing with its own routines. Thus, it is helpful to view authentic assessment as a creative action for it involves the entire being of the learner much like any artistic activity requires the entire being of the artist.

Educators would be well served to use authentic assessment techniques in classrooms. We know from research, experience, and plain common sense that high stakes testing is harmful to our children and, ironically, our future as a nation. Authentic assessment offers the best viable alternative to one-shot, high stakes tests. It has been well documented that the high stakes test do only two things well:

1. High stakes, standardized, one-shot tests make money for test makers.
2. High stakes, standardized, one-shot tests tell us the size of houses and incomes near a school. Many studies document the fact that all you need to know is the poverty level of a school to determine with about 90 percent accuracy the results on such tests.

Likewise we know that high stakes testing gets quite a bit wrong:

1. High stakes testing gets learning, growth and development wrong.
2. High stakes testing gets child development wrong.
3. High stakes testing gets special education, bilingual education, English as a foreign language, and minority issues wrong.
4. High stakes testing cannot measure deep critical thinking or test multiple intelligences.
5. High stakes testing cannot show how students connect the dots between main ideas and what they are learning.
6. High stakes testing cannot appraise creativity, imagination, or common sense.
7. High stakes testing encourages false reporting.
8. High stakes testing contributes to high dropout rates.
9. High stakes testing encourages teaching to the test, for the moment, not for long-term learning.
10. High stakes testing erases the teacher's voice, and trivializes what we know about childhood learning and development.

Thus, taking this into account and taking into account the many resources, web sites, research reports, lawsuits, and what we know about children, is it not time to look at the most solid alternative, authentic assessment? With the overt problems of high stakes testing, I can only see high stakes testing as a form of child abuse.

Closing Thoughts on the Tragedy of a Flawed Law: No Child Left Behind or No Child Left?

It has always amazed me that bureaucrats and businessmen have the audacity to meddle in the work of professional educators and in that process demean and

How Can Assessment Work in Urban Schools?

criticize the nearly entirely female work force. Would they do this in the field of architecture, medicine or law, for example? Would they try to do this in engineering or the arts? The fact is that education is easy to pick on. The reverie these sometime critics revert to in terms of how wonderful the good old days were is astonishing when you look at the evidence. Were there ever any good old days? In addition, the media seem to love stories about failures in public schools. Is it not surprising that the failures in private schools receive little if any press coverage? For example, in a recent situation in the State of Florida, a faith-based private charter school was found to be ludicrously wanton in use of public funds, with nothing to show for it. It was closed following investigation and public outcry. The bloated promises of higher achievement were not met, and in fact the students in this publicly funded private venture actually were described as below standard. This is not surprising given the planned attack on public education which began in the Reagan era of the 1980s. Reagan, his paid employees, and subsequent conservative leaders have, to the present day, attempted to:

1. denigrate public education in order to move toward an agenda of privatization, and corporatization of public schools;
2. erase the U. S. Department of Education, which met with such opposition Reagan and his boys had to give it up, but I imagine this attempt will be made again;
3. develop an ongoing agenda of failure stories rather than success stories about public education, especially in urban settings, in effect, demonizing urban youth;
4. use high stakes testing as the only measure of effectiveness and when this was found problematic, dumb down the test to make it appear that more students were passing;
5. marginalize people and programs which offered solid evidence of the waste and mindlessness of high stakes testing, for example, the G.W. Bush Administration's scrubbing of the ERIC database of educational research in April 2002, basically erasing all research which "does not agree with the administration's policy on education and testing";
6. remove teachers from actually teaching the subject matter of the curriculum in order to prep for high stakes testing and live by the corporate creed that if you pass the test, you get the big money and if not we publicize and name your schools as failures;
7. use high stakes tests as a cover up for what is really going on with dropouts, special needs learners, minority students, and children whose native language is not English;
8. foist on the public the erroneous belief that more tests make better schools, which amounts to a wooden-headed and transparent marketing ploy;
9. cover up the reporting of the profits and sometime conflict of interest of individuals and companies that make millions of dollars from the testing business, such as in Florida, where the Florida test, Florida's Comprehensive

Assessment Test, was owned and operated by Neil Bush, the brother of the then Governor of Florida (since then the test has been sold to a larger conglomerate);

10. deny research that shows clearly all the problems with high stakes testing and its effects described earlier—in other words, denial trumps science.

Sadly, even with the voices of Deborah Meier, Alfie Kohn, Susan Ohanian, the professionals at FairTest, and all of us who write about the problems with high stakes testing, the public is largely unaware of the nature and harm of high stakes testing. Yet hopeful signs continue to spring up in that states that have experienced the serious and harmful effects of high stakes testing are taking control of matters and saying no to high stakes testing. Several sites from the states that are fighting the mindlessness of high stakes testing are presented below. Taking a look at the national FairTest database at www.fairtest.org, the Florida Coalition for Assessment Reform at www.fcarweb.org, the California Coalition for Authentic Reform in Education at www.calcare.org, and others, you see that overall they:

1. monitor the uses and abuses of high stakes standardized tests,
2. advocate for children,
3. promote public policies that support constructive, authentic assessment,
4. increase public awareness of alternatives to high stakes testing,
5. publicize the onerous burdens and the negative effects of NCLB,
6. offer opt out options for students to opt out of high stakes standardized tests.

There is hope in the quagmire.

At the sophisticated site FairTest, citizens may find sample letters to send to Congress, businessmen, and particular textbook companies that have recently changed textbooks to match the state tests, thus insuring a brain-dead student population. These textbook makers do not allow for the use of creativity or imagination in the learning process. Sadly, they have trivialized learning for children by reducing schooling to memorizing facts, drilling for the tests, and trying to get that one right answer. Thus, the books and tests are actually formulated to keep children from exercising critical and higher order thinking skills. FairTest also provides the latest updates on legislation, lawsuits, ethical problems, resources, and links to other key sites in individual states. To use just one more example, let us turn to the State of California.

California educators and citizens organized the comprehensive site www.calcare.org, where you will find the California Coalition for Authentic Reform in Education battling against high stakes testing, ethical improprieties in the administration and scoring of the standardized SAT-9 (Stanford Achievement Test-9) used in California, exposing the harmful effects felt by children as well as cogently describing the arguments on cultural bias in the test. California is the most diverse state in the United States and is a good case to study and learn about the negative side effects of high stakes testing. In fact, on that site you may read about how a grassroots citizens' movement changed high stakes testing in

California. It is now possible to opt out of the entire process. Check the web site for more data and the process involved.

Hope for the Future

One of the most hopeful signs regarding educating people about the dangers of high stakes testing and the strengths of authentic assessment is the vast number of resources available online. List servs, web sites, training sessions, samples of authentic assessment, and lists of all the lawsuits against individual states for not providing equal educational opportunities in urban settings are readily available. Any person reading this chapter can surely find information to help fight the negative effects of high stakes testing. If nothing else, the exposure of the greed and corruption involved in high stakes testing is well documented. In addition, the grassroots citizen groups, which are well organized against high stakes testing, are also documented state by state. Who benefits from high stakes testing? Test makers who are making billions in testing materials. This too is exposed online. You may be brought to tears when you see the salaries of the CEOs of testing conglomerates. Wealthy individuals can go to tutoring centers to cram for a test or practice taking tests. These are not options for poverty-dense urban neighborhoods. Visit FairTest for almost anything touching on the problems with high stakes testing. All the negative side effects of high stakes testing are well documented on this jewel of a resource. There are so many links, resources, fact sheets, and summaries of research reports, it would take another entire book to list them. Once you arrive at the site, you can begin your own journey toward educating yourself and others about what we should know about high stakes testing and assessment in the urban setting. Know that this journey is a critical and nuanced journey and will take dedication, persistence, diligence, and a strong vision of hope for our children. More than anything, as a sign for hope, know that you and I are not alone. There is a growing body of critique, literature, resource sites, and community members engaged in the process of finding good assessment practices such as authentic assessment rather than fragmented and ill-conceived prepackaged tests for evaluating our students. We can and should change the dehumanizing aspects of high stakes testing in the urban setting and in all settings. If we are to arrive at Freire's (2007) conscientization, this would be a good project to begin with for the urban setting. Thus, we can stem the effects of this unnecessary child abuse practice.

REFERENCES

Apple, M. (2009). Some ideas on interrupting the right: On doing critical educational work in conservative times. *Education, Citizenship, and Social Justice.* 4(2), 87–101.

Freire, P. (2007). *Pedagogy of the oppressed.* 30th Anniversary Ed. New York: Continuum.

Harding, S. (1991). *Whose science, whose knowledge? Thinking from women's lives.* Ithaca, NY: Cornell University Press.

Horn, R. A. (2004). *Standards primer.* New York: Peter Lang.

Horn, R. A. & Kincheloe, J. L. . (2001). *American standards: Quality education in a complex world, the Texas case.* New York: Peter Lang.

Janesick, V. J. (2000). *The assessment debate: A reference handbook.* Santa Barbara, CA: ABC-CLIO.

Janesick, V. J. (2006). *Authentic assessment primer.* New York: Peter Lang.

Kohn, A. (1993, 1999) *Punished by rewards: The trouble with gold stars, incentive plans, A's, praise, and bribes.* Boston: Houghton Mifflin.

Kohn, A. (2000). *The case against standardized testing: Raising the scores, ruining the schools.* Portsmouth, NH: Heinemann.

Kohn, A. (2004). *What does it mean to be well educated? And more essays on standards, grading, and other follies.* Boston: Beacon Press.

McNeil, L. (2000). *Contradictions of school reform: Educational costs of standardized testing.* New York: Routledge.

Meier, D. (2004). NCLB and democracy. In Meier, D. & G. Wood, (Eds.) *Many children left behind: How the NCLB Act is damaging our children and our schools* (pp. 66–78). Boston: Beacon Press.

Ohanian, S. (1999). *One size fits few: The folly of educational standards.* Portsmouth, NH: Heinemann.

Tharp. T. & M. Reiter. (2003). *The creative habit: Learn it and use it for life.* New York: Simon & Schuster.

Wiggins, G. (1993a). *Assessing student performance: Exploring the purpose and limits of testing.* San Francisco: Jossey-Bass.

Wiggins, G. (1993b). Assessment authenticity, context, and validity. *Phi Delta Kappan, 75*(3), 200–214.

Wiggins, G. (1998). *Educative assessment: Designing assessments to inform and improve student performance.* San Francisco: Jossey-Bass.

CHAPTER SIX

Priya Parmar

Does Hip Hop Have a Home in Urban Education?

Rap is something you do.
Hip Hop is something we live.
Hip Hop is a state of mind.
I AM HIP HOP!
　　　　—KRS-One

Poor academic achievement, low graduation rates, and high dropout rates, among other problems, have always plagued urban school districts. While social, political, and economic conditions certainly contribute to failing schools, some critics ignore such factors and unjustly place much of the responsibility on the shoulders of teachers (i.e., teacher accountability), students (i.e., deficit theory), and their families (i.e., "parents don't care" or "are not involved"). The demographics of urban schools comprise largely African American, Hispanic, and immigrant youth, yet a close examination of school curricula reveals their knowledge, experiences, and history remain marginalized, subjugated, or altogether untold. A counter-approach to address these challenges involves a reconceptualization of the school curricula. This chapter encourages all teacher educators, regardless of subject matter, to engage in a cultural pedagogy that explores, learns, acknowledges, and respects the rich and varied cultural identities, experiences, and knowledge that their students bring to school. One form of cultural pedagogy is the acknowledgment that Hip Hop *culture* is intricately tied to one's social and cultural identity. Given this reality, teacher education programs and educators in K-12 schools can no longer expect students to "leave that rap-stuff outside the school building."

The remark insisting that rap was not welcomed within the "sanctuary" of her high school walls was made by an African American female principal in Brooklyn, New York, in 2006 when I approached her about having a few of her teachers participate in a literacy program I created in 2004. The program, *Lyrical Minded: Enhancing Literacy through Popular Culture and Spoken Word Poetry,* is intended to enhance literacy and critical thinking skills using a cultural pedagogy that incorporates critical literacies, including media literacy. Teachers from all content areas attend a six-week summer course that introduces them to critical pedagogy, critical literacies, and the importance of cultural pedagogy. The purpose is to use alternative texts that "speak" to their students while also meeting New York City and State standards. Participants are encouraged to use popular culture (e.g., music, film, television, comics, and video games) and Hip Hop culture as cultural pedagogical texts. Cultural texts are not meant to be used passively in the classroom; in fact, critical pedagogy helps students develop critical literacy skills that enable them to explore and understand different ways of looking at culture which can take the form of written, visual, or spoken texts. Students are then able to question the attitudes, values, and beliefs that lie beneath the surface of such texts. All teachers in the program incorporate spoken word poetry into their lessons as a vehicle that allows students to express their thoughts in an unconstrained, uninhibited manner. Each teacher develops nine to twelve week-long units in his/her respective disciplines and then implements them in the upcoming school year with assistance from me and another literacy professor. Local spoken word artists are also available to conduct workshops in each teacher's class. Upon completing the unit, all participating schools and students attend a spoken word performance at the legendary Nuyorican Poets Café in the Lower East Side of Manhattan. The annual fieldtrip serves as a culminating event that brings teachers and students together to share and celebrate the poetry students created during the implementation phase of the Lyrical Minded program.

Before I even had an opportunity to explain the goals of the program to the principal, she had already made up her mind once she heard that Hip Hop was a choice teachers could use as a source of cultural texts in the classroom. She automatically assumed that Hip Hop was "rap," and in a somewhat elitist tone stated, "I don't want that rap-stuff in my school! These kids have to leave it outside!" Sadly for her students, this principal failed to realize that many of her students *were* Hip Hop. They lived and breathed it; it was how they identified themselves. It was impossible to separate the two; asking them to do so was like ripping a part of their being out, asking them to sell out to be something they were not. Rather than stay and clarify the misconceptions she held about Hip Hop—and about her students—I left, partly due to my resistance to humbling myself and *convincing* her to validate her own students' culture, and partly because of her attitude in refusing to acknowledge her students! At that point in time, my desire was to work with administrators who were open to possibility and innovative pedagogies, even if they were unfamiliar with Hip Hop culture. Fortunately for me, there were plenty of schools willing to learn from—and with—their faculty and students. Recognizing, understanding, validating, and including the experiences, knowledge, culture, and subcultures our students come from is the first line of action of a cultural pedagogy.

This chapter will share ideas and pedagogical strategies stemming from ethnographic research conducted from the Lyrical Minded program as well as my own teaching of high school students. For the past several years, in addition to my responsibilities as a literacy (assistant) professor at Brooklyn College's School of Education, I have also served as a part-time English teacher in select Brooklyn high schools teaching a course I developed entitled "Hip Hop 101." The course is guided under the theoretical foundation of critical and cultural pedagogy, has similar objectives to the Lyrical Minded program, and has been offered both during regular school hours and as an after school program in which students receive English credit toward their graduation. The majority of my Hip Hop 101 students, as well as those students participating in the Lyrical Minded program, come from working class backgrounds and are of African American or Hispanic descent.

The critical and cultural pedagogy I advocate here is discussed with, and explained to, my students, in age appropriate language. It is important to include their voices in my lesson planning as it only creates more engaged, thoughtful, and critical participation—all a part of a critical and cultural pedagogy. My students have written powerful poetry illustrating the importance of recognizing and including their cultural knowledge and identities, specifically Hip Hop as cultural text. As such, select poems will be shared as a means to reinforce some of my points, and more importantly, to hear their voices and concerns.

In fact, let us begin by sharing a poem written by Laron, a tenth grade student at the time, participating in the Lyrical Minded program (2004–2005). He shares his feelings about school as a place that is decontextualized and culturally irrelevant for him. In a poem titled simply *"High School,"* he writes:

> High school is a place where work is done
> All work no play, no time for fun.
> I travel an hour just to get here
> I stay for six hours and get nowhere.
> And every week there's a test to take
> But when it's done, I have plans to make.
> There are so many rules about what not to do
> How is chewing gum even bothering you?
> And then there are people in the school
> They come here, don't work, and act a fool.
> But I'm "told" that I'm not a person with the right to complain
> So sometimes I take school as just a game.
> Now I'm writing this poem and wasting my time
> But a good thing is, I'm making it rhyme!
> And when tomorrow comes they got work to give
> But I'm a teenager with a *real* life to live!

Laron's feelings about traveling one hour to school only to be met with mundane, test-driven, rule-bound, and mechanistic routines are shared by many students who attend schools that are technocratic and positivist in nature. This approach to education pushes teachers to use their time wisely and efficiently in a way that forces rote learning, memorization, and drilling of skills necessary to pass standardized exams. Often the result is decontextualized content that is rendered meaningless and boring. If students are not acting out due to boredom, they are passively sitting, trained to behave according to a set of rules and standards that ultimately produce compliant, complacent citizens who know their place. Is this the type of educational environment we want to support? Or do we wish to provide democratic education where the goal is to create civic-minded, critical thinkers that are socially, culturally, economically, and politically active in society?

Critical pedagogy supports the latter, arguing for fair, just, and inclusive curricula that represent multiple and alternative perspectives and knowledge. Ignoring, excluding, or marginalizing these "other" perspectives and knowledge produces schools that center or confirm certain cultures while devaluing others. The valuing of particular forms of knowledge, language, and experience familiar only to certain (privileged) students is legitimized, thereby reproducing what French sociologist Pierre Bourdieu refers to as "cultural capital," or cultural reproduction (Aronowitz & Giroux, 1993). Kincheloe and Steinberg (1997) offer awareness of how cultural pedagogy can counter the cultural capital of privileged groups by having educators and our students understand (p. 87):

- The complex relationship between power and knowledge.
- The ways knowledge is produced, accepted, and rejected.
- The ways individuals receive dominant representations and encodings of the world—are they assimilated, resisted, or transformed?
- The manner in which individuals negotiate their relationship with the "official story," the legitimate canon.
- The process by which pleasure is derived from engagement with the dominant culture—an investment that produces meaning and formulates affect.

This sort of cultural pedagogy validates marginalized voices, histories, and experiences and helps students map their relation to the social worlds around them. They do this by realizing the complex ways in which they are connected to both people like themselves and those radically different from them (Kincheloe & Steinberg, 1997; Parmar, 2009). The following spoken word piece, titled "Where I'm from," illustrates the importance of this point nicely. It was written in 2006 by two of my tenth-grade Hip Hop 101 students, Sharlene and Chantelle. They engage in a dialogue reflecting mixed feelings of frustration, marginalization, exclusion, and awareness:

Chantelle:
Where I'm from people come from all different places
It's so diverse here I see so many different faces;

But through all the diversity we live in different sets.
We got people who get divided into color then divided in gangs
One big controversial net.

Sharlene:
Where I'm from these dirty bums are always trying to holla.
Their pants are always saggin' talking about how they bangin.'
I can't walk down the street without being acknowledged
I feel fear in my heart 'cause what society has built in me
Showing me that our men are rapists, molesters, and killers
Everything I won't dare to be.
I cross the other street when I see thug looking boys walking
'Cause deep inside I want to live another day and still be talking
It's more than just my neighborhood, it's a nightmare
I want to wake up from.
Where I'm from I have to work twice as hard to make it in life
I have 2 strikes against me
I'm a female and I'm African American
So where I'm from it's not a game
You either living for today or forget that in this world you ever came.

Chantelle:
I listen to music people say it's trash
Saying we are Negro's who need to go back to being lashed
People say things like don't judge a book by its cover
I say the same from not judging my music because of my color
Where I'm from I'm telling you it's a real diverse place
Beautiful for the people that love and a punishment for the people that hate.

The last verse by Chantelle moves the girls' critique of their neighborhoods to outsiders' perceptions of their music—Hip Hop. The assertion "I AM HIP HOP" made by the Hip Hop generation and youth identifying with Hip Hop culture is a growing proclamation demanding the serious recognition and inclusion of Hip Hop as a form of cultural identity in the urban school curriculum. The MC, artist, and activist, considered by many to be the "Teacha" of Hip Hop culture, KRS-One (formerly of the group Boogie Down Productions), has declared himself—and the Hip Hop generation—to be Hip Hop. The proclamation I am *Hip Hop* is a state of mind, being, and identity—a culture. KRS-One and his Temple of Hip Hop declared Hip Hop as an official "Kulture" when presenting the document known as "The Hip Hop Declaration of Peace" (written in consultation with community activists and founding members of the culture) to the United Nations on May 16, 2001 (HipHop Ministries, Inc., 2004; TheSearchForTheLight, 2008).

When making such declarations, however, we must first begin with demystifying the myths and fears that surround Hip Hop. What *is* Hip Hop? What does it mean *to be* Hip Hop? Who can make that claim? Why does Hip Hop evoke moral panic? I often begin my discussions about Hip Hop by asking my audience (youth and adults) how they define or see Hip Hop. Here are some of the more informed comments I have received:

- Hip Hop is a culture. It's a lifestyle . . . a movement.
- Hip Hop is a way we act, live, speak, and dress.
- Hip Hop originated in the South Bronx from African American and Latino youth expressing artistic forms in a variety of ways such as deejaying, MCing, graffiti-writing, and break-dancing.
- Hip Hop is self-expression through a variety of means (poetry, spoken word, MCing, art (graffiti), dance, and music).
- Hip Hop is a cultural, social, and political movement expressing the unheard, ignored, or exploited voices of the oppressed.

It is difficult to provide a narrow or definitive definition of Hip Hop just as it is if asked to define any culture or subculture. Most "Hip Hoppas" will agree that the four original, or foundational, elements that comprise the culture are:

1. Taggin,' writing, or mainstream's use of the term, graffiti art;
2. DJing ("deejaying") or turntablism;
3. MCing ("emceeing"), rhyming, or mainstream's use of the terms "rap," "rapper," or "rapping"; and
4. Breakin,' B-boys, B-girls (Break-boys and Break-girls, respectively), or mainstream's use of the term break-dancing.

Hip Hop culture has evolved to include many more elements and principles such as fashion, language, lifestyle, and more, sustaining itself as an (inter) national community of entrepreneurs, professionals, activists, educators, scholars, poets, and artists from all ethnic and class backgrounds. This list is not meant to be exhaustive by any means, as it is understood that the culture is continuously growing and developing. The Hip Hop Declaration of Peace outlines eighteen principles that serve to guide and protect the culture as well as provide additional clarity as to the meaning, purpose, and intentions of Hip Hop. The document serves as a framework of expectations of what it means *to be* Hip Hop. KRS-One acknowledges that these principles are not meant to be static or definitive; rather, he expects the community to engage in intellectual debate about the contents of the Declaration. In fact, in an interview with Hip Hop historian and journalist, Davey D, KRS-One explained that it is up to the individual to "determine for ourselves our place and subsequent actions within Hip Hop . . ." (Davey D, 2001).

As I have expressed in previous publications, all four foundational elements of Hip Hop have the potential to be used as cultural texts that can be read, analyzed, and interpreted due to the deep historical roots, experiences, and knowledge that pioneers from each element contribute and/or were influenced by. From an aesthetic perspective, each element provides opportunities for students to read and interpret the creative, energetic, and expressive nature of the art form to excite crowds—visually, verbally, kinesthetically, and aurally (Parmar and Bain, 2006; Parmar, 2009).

More important than finding a common definition of Hip Hop, is recognizing and learning its history and origin if we expect any level of education (K-12 and academe) to view it as credible or valuable cultural texts. Taking an inter- and counterdisciplinary approach to studying Hip Hop will inevitably open doors of discovery to the forebears of the culture, stemming back to West African and Jamaican historical roots, as well as acknowledging the influence of the African American literary tradition. Several genres of music, including rock, funk, soul, jazz, reggae, and rhythm and blues must be recognized as heavy influences on the pioneers of Hip Hop, along with poets from the Black Power Movement (e.g., Gil Scott-Heron, The Last Poets, and Amiri Baraka). There are countless resources available online and in print that provide detailed and comprehensive historical information on Hip Hop culture and that serve as prerequisite reading prior to pursuing Hip Hop as a cultural pedagogy (see The Universal Zulu Nation, 2009; George, 1999; Fricke, 2002; Forman & Neal, 2004; Chang, 2005; Davey D, 2009).

I want to return to the list of common responses I receive when asking students to define Hip Hop. Listed below are some of the more stereotypic comments:

- Hip Hop is music—rap.
- Hip Hop is misogynistic.
- Hip Hop is violent, sexist, and homophobic.
- Hip Hop is ripe with "gangsters" and youth acting "wild."
- Hip Hop is all about gaining material wealth and showing off the "bling-bling"—money, cars, clothes, jewelry, women, and mansions.
- Hip Hop objectifies women as mere sexual objects by referring to them as "bitches" and "hos."
- Hip Hop is "their" music; it is ghetto music.
- Hip Hop is a bunch of slang.

As you can see, the statements listed above are heavily concentrated on the MCing element of Hip Hop and informed by mainstream (mis)representations of this particular element. The one-sided depictions of MCing propagated in mainstream media outlets have portrayed this art form as perceived above; however, it does not accurately represent Hip Hop culture or even the MCing element of the culture. It should be noted that the interchangeable use of the terms "rap" and "Hip Hop" is incorrect, partly due to the lack of recognition the other elements receive. The terms are not synonymous. Rap is not solely Hip Hop, and MCing is only one aspect of a culture that is complex, rich in history, and ever-evolving. Moreover, many Hip Hoppas differentiate between "rappers" and "MCs." Ryan, a tenth grade Hip Hop 101 student who *is* Hip Hop and astute for his young years, explains the distinction in a poem called *Hip Hop* (2006):

> Rappers talk about guns, sex, and how life is hard
> But rappers are nothing but modern day "fake" bards
> Telling stories through song and rhymes
> Telling other people's stories, talking about
> Other people's life and times
> So can you tell me why the media
> Portrays them so bad?

Is it something they can't understand?
Most of them never had the life some of these rappers had
Through all the negativity there is some positivity
MCs like Kanye, Common, Talib, and Def
They express themselves from their minds and creativity
So through all the darkness
There is some light
Through all the wrong
There is some right.

Many Hip Hop cultural critics, including artists, have argued that Hip Hop is dead, as seen or heard on mainstream airwaves. Unfortunately, what is left over is "Hip Pop." Hip Pop refers to a "mainstream or commercial artist who 'sells out' to corporate interests" (Parmar, 2009, p. 35). Examples of artists who may arguably be considered as Hip Pop: P. Diddy, Chingy, Lil Jon, Nelly, Cash Money Millionaires, and others. Hip Hop, as opposed to Hip Pop, refers to the MCing element and can be defined as, " . . . a Hip Hop artist who may have gained commercial appeal but has not sold out to corporate interests" (p. 35). Examples of Hip Hop MC's are KRS-One, Rakim, Mos Def, MC Lyte, Hieroglyphics, The Roots, Wu-Tang Clan, Talib Kweli, Nas, Common, and too many others to list here. KRS-ONE has also argued that an artist can move from MC to rapper back to MC and vice versa. He cites examples such as Tupac, 50 Cent, and even himself (ibid). Mainstream media have appropriated and commodified the culture to such an extent that the true spirit of Hip Hop has been "raped" or stripped of its art form, all for capitalistic gains. From a critical lens, the culprits aiding in commercializing this art form are named as the record labels and the corporations that own them, upper and middle management of artists, and to some degree, rappers themselves. Creating awareness of what Hip Hop was and is, learning its history, and understanding how power operates in shaping beliefs, perceptions, unwarranted fears, and stereotypes of the culture will create, critical, informed consumers who can distinguish between Hip Hop and Hip Pop.

Cultural pedagogy manifests itself in a variety of creative, thought-provoking, contextual ways. One of my favorite ways to begin the Hip Hop 101 class is by having students discuss how power situates itself in their lives, whether it is in school, their neighborhoods, or in the larger society. Teachers participating in the Lyrical Minded program do the same. Students are asked to bring in texts that reflect dominant culture's definition of beauty as perpetuated by media. They bring in various texts ranging from magazine advertisements to pictures of popular celebrity actresses or entertainers, to rap lyrics that describe the object of the rapper's affection. The visual texts have similar characteristics: white female models or light-skinned African American celebrities that are pictured with clear, flawless skin and perfectly proportioned figures, smiling either innocently or seductively into the camera. The printed texts (lyrics) often describe physical and personal characteristics that make a female desirable, distinguishing between sexually promiscuous women, and girlfriend or "wifey" material. We examine the explicit and implicit messages promoted in these texts, differentiating between generalizations and stereotypes, naming the people responsible for producing or constructing the images (i.e., corporations, advertisers, and consumers), identifying groups who are represented and excluded, designating the intended audience, and discussing accessibility or product placement. We talk about potential consequences of being overexposed with these messages about beauty (i.e., how they shape identity, perception, and poor or strong self-image, contribute to cultural reproduction of the dominant culture or empowerment, and lead to internalizing unhealthy beliefs of what beauty is and is not), and about gender roles (i.e., perceptions and expectations from both sexes). Students engage in lively, insightful, and critical debate, questioning the intent of corporations. They are asked to reconstruct images they find to be problematic by expressing them in diverse forms, including art, written poetry or rap, performance or spoken word poetry, skits or role plays of commercials and news stories, or movement (dance) without expressing words. All assignments include a written component explaining their rationale. One of my English teachers in the program designed critical lessons challenging mainstream standards of beauty and debating the impact media has on youth (i.e., internalized hatred for self or others) using Toni Morrison's novel, *The Bluest Eye*. Critical activities examining dominant representations and cultural and social reproduction followed.

In my Hip Hop 101 class, I usually have pre-selected lyrics from underground or conscious artists such as KRS-One, Immortal Technique, Nas, Talib Kweli, or Queen Latifah prepared for students to analyze. I also respect my students' knowledge and expertise, and will often ask them to bring in printed or audio versions of Hip Hop songs that are reflective of the theme covered during the lesson. I provide guidelines that students are to abide by when selecting their texts, always being mindful and respectful of school policies and administrators' wishes. Fortunately, the administrators I have worked with are open to the diversity of content and language found in the lyrics, understanding that their students are, like it or not, exposed to harsh, violent, and sexual images found in *all* media, not only in Hip Hop. They insist we take a critical approach in analyzing, deconstructing, and recreating these texts, in the hope of creating spaces where students are acquiring essential skills for success in and out of school. Teachers report increased participation, more thought-provoking discussions and debates, and willingness from students to read, write, and attend their classes.

Preparing students to perform well academically and on standardized exams is a serious issue. I have a hand in preparing my students to perform well on the English Regents exam, but I refuse to resort to using mechanical teaching-to-the-test methods. Critical and cultural pedagogical strategies impart valuable skills that will prepare students to take standardized exams. For example, the English Regents exam requires students to organize their ideas in a logical and coherent manner, to use a tone or level of language appropriate for an English class, to follow the conventions of standard written English, and to indicate any words taken directly from class readings or documentaries by using quotation marks or referring to the speaker. My students are required to research Hip Hop culture and its history, preparing reports that are coherent and logical. They are required to write in formal Standard American English and are taught how to reference and quote appropriately. We discuss the level of language that is appropriate depending on the requirements of the assignment. Research reports, essays, or formal letters are to be written using Standard American English. Creative writing, journal writing, and reflections can incorporate home dialects. We have extensive discussions of the use of language found in select mainstream Hip Hop lyrics, questioning intent and debating whether certain language should be left in or omitted. This opens doors to debate issues of censorship. Does censoring certain words or language suppress the realness or flavor of the message? Who determines what words are censored and why? There are times that I require my students to rewrite or summarize the lyrics using conventions of Standard American English, and there are other times that I ask them to write freely using their own language and dialect. At times I will assess only content because I want them to write with no inhibitions or reservations; yet at other times, I will assess for both content, spelling, and grammar because I want them to be prepared and confident as they prepare to enter institutions that uphold only "standard" conventions of the language.

It is important to discuss the role of power in terms of language use. We talk about what Standard American English is from a sociolinguistic perspective. My students understand that the Standard English required of them by schools is merely a dialect of the English language that was proclaimed standard by power constructs. We learn why it is important to navigate between different dialects, or "code-switch," depending on the audience to whom we are addressing. At the same time, home dialects are valued and validated by providing examples of successful individuals who are from the same dialectical background as my students. We discuss the political nature of language by asking who determines language as standard and non-standard. We understand there are codes of convention in terms of language, and even in dress and mannerisms that are accepted in certain situations and frowned upon in others. I ask students to reflect on *why* such codes are in effect and *to whom* these codes apply. Why are certain groups relegated to conform to these codes, while others are not? Are conditions based on race, class, or gender? Are there double standards?

An integral part of a critical and cultural pedagogy is to encourage student agency (activism). We can analyze, deconstruct, reconstruct, and question dominant power and ideologies over and over, but after creating this consciousness, the burning question is: What are we going to do about it? What actions can we take? Some ideas include:

- writing letters to politicians, magazines, newspapers, or school officials;
- organizing petitions;
- canceling subscriptions;
- turning off the television;

- refusing to buy products from companies we feel exploit workers;
- refusing to buy or download music from artists we feel contribute to the demise of Hip Hop;
- boycotting products;
- producing Public Service Announcements and airing them in school, the local community, and other alternative media outlets;
- advocating for programs that promote cultural and media awareness and inclusionary texts.

As I write these words, I am reminded of the profound words spoken by internationally known slam poet and queer activist Alix Olson:

> I think U.S. citizens are trained at a young age to fully inhale the system, the rhetoric and ideologies surrounding democracy, capitalism, religion, family life. . . . If the wizard is exposed, and we realize we've been lied to, it's frightening, like political vertigo or instantaneous sobriety. After all, once you've seen the light, there's no going back and, at that point, whether you like it or not, you are accountable to truth and responsible for creating change (2006).

I, too, hope to compel my students to act and create change.

In conclusion, issues of cultural pedagogy within the framework of Hip Hop include, but are not limited to: analyzing, critiquing, and interpreting the complex relationships between power, knowledge, identity, and politics. In relation to the MCing or rap element of Hip Hop, students can take a closer look at the relationships among corporate record labels, middle management, writers, producers of artists, the artists themselves, and even the models paid to be in the music videos (since ironically, much of the focus and blame appears to be placed on them). A central role when examining Hip Hop or any cultural text is examining the role of power. Who holds it? How do they use it to shape, control, reward, and normalize perceptions of self and others? Examining ways in which identity and knowledge are produced and validated or invalidated can be accomplished by examining mainstream media's appropriation, commercialization, and capitalization of the culture, resulting in reductionist or simplified definitions of Hip Hop with "rap" as its sole signifier and identifier. The production and maintenance of cultural hegemony can be challenged, questioned, and resisted. Educators can validate and empower subjugated and/or indigenous bodies of knowledge by centralizing them in the school curricula and exposing students to the contributions of those that have gone unrecognized and excluded in dominant cultural texts. This involves incorporating historical analysis across disciplines and naming the silenced or marginalized voices, cultures, and ideologies in mathematics, science, history, English literature, art, and music classes. Cultural pedagogy results in the development of a critical consciousness and self-consciousness by challenging hegemonic practices, which ultimately helps students recognize their position in the world. And finally, critical and cultural pedagogy encourages teacher and student agency.

I end this chapter with a powerful critique and defense of Hip Hop written in 2006 by Jessica, another tenth grade Hip Hop 101 student who began the semester quiet and reserved, due to insecurities she felt as a result of suffering from a lisp. She was never at a loss for words on paper though! As each week passed, I noticed Jessica slowly coming out of her shell, at first volunteering to read her poems aloud and then gradually moving towards thoughtful and critical debate as the semester progressed. My once reserved, self-conscious Hip Hoppa performed this poem, called "Hip Hop," on stage in front of 200 peers and teachers from different Brooklyn high schools at the Lyrical Minded annual culminating event at the Nuyorican Poets' Café. I was like a proud older sister! Jessica's poem captures the essence of my argument and the empowering potential of our students if we only hand over, or share, the mic.

Hip Hop, what is it you may ask?
It's a language, type of music, dance, style, swagger, and flavor.
It's a culture; it's how I live my life, my past, present, and future.
Because I am Hip Hop people think I am less than them
They think I am beneath them, like some kind of ghetto hood rat
I don't think of myself as a poor deprived ghetto girl from the hood
I may fall down seven times but I'll stand up eight
And you don't know I gotta brush these players off and haters too
Stay true to my peoples, my whole crew
Haters you know they the ones who are false
Claiming Hip Hop and giving me mean mugs while we're in class
They share each other's clothes and still be looking like trash
And with how some Hip Hop lies they look in the mirror and see misconception
'Cause see these chicks spend hours perfecting them features, yet I get more
glances in a hoodie and some sneakers!
Hip Hop all day every day, got me contemplating
I'm in school, sometimes not listening, not even concentrating
Sometimes I wish I could stop, rewind, go back in time and re-write the story of my life
And the people in the suburbs, they think they know Hip Hop
'Cause what they see on TV
But it's really not all they conceive it to be.
Then you got fake Hip Hop
Fake Hip Hop is bumpin' to materialistic expectations
Forget that 'ish and the ignorant faces
Forget a gangsta reputation
True Hip Hop can speak of things like love and poverty
A skateboard or a country illusion or reality
Hip Hop, what can I say, the words are right there
But I can't say them on the tip of my tongue like I can taste them
I see them before me but I can't reach them
I'm trying to get it out so I can show those in our generation
But it's kinda hard 'cause I'm suffering from what I like to call poetic constipation.
Hip Hop is about love too—that person who has your heart
You called those people "niggas," they weren't "niggas"
They were my family, my ancestors, my roots
I been through so much you don't even know
I've been hurting so long but it just don't always show
And there's only one place I can escape and go

What am I talking about you may ask?
Hip Hop—only alive to those who see
True Hip Hop and its mentality.
Maybe one day Hip Hop will be seen as positive
And we'll win the fight
An idea that will turn into day from the dark, lonely night.

REFERENCES

Aronowitz, S., & Giroux, H. (1993). *Education still under siege* (2nd ed.). Westport, CT: Bergin & Garvey.

Chang, J. (2005). *Can't stop, won't stop: A history of the Hip-Hop generation.* New York: Picador.

Davey D. (2001). KRS to go to UN. Retrieved July 20, 2009 from http://www.daveyd.com/FullArticles\articleN771.asp

Davey D. (2009). Davey D's Hip Hop history. What is Hip Hop . . . directory. Retrieved July 20, 2009 from: http://www.daveyd.com/hiphophistory09.html

Forman, M., & Neal, M.A. (2005). *That's the joint! The Hip-Hop studies reader.* New York: Routledge.

Fricke, J. (2002). *Yes yes y'all: The Experience Music Project's oral history of Hip-Hop's first decade.* Cambridge, MA: Da Capo Press.

George, N. (1999). *Hip Hop America.* New York: Penguin.

HipHop Ministries, Inc. (2004). *The Hip Hop declaration of peace.* Retrieved July 20, 2009 from http://www.hiphopministries.org/gpage.html

Kincheloe, J., & Steinberg S. (1997). *Changing multiculturalism.* London: Open University Press.

Olson, A. (2006). *Alix Olson Quotes.* Retrieved August 15, 2009 from http://thinkexist.com/quotation/i-think-u-s-citizens-are-trained-at-a-young-age/821940.html

Parmar, P. (2009). *Knowledge reigns supreme: The critical pedagogy of Hip Hop activist KRS-One.* Rotterdam: Sense Publishers.

Parmar, P., & Bain, B. (2006). Spoken word and Hip Hop: The power of urban art and culture. In J. L. Kincheloe & K. Hayes (Eds.). *City kids: Understanding, appreciating, and teaching them.* New York: Peter Lang.

TheSearchForTheLight (2008). KRS-One—Hip-Hop's Declaration of Peace. Retrieved July 20, 2009 from http://www.youtube.com/watch?v=UM_2–52v_iM

The Universal Zulu Nation (2009). Retrieved July 20, 2009 from http://www.zulunation.com/

CHAPTER SEVEN

Christopher Emdin

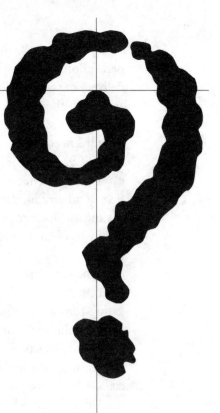

What Is Urban Science Education?

 As a student of science teaching and learning in urban settings, and a scholar within the field of urban science education, one would imagine that most of my academic work surrounds uncovering new approaches to science instruction and then implementing these approaches within urban classrooms. Some may see the work as requiring the creation of science curricula that will be taught in schools, or even creating science texts for schools. The more progressive educator would probably imagine that the work requires finding out what students are interested in, and then connecting them to science through these interests. Based on these very logical perspectives of what an urban science educator does, or should do, defining urban science education seems simple. It appears as though it is merely an extension of science education in general. Therefore defining urban science education should be simple. It can be viewed as a study of pedagogical approaches to delivering science content that just so happens to be done within urban contexts. The problem with this definition is that the placing of the word urban before the phrase science education disturbs traditional notions of science education and requires us to redefine established notions and refocus on what the goals of urban science education truly should be.

The underlying yet widespread notion that many science educators hold is that whatever practices are used in non-urban settings should be the same ones that are used in urban settings. The mode of thinking that supports this argument is difficult to challenge. It maintains that science is an objective discipline, and that all students should be taught science essentially the same ways because it is equitable and fair to all students to do so. Essentially, there is an underlying perception that no students should receive special treatment in regard to the delivery of science. The focus on inquiry and hands-on science makes it appear as though the field is welcoming to all and meets the needs of all children. In actuality, much of the existent practice in science education does not truly consider the needs of urban youth. While this may not be explicitly stated in bylines of prolific scholars or beautifully succinct article abstracts of "urban science educators," any science education literature classified as the significant pieces in the field of urban education reveals an overwhelming exclusion of urbanness beyond the title or description of the setting. While it is easy to gloss over this fact, or excuse its blatant disregard for urban youth because science is considered to be an objective discipline and science educators are scientists by training at their core, the reality is that much of the work in the field is not truly Urban Science Education. I argue that if the work of science educators does not consist of navigating through the ever-changing dynamics of the political spectra, does not consider the sociocultural dynamics of being urban, and does not function to combat the effects of newly packaged versions of age-old approaches to teaching and learning science that do not meet the needs of urban youth, it should not be classified as Urban Science Education.

Urban Science Education is the work of teachers and researchers who believe in providing students of all racial, ethnic, and sociocultural backgrounds equal access to science and who have considered the historical inequities in science education and the fact that teaching urban youth without considering the complexities of their existence defeats the purpose of teaching. It is the work of those who view science education as a social justice issue (Tate, 2001) and those who consider dynamics such as sociolinguistic issues and ethnicity (Rodriguez, 2003), sociocultural dynamics within the urban context, democracy in urban science classrooms (Basu, 2008), and specifically urban issues such as homelessness (Barton, 1998), sociopolitical action (Hodson, 1999) and hip-hop culture (Emdin, in press).

Urban science educators realize that the academic/educational challenges that have plagued communities where urban youth live are compounded by years of disregard, invalidation, and a positioning of the urban student as being other than the "normal" student. While the "normal" student is perceived as interested in success in school, able to achieve in science, and having appropriate behavior, urban students are perceived (in both media and academic venues) as uninterested in school, hard to teach, and unable to do well in challenging academic subjects. The collateral effects of being perceived as other than the norm (not being a normal student) in conjunction with the absence of material resources for engaging with a discipline like science causes many urban students to become alienated from schools and creates huge gaps between the culture of school and that of the students. On one level, students are not perceived or treated as full participants in science. On another level, inequities in the distribution of resources do not provide them with the tools to become full participants in science. In response to this multilayered attack on the participation of urban youth in science, Urban Science Education as a field of study, and urban science educators, begins with urban youth's realities as the point from which they are connected to science.

The Effects of Perceptions of Urban Youth

Inaccurate perceptions of urban youth realities that focus on the perils of being urban, like crime, violence, and being poor, often cause the teaching of urban students to be presented as challenging. In other instances it is presented to the public as a labor of love that requires enduring hardship and providing charity to the socioeconomically deprived and the academically uninterested. In fact, efforts to recruit teachers to urban schools such as Teach for America and the Teaching Fellows in New York City play on these myths and misconceptions of urban youth and present teacher recruits with a perception that they are the most promising college graduates (mostly of racial and ethnic backgrounds that vary from those of students in urban schools) who are providing a charity to deprived urban youth by committing to teaching the least promising of people (youth of color in urban public schools). Perceptions of urban youth as academically and intellectually challenged, and in need of being saved from themselves, have grown to become so pervasive that evidence to support these deficit perspectives has infiltrated teacher perceptions of urban youth, often before these teachers even enter urban schools.

In response, I argue that because urban youth are continually perceived as hard to teach, unable to comprehend challenging subject matter like science, and uninterested in school, they are treated as such by teachers. I extend this argument by suggesting that the practices teachers enact in urban science classrooms are often much less focused on what is best to do for students in a particular classroom and more on what is perceived as best practice based on a caricature of urban students, urban science classrooms, and urban schools in general. This ideology does not provide opportunities for teachers to see that urban youth are embedded in a culture that supports critical thinking and questioning, which are necessary attributes for understanding science. Furthermore, urban communities are filled with resources for teaching science that are often ignored by teachers. Instead, the practices of teachers in urban schools are often oppositional to practices that are part of urban youth culture and aligned to what is best for teaching students from non-urban and more affluent backgrounds. Over time, these practices become the normalized ways of teaching science in urban settings and have a deleterious effect on the teaching and learning of science for urban youth. In response, I argue for an approach to science pedagogy that is rooted in students' realities.

Pedagogy, the science of teaching, gets enacted in ways that ascribe to a method of teaching designed for a population perceived as the norm and does not consider the ways of knowing and being of urban youth of color in urban settings. These students are traditionally not considered in the design of curriculum or the implementation of pedagogy and therefore, are not being perceived as normal. I draw this conclusion based on Goffman's (1997) description of the "normals" as populations who are the societal norm and science education's lack of a concerted focus on urban youth that positions them as not the norm. Urban Science Education requires a transformative pedagogical approach that challenges those who perceive themselves as, or who are traditionally perceived as, normal to reinvestigate their relegation of women, people of color or any other groups that vary from an established norm to subaltern positions. This approach to pedagogy is concerned not only with subject matter delivery but also with challenging hierarchies that are inherited by the placing of science education for non-urban socioeconomically advantaged students as the primary way through which those who do not fit into this mold are taught science.

In describing Reality Pedagogy, it is necessary to describe the concepts of reality and pedagogy as distinct concepts that must converge. The amalgamation of these concepts is the first step to creating an approach to the teaching of science that benefits populations that have been removed from achievement in, or access to, science. Reality Pedagogy acknowledges non-dominant standpoints and utilizes the position of those viewed as 'other' as the point from which pedagogy is birthed, and once developed, transformative teaching and research continue to feed. This process involves a positioning of the other to the norm. This repositioning of standpoints in favor of those not considered the norm, and their being repositioned as the norm, is valuable in enacting pedagogy that is responsive to the needs of the marginalized. While engaging in this task may sound uncritically altruistic, or even worse superficial (because of an age-old similar message about focusing on students' interests to improve science education), I argue that focusing on student realities is not the same as focusing on their interests. While students' interests may be fleeting, Realities are where interests grow from. They remain the same while youth of color live within the social fields that make them urban and deal with the societal structures that relegate them to subaltern positions. Realities for urban youth of color, particularly as they relate to being seen as unable to do well in science, are similar today to what they were immediately after the post-*Sputnik* era, when students of color were not viewed as part of the "best and brightest" in the nation. In a sense, realities remain the same. Williams (1991) describes how one's subject position is directly related to his/her reality and how each individual's reality is shaped by the position one is granted within society. Urban Science Education, and the Reality Pedagogy it spawns, begins from the standpoint of urban youth of color in order to find ways to connect them to science.

Urban Youth Reality: Hip Hop and Urban Science Education

When urban student realities are considered in teaching and learning, it becomes necessary to also study hip hop. Hip hop, which is usually misclassified as a type of music urban youth listen to, is actually the dominant culture of minoritized urban youth. While rap music (the music misclassified as hip hop) is the chief artifact of hip hop, it merely provides insight into student realities. Therefore, rap music should be a tool that is combined with other studies of the urban youth culture to help the outsider to hip-hop culture to understand the experiences of urban youth and phenomena like the closed set of heroes, rules, and ways of teaching and learning that are a part of hip hop.

I find that hip hop is such a fundamental component of the lives of urban youth because it stands as an entry into a world that is an escape from the harsh realities of the conditions and circumstances within urban contexts. In this other world that hip hop provides, students who are considered to be outside the norm in spaces like science classrooms are viewed as integral parts of something that is bigger than they are. Hip hop then becomes the immediate alternative to, and means of expressing agency in response to, any oppressive scenario. In science classrooms that do not allow urban youth to be a part of their inner workings, the class becomes an oppressive space, and students turn away from the classroom and towards hip hop.

When one studies hip hop, a bond between those who are marginalized from society and certain subcultures of hip hop like rap, graffiti, dance, and spoken word becomes evident. Youth become completely engulfed in the unique culture of the particular hip hop field they are engaged in, and an expression of, and passion for, hip hop at large becomes poured into their interactions with their peers within these subcultures. The passion for hip hop described by participants in the culture (often expressed by rap artists in songs) is similar to the "love of science" or feeling of belonging to a "community of scholars" (DeMichele, 2002) that is often described by scientists when they are asked about their choice of science as a profession. I argue that the passion exhibited by those invested in hip hop for the sake of hip hop can be expressed in science and used to develop interest and participation in science if hip hop and other pieces of student realities become a part of the classroom. This happens if the structures of the science classroom are amenable to hip hop culture. By this, I mean that in order to focus on students' realities in the instruction of science and become an urban science educator, it is necessary to allow significant parts of urban youth lifeworlds such as hip hop to be a part of the science classroom.

This requires an understanding that certain students' struggles with engaging in the science classroom are rooted in the fact that the traditional science curriculum is scripted and follows a strict question–and-answer protocol. In hip hop, everything from dance and art to rap (even when it is confined to the generic five-minute verse-and-chorus formula of popular music) contains prolific improvisation and constant references to the shared experiences of participants in hip hop. When students have to deal with teacher-centered, strict, and outcome-based instruction, the ability to create solutions to problems as they unfold, and work together with peers to improvise in finding solutions as they do in hip hop, is lost.

In one of my research projects in a chemistry laboratory and classroom, the students would rush through the specific steps of a scripted chemistry lab so that they could conduct their own mini experiments when the assigned lab was over. In these impromptu sessions, they would gather around in a group that mimicked spaces where they would rap and conduct their own experiments with the materials from the classroom lab. The students would pose questions to each other, present possible answers to the questions posed, and perform experiments to prove and disprove each other's hypotheses. These students would nod in unison while counting the number of drops being placed into a beaker as though they were nodding to the rhythm of a rap song and discuss their observations in cadence as though they were rapping. They collectively sighed when the results of their classroom experiments produced expected results and cheered when they felt like they were embarking on something that was not part of the prescribed science lab. The creation of this type of space, where students can explore science in ways that they communicate outside of the classroom, values their realities and allows for their connection to science in more profound ways than the regular science classroom.

Within the conventional chemistry classroom, with an established state curriculum and state-approved pacing calendar, these same students would sit silently, refuse to answer questions, and fail to interact with the teacher. They would talk to the teacher in ways that were almost opposite to the ways that they interacted in the laboratory when they had the opportunity to engage in authentic science on their own. Urban Science Education focuses on moments like the ones where students are engaged and functions to replicate that type of practice for other urban youth who struggle to connect to science in the classroom.

In my experiences as a secondary school physics and chemistry teacher, I often found that the students who exhibited the most resistance to school were often the ones most entrenched in hip hop. These were the students who wanted to be rappers, were part of rap groups, were dancers, poets, graffiti artists, or beat boxers. By focusing on a Reality Pedagogy approach, these students were allowed to display their connection to hip hop in the classroom on a weekly basis. They were allowed to rap concepts in science, draw graffiti caricatures and pictures that described science concepts, and even celebrate their academic successes through dance. Once these students were presented with the fact that their stance as participants in hip hop did not mean they were outside of what is appropriate or normal in school, their level of achievement in science classes tremendously increased. These students were able to realize that they were not being blamed for issues of low achievement that they may have come to the classroom with. Rather, they were shown that the chief reason for their lack of success in science was the method of subject matter delivery. This process allows students to see that their participation in hip hop provides them with more insight and a deeper understanding of science than their peers in other settings because of their ability to improvise and deeply inquire about phenomena.

Prerequisites for Reality Pedagogy

Enacting Reality Pedagogy requires not only an understanding of the ways of knowing and being of urban youth who are embedded in hip hop but also an attentiveness to the researcher's or teacher's epistemological beliefs. This involves an awareness that one's background may support a view of the world that distorts, dismisses or underemphasizes the positive aspects of other ways of knowing. This awareness of one's self is also the fundamental point of the teacher's or researcher's situating self and developing into a Reality Pedagogue or urban science educator. The goal for teachers of urban youth who are a part of hip hop is to begin with a focus on self. Becoming an urban science educator firstly requires an understanding of what makes one want to be a teacher and, more importantly, what causes one to believe what they do about students and about science. This self-interrogation about one's view of science allows the teacher to consider what learning or understanding science truly is and whether or not science and its tenets of dialogue, questioning, and inquiry align with the types of practices the teacher enacts in the classroom.

Urban Science Education requires educators to tell students where they come from, how they were raised, why they love science, and their previous experiences with urban settings and hip hop culture. This is necessary even if there is no familiarity with hip hop and urban contexts because it presents a true picture of self that participants in hip hop appreciate. This use of autobiography as an instructional tool functions to create spaces in the classroom where students are allowed to present their own autobiographies and begin to see that it is acceptable to present their true selves in the science classroom. This process not only provides a deep understanding of where the teacher or researcher stands but also helps students to understand that they are just as valued as the teacher. Furthermore, the vulnerability that the teacher or researcher exposes to the classroom closely aligns to the ways participants in hip hop express their innermost selves to other participants in the culture. For example, on any given rap album, the listener is given information about where an artist comes from, the struggles in the artist's life, details about family, and even that person's goals, dreams, and fantasies. By presenting the role that science has played in the teacher's life as a part of an autobiography that is shared in the classroom, the significance of the discipline becomes expressed to students and they see science as an extension of life outside of the classroom and not an entity that is outside of real life.

Urban Science Education Practices:
The Enactment of Reality Pedagogy

Because Urban Science Education focuses on student realities as the point from which pedagogy is enacted, I outline some of the practices rooted in urban youth hip-hop culture that I have enacted and that can be employed in urban science classrooms. While this is neither an exhaustive list nor a set of practices that should be replicated without the educator studying the realities of their students' experiences, it does provide information on the potential of practices that develop from studying realities that will be helpful for urban science educators.

One of the most practical approaches to student involvement that I have used is the use of the call and response model of communication; which has roots in black culture and is a part of hip hop. In this process, the teacher calls out a phrase or saying and invites students to respond with their own phrase. This practice conjures up the structures within the out-of-school social fields that allow students to actively communicate with each other and subsequently draws students into active engagement within the classroom. When I teach, I transition from one part of the lesson to the other by shouting out a phrase like "Shall I proceed?" The students then respond by saying "Yes, indeed." After this practice is enacted, it becomes a prompt that allows the entire class to be focused on the teacher and prepare for the next phase of the lesson. This call and response model may also revolve around a science formula by having students respond to a phrase like "force equals" by saying "mass times acceleration." This call and response practice is rooted in hip hop modes of communication that urban youth enact in the neighborhood as they call to each other, and in hip hop spaces like rap performances.

In other instances, I have appropriated the b-boy pose of standing with arms folded that is used in hip hop, given a salute, or have even done a short dance as a way to quietly celebrate a successful experiment or activity in the class. After I deliver a concept to the student, ask them if they understand, and get a positive response from them, I fold my arms and give a b-boy pose in front of the class and allow them to celebrate in whichever ways they see fit. Without inviting students to give a pose, or encouraging them to do as I do, they enact the same practices after they have been successful in a class activity. Since this practice originates in the out-of-school hip hop field, the teacher who enacts a b-boy pose or permits it or other forms of celebration and excitement in the classroom allows for a natural infusion of hip hop culture into the science classroom and allows for this phenomenon to become one of the established classroom structures.

I have also allowed students to come to the board with their "crew" to work on and answer a problem. Since I am aware that students work and move together outside of school in a communal way, I focus a bulk of my class assignments on group work presentations, allow students to sign their "tags" (graffiti nicknames) on the board when they solve questions or provide answers, and allow their final grades on certain assignments to be based on group work. Students welcome these communal structures and become invested in the achievement of their peers just as they have a responsibility for each other's safety and well-being outside of the school.

I have been able to allow hip hop students to see themselves as scientists simply by welcoming students in the classroom with "Good morning, scientists" and referring to them as scientists throughout the classroom lesson and in the hallways. While this practice may appear superficial, it is a first step indicating acknowledgment and recognition of the students' selves that are normally dismissed. I also start each of my classes by asking what the students had experienced the night before or what was going on in the neighborhood. This timed activity may only take two minutes out of a 40-minute lesson but sets the tone for the classroom that the students are valued. In addition, these conversations provide the teacher with culturally relevant examples that can be drawn upon during the lesson. This practice also allows the teacher to gain a sense of how the students are feeling that day and whether or not they have had experiences that day that may prevent them from being active participants in the classroom or that may make them particularly engaged and excited.

I also find that understanding students' passion for rap music and welcoming it in the classroom is important. Therefore, I play hip-hop music at a low volume in the background while students are doing problems or working on a group activity. This practice causes students to speak at low volumes so that they can hear the music and inhibits the need for strict classroom management during activities where students move a lot and are more likely to speak loudly.

When this approach is combined with references to the students' neighborhoods in the creation of science questions or examples being used in the class such as, "I was walking down Jerome Avenue (South Bronx, New York), right by the deli shop where the guys on the corner are usually rapping and I saw a rock" rather than "I was walking down the street and saw a rock," the teacher indicates to students that there is an appreciation of who they are and where they come from.

The combination of these types of activities and a more focused effort to literally bring the community into the science classroom combines to create a science classroom that is not only relevant to students' lives but that values their culture and welcomes it into the science classroom. In the following section, I outline some ways that I have been able to bring the community into the science classroom.

The School Community as a Science Curriculum Resource

As alluded to throughout this chapter, one of the major themes of the discussions surrounding Urban Science Education is the importance of reaching out to the students' realities through their community. The primary way that I have accomplished this goal has been by inviting members of the community that students respect to come to the classroom to co-teach with me. While these individuals may not be experts in science, their stature within the community and their information about what is happening in the neighborhood can serve as a conduit for relating students' realities to science.

I have identified participants in hip hop culture within the community of the school who have jobs, careers, and interests that are directly or indirectly related to science. This process requires visiting the neighborhood that students come from, talking to community members, and immersing oneself in their community so much that the teacher becomes a part of students' realities. By taking this approach, I have been able to invite graffiti artists who are experts at painting with aerosol paint, people who work with harsh chemicals in working with cleaning equipment, and local rap artists. They have contributed to science lessons discussing the chemistry of containers made of tin-plated steel or aluminium used for aerosols, the chemistry of the dyes and pigments that they use in their work, and the chemistry of solvents. In every situation where these individuals have been given the opportunity to be a part of classroom discussions, the levels of engagement for students who are a part of hip hop have been substantially increased when compared with other classroom lessons.

Conclusions: On Reframing Urban Science Education

To meet the larger goal of addressing the needs of a hip hop generation in urban science classrooms, science education must allow for the growth of Urban Science Education into a distinct academic field that is aligned to, yet separate from, science education. In this effort, enacting a hip hop based Reality Pedagogy is the most important piece of teaching science for urban youth. This approach moves Urban Science Education to a place where there is an understanding that existent belief systems and practices that position urban youth as outside of success in science have the potential to be addressed by educators and researchers. By using a sociocultural framework that considers the everyday practices of students and teachers in urban science classrooms, the power of urban youth networks is strengthened, and teachers in urban schools become prepared to move beyond existent approaches to teaching that exclude urban youth from science.

REFERENCES

Barton, A. C. (1998). Teaching science with homeless children: Pedagogy, representation, and identity. *Journal of Research in Science Teaching, 35*(4), 379–394.

Basu, S. J. (2008). Empowering communities of research and practice by conducting research for change and including participant voice in reflection on research. *Cultural Studies in Science Education, 3*(4), 859–865.

DeMichele, J. (2002). Why scientists do science: A trek for answers. *Journal of Young Investigators, 1*(6), 1–6.

Emdin, C. (in press). Affiliation and alienation: Hip hop, rap and urban science education. *Journal of Curriculum Studies.*

Goffman, E. (1997). Social life as drama. In Lemert, C. & Branaman, A. (Eds.), *The Goffman Reader*. Oxford: Blackwell.

Hodson, D. (1999). Going beyond cultural pluralism: Science education for socio-political action. *Science Education, 83*(6), 775–796.

Rodriguez, A. J. (2003). "Science for all" and invisible ethnicities: How the discourse of power and good intentions undermine the national science education standards. In Maxwell S. Hines, (Ed.), *Multicultural Science Education: Theory, Practice, and Promise*. New York: Peter Lang.

Tate, W. (2001). Science education as a civil right: Urban schools and opportunity-to-learn considerations. *Journal of Research in Science Teaching, 38*(9), 1015–1028.

Williams, P. (1991). *The Alchemy of Race and Rights*. Cambridge, MA: Harvard University Press.

CHAPTER EIGHT

Linda Ware & Jan W. Valle

How Do We Begin a Conversation on Disability in Urban Education?

Recognizing that disability is a central feature in the everyday business of schools where among the most frequent issues are those that include placement decisions, curriculum development, co-teaching considerations, building access, parent interactions, and hallway talk, our chapter asks: *How might schools begin to encourage a new understanding of disability without defaulting to the traditional paradigm of special education and the metanarrative embedded in general and special education?* We suggest that in order to begin such a conversation on disability educators must understand disability through an entirely new lens informed by the interdisciplinary field of disability studies and the subfield of disability studies in education (hereafter DSE).

Disability studies, regardless of its disciplinary home in the humanities, social science, rehabilitative medicine, and law—begins with the task of interrogating normalcy and exploring ableism—the assumed privilege afforded to non-disabled individuals in society (Davis, 1997; Linton, 1998). Disability studies research encourages a departure from exclusively medicalized meanings of disability and instead invites understanding disability through radical analyses and insights about the body, society, and culture. In a society that has yet to fully disentangle the historic discourse about cultural difference as subordinate to the dominant culture, the challenge of understanding disability as difference that need *not* assume a less worthy life can seem too complex for many in society to disentangle. Such a conversation among educators holds even greater urgency. DSE offers a way into such a conversation because it invites new questions about disability specific to educational settings and the practical concerns of teaching.

Described elsewhere as the long overdue project in education to *restory* special education (Ware 2005), such a project would signal a shift in emphases. One such shift is described by Reid and Valle (2004) who call for renewed emphasis on redesigning the context, not on 'curing' or 'remediating' individuals' impairment in the example of learning disability (LD). In a recent special issue of the *Journal of Learning Disabilities*, "Discursive Practices of Learning Disability" (Wong, 2004), these authors recommend a "comprehensive and more openly political vision of the LD field" (Reid and Valle: 466). The special issue was built on the following assumptions: "Education in a representative democracy is inevitably a political enterprise; social justice is everyone's responsibility, but educators have a special role to play; and segregated schooling is neither equal nor equitable" (466). The contributors addressed disability, in the example of learning disability, as it is constructed in schools through the reification of conceptions of *ability, of abnormality and normalcy*. Informed by DSE and the cultural demands of the urban context, this chapter raises a related question: *How do educators grapple with schooling at the intersections of culture, learning, and disability?*

Cultural Difference, Learning and Disability

Efforts to disentangle what amounts to intersecting and complex analyses about the fundamental question of how to respond to cultural differences in education suggests a review of the educational researchers who study the persistent over-representation of students of color in special education—a problem that is particularly pernicious in urban contexts (Artiles, 1997; Connor, 2009; Harry & Klinger, 2006; Losen & Orfield, 2002; Parrish, 2002; Rueda et al, 2002). The overrepresentation challenge has evolved from the mere calculation of student bodies to a more complex and comprehensive excavation of P-12 educational context as a site that produces disproportionality. Informed by these researchers, educators would have to be willing to disentangle the mandated meaning of disability informed by policy, procedures, and institutional protocols that author disability in the narrowest terms of human understanding (i.e., abnormality, impediment, limitation, deficiency, dependency, needs)—and willing to challenge the status quo meanings constructed through the institutional, bureaucratic and discursive structures of general and special education. Such conversation on disability in urban education would necessitate the recruitment of allies in general education willing to grapple with the larger meaning of "acceptance" and who "belongs" in society and in schools (Kluth, 2003; Oyler 1996, 2006; Sapon-Shevin, 2007; Ware, 2003a)—while simultaneously enacting personal beliefs in response to the mandate for the inclusion of previously excluded children from the general education classroom as the consequence of mandates for inclusion. Efforts to broaden the perspective for educators would also necessitate consideration of the insights of disability rights activists who persist in their efforts to win equal access to education, employment, fair housing, and transportation. Despite the decades-old federal legislation enacted in law through the Americans with Disabilities Act (ADA), disability activists remind us that understanding disability and acceptance of disability as a value-added lived experience remain an elusive goal in American society. Clearly, such an initiative located within education would yield nothing short of a refusal to accept the meaning of disability in the institutions where they work (Baglieri, et al., forthcoming; Ware, 2006a, 2006b, in press).

Given our collective experience working in the very sites we hope to *restory,* this chapter describes both the challenges and the rewards of educating urban educators about DSE. Our theoretical work in disability studies is very much informed by our ongoing efforts with educators as we introduce the field of disability studies and more specifically, DSE. We recognize that we cannot begin a conversation on disability in P-12 education that departs from the traditional special education paradigm unless educators and school administrators join with us to make the lived experience of disability matter in schools and society and to move beyond the reductionist rhetoric that frames the existing discourse.

Disability Studies in Education

Numerous and varied interdisciplinary scholarly threads have been woven together over the past ten years to inform DSE. Influences include those advanced by disability studies in the arts and humanities—including history and philosophy—as well as disability studies in the rehabilitative and social sciences, and elsewhere, including cultural studies, economics, critical legal studies, geography, and critical/activist scholarship in all disciplines. As a subfield of disability studies writ large, DSE scholars "investigate *what disability means;* how it is interpreted, enacted, and resisted in the social practices of individuals, groups, organization, and cultures." Gabel & Danforth (2008) notes that because DSE examines disability in social and cultural context, existing "constructions of disability are questioned and special education assumptions and practices are challenged (xix)." Although DSE is informed by the scholarship and activism of critical special educators and their decades-old criticism of traditional special education and the limits of understanding disability through an exclusively reductionist lens; Taylor underscores an important point for educators: *disability studies is not special education.* Although disability is central to both and claims are made to improve outcomes for disabled people, congruence should not be assumed. Ashton (in press) disentangles the incongruence by examining the role played by CEC and their professional standards in the construction of the special educator and the student with disabilities. She contends that these constructions ensure inclusive education will remain unrealizable as long as special education remains at the helm.

In an effort to legitimize DSE as a professional organization, critical special education scholars, disability studies scholars and educational researchers, formed the DSE special interest group (SIG) in conjunction with the American Educational Research Association (AERA). The mission of the DSE SIG is to promote understanding of disability from a social model perspective drawing on social, cultural, historical, discursive, philosophical, literary, aesthetic, artistic, and other traditions to challenge medical, scientific, and psychological models of disability as they relate to education. Since 2001 the DSE members have sponsored an annual international conference (see *http://www. disabilitystudiesineducation.org/history.htm*) in conversation linked to the DSE tenets that are included below.

DSE SIG Tenets

To engage in research, policy, and action that

- contextualize disability within political and social spheres
- privilege the interest, agendas, and voices of people labeled with disability/disabled people
- promote social justice, equitable and inclusive educational opportunities, and full and meaningful access to all aspects of society for people labeled with disability/disabled people
- assume competence and reject deficit models of disability

The DSE SIG operates as an organizational vehicle for networking among Disability Studies researchers in education and to increase the visibility and influence of Disability Studies among all educational researchers.

Approaches to Theory, Research, & Practice in DSE

Examples of approaches to theory and DSE may include:

- Contrasts medical, scientific, psychological understandings with social and experiential understandings of disability
- Predominantly focuses on political, social, cultural, historical, social, and individual understandings of disability
- Supports the education of students labeled with disabilities in non-segregated settings from a civil rights stance.
- Engages work that discerns the oppressive nature of essentialized/categorical/medicalized naming of disability in urban schools, policy, institutions, and the law while simultaneously recognizing the political power that may be found in collective and individual activism and pride through group-specific claims to disabled identities and positions

How Do We Begin a Conversation on Disability in Urban Education?

- Recognizes the embodied/aesthetic experiences of people whose lives/selves are made meaningful as disabled, as well as troubles the school and societal discourses that position such experiences as "othered" to an assumed normate
- Includes disabled people in theorizing about disability

Examples of approaches to research and DSE:

- Welcomes scholars with disabilities and non-disabled scholars working together
- Recognizes and privileges the knowledge derived from the lived experience of people with disabilities
- Whenever possible adheres to an emancipatory stance (for example, working with people with disabilities as informed participants or co-researchers, not subjects)
- Welcomes intradisciplinary approaches to understanding the phenomenon of disability, e.g. with educational foundations, special education, etc.
- Cultivates interdisciplinary approaches to understanding the phenomenon of disability, e.g., interfacing with multicultural education, the humanities, social sciences, philosophy, cultural studies, etc.
- Challenges research methodology that objectifies, marginalizes, and oppresses people with disabilities

Examples of approaches to practice and DSE may include:

- Disability primarily recognized and valued as natural part of human diversity
- Disability and inclusive education
- Disability culture and identity as part of a multicultural curriculum
- Disability Rights Movement studied as part of the civil rights movement
- Disability history and culture and the contributions of disabled people as integral to all aspects of the curriculum
- Supporting disabled students in the development of a positive disability identity

From Talking Points to Practice

The DSE tenets represent a radical departure from special education's emphasis on pathology, problem, cure, and care. In our work with practicing teachers we have found that many teachers have never been asked to reflect on the collateral "damage" done to children as a consequence of the everyday practices in special education. Many are unaware of the decades-old critical special education scholarship that outlined the limits of understanding disability through a reductionist lens which is now credited as foundational to DSE (for a more comprehensive discussion see Ware 2005; in press). Rather than implicate the teachers we note that this critique of special education has been elided from the typical fare offered in general and special education teacher preparation (Brantlinger, 1997, 2006;

Gallagher et. al, 2004; Ware, 2005, 2003a; Slee, 2004, 2006). Recognition of the influence of critical special education literature on the evolution of DSE scholarship (Gabel & Danforth, 2006) has returned many scholars to this oeuvre of critical constructivist special education literature in an effort to better understand the need to promote DSE and the challenge of introducing new areas of scholarly inquiry in schools of education (Gallagher et. al 2004; Ware, 2003b). Ware (in press) parallels the DSE "recovery project" to the "recovery project" outlined by Davis (1997) in the example of disability studies in the humanities. Davis notes that despite the historic oppression and marginalization of disabled people, disability was all but a disappeared category in the humanities until scholars realized that the "'problem' is not the 'person with disabilities' the problem is the way that normalcy is constructed to create the 'problem' of the disabled person" (1997).

The parallel drawn by Davis holds in the example of education, where intra-disciplinary approaches to understanding disability have been introduced that draw on similar arguments to faculty in educational foundations, multicultural education, social justice education, bi-lingual education, literacy, and educational administration. However, at present, only a handful of schools have forged such connections at the level of curriculum and program development. Following a brownbag presentation for faculty and staff in the school of education (SOE) at The City College of New York (CCNY), Ware and Valle (2005) found that faculty were quick to recognize that disability operates as an all but disappeared category in schools of education in general. With the exception of our colleagues in special education and education psychology, none were able to recall any prior discussion of disability in their own professional preparation. When considering disability through a DSE lens, many SOE faculty moved with relative ease from a general discussion about the societal impulse to dismiss disability as a fundamental societal concern, to a discussion linked to existing program and course offerings. Some recognized the need to interrogate individual/collective complicity with this erasure, assuming others held firm to the belief that education is walled off from politics, and so too, is disability. Within this space of opposing ideas, it became productive to consider Davis' dictum, that the *problem is the construal of normalcy, not the person with disabilities.* Our presentation ignited broad interest in DSE and it ultimately served as the impetus for a curriculum makeover in the special education Master's program tied to DSE (Ware, 2006a; Ware & Valle, 2005).

Disability Studies in Conversation with Educators

DSE, like disability studies in the humanities and in the social and rehabilitative sciences may not be prominent on every college campus, however, disability studies is very much a part of the makeover on many campuses (Berube, 2002; 2005). Efforts to integrate disability studies throughout higher education coursework require that we turn our attention to the myriad ways that disability matters beyond personal tragedy, pathos, or deviance. Once the intellectual will is summoned to challenge the existing view of disability and the disabled individual as a marginal subject in higher education, the makeover Berube promises will be quite extensive. Specific to education such makeovers in higher education have been located on a continuum between trouble and triumphalism (Ferri, 2006; Ware, 2006a). In "Teaching to Trouble," Ferri (2006) noted her interdisciplinary approach as troubling to her pre-service teacher education students. Her students are unaccustomed to non-textbook based instruction and to that which links critical theory to practice. Ferri noted that students come to class with the expectation that they will obtain "'practical knowledge' about what to do in the classroom" (299). In an analysis similar to Brantlinger (2006) who outlined the discomfort students felt discussing political aspects of inclusion, Ferri also found that her students reported confusion and frustration because they do not expect a class in education to be "political." Ferri observed that this is an important distinction between disability studies and other identity studies courses:

> [W]hen students first encounter the term ableism and concepts such as able-bodied privilege and the social construction of ability/disability they must confront their own attachments and identifications to these categories and trouble their own ways of knowing about disability (299).

Ferri observes that even when students have previously completed gender or multicultural coursework, they grapple with ableism because it "complicates their ideas about difference" (301) and reveals some of the "stuck" places in our thinking about difference (304). The double meaning in her title, "Teaching to Trouble," suggests the obvious challenge when we invite teachers to trouble— both as a verb in which they will have to explore meanings and matter that they might rather leave unexplored and as a noun, leading students to a problematic, political place.

Elsewhere Ware (2003a, 2005, 2006a) has noted that following an introduction to DSE, many educators, who previously ignored the political patina that washes over their work in P-12 educational settings, found that they were unable to continue to ignore the obvious contradictions posed by the demands of practice in both general and special education. Ware's accounts of teacher transformation informed by interdisciplinary humanities-based disability studies is more triumphant than troubling; however, like Ferri and Brantlinger she offers are way into a conversation on disability that departs from the traditional special education paradigm.

As university professors we enjoy considerable leeway in structuring our courses to push the boundaries of student comfort zones when introducing new content. We take the responsibility seriously when asking our students to "think outside the box." However, when we support professional development in P-12 public education, greater caution is exercised as radical new ideas are rarely delivered in the context of district-initiated professional development. DSE offers a radical interpretation of disability, one that challenges the hierarchical knowledge authority that resides in large public education bureaucracies (Ware, 2003a; 2003b; 2006a). Given the context of urban school districts where reform by fiat is commonplace, it is typical that little or no input will be considered from the individuals charged to implement the reform. Canned curriculum and technicist teaching strategies are oftentimes delivered after mandated changes have been decreed, leaving teachers and professional development staff scurrying to obtain the needed expertise. Given these conditions, SOE faculty who seek to partner with urban school districts to promote radical reform can face numerous challenges. In the section that follows, we describe one such partnership with urban educators as an example of how we might address the question taken up by this chapter.

Disability Studies Conversations in Professional Practice

Randi Weingarten, the former president of the United Federation of Teachers, recently noted that the most "rewarding (and exhausting) aspects of working in public education in New York City is that it is the best laboratory for trying new things" (2009). The system boasts of having the most diverse student population in the world with "1.1 million kids from every kind of household, economic background and skill level. . . . [and] more than 150 languages are spoken in our schools. . . . it is also one of the toughest, most watched school systems there is" (ibid.). We concur with much of the sentiment about the value of working with schools in New York City; however, our experience has proven that both the challenges and the rewards increase exponentially when attempting special education reform.

The historic reliance on the medical model in the delivery of services for students with disabilities has served to be the greatest obstacle to the implementation of educational inclusion. Following their evaluation of the New York City Department of Education, Hehir et al. (2005) underscored the need to attend to reform of the existing philosophy on disability. These researchers urged a shift in focus from a medical model to a "social systems" model. The report was heralded by many in the New York City Department of Education who have begun the slow process of translating the report's recommendations into practice. However, given its emphasis on re-examining ideology, the conversation on reform has proven challenging. In truth, the recommendations made by Hehir et al. would apply to any urban, suburban, or rural district in the United States as the medicalization of disability in P-12 education is uniformly institutionalized nation-wide. In much the same way as noted above, the inability to disentangle cultural difference from the "problem of the individual" results in a similar construction of "difference as problem" in the example of disability.

By coincidence, there has been a return to collaboration among educators across New York State and the nation, as a way to support teachers in inclusive education classrooms. Urban, suburban and rural school districts have shown an increase in the number of co-taught classrooms—a reform that actually challenges the structure of instruction and the institution of schooling. According to a report posted on the New York City Department of Education website (July 2007), more than 400 co-taught classrooms were expected to open during the 2007–2008 school year alone. Such a rapid increase in the number of Integrative Co-Teaching Services[1] classrooms has led to an increased need for professional development throughout the state. The impetus for the workshop described in the section that follows evolved from a co-teaching seminar Valle organized with Ellen Rice—an adjunct City College professor and an inclusion-support professional with the New York City Department of Education. Valle and Rice co-taught a collaborative team teaching (CTT) seminar for teachers offered through City College (2008–2009) to introduce teachers to the meaningful application of DSE tenets in inclusive settings through the implementation of "best practices" in CTT classrooms.[2]

Staging a Workshop

Teachers enrolled in the CTT workshop of their own volition, and much like the students described by Ferri, they were expecting to amass the practical knowledge to enhance their own co-teaching efforts in the upcoming school year. What many did not expect was an introduction to DSE that ran like a fine thread throughout the workshop. None expected that once DSE topics were raised, as the backdrop to reframing questions and concerns about best practices to support inclusion, they too would be asked to confront their own attachments and identifications to the categories they use every day in the workplace. And much like the work described by Ferri, the workshop participants found the content stimulating, albeit challenging as they began to trouble their own ways of knowing about disability. Such reflection was welcome in a setting framed by Valle's opening remarks and the question: "Is inclusion a practice or an ideology?"

For the workshop participants the conversation readily turned to consideration of the ways disability is constructed in schools, and their questions that followed revealed much about their philosophy in the example of inclusion and disability. Reflection gave voice to important questions that had not been considered in prior workshops. Too often, educators attend workshops on professional development in the absence of self-reflection on *personal development,* as if the two were unrelated. The CTT workshop made explicit this connection by encouraging the teachers to engage in new conversations on disability embedded in the agenda. The key learning outcomes for the participants included:

- reframing inclusion through disability studies
- establishing a working philosophy of inclusion
- building and maintaining an effective co-teaching relationship
- building classroom community, routines, and procedures
- understanding and implementing the Six Co-Teaching Models
- differentiating instruction for all students

- integrating assessment data into the curriculum
- implementing the Individuals with Disabilities in Education Improvement Act (IDEIA) into the Integrated Co-Teaching Services classroom
- understanding, preventing, and responding to challenging behaviors

With the exception of the first two outcomes, the remainder were extrapolated from professional development materials commonly used in many school districts (e.g., Friend, 2007; Friend & Cook, 2009; Tomlinson et al. 2008; Tomlinson, 2003; Villa, Thousand & Nevin, 2004). Afternoon sessions included DOE professional development staff presenting on "best practices for urban classrooms"—but at every opportunity, we underscored the application of these practices informed by DSE insights and activities introduced in the morning sessions. This included understanding the limits of the medical model embraced by special education in contrast to the social construction of disability embraced by DSE. Valle introduced disability activists such as Harriet McBryde Johnson framed by her article in the *New York Times*, "Unspeakable Conversations: Should I Have Been Killed at Birth? The Case for My Life." and in an example of inclusion, Valle drew from another *New York Times* article, "The Lessons of Classroom 506" (Belkin, 2004). The expectation for the workshop was to facilitate, strengthen, and sustain strong and effective team-teaching partnerships in inclusive settings; therefore, it was imperative to position disability and inclusion as relevant issues in society and in schools across the lifespan. This presentation would serve to anchor the participants and the ideology that shaped their teaching practice.

Informed by DSE, reframing disability and inclusive practice entailed *(re) presenting* the history, rationale, and philosophy of inclusion as it has been implemented within the institution of special education (taken up in the workshop as a failed initiative). DSE provided the framework within which to deconstruct the medical model of disability and its consequences within special education— toward the goal of implementing *truly* inclusive practices within schools. The section that follows highlights some of the DSE activities framed by participants' questions posed during the workshop.

Where in the curriculum and the course of a day?

In one morning activity the participants worked in small groups to identify and list characterizations of disability in literature, print media, history, the arts, film and television, and one group was asked to identify the characterizations of disability in schools. Much chatter erupted across the room as some groups were quick to draw up their list and others were stymied by the activity. We have utilized this activity in our teaching and typically, film and television are the easiest lists to create while literature and the arts prove more challenging. As the lists were posted around the room and read aloud, animated exchange followed as the participants continued to add to each list. We troubled the lists further by asking: *Who tells the story and why does it matter? How many of these characters are children? Latino? Women? How is class featured? What roles are stereotypical?* The activity is further troubled when we ask teachers where in their curriculum is disability experience integrated or taught? Once the last list was posted in response to the question, *How do we characterize disability in schools?* Silence permeated the room as it was read:

> 8:1:1, 12:1:1, testing modifications (QRA, extended time), self contained, at risk mandated, bus kids, adapted/modified/differentiated curriculum; Assisted Technology, non-linguistic representation; crisis intervention specialist, ED, LD, Autistic, physical disability, LRE, speech impaired, people first language, mentally retarded, requires constant redirection, ADHD academically delayed, OT, PT, ST, Counseling, therapeutic intervention, SBST, SETSS, PBS, IEP, BIP, FBA, D75[3]

The activity served on many levels to dramatize the point that a fundamental shift was needed in the way that schools characterize disability. That is, between the missing accounts of productive and proactive living with disability represented in the curriculum and against the labels that are assigned to disabled people in society at large, Ware asked: *How likely might it be that children become known in schools only by their labels? Do children risk losing their own identity in the process of attending school? What is the collateral "damage" for children identified with "special needs" as they move through our classrooms? Is the medicalization of disability the only viable language in schools?* The participants were left to consider where in the curriculum and in the course of a day, disability might be offered as a value-added[4] experience.

Why do we look at disability as loss?

The discussion on day two was framed by the following questions:

> Why is it that when we think about living with a disability, we think in terms of loss? Why are we quick to assume that something is "missing" for those who might be born with a disability, or for those who acquire a disability later in life?

The discussion touched on a number of related points about the social construction of disability as a theme that invited the participants to speculate about notions of loss and a less–than valued life experience. With our focus in special education on deficiency, pathology, cure, and intervention in pursuit of a mythological norm, Ware asked: *"Do we really mean to tell children at every turn that they are not acceptable the way they are?"* Valle added: "If we associate disability with lack, it will be difficult to view the children as anything but damaged." Our discussion was shaped by the handout below taken from *Rethinking Difference: A Disability Studies Approach to Inclusive Practices* (Valle and Connor, in press) which prompted the participants to discuss the unconscious messages sent by everyday schooling practices in general and special education and in particular to answer the larger question posed by Valle: *Why does loss permeate our conversations on disability?*

The world is meant for us, not others.

Persons with disabilities can be with us, but we do not have to be with them.

The needs of persons with disabilities are secondary to our needs.

Disability is not something we talk about, especially not to the person with a disability.

We do not have anything in common with persons with disabilities.

Persons with disabilities do not have feelings or opinions. They are not like real people to be friends with.

People with disabilities cause problems for everyone else.

It is not our responsibility to engage people with disabilities. They have issues that are beyond us.

It really does not work for people with disabilities to be with us.

People with disabilities take up too much of our time.

We have nothing to learn from people with disabilities.

People with disabilities make us uncomfortable. We do not know how to talk to them.

We do not know why people with disabilities have to be in our class.

In their new role as CTTs they would have the opportunity to bridge the divide between general and special education through practices that welcomed difference. Their peers, as well as their students, would be imprinted by the context they created in classrooms where inclusion might, indeed, mean belonging. Thus it was imperative that the workshop participants recognize the implicit as well as the explicit messages that schools convey. All the while schools herald inclusion, they visibly enforce exclusion, however, few recognize this inherent contradiction of schooling (Slee, 2004, 2006; Slee & Allan, 2001). Throughout the workshop this phenomenon became more transparent as a consequence of listening to those who lived the experience of "difference-as-problem."

"Do they really think that?"

Finally, in what proved to be the most powerful and troubling activity of the workshop, we organized the "Gallery Walk" featuring the cartoon images provided by our colleague at Hunter College, David J. Connor. In his research with adolescents and young adults with learning disability in New York City, Connor creates cartoons informed by their interview data recounting their experiences in special education (2008; 2009). The images render students with learning disabilities as they have come to view themselves—shamed and constrained by the everyday practices in special education. Connor's images were displayed on one side of the room in a minimally appointed gallery. On the opposite wall, one to two line sentiments were posted beneath the heading "New York City high school 'special education' students labeled LD." Samples of the written text include:

> In my junior high, I was completely isolated, yo. They treat you like a baby, yo. Some teachers think you are not capable of doing papers and stuff, like you can't be responsible.

> I'm embarrassed for real, but now I'm not so much because everybody's got problems. They just give *us* a name and I think about it every night like what is the matter with me?

> It's like teachers and other students have doubts like that we can't go to college. You get the message like you don't have the intelligence to go to college.

As the teachers moved between the two walls, silence was once again palpable. Connor's graphic work is unique in the DSE literature as he strives to capture the representations articulated by disabled youth talking back to the unwanted and unwarranted scripts that mark their lived experience in special education. His renderings convey the abject refusal by his "subjects" to accept that their schooling experience was designed with their interests in mind. Positioned against the commentary of students, the "Gallery Walk" activity left many participants unable to reconcile their beliefs about the purpose of special education with those expressed by the students. One teacher offered his own experience as a special education student to confirm the students' perspective. "So much of this is very familiar," he explained and offered one subtle, yet salient memory of exclusion prompted by the Gallery Walk experience. He recounted that when he was a senior in high school he was not among those called to the college recruitment assembly at his high school, although he was among those called when the Army recruiters arrived. For this participant who spent the bulk of his schooling in special education, the Gallery Walk activity confirmed how the discussion on difference proved to be a problem. It was only later in life, after early career stints in law enforcement and private investigation that he realized that he was not the *problem*. His decision to become a teacher was very much motivated by the realization that many students are devalued on a daily basis in schools—whether intentionally or not—the effect endures.

This participant's candid reflection provided considerable authenticity to the insights we hoped the DSE component of the workshop would provide. That the participants would be as forthcoming as many were was both expected and unexpected. In earlier work at CCNY with special education Master's students, Ware (2006b) elaborated on classroom exchanges and student engagement with DSE content that tapped into similar multiple perspectives on disability experience. The reactions in the CTT workshop paralleled those earlier accounts as teachers realized that the traditional special education knowledge base is fixed outside the translation many disabled people make of their lives; sadly, that knowledge is too often excluded from teacher preparation coursework. What is perhaps most troubling is realizing that when disability is framed in terms of loss or individual deficiency we send a powerful message to children with disabilities and their families about human worth. As the workshop neared an end, Valle's question of why the disability experience is always framed in terms of loss or individual lack could then be readily answered as the pieces began to fall into place—those who have no lived experience of disability author such accounts.

Disability Studies Conversations—Making More Trouble

On the final day of the workshop, teachers wondered how they would begin to change their practice in ways informed by DSE. They grasped the difference between the medical and social models of disability; they recognized the difference between a children's book focused on overcoming disability and one that enacted empowering scenarios told in the first person; they left with a toolkit that would help them to differentiate instruction. More importantly, they left with a new understanding that the toolkit would work for all children and not just those schools name disabled. If student diversity in learning is perceived as a value-added feature of their teaching and embedded in the community they created in their classroom, then the diversity of their students would likewise be characterized as difference that mattered and difference that makes the classroom a more dynamic place. Simply put, student diversity would be reflected as difference that mattered and not difference as problem.

Others left with an unsettled feeling that they were "foot soldiers" for a system they did not create, and yet, they were nonetheless expected to maintain it. Throughout the workshop we were asking them to be revolutionary in their thinking about disability, yet, we could not guarantee that the system would allow them to be radical in any way. The sorting and categorizing of students along the socially constructed binaries of typical/deviant, average/below average, and normal/abnormal would continue even if they refused their status as the "card-carrying designators" of difference (Slee, 2006). We did not hush these concerns but reminded them of Ferri's advice to find other like-minded thinkers in their schools—and to maintain the web-based connections organized for the participants through the workshop organizers. We encouraged them to work with us to begin this long overdue conversation on disability that departs from the traditional special education paradigm that locates the "problem" of disability inside the individual. As this project continues, the participants will be supported in large-group meetings and through individual class visits to find ways to minimize the contradictions evident in a system that aims to include all children while it simultaneously enacts the mandate to name difference as "problem" in everyday schooling practices.

Conclusion

This chapter explored how P-12 general and special education has uncritically accepted special education's default paradigm, one that has disqualified the voices and discredited the perspective of individuals with disability in schools and society. We suggested that by engaging educators in disability studies writ large and that which we know of as DSE in particular, we might find a way to privilege the perspective of disabled children and youth whose theorizing about disability matters. In order to ask new questions about the multiplicity of disability experience, we must include the questions of those who live inside the experience. DSE, as the tenets above suggest, continues to document the value of this approach for urban educators and for all who are willing to reexamine the meaning we make of disability in the political and social spheres we occupy as educators. We look forward to the opportunity to consider a similar project with school administrators and other district personnel, as they possess considerable influence on the structures that enable or constrain new conversations on disability in P-12 education.

NOTES

1. Although the term Integrative Co-Teaching Services is exclusive to usage in New York State, it is for all intents and purposes a renaming of the decades-old practice of collaborative team teaching initially introduced in the early efforts at educational inclusion during the early to mid-1980s. Villa, Thousand & Nevin (2004) provide a brief history.

2. The program requirements for the Master's in special education at City College included a two–semester course on differentiated instruction that was co–taught by two faculty members. The design of the course was intended to model the fundamental principle of two teachers working in practice of collaborators.

3. The terminology and descriptors provided by the participants included a mix of typical terms used by schools to describe children with disabilities. These included: Emotionally Disturbed (ED), Learning Disabled (LD), Attention Deficit Hyperactive disorder (ADHD). Those exclusive to New York City included the designation of special education classrooms by the ratio of students, teachers, and paraprofessionals. Thus an 8:1:1 classroom would indicate a high needs settings given that eight students would be configured with two adults that include a teacher and a paraprofessional. Over the years, a variety of service delivery models unique to New York City Special Education included, for example, SETTS, SBTS although many teachers found it difficult to recall the exact terminology. The Committee on Special Education (CSE) is the organizational configuration of the team that decides appropriate educational needs. It typically includes parents, teachers, and various service providers such as the occupational therapist (OT), physical therapist (PT) or speech therapist (SPT). The CSE decides what testing modifications are appropriate including extended time on tests, access to assisted technology, counseling, etc., which are then spelled out on the child's Individual Education Plan (IEP). Students are subsequently identified with the need for: a Functional Behavioral Analysis (FBA), a Behavioral Improvement Plan (BIP), counseling, adapted/modified/differentiated curriculum, assistive technology, job-coaches, etc. District 75 (D75) is the entity that administers special education in New York City.

4. Valle introduced the 'disability as-loss' narrative as one typically authored by non-disabled people because "we see someone with a disability and immediately think tragedy and misfortune." Ware contrasted this to understanding disability as a "value-added" experience authored by many disabled young adults and adults recounted in the disability studies literature. This narrative suggests that living with a disability has informed their identity in an enabling rather disabling way. They value the life lived differently—one in which difference is not constructed as problem. Their insight stands in marked contrast to the sentimentalized "special-ness" typically ascribed to their lives.

Artiles, A. J. (1997). Learning disabilities empirical research on ethnic minority students: An analysis of 22 years of studies published in selected refereed journals. *Learning Disabilities Research and Practice,* 12(2), 82–91.

Ashton, J. (in press). The CEC professional standards: A Foucauldian genealogy of the Re/Construction of Special Education. *International Journal of Inclusive Education.*

_____. (1998) The dilemma of difference: Enriching the disproportionality discourse with theory and context. *The Journal of Special Education,* 32, 32–36.

_____. (2003). Special education's changing identity: Paradoxes and dilemmas in views of culture and space. *Harvard Educational Review,* 73 (2), 164–202.

Baglieri, S., Bejoian, L., Broderick, A., Connor, D. J. & Valle, J. W. (in press). [Re]claiming "inclusive education" toward cohesion in educational reform: Disability studies unravels the myth of the normal child. *Teachers College Record.*

Belkin, L. (2004). The Lessons of Classroom 506. *New York Times Magazine.* September 12.

Berube, M. (2002). Afterword: If I should live so long. In S.L. Snyder, B. Brueggemann & R. Garland-Thomson (Eds.), *Disability studies: Enabling the humanities,* (337–343). New York: Modern Language Association.

_____. (2005). College makeover. *Slate.* November 15, 2005.

Brantlinger, E. (1997). Uses of ideology: Cases of non-recognition of the politics of research and practice in special education, *Review of Educational Research,* 67, 425–459.

_____. (2004a). Ideologies discerned, values determined: Getting past the hierarchies of special education. In L. Ware (Ed.), *Ideology and the politics of in/exclusion* (11–31). New York: Peter Lang.

_____. (2004b). Confounding the needs and confronting the norms: An extension of Reid and Valle's essay. In the special series, Discursive Practices of Learning Disability, *Journal of Learning Disabilities,* 37(6), 490–499.

_____. (2006). *Who benefits from special education? Remediating (fixing) other people's children.* New York: Routledge.

Connor, D. J. (2009). Breaking containment—the power of narrative knowing: Countering silences within traditional special education research. *The International Journal of Inclusive Education,* 13(5), 449–470.

_____. 2008). *Urban narratives: Portraits in progress, life at the intersections of learning disability, race, and social class.* New York: Peter Lang.

Davis, L. J. (1997). *The disability studies reader.* New York: Routledge.

Ferri, B. A. (2006). Teaching to trouble. In S. Danforth & S.L. Gabel (Eds.), *Vital questions facing disability studies in education* (289–306). New York: Peter Lang.

Friend, M. (2007). *Co-Teach! A handbook for creating and sustaining classroom partnerships in inclusive schools.* Greensboro: North Carolina: Marilyn Friend, Inc.

Friend, M., & Cook, L. (2009). *Interactions: Collaboration skills for school professionals* (6th ed.). White Plains, NY: Longman.

Gallagher, D. J., Heshusius, L., Iano, R. P., & Skritic, T.M. (Eds.) (2004). *Challenging orthodoxy in special education: Dissenting voices.* Denver, CO: Love Publishing Co.

Harry, B. and Klinger, B. (2006). *Why are there so many minority students in special education?* New York: Teachers College Press.

Hehir, T. (2005). IDEA and disproportionality: Federal enforcement, effective advocacy and strategies for change. In D. J. Losen and G. Orfield (Eds.), *Racial inequality in special education* (219–238). Cambridge, MA: Harvard University Press.

Johnson, H. McBryde (2003). Unspeakable conversations. Should I have been killed at birth? The case for my life. *The New York Times Magazine*. February 16, 2003.

Kluth, P. (2003). *You're going to love this kid: Teaching students with autism in the inclusive classroom.* Baltimore: Paul H. Brookes Publishing Co.

Linton, S. (1998). *Claiming disability: Knowledge and identity.* New York: New York University Press.

Losen D. J. and Orfield, G. (Eds.), (2002). *Racial inequality in special education.* Cambridge, MA: Harvard Education Press.

Oyler, C. (1996). *Making room for inclusion: Sharing teacher authority in room 104.* New York: Teachers College Press.

Oyler, C. (2006). *Learning to teach inclusively.* Mahwah: New Jersey: Lawrence Erlbaum Associates.

Parrish, T. (2002). Racial disparities in the identification, funding, and provision of special education. In *Racial inequality in special education*, D. J. Losen & G. Orfield (Eds.), 15–37. Cambridge, MA: Harvard Education Press.

Reid, D.K., & Valle, J.W. (2004). The discursive practice of learning disability: Implications for instruction and parent-school relations. The Discursive Practices of Learning Disability, Special Issue, *Journal of Learning Disabilities*, 37(6), 466–481.

Rizvi, F., & Lingard, B. (1996). *Disability, education and the discourse of justice.* Buckingham, England: Open University Press.

Rueda, R., Artiles, A. J., Salazar, J. & Higareda, I. (2002). An analysis of special education as a response to the diminished academic achievement of Chicano/Latino students. An update. In R.R. Valencia (Ed), *Chicano school failure and success: Past, present, and future* (2ⁿᵈ ed., 310–332). London: Routledge/Falmer.

Sapon-Shevin, M. (2007). *Widening the circle: The power of inclusive classrooms.* Boston: Beacon Press.

Slee, R. (2004). Meaning in the service of power. In L. Ware (Ed.), *Ideology and the politics of in/exclusion.* New York: Peter Lang.

Slee, R. (2006). Limits to and the possibilities for educational reform. *International Journal of Inclusive Education*, 5(2–3), 167–177.

Slee, R. & Allan, J. (2001). Excluding the included: A reconsideration of inclusive education. *International Studies in Sociology of Education*, 11(2), 173–191.

Tomlinson, C. A., (2003). *Fulfilling the promise of the differentiated classroom: Strategies and tools for responsive teaching.* Alexandria, VA: Association for Supervision and Curriculum Development.

Tomlinson, C. A., Brimijoin, K., & Narvaez, L. (2008). *The differentiated school: Making revolutionary changes in teaching and learning.* Alexandria, VA: Association for Supervision and Curriculum Development.

Valle, J. W. (2009). *What mothers say about special education: From the 1960s to the present.* New York: Palgrave Macmillan.

Valle, J. W. & Connor, D. J. (in press). *Rethinking Difference: A disability studies approach to inclusive practices.* New York: McGraw–Hill.

Villa, R., Thousand, J., & Nevin, A. (Eds). (2004). *A guide to co-teaching: Practical tips for facilitating student learning.* Thousand Oaks, CA: Corwin Press

Ware, L. (2003a). Working past pity: What we make of disability in schools. In J. Allan (Ed.), *Inclusion, participation and democracy: What is the purpose?* (117–137). Amsterdam: Kluwer Academic Publishers.

Ware, L. (2003b). Understanding disability and transforming schools. In T. Booth, K. Nes, & M. Stromstad (Eds.), *Developing inclusive teacher education* (146–165). London: Routledge.

____. (2005). Many possible futures, many different directions: Merging critical special education and disability studies. In S.L. Gabel (Ed.), *Disability studies in education: Readings in theory and method* (103–124). New York: Peter Lang.

____. (2006a). Urban educators, disability studies, and education: Excavations in schools and society. *The International Journal of Inclusive Education,* v10 (2–3), 149–168.

____. (2006b). A look at the way we look at disability. In S. Danforth & S.L. Gabel (Eds.), *Vital questions facing disability studies in education* (271–288). New York: Peter Lang.

____. (in press). *Disability Studies in Education.* To appear in S. Tozer, A. Henry & B. Gallegos (Eds.). *The handbook of research in the sociocultural foundations of education.* New York & London: Routledge Press.

Ware L. & Valle, J., (2005). *Theorizing and Politicizing Disability in Education and Rehabilitation.* Plenary session. 5th Annual Second City Conference on Disability Studies in Education. Teachers College, Columbia University. New York. May 19–21.

Wong, B. (Ed) (2004). Special Series: The Discursive Practices of Learning Disability, *Journal of Learning Disabilities,* 37 (6).

CHAPTER NINE

Elizabeth Quintero

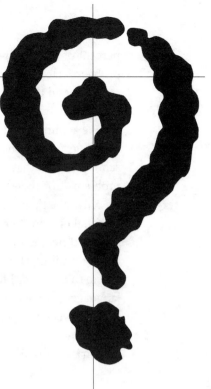

How Can Multiple Literacies Be Used for Literacy Learning in Urban Schools?

 It is the worst of times, and politicians are working hard to say there is opportunity in the challenges we face. The economy is tenuous; unemployment is rising, and we have a governance system that seems, at best, out of touch with all of us, and, at worst, dysfunctional. At the beginning of this dark time, the Fall of 2008, our university was visited by a politician, a native son who clearly respected learning and was happy to be addressing an audience in his childhood environs. Rumor preceded him, saying that he hoped to run for a higher political office. He spoke of the strengths of, and challenges facing, our state and particularly our educational system. He spent 30 minutes talking about the diversity of the population in the state and stressed that a diverse workforce is a very strong asset to have. Then he put a slide on the projector that showed that in our state, 34 percent of the students in K-12 education "go home after school to a family that doesn't speak English." (Actually, the number is higher.) He went on, "This is a problem for our teachers and our schools."

My friends and I, who were sitting on the first row, glanced at each other in barely concealed fury. He continued for a few more minutes discussing the challenges for education in such a diverse society as ours and offered a few worn-out solutions to alleviate these "problems" for teachers of English Language Learners. After he finished his remarks, I joined several people who waited to speak to him personally. When it was my turn, I introduced myself, offered my hand, and commented on my agreement with his opening remarks about the strength and potential of a diverse workforce. Then I said, "However, I have to tell you some of my colleagues and I adamantly disagree with your comments about the 34 percent of students going home to speak a language other than English being a problem." He blinked, the smile only slightly fading. So I went on, "We feel very strongly, and there is a huge body of research that supports our stance, that students going home to speak other languages are an asset, not a problem or a liability. We acknowledge that for some teachers who have not been educated about teaching multilingual students or school districts whose funds are tied to test scores on tests that are not appropriate for English Language Learners this is a problem—for them. The children are on their way to being multilingual and if we only take their lead, we could have a population of cognitively flexible, multilingual citizens." His smile faded and he dismissed me. It is unacceptable that educated people in positions of power still perpetuate the misinformation that being multilingual is a problem.

In this chapter I focus on literacies (my main focus of research and teaching), languages (home languages and target languages of host countries), the connections between personal and communal history and experience, on the one hand, and learning texts or the canon on the other, and how all of the above relate to the curriculum in various learning situations.

In These Times

Literacies and languages are two of the most important aspects of all learning, and can be an important structure for teachers, parents, and families to support learning for all. This learning must encompass the many varied sources of knowledge that have come before; it must also include new, creative, and often not yet conceived, forms of knowledge and skills. This requires rethinking the meaning of literacies and certainly the aspects of literacy involvement that make learning endeavors meaningful. Many literacy scholars today consider literacy to be much more than decoding words, reading and writing. Many believe that literacy in a variety of languages is a rich context for learning. Many believe that personal and communal history must be a part of literacy's work. Many even believe that the only way to delve into authentic learning is by including personal story as an important form of literacy.

A student teacher writes about the rich literacy history she experienced in her family in southern California. She remembers:

> I have always been surrounded by literacy in my life. I can remember as far back as when I was three years old or younger. I remember my dad listening to the Dodger games in Spanish over the radio. My dad would have me turn on the radio and he would tell me [to] turn the dial until he was able to hear the game without static.

> Another memory I have of my father was when I was four years old. My dad would sit me on his lap with a note pad on mine. He would write my full name in cursive and have me trace it. I also remember my dad teaching me English at home. He would say "Spoon," "Apple" and "Teacher." He would have me repeat it after him. My dad had very beautiful penmanship.

My mother, on the other hand, did not know how to read or write. They had an agreement that my dad would teach us how to read and write while she taught us how to be honest and responsible people.

A memory I have of my mother with literacy is her singing and dancing while doing chores. I remember her dancing around with the broom and whistling. She taught me how to whistle and hum to music. My mother did not read or write but she would always sit down with us to do our homework. My mother would also buy the newspaper and read it, little did I know that all she did was look at pictures and cut the coupons. Now I understand a lot of things that happened when I was younger and appreciate my mother more. (Quintero, 2009b, p. 94–95.)

Communication through literacy can be enhanced by story as a way to make language and culture visible. This is crucial for all learners and especially for immigrant students in school. To belong is to be recognized as a full participant in the practices that shape knowledge, identities, and action. Yet to learn is to draw upon one's own and others' knowledge sources, to transform these, and formulate conceptual frames for future learning. Urban neighborhoods and schools around the world have increasing numbers of people representing ethnic, racial, and religious diversity. Many students today in schools around have exquisitely complex stories of going and coming. They have left a home country for a myriad of reasons, and they have come to their new country with a multitude of experiences. Teachers and students can use multicultural story and literacy as a way to enter neighborhoods and begin to learn from other stories of the various groups of people. Furthermore, the study of our students' histories must be ongoing and a part of literacy education. What does history mean when studying literacy curriculum and learning? Is not the most important goal in literacy education helping students critically "read" what they are learning in and out of school? How does the information in the curriculum relate to personal and family prior knowledge? How does the information differ from that knowledge?

For many students and their teachers in the United States and around the world, there is confusion and often dissonance concerning multiple language use, learning, and the academic requirements for success. A student teacher working in a kindergarten in New York City remarked:

Here in New York, there are so many different languages all over the place. From what I have seen in the classroom that I work in now, is that all of the children are all very culturally different. I have not seen any lessons or sharing time to have children discuss their home language. However, I am aware that the kindergarten teacher has discussed a couple of different places where children are from, or where their parents come from, and their cultural differences. For example, one of the students parents are from Ethiopia, and the teacher has discussed this on several occasions. I think that this is so great because then the child feels proud about his origins.

Yet, she worried,

This is similar to but different from language use, . . . both culture and language should be shared and taught whenever possible . . . Within our use of language is our value system . . . if English is the only language accepted in school, this implies other languages are not as valued (Quintero, 2009b, p. 62).

The teachers I work with and I support students' multiple languages and recognize ways that multiple knowledge sources, identities, and language forms can contribute to the formation of new relationships and meanings. As a community of scholars in a wide variety of classrooms, we respect learners' backgrounds, plan carefully for their current experiences in school, and prepare them for the future challenges of standardized testing, competitive learning programs, and a variety of future journeys. Our work uses critical literacy as a framework. We define critical literacy as a process of constructing and critically using language (oral and written) as a means of expression, interpretation, and transformation of our lives and the lives of those around us. Critical literacy is a process of both reading history (the world) and creating history (what you believe is important?).

Some of the teachers and student teachers I work with have had past experiences similar to the experiences of the children from migrating families. By the year 2030, over half of students in schools in the United States will be students of multicultural and multilingual backgrounds. González et al. (2005) declare that "funds of knowledge" of all families in our communities must be recognized and built upon. Acculturation and language acquisition are impacted by the process of aligning new societal expectations and requirements with previous cultural norms, individual perceptions, and experiences preeminent in immigrants' lives. Yet these urgent issues are often ignored (Ullman, 1997; Zou, 1998). Franken and Haslett (2002) report research documenting that when students are faced with a topic on which they have little domain-specific knowledge, interaction significantly helps students' understanding of text.

We who are dedicated to, and immersed in, critical pedagogy have internalized that knowing, meaning, and meaning-making are pluralities. Scholars and advocates who work with migrating families have learned over the years about "funds of knowledge," and many critical pedagogues have emphasized the strengths of all learners when their histories, languages, and cultures are valued and included (Grinberg, 2005; Freire and Macedo, 1987; Kincheloe, 2000, 2002; Naiditch, 2006; Soto, 2000; Steinberg, 2001). Yet, here we are in late 2009, in a context in which power brokers create, proselytize, and use as threats standards based on a very narrow knowledge base that ignores much of the history, art, and information of human experience.

By virtue of the fact that many immigrant students come from such a variety of backgrounds with such different strengths and experiences, it is almost inevitable that many occasions will arise in the literacy classroom when one or more students have a lack of background knowledge on a topic and at the same time a source of knowledge from past lived experience that is unique to that learner. In order to rethink the meaning of literacy and ways to encourage all learners' development of literacy in one or more languages, we must ask research questions based upon critical literacy such as: whose stories are important and in what ways? What can we learn from the stories? Whose background knowledge will we respect and include, and in what ways? Whose and which knowledge is power, and in what ways? What ways can we use literacy for specific transformative action?

In a previous study of the beliefs and practices of effective literacy teachers (Rummel & Quintero, 1997), we found that family history and literacy are an interwoven fabric of cultural practices. This family knowledge and related literacy practices promote strength, encourage nurturance, and support risk taking. The teachers in our study, like many well-known writers and visionaries, talked about the importance of parents and grandparents passing on stories. They felt that this was an important legacy passed down through the generations. One teacher smiled as she reported that her West Indian grandmother passed on teachings through folk tales. Another teacher talked about both grandfather and grandmother. He noted that in his American Indian family passing on stories was done orally during his youth. The family gathered around a campfire, and the eldest would talk and tell stories.

Critical theorists, as well as New Literacy Studies proponents, believe that literacy is about personal and communal knowledge. We believe that the ways in which people address reading and writing are themselves rooted in conceptions of knowledge, identity, and being. Literacy is always contested, both its meanings and its practices, hence particular versions of it are always "ideological"; they are always rooted in a particular world-view and in a desire for that view of literacy to dominate and to marginalize others (Gee, 1991; Besnier & Street, 1994). The way in which teachers or facilitators and their students interact is already a social practice that affects the nature of the literacy being learned and the ideas about literacy held by the participants, especially the ideas of new learners regarding their position in relations of power. It is not valid to suggest that literacy can be "given" neutrally and that its social effects are only experienced afterwards.

So what does this mean for promoting literacy practice and teaching and learning? Critical pedagogues advocate "Reading the World" (Freire & Macedo, 1987). We believe that the texts students and teachers decode should contain images of their own concrete, situated experiences with the world and the transnational global realities of neighbors, far and near. This is a way to radically redefine conventional notions of print-based literacy and conventional school curricula. This does not mean throwing out, ignoring, or not providing access to accepted bodies of information and canon in learning events. It means sharing the space, the time, and especially the importance between the old and the new.

For example, a university student in a teacher education class studying bilingual theory and methods wrote about a project she designed based on Ada and Campoy's (2003) *Authors in the Classroom:*

> In order to connect the project personally I chose to make a book for my little brother called "Baseball (Béisbol)." The book is about what he wants to be when he grows up, a baseball player. I decided to write it in English and Spanish in order to involve him in the half of our family that is Cuban. I want him to have more exposure to the Spanish language than I did. At first I was hesitant because although my family speaks Spanish, they can't write it. I know that some of the words in the book I made probably aren't the correct Spanish, but it's my family's Spanish.

A project like this is a great way to get the family involved all together. If I had had the opportunity (I am studying in a different city from where my family lives), I would have enjoyed making the book with my brother instead of for my brother. I know that he would have really enjoyed writing about himself because what child doesn't like to talk about himself and say the things he is good at?

My ultimate goal as a teacher would be to incorporate the families into the learning as much as possible, to bring their creative minds out as much as possible, and to encourage them to never stop learning.

As a side note, the student revealed on the final night of class that she had been to her parents' home the previous weekend and had shown her parents the almost finished book (which was going to be a surprise for the brother). Because she had been unsure about some of the Spanish words, she had consulted various web sites and dictionaries. Her father saw the book and said, "No, those words aren't right. Here, let me do this." She had previously asked him to help translate, but he'd declined saying his Spanish wasn't good enough. But he was not going to let his son's book have inaccurate vocabulary in it! Now, the book had really become a family project for her family, using both languages the family speaks in their home context.

Family knowledge and literacy are an interwoven fabric of cultural practices. This is an authentic way to encourage literacy. And this brings us to a brief discussion of languages. We have much research about language acquisition, home language influence on target language literacy, and learning in multilingual environments. Emerging research in neuroscience informs this field as well. The information is almost overwhelming in its vastness. However, we must begin to refine practice based upon the research.

Language/s

According to Bakhtin (1988), the production and reception of meaning are what truly establishes language. Language has a dialogical and ideological dimension that is historically determined and built. Comprehension implies not only the identification of the formal and normative aspects and signs of language, but also the subtexts, the intentions that are not explicit. Discourse always has a live meaning and direction. At the same time, meaning and communication imply community. One always addresses someone, and that someone does not assume a purely passive role; the interlocutor participates in the formation of the meaning of the utterance, just as the other elements of speech do. Bakhtin (1988) says that language is constitutively intersubjective and social. It is not experience that organizes expression. On the contrary, expression precedes and organizes experience, giving it form and direction. Again, this structure helps in the connection of critical theory to critical literacy.

This leads to the issue of home language use, the cognitive and socioemotional aspects of native language, and how they affect schooling. Unfortunately, much of the information publicized in the United States media, both

How Can Multiple Literacies Aid in Literacy Learning in Urban Schools?

about language and literacy of non-English-speaking people and about the best schooling programs for these students, is false. Students and their families who speak languages other than English can, and should, continue to nurture their home language while their English acquisition is in progress. The languages and literacies enrich each other; they do not prohibit the students from becoming fluent and literate in English.

In the area of language development, we now know that at age six, children have not yet begun to complete full cognitive development in their first language (Collier, 1989). When children's first language acquisition is discontinued before cognition is fully developed, they may experience negative cognitive effects in their second language development; conversely, children who have an opportunity to learn in their native language and learn a second language reach full cognitive development in two languages and enjoy cognitive advances over monolinguals (Collier, 1989). Making the issue of learning in a student's first language more urgent, research now shows that it may take as long as seven to ten years for nonnative speakers to reach the average level of performance by native speakers on standardized tests (Collier, 1989; Collier & Thomas, 1999). Research (Baker, 2000; Cummins, 2000; Skutnabb-Kangas, 2000; Quintero, 2004) documents ways in which students learning English as a new language can become more effective writers, readers, and participants in English literacy as well as in their native language literacies.

The contextual reality of many English Literacy classrooms in the United States and all over the world is that a large variety of native languages are present. Sometimes a classroom teacher speaks the native languages of the students. However, it is almost always impossible for each teacher to be knowledgeable of every language represented in the classroom. Reyes (1992) and Quintero (2002) document that it is rarely crucial for the classroom teacher to be proficient in all languages represented by students in the classroom. Using critical literacy is one way any classroom teacher can orchestrate a meaningful English Literacy lesson that includes speaking, reading, and writing in the students' native languages— even when the teacher does not know the native languages. Critical literacy uses native language as a scaffolding technique to promote English literacy while exposing students to important content information in their home language, thus giving value to each student's personal experience. The approach allows for adaptations to be made regarding language and background knowledge, such as cultural experience and experience in formal literacy instruction. It also allows for flexibility in terms of the educational aspirations of the students.

To reiterate, research evidence does not support the notion that the first language interferes with learning a second language (Larsen-Freeman & Long, 1991). It is clear that the first language serves a function in early second language acquisition, but it is a supportive role rather than a negative one (Ovando & Collier, 1998).

> In the beginning stages of L2 acquisition, acquirers lean on their L1 knowledge to analyze patterns in L2, and they subconsciously apply some structures from L1 to L2 in the early

stages of interlanguage development. Most linguists look upon this process as a positive use of L1 knowledge (Ovando & Collier, 1998, p. 95).

Ovando and Collier (1998) go on to state the need to educate school staff and parents who are unfamiliar with this information about the importance of students using their native languages in learning.

Research by Cashion and Eagan (1990) on Canadian French immersion programs and by Verhoeven (1991) with minority language students in the Netherlands show that transfer across languages is two-way (from L1 to L2 and then back from L2 to L1) if the sociolinguistic and educational conditions are right.

Literacies, Languages, and Curriculum

Comber and Kamler (1997) maintain that we must continue to examine the different versions of critical literacy that emerge and show the complex pictures of what pedagogies for critical literacy look like in different settings and educational contexts. In addition, they say that it is urgent that we continue to discuss the way in which power is exercised through textual practices during these times of demands for accountability in the production of students with particular sets of competencies and in the context of managerialist discourses which threaten to inhibit the freedom and power of individual and group student texts in the literacy classroom (Comber & Kamler, 1997).

I have found that Freire's (1973) approach based on critical theory and critical literacy is effective in teaching. The pedagogical method leads students of any age, experience, or ability level to base new learning on personal experience, expressed in a variety of languages, in a way that encourages critical reflection. All activities focus on participation. This method lends itself well to integrated literacy development and curriculum activities. It combines reflective thinking, information gathering, collaborative decision making, and personal learning choices. The method encourages students to choose, examine, and analyze information in all subject areas, focusing on authenticity of multiple experiences in multiple contexts. It also encourages an investigation into personal and communal historical memory. This combination of story, literature, academic information, and critical theory allows readers to use autobiography as a way to move beyond a neutral conception of culture (Willis, 1995). Critical literacy learning activities often begin with self-reflection; therefore, the stories generated by participants become sources of autobiographical narrative (Rogers, 1993). Through the semi-structured learning activities, a pattern of events, beliefs, or behaviors can be traced through a series of reflections (Reed-Danahay, 1997).

Previously, I defined critical literacy as a process of constructing and critically using language (oral and written) as a means of expression, interpretation, and transformation of our lives and the lives of those around us. Critical literacy and critical learning encourage a natural movement from reflection toward action. My work in teacher education uses critical literacy as a framework for integrated curriculum that includes all the traditional content areas of study, the arts, and new forms of cross-disciplinary ways of knowing, and grapples with the ways in which the canon is included in the areas of study. Using a critical literacy approach with multicultural literature and the words of many community members who are not currently heard supports an environment of possibility for learners. Critical literacy can be a powerful tool for learning and instruction for English Language Learners. The approach helps students express their voice in oral and written ways (Torres-Guzmán, 1993). Kuiken and Vedder (2002) show that when a writing task involves collaboration, there are a number of pedagogical advantages. This collaboration helps to assure the language skills are integrated rather than practiced in isolation (Kuiken & Vedder, 2002). This approach is not a prescriptive lesson planning format but is a way to facilitate student choice and generative work that is related to students' lives whatever the age or context of the students.

Critical literacy encourages students to experience and make conscious the transformations that often occur through the reading of and reflection on literature, academic texts, and other forms of literacy including biographies. This natural outcome is not causal, but our thinking, understanding of events, and behavior, are influenced by the process. It is always important to keep an open mind regarding what we are all learning and we must always ask what is really going on here? This is true in terms of policy and politics and it is true in terms of the multicultural children's literature we use in our classrooms.

This brings us to student writing and the creation of texts. Edelsky (1986) maintains that writing is a recursive process in which students actively hypothesize about the aspects of writing that can be applied across languages. DeSilva (1998) and Pérez (1998) maintain that learners can develop their knowledge of second language writing and speaking conventions by using what they understand about writing in their native language. Many researchers and classroom teachers have shown that language interaction in the form of student-centered discussions and demonstrations, language experience story writing and reading, and holistic literacy development allow for native language literacy to enhance English language literacy development (Hakuta, 1986; Hakuta & Garcia, 1989; Hudelson, 1986; Peregoy & Boyle, 2000; Quintero, 2002).

Freire's approach that has guided critical literacy work over the years is curriculum based, in spite of the emphasis on participatory knowledge sharing and dialogue. It is the relating of curriculum-specified information to the knowledge and strengths of the learners that accounts for its brilliance. The mutual responsibility for learning activities and shared information place at the fore of all lessons the learners' strengths and prior knowledges and the target body of knowledges required in a certain learning context.

A brief example taken from a case study (Quintero, 2002) shows one way to structure a class of multilingual learners using critical pedagogy and critical literacy. The adult education class in the study was composed of immigrant learners studying English. There were 20 students, some of whom spoke Hmong, Vietnamese, Spanish, Mandarin Chinese, Polish, and French. They were studying content such as U.S. history, government, and civic principles, to prepare for the U.S. Citizenship Test, which is required for becoming a naturalized U.S. citizen.

The teacher of this class opened the class session by telling a story about her family's historical home, Serbia, that she had learned from her grandfather. She explained that she had heard her grandfather's comments about the old country for years, but then when she was in college and was working on an assignment about historical information not found in history textbooks, she decided to interview him regarding specific historical questions. She showed the students some of the questions she had created. Then she made a visual depiction in the form of a mural of what she learned about life and governance in the small Serbian village that the family had come from.

Then she showed the students a list she had made that showed two categories—facts commonly found in history textbooks about Serbia during the late twentieth and early twenty-first centuries, and facts not found in these textbooks. For a short time they discussed different students' ideas about why this was so.

Then the students were asked to think of a historical event or aspect of their own countries and make a rough visual sketch depicting this. They were asked to write descriptions of what the sketches showed in their native languages. During this part of the lesson, the students who shared home languages were encouraged to work together so that they could use their home language to support their thinking and expression during the exercise. They then formed small groups to tell the stories in English.

Finally, the teacher distributed printed information about the United States citizenship lesson, a lesson on local, state, and federal governance. She asked students to read the information and then discuss in small groups the differences between the system in the United States and their home countries. Then as a class, the students contributed to a list of characteristics of the United States system, written in English on a large tablet displayed in the front of the class. As the class progressed over the next weeks, the participants worked on several collaboratively written texts relating the information about the United States government to governments in their home countries. These texts became future models and resources for future classes. The teacher used native language writing as a scaffolding exercise in many of her future lessons and collected data indicating an increase in the success of the students' English literacy and content learning for the citizenship exam.

Critical literacy does not just provide a possibility for expository writing and writing for studying content area information. A critical literacy framework, based on participant history, multiple sources of knowledge, and transformative action, also has great potential for creative and fiction writing contexts. All learners, from all backgrounds and histories, learn through their stories while engaging in daily activities, storytelling, and play. They experience development in multiple domains and engage in multidimensional learning when given the opportunity and encouragement. Adler (2009) argues that adolescents learn through their personal stories while engaging in play and daily activities. This is particularly true, she says, for adolescent writers.

> Their intellectual, personal, *and* social growth are likely to flourish in the playful world of imagination. Within this world, rules are bent and reconfigured such that impossible ideas become possible. Within this world, writers are motivated and engaged in experimenting with and constructing an imaginary reality that responds to their needs (Adler, 2009, p. vii).

In her research, she found that regardless of achievement levels, gender, or economic status, students proclaimed the importance of imaginative play in their lives. She noted that Sadie explained that writing fiction is "good; it's an outlet for my anger and my issues." Matthew said that fiction, as well as athletics, helped him cope with the anger he felt after his parents' divorce. Jack reported that he used fiction to rewrite his life in a positive way, noting that, "I am not a very agile person so I always dream about being very fast and very hero-ish. Like Indiana Jones or James Bond or something like that. I like to write about those guys or write about my own characters like that" (Adler, 2009, p. 78).

To come full circle with my thoughts here, I believe that this idea of learner/writer agency and more developed selves supports my own belief that when I speak of literacy, all literacy is—or should be—critical literacies. This constructing of personal and communal meaning (in a variety of languages) and taking action according to that meaning is the most authentic way to personalize literacy.

Critical literacy lends itself to ongoing scholarly research on teaching and learning. Teachers can and should join the culture of researchers if a new level of educational rigor and quality is ever to be achieved. In such a culture, teacher–scholars will begin to understand the power implications of technical standards. In this context, they gain heightened awareness of how they can contribute to the research on education. Perhaps learners and scholars can begin to put on the table the reality that all school textbooks are political (Schissler, 2006). As Schissler says, "A new knowledge frame that is more conducive to the ambiguities and the complexities of the world needs to be developed . . ." (2006). I believe that students, through family stories, personal responses to their changing worlds, and connections made to continually emerging new knowledges, can be the creators of much of our new knowledge frames.

Adler (2009) articulates the duality and dilemma that most educators, especially literacy educators and writing instructors, face in these difficult times. She says,

> One voice intones, "Let's get serious—we must get our nation's youth equipped with basic literacy and communication skills to succeed in the workforce." Simultaneously, another whispers, "Hang on a minute—let's also cultivate higher-level thinking in our students, equipping them to handle the kinds of imaginative problem solving they'll need to survive intellectually in our complex twenty-first century world" (Adler, 2009) p. viii).

From where I stand, it is the second voice that is screaming at us to listen. My years of experience and research help me to be absolutely sure about this. Adler (2009) believes that:

> What students need is to find the payoff, to see how carefully selected details and events drawn from real experience give fiction breath and form. This is where our writers need help—not exclusively with exercises or formulas for stories, though these have their uses, but with instructional support that overtly addresses the relationship between the two worlds, the verisimilitude that grows out of well-anchored fiction (Adler, 2009, p. x).

According to Freire (1997), freedom can occur only when the oppressed reject the image of oppression "and replace it with autonomy and responsibility" (p. 29). Those who adopt Freire's pedagogy need to be aware that it is not made up of techniques to save the world. Instead, he felt that "the progressive educator must always be moving out on his or her own, continually reinventing me and reinventing what it means to be democratic in his or her own specific cultural and historical context" (Freire, 1997, p. 308). A philosophy and teaching practice based on critical literacies makes the "continually reinventing me and reinventing what it means to be democratic" possible.

REFERENCES

Ada, A. A., & Campoy, F. I. (2003). *Authors in the classroom: A transformative education process.* New York: Allyn & Bacon.

Adler, M. (2009). *Writers at play: Making spaces for adolescents to balance imagination and craft.* Portsmouth, NH: Heinemann.

Baker, M. (2000). Towards a methodology for investigating the style of a literary translator. *Target, 12*(2), 241–266.

Bakhtin, M. (1988). From the prehistory of novelistic discourse. In David Lodge (Ed.), *Modern criticism and theory.* New York: Longman.

Banks, J., & Banks, C. (1995). *Handbook of research on multicultural education.* New York: Macmillan.

Benjamin, W. (1987). *Obras escolhidas I, Magia e ténica, arête e poíitica.* São Paulo: Brasiliense.

Bransford, J., Brown, A., & Cocking, R. (1999). *How people learn: Brain, mind, experience and school.* Washington, DC: National Academy Press.

Besnier, N., & Street, B. (1994). Aspects of Literacy. In T. Ingold, (Ed.), *Companion Encyclopedia of Anthropology: Humanity, Culture, and Social Life* (pp. 527–562). London: Routledge.

Cashion, M., & Eagan, R. (1990). Spontaneous reading and writing in English by students in total French immersion: Summary of final report. *English Quarterly, 22*(1), 30–44.

Collier, V. P. (1989). How long? A synthesis of research on academic achievement in second language. *TESOL Quarterly, 23,* 509–531.

Collier, V. P., & Thomas, W. P. (1999). Making U.S. schools effective for English language learners, Part 3. *TESOL Matters, 9*(6), 1, 10.

Comber, B., & Kamler, B. (1997). Critical literacies: Politicising the language classroom. Paper submitted for Interpretations. Language and Literacy Research Centre, University of South Australia, Underdale.

Cummins, J. (2000). *Language, power, and pedagogy: Bilingual children in the crossfire.* Clevedon, England: Multilingual Matters.

DeSilva, A. D. (1998). Emergent Spanish writing of a second grader in a whole language classroom. In B. Pérez (Ed.), *Sociocultural contexts of language and literacy* (pp. 223–248). Mahwah, NJ: Lawrence Erlbaum.

Edelsky, C. (1986). *Writing in a Bilingual Program: Habia Una Vez.* Norwood, NJ: Ablex.

Franken, M., & Haslett, S. (2002). When and why talking can make writing harder. In S. Ransdell & M. L. Barbier (Eds.), *Psycholinguistic approaches to understanding second language writing* (pp. 34–46). Amsterdam: Kluwer Press.

Freeman, R. D. (1998). *Bilingual education and social change.* Clevedon, England: Multilingual Matters.

Freire, P. (1973). *Education for critical consciousness.* New York: Seabury.

Freire, P. (1985). *The politics of education.* Westport, CT: Bergin & Garvey.

Freire, P. (1997). *Pedagogy of hope.* Westport, CT: Bergin & Garvey.

Freire, P., & Macedo, D. (1987). *Literacy: Reading the word and the world.* Westport, CT: Bergin & Garvey.

Gabel, S. and Danforth, Scot. (2008) *Disability and the Politics of Education: An International Reader.* New York: Peter Lang Publishing

Gee, J. (1991). Socio-cultural approaches to literacy. *Annual Review of Applied Linguistics, 12,* 31–48.

Giroux, H. (1988). *Teachers as intellectuals: Toward a critical of learning.* Westport, CT: Bergin & Garvey.

González, N., Moll, L. C., & Amanti, C. (2005). *Funds of knowledge: Theorizing practices in households, communities, and classrooms.* Mahwah, NJ: Lawrence Erlbaum.

Goodman, K. . (1987). *What's whole in whole language?* Portsmouth, NH: Heinemann.

Grinberg, J. G. (2005). *Teaching like that: Progressive teacher education at Bank Street during the 1930s.* New York: Peter Lang.

Hakuta, K. (1986). *Mirror of language: The debate on bilingualism.* New York: Basic Books.

Hakuta, K., & Garcia, E. (1989). Bilingualism and education. *American Psychologist, 44*(2), 374–379.

Hudelson, S. (1994). Literacy development of second language children. In F. Genesee (Ed.), *Educating second language children: The whole child, the whole curriculum, the whole community* (pp. 129–158). Cambridge, England: Cambridge University Press.

Kincheloe, J. (2000). Certifying the damage: Mainstream educational psychology and the oppression of children. In L. D. Soto (Ed.), *The politics of early childhood education* (pp. 75–84). New York: Peter Lang.

Kincheloe, J. (2002). *Teachers as researchers: Qualitative paths to empowerment* (2nd ed.). New York: RoutledgeFalmer.

Kincheloe, J., & Steinberg, S. (1997). *Changing multiculturalism.* Philadelphia: Open University Press.

Kuiken, F., & Vedder, I. (2002). Collaborative writing in L2: The effect of group interaction on text quality. In S. Ransdell & M. Barbier (Eds.), *New directions for research in L2 writing* (pp. 169–188). Amsterdam: Kluwer Academic Publishers.

Larsen-Freeman, D., & Long, M. H. (1991). *An introduction to second language acquisition research.* New York: Longman.

Lee, C. D. (2008). The centrality of culture to the scientific study of learning and development: How an ecological framework in education research facilitates civic responsibility. *Educational Researcher, 37*(5), 267–279.

Naiditch, F. (2006). *The pragmatics of permission: A study of Brazilian ESL learners.* Ph.D. Dissertation. New York: New York University.

Ovando, C. J., & Collier, V. P. (1998). *Bilingual and ESL classrooms: Teaching in multicultural contexts.* New York: McGraw-Hill.

Peregoy, S. F., & Boyle, O. (2000). *Reading, Writing and Learning in ESL: A Resource Book for K-12 Teachers.* New York: Addison-Wesley.

Pérez, B. (1998). (Ed.), *Sociocultural contexts of language and literacy.* Mahwah, NJ: Lawrence Erlbaum.

Quintero, E. P. (2002). A problem-posing approach to using native language writing in English literacy instruction. In Ransdell, S. and ML Barbier (Eds.) *Psycholinguistic Approaches to Understanding Second Language Writing.* Amsterdam: Kluwer Press.

Quintero, E. P. (2004). *Problem-posing with multicultural children's literature: Developing critical, early childhood curricula.* New York: Peter Lang.

Quintero, E. P. (2007). Qualitative research with refugee families. In Hatch, A. (Ed.) *Early Childhood Qualitative Research.* New York: Routledge/Taylor and Francis.

Quintero, E. P. (2009a). *Critical literacy in early childhood education: Artful story and the integrated curriculum.* New York: Peter Lang.

Quintero, E. P. (2009b). Young children and story: The path to transformative action. In S. Steinberg (Ed.), *Diversity: A reader,* pp. 161–170. New York: Peter Lang.

Reed-Danahay, D. (Ed.) (1997). *Auto/ethnography : Rewriting the self and the social.* Gordonsville, VA: Berg Publishers.

Reyes, M. (1992). Questioning venerable assumptions: Literacy instruction for linguistically different students. *Harvard Education Review, 2*(4), 427–444.

Rogers, A. (1993). Voice, play, and the practice of ordinary courage in girls and women's lives. *Harvard Educational Review, 63*(3), 265–295.

Rummel, M. K., & Quintero, E. P. (1997). *Teachers' reading/teachers' lives.* Albany, NY: SUNY Press.

Schissler, H. (2006). Containing and regulating knowledge or tapping into the human potential? Some thoughts on standards, canonization, and the need to develop a global consciousness. Paper presented at the conference National History Standards: The Problem of the cannon and the Future of History Teaching, UCLA-Utrecht Exchange Program and the Netherlands Institute for Teaching and Learning History, Amsterdam, The Netherlands.

Skutnabb-Kangas, T. (2000). *Linguistic genocide in education—or worldwide diversity and human rights?* Mahwah, NJ: Lawrence Erlbaum.

Soto, L. D. (2000). *The politics of early childhood education.* New York: Peter Lang.

Steinberg, S. (2001). *Multi/Intercultural Conversations: A Reader.* New York: Peter Lang.

Torres-Guzmán, M. E. (1993). Critical pedagogy and Bilingual/Bicultural Education Special Interest Group update. *NABE News, 17*(3), 14–15, 36.

Ullman, C. (1997). Social Identity and the Adult ESL Classroom. *ERIC Digest.* National Clearinghouse on Literacy Education, October 1997, ED413797.

Verhoeven, L., (1991). Acquisition of biliteracy: A comparative ethnography of minority ethnolinguistic schools in New York City. *AILA Review 8,* 61–74.

Willis, A. (1995). Reading the world of school literacy: Contextualizing the experience of a young African American male. *Harvard Educational Review 65*(1), 30–49.

Zou, Y. (1998). Rethinking empowerment: The acquisition of cultural, linguistic and academic knowledge. *The Teachers of English to Speakers of Other Languages Journal 7*(4), 4–9.

CHAPTER TEN

Vanessa Domine

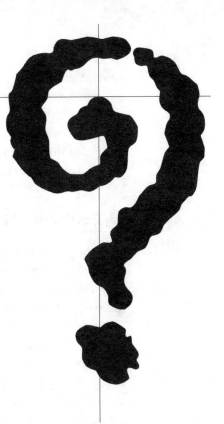

How Important Is Technology in Urban Education?

To question the importance of technology in urban education is to administer a pedagogical Rorschach test. The responses that ensue reflect deeper assumptions and beliefs about teaching, learning, and the purposes of schooling. More than a century ago, technicians introduced slate boards into classrooms, followed by film, television, teaching machines, and computers with the vehement hope that each new technology would revolutionize teaching and learning. Fast forward to the present, when government and industry on a global scale continue to exert pressure on educators and administrators to perpetuate technology through policy, curriculum, and standardization. The U.S. federal and state governments now designate technology as a separate subject area to be formally assessed—heightening already steep challenges such as overcrowding, high dropout rates, low test scores, and racial, ethnic, cultural, and linguistic diversity within urban schools. Designating technology as a separate subject area is myopic since curriculum cannot be separated from the technologies through which it is mediated—whether spoken, printed, electronic or digital.

Positioning technology as an educational panacea is also problematic in that it shifts much-needed attention away from the political, economic and social motivators that compel urban education. Today most people use the word *technology* to reference something computer-related, but the word was not associated with machines until the Great Exhibition of 1951 in London. Prior to that, *technology* denoted a methodology or a process of doing things that represented a particular way of thinking about the world.[1] Defining technology as methodology liberates its reference to one specific machine or discipline of study or even a course subject area and instead implies that political, social and cultural ideologies are woven throughout all bodies of knowledge, throughout all of education and even throughout our daily lives.[2] Through this chapter I assert the extent to which technology is an asset or liability to urban schooling hinges upon our ability as educators to achieve equitable access, overcome excessive standardization, embrace media literacy, and commit to professional development.

Achieving Equitable Access

Over the past ten years, the U.S. government has spent more than 40 billion dollars to place computers in schools and to connect classrooms to the internet. In 1997 the government subsidized a 2 billion dollar program called Educational Rate (E-Rate) to help schools and libraries obtain internet wiring and services. The program provided an up to 90 percent discount to schools with the largest number of poor children. The goal of E-Rate was to increase equity of access—to bridge the digital divide—across poor and wealthy communities within the United States. It accomplished this goal in many poor communities across the United States; however, the lack of administrative oversight in its implementation allowed for widespread fraud and abuse.[3] As of 2004, there were more than 40 cases of fraud and abuse being investigated by the Federal Communications Commission, the Department of Justice, and the Federal Bureau of Investigation. In some cases, telecommunications companies aggressively marketed unnecessary equipment to school districts, and in other cases never installed purchased equipment in the schools. As recently as 2009, a Texas school district's technology officer was convicted on bribery charges related to E-Rate contracts. The exploitation and abuse of E-Rate ultimately denied access to those with the greatest need for internet access.

Despite the challenges with E-Rate, nearly 100 percent of public schools in the U.S. currently have access to the internet as compared with only 35 percent of public schools in 1994.[4] Internet access has also expanded to classrooms, with 94 percent having internet access in 2005 compared with only 3 percent of classrooms in 1994.[5] Schools may be equipped with internet connections, but less than half of the U.S. student population actually accesses the internet while at school.[6] The U.S. Department of Education in 2004 decided to promote "ubiquitous access to computers and connectivity for each student," the U.S. Department of Education in 2004 unveiled a National Educational Technology Plan (NETP) that boldly identifies itself as a "technology-driven" educational reform (in noted contrast to educationally-driven uses of technology). Among the action steps recommended by the NETP are "creative" technology partnerships with the business community, improving professional development through online learning, and encouraging broadband internet access.

Broadband, or high-speed, internet access within urban education further complicates the discussion, as it is dramatically more efficient in handling *rich media*—a combination of text, audio, and video that supply interactive experiences for the user—yet it is also substantially more expensive. Data show urban dwellers have less access to high-speed internet than suburbanites, in part due to the cost to the consumer.[7] In Washington, DC, the nation's capital, nearly 160,000 residents have no internet access at all, more than 240,000 residents do not have internet access at home, and only 52 percent of homes have high-speed internet access.[8] Specific populations without high-speed internet access are identified as low-income households, immigrant populations and senior citizens. More than a decade after the establishment of E-Rate, the U.S. Government set aside stimulus money for increased broadband access in "underserved" and "unserved" areas as part of the American Recovery and Reinvestment Act (ARRA). The language used to explain the criteria for eligibility to receive stimulus money excludes many urban areas, however. An area was defined as unserved if at least 90 percent of its households lack access to minimum-speed broadband service of any kind. If more than 50 percent of the households already have physical access to broadband service (e.g., the capability to subscribe to the service upon request), then it does not qualify for stimulus money.[9] Economic stimulus to expand the availability of broadband networks in urban areas is a step towards increased equity, yet at the same time it does not address the fiscal inability of many urban families to actually subscribe to the broadband service. In this case, access does not equate service.

One alternative technological solution to the lack of internet access in urban communities is wireless broadband, or Wi-Fi. Wi-Fi is particularly beneficial for inner cities where schools and apartment buildings may be heavily laden with asbestos, thereby making it difficult, if not impossible, to install wiring and cable. From a technical standpoint, school administrators can create fairly easily large areas of wireless internet access, or *hot spots,* using an internet access point, a high-speed internet connection, and some form of password protection (to restrict outsiders from accessing the network). Densely populated urban communities can also benefit greatly from hot spots of free Wi-Fi service. One challenge is that it requires public–private partnerships between cities and telecommunications companies. Such partnerships may yield potential customers and therefore be a boon to the technology industry, yet the reality is that some internet service providers refuse to offer service to urban communities that may not be as profitable as their suburban counterparts.[10] A more civic-minded approach entails the implementation of Wi-Fi hot spots in parks, libraries, community centers, and small businesses can support the revitalization of urban centers by connecting citizens to services and to one another. In theory, city officials could purchase bundled hot spots to make a wireless community network and then allocate those services to the areas of greatest need within the city. Although socially transformative in theory, critics question the ability of public officials to compete with the private sector for the citizen-as-consumer. Currently, hot spots serve the travel and tourism industries—as evidenced by their relatively exclusive presence in hotels, restaurants, airports, and coffee shops. Critics also suggest the possibility of overburdening taxpayers with high maintenance systems, given the looming obsolescence of wireless broadband at the hand of smartphone (computer + phone) technology.

The use of mobile devices is expected to surpass the use of Wi-Fi to access the internet. In 2004, 66 percent of American adults owned a cell phone.[11] Current estimates are as high as 82 percent. In 2009, one-third of Americans used a cell phone or smartphone to access the internet for e-mailing, instant messaging, or information seeking. The dramatic increase in access to cell phones and their increased use for internet access begs the question, "Should cell phones be used in schools?" Some school districts ban the use of cell phones in the classroom, as it enables students to access controversial material on the web. Cell phones have created an easy avenue for cheating, as students capture digital photos of exams to circulate and text answers to one another. While the jury is still out on the (non)uses of smartphones in schools, it is quite possible that the mobility afforded through their use may translate into social and economic mobility for urban students and their families. Industry-sponsored digital pioneers are currently experimenting with smartphones in the classroom. In one study, ninth- and tenth-grade students in low-income neighborhoods were given high-end smartphones running programs specifically for algebra studies. The students recorded themselves solving problems and posting the videos to a private social networking site for viewing by their classmates. The study found that students with the smartphones performed 25 percent better on the algebra final examination than did students without the devices.[12] Looking ahead, we see that the digital divide of the late twentieth century may be only partially closed, as there remain significant barriers to internet access among urban populations. According to the 2008 *Technology Counts* report, technology access, use, and capacity in U.S. schools is merely average (76.9 percent). Despite federal efforts to level the playing field through policy efforts (e.g., E-Rate and the ARRA), internet access in urban areas remains a complicated and still unresolved issue. Meanwhile, technological developments move forward at a rapid pace.

A closer look at internet access *outside* of schools suggests socioeconomic, racial, and cultural disparities. While 99 percent of U.S. schools have access to the internet, only 60 percent of U.S. households have internet access.[13] Nearly all college graduates use the internet, as compared with only one-third of high school dropouts.[14] Nearly 100 percent of those who earn at least $75,000 per year use the internet, while only half of the population who earn less than $30,000 per year use the internet. Blacks and Hispanics are also less likely to access the internet than Whites.[15] Failure to resolve issues of internet access denies urban students and their families access to information, knowledge, opportunity, and the world at large. On a practical level, students cannot complete their homework assignments; families are prevented from taking online courses; parents cannot secure employment, and binational families cannot connect with relatives in other countries. On a pedagogical level, lack of access to the internet denies urban teachers and their students a global connection to a worldwide community and ultimately denies them an identity that extends beyond the self, something educators argue is essential to achieving social and political democracy.

The value of the internet, computers and smartphones lies in their capability to interconnect and consequently strengthen urban communities through a strategic use of communication technologies, such as e-mail, text-messaging, discussion boards, and live chat. We must remind ourselves that urban schooling is one component of a larger system that includes families, housing developments, community centers, schools, religious organizations, libraries, universities, and business professionals. One urban high school principal in Detroit was inspired by the technological savvy of her college-age children and chose to acquire computers and internet access specifically for increasing parental involvement in schools within the district.[16] The principal creatively assembled Title I funding and business partnerships to build networks between district schools and neighborhood housing developments. This orchestration of funding included monies for a technology coordinator and two computer labs both in schools and within housing developments. The principal supported community professional development where parents, teachers, and families collaborated on web pages for their classrooms and schools. The web pages announced school activities, and provided discussion threads for teachers, students, and parents to interact. What is particularly powerful about this systemic approach to technology is its insight into the importance of parental and family support in student achievement and reframing professional development as a communal activity. As shown in this example, most urban schools can compensate for the lack of equipment through localized school–community partnerships with public libraries, community centers and nonprofit organizations. If such networks can be forged and equity of access to computers and the internet can be accomplished by combined efforts and technologies within homes, libraries, churches, and community centers, then the educational value of the internet increases exponentially. The purpose is not to derive a formulaic vision or template for technology to then apply all urban settings or even urban education. Rather, the value of technology lies in facilitating and supporting a shared purpose within the larger urban community and an authentic educational need within the school classroom. Whether these connections happen through face-to-face communication or digital communication (or both) is secondary to the larger goal of building bridges between students and the communities in which they live.

Overcoming Excessive Standardization

According to the Education Commission of the States (ECS), low achievement of minority students is one of the most pressing problems in education. Of major concern in this regard is the *achievement gap,* or the disparity among student performance (e.g., test scores, grade point average, dropout rates, and college enrollments) and gender, race, ethnicity, ability, and socioeconomic status.

Currently the data show Black and Hispanic high school students achieve at about the same level as the lowest achieving White students.[17] To close this achievement gap the U.S. federal government enacted in 2002 No Child Left Behind (NCLB), requiring every identified racial and ethnic group to perform on grade level (or make adequate yearly progress). By 2014, all students must achieve proficiency in the subject areas of reading, math, science and technology. Under NCLB, students are also required to participate in the National Assessment of Educational Progress (NAEP), also known as the Nation's Report Card. Beginning in 2012, technology literacy will be assessed separately as part of the NAEP. In essence, within the next five years, students will be tested for technological literacy at both the state and federal levels. Ultimately, states develop their own standardized tests for technological proficiency. As of 2009, 44 states have either stand-alone technology standards for students or technology standards that are integrated into other student academic standards, and 56 percent of school districts meet the state definition of effective integration of technology.[18] Research indicates that technology is at its most powerful when used as a tool for problem solving and critical thinking.[19] Problem solving and critical thinking are key concepts woven throughout standards in other core disciplines and are now sanctioned by technology standards. Whether or not our high stakes tests adequately measure the use of technology to enhance critical thinking and problem solving remains to be seen.

The definition of *technological literacy* remains unclear. Under NCLB, technological literacy means young people are able to "exploit new technologies" and "enter the workforce and be competitive economically." Technology can refer to both a discipline of study as well as a set of skills to be acquired. If one subscribes to technology as a separate subject area then the focus is technology education—learning *about* technology and acquiring job skills. If one views technology as subordinate to subject area curricula then the focus is technology and curriculum integration—learning *with* technology for the purpose of academic achievement. To a certain extent, both of these approaches are reflected in National Educational Technology Standards for Students (NETS-S) created by the International Society for Technology in Education (ISTE) in 2000 and later updated in 2007. Following the creation of NETS-S in 2000, ISTE subsequently developed collateral NETS for teachers and administrators, illustrating the need for a systemic approach in standardizing the uses and study of technology in schools. The NETS-S cluster around core areas: creativity and innovation, research and information fluency, critical thinking, problem solving and decision making, digital citizenship, and technology operations and concepts. The first five areas lend themselves primarily to the integration of technology across curricula, whereas the sixth area (operations and concepts) caters to the vocational side of technology education.

Although technology is now a formal subject area with a growing body of state and federal standards, it is not necessarily fiscally valued or supported at the federal level. One federal mechanism for facilitating technological literacy under NCLB is the federal Enhancing Education Through Technology (Ed-Tech) State Program, the purpose of which is to improve student achievement through the use of technology in elementary and secondary schools. The original appropriation in 2002 was 700 million dollars to fund continuing, sustained professional development programs, public–private partnerships, and the use of new or existing technologies to support academic achievement (and standards).[20] Funding for Ed-Tech has decreased significantly, as is the case with many NCLB initiatives. The original 700 million dollars was reduced to 496 million dollars in 2005 and by 2008 appropriation was down to 267 million dollars.[21] While the federal government cuts funding, the clock continues to countdown to 2014 when all (100 percent of) eighth graders must be proficient in technology.

It is paradoxical that one of the most industrialized countries in the world is severely underfunded in educational technology. The increased standardization and assessment of technology as curriculum coupled with a reduction in federal funding sends a mixed message not only about the importance of technology in education but also about the value of those students and teachers within communities without access to current technologies. Increased standardization and reduction of funding have also created inroads for private sector sponsorship of public education. In 2002, leaders in business, education and policymaking assembled the Partnership for 21st Century Skills (P21) as a "leading advocacy organization" with the goal of "infusing 21st century skills into education."[22] The P21 organization is self-described as a "partnership," yet it is worth noting there are more partners from the technology industry than from education. The P21 vision implies learning with technology to support overall academic achievement, yet at the same time the mission of the organization is aligned with the vocational side of technology. The dual focus on citizenship and career skills plays out in the set of P21 standards or "Framework for 21st Century Learning" created in 2004. The framework "holistically" combines student outcomes with support systems. The student outcomes include information, media, and technology skills that are further defined as creativity, innovation, critical thinking and problem solving, communication, collaboration, and media literacy. The P21 framework is unique in its inclusion of media literacy and its alignment with NETS and NCLB technology standards.

Questioning the purposes and outcomes of increased standardization and assessment in the area of technological literacy is essential—particularly when business and industry are major stakeholders of public education in the United States. The economic imperative of technological literacy is understandable given the capitalistic, free market economy of the United States. However, the need for technological literacy for all students as driven by future economic need may not be a valid argument. The U.S. Bureau of Labor Statistics (USBLS) projects that more than three out of every ten new jobs created in the U.S. economy during 2006–2016 will not be technology related but rather in the healthcare, social assistance and educational services sectors.[23] The largest increases in employment will be in the professions of nursing, retail sales, customer service, and food preparation. Interestingly, computer software engineering trails way behind with the fifteenth largest increase in projected employment. Given these figures, we can see that even from an economic perspective, technology plays a minimum role in the future workforce for many young people. What these occupations do require, however, are communication competencies—both on interpersonal and intercultural levels. The workforce will become more diverse within the next decade. The White (non-Hispanic) labor force will decrease while Hispanics are projected to be the fastest growing ethnic group—with a 30 percent projected growth rate by 2016.[24] The questions we should therefore be asking are, "How do our standards and assessments address the market need for multicultural and intercultural literacies?" and "How can new technologies support multicultural education?" As technology standardization and assessment gain momentum during the next few years, it will be difficult (if not impossible) to make sense of the disaggregated test data given the characteristics of urban student populations as increasingly diverse, nonnative English-speaking, and with little or no access to technology.

Embracing Media Literacy

To view technology as merely a collection of tools or skills for teaching and learning ignores their tremendous power to *mediate* the communicative processes that comprise education. Calling attention to the *mediated* nature of education and curriculum questions the ways in which students, teachers, administrators, and policymakers make sense of the world. It also creates an awareness of ownership in the sense that those who control our technologies influence the information we have access to, and therefore have access to social, political, and economic power. Once students and their families have access to technologies (including the internet), they need more than research and information literacy skills to help them make sense of all the information. They need a process of inquiry and the ability to express understanding about the world at large. The more important question for urban educators is: "How can we simultaneously cultivate critical thinking, multicultural education, and technological literacy among students, given the challenges confronting them on a daily basis?"

The answer lies in *media literacy*—the ability to access, analyze, evaluate, produce, and communicate information using a variety of technologies.[25] Students might access and analyze crime statistics within their neighborhood and look at news media portrayals of crime within the larger community. They can evaluate to what extent the information about their community is not reported and how those representations compare with other communities. Are such portrayals accurate? Are they fair? Using technologies, students could produce a web site or documentary illustrating the results of their investigation. Other production and communication activities might include students using their cell phones to text one another as part of a collaborative writing assignment in the field. A teacher might ask students to use their cell phones to take photos to upload to their course blog or post updates on Twitter. Regardless of the technological device, it is within the progression of access, analysis, evaluation, production, and communication of information and ideas that students transform information into knowledge and knowledge into social change. In this regard, media literacy as *critical pedagogy* promotes a more active, participatory, and responsible student-citizenry than do the current government-sanctioned technological literacy standards. Policymakers have finally realized that technology skills alone cannot cultivate the type of citizenry required in the twenty-first century. Federal Communications Commissioner Michael Copps recently called for a

> sustained K-12 media literacy program—something to teach kids not only how to use the media but how the media use them. Kids need to know how particular messages get crafted and why, what devices are used to hold their attention and what ideas are left out. . . . No child's education can be complete without this.[26]

School-based conversations about technology therefore need to move beyond skill acquisition to include habits of mind that allow students to thoughtfully navigate the mediated world in which they live. The issue of inequitable access emerges yet again, as many urban schools have neither computer labs nor computers in the classroom and therefore struggle with achieving technological literacy for all students. Using technologies in the context of student-produced media requires reconfiguring classroom time and space and allowing students to immerse themselves in the content and to experiment with technologies they may not have access to outside the classroom. Such teaching and learning demand extended blocks of time—not the standard 40 minutes during the school day. In addition, media literacy renders obsolete the traditional role of the computer teacher and instead positions all teachers as educational leaders that orchestrate a variety of technologies to support classroom goals. A media literate view of technology empowers teachers to select what tools or devices will shape the classroom environment and how they impact students beyond the four walls of the classroom. Media literacy requires that educators abandon the technological elitism associated with computers in the classroom and embrace higher-level thinking skills across all media forms. It also requires us to ask critical questions such as: "Whose stories are told and whose stories are left untold by history textbooks? Through live and online museum exhibits? Through instructional films?" and "What publishers, producers and corporations are most likely to support the goals and interests of this particular urban community and least likely to commercially exploit it?" From a media literacy perspective, academic achievement has less to do with the physical mobility associated with laptops and wireless networks and everything to do with social, political, and economic mobility into a world of the student's own creation. Although some students may be more technologically proficient than their teachers, those students still crave the leadership and example of adults in their lives.

Equity of access, standardization, and media literacy all converge in the current technological climate of *Web 2.0*, which refers to web-based applications that are readily accessible on demand and allow users (learners) to produce their own content and then communicate it to a worldwide community. The most popular Web 2.0 features are the social networks (e.g., MySpace, Facebook, Xanga, and Bebo). In theory, social networks provide an opportunity for teachers and students to create and disseminate powerful messages using their own voices and perspectives and thus contribute to the social, economic, and political discourse. It is immediate and wide-reaching and creates a sense of individual empowerment as well as community belonging that can be stifled by the overcrowding, poor teacher quality, and language barriers that often exist within urban schools. Social networks can serve as a *third space* where educators can mentor young people and connect curriculum to everyday life.[27] The reality differs in that most educators find students' access to social networks during the school day to be a distraction and a liability. Most districts use filtering software to block student access to those web sites from the school network—although students can still access that content from smartphones. Only 50 percent of schools use honor codes to prevent students from accessing inappropriate material on the internet, suggesting that there is much work to be done in cultivating a sense of moral responsibility and digital citizenship.[28] Educators are, at best, cautiously optimistic about social networking in education. From a media literacy perspective, social networking technology may foster racial division; a recent study of users of social networking sites found Whites, African Americans and Asian Americans use Facebook, but that Hispanics are much less likely to use Facebook and much more likely to use MySpace.[29] Facebook users had parents with significantly higher levels of education than those of MySpace users, suggesting that social networking may also generate socioeconomic stratification among participants. These data are critical in coming to an understanding about the purpose and role of social networking technologies in urban education. If our task as urban educators is to interconnect with diverse groups of people and encourage students to seek world views that are different from their own, then social networks may not be the most appropriate technologies for the task. Regardless of the choice, without achieving a deeper technical and social understanding of social networking technology, educators will fall victim to runaway technology instead of focusing on diversity as the mechanism for social transformation.

Committing to Professional Development

We know from decades of research that technologies themselves do not cause substantial changes in schools.[30] Teacher professional development has been acknowledged as essential to pedagogical success with technology. It is not surprising that a lack of professional development and support in this area has been the biggest stumbling block to fully implementing technology in schools. Education programs do not adequately prepare preservice teachers to integrate technology into their teaching.[31] In the United States only 19 states include technology in their initial teacher licensure requirements. According to a 2007 U.S. Department of Education study, barriers to practicing technology during preservice teachers' field experiences include competing priorities in the classroom, lack of technology infrastructure in the schools, lack of training or skill, lack of time, and unwillingness on the part of supervising teachers to integrate technology in their classrooms.[32] Another government report notes the biggest gap in needs between high-poverty schools and low-poverty schools is the need for professional development in the area of using technology to meet the needs of English language learners, particularly in the areas of science and math. A similar gap exists in teachers' perceived need for professional development in improving students' technology literacy.[33] Teacher education is even sparser in the area of media literacy. Out of approximately 4,300 higher education institutions, only 61 report offering media literacy curricula. Of those media literacy curricula reported, only 20 percent are offered through education departments.[34] There is much progress yet to be made in the area of teacher preparation and learning technologies.

If teachers are informally learning about technology on a daily basis within their classrooms, professional development must be grounded in the reality of daily teaching experiences and allow for immediate transformation of what happens in the classroom. One-day district workshops where teachers are "released" from their classrooms to watch demonstrations of the latest technological tool are no longer relevant. Teachers need time and the freedom to experiment with a variety of technologies to discover their authenticity and impact on personal, professional, and ultimately pedagogical levels. Learning about technology is a transformative process that begins with experimentation at a basic level and grows over a period of time. The bureaucratic constraints of urban education make such experimentation close to impossible. In contrast, the democratizing structure of the internet creates a bottom-up mechanism for teachers to renew their practice and enact curricular and social change.

Web 2.0 offers tremendous possibilities for teacher education, particularly with little to no funding available to support professional development. Instead of districts hiring technology experts, teachers can access them (for free) on the internet and on demand. Instead of sitting through one-day workshop presentations, they can participate in live webinars or access streaming video archives when needed. Teachers can also create their own online communities of practice (in the form of blogs, wikis, and other online tools) based on their own professional needs, subject areas, and pedagogical interests. In theory, an online social network of teachers is ideal for technology professional development, as members can informally meet (online and offline) over time to contribute, collaborate, and reflect on their classroom teaching and technology practices. This supports a model of professional development that is transformative, fluid and focused on felt needs rather than top-down dispensing of information. The catch is that the value of any community of practice is determined by the contributions made by its members, which requires urban teachers to invest their time, effort, and technology. The payoff is that teachers can ultimately model the technology use and behavior they in turn expect from students.

Looking Ahead

The greatest potential for technology in urban education is not the top-down, bureaucratic approaches represented by increased standardized testing. Rather, it is the idea of knowledge as a social network that is collaborative, fluid, and systemic. As urban educators, we need to acknowledge the disparity between our students' digital reality outside of school and their lives within school. In addition, we need to acknowledge the socioeconomic, racial, and ethnic divides created and perpetuated through the uses of the internet and other technologies. Once we recognize these inequities, we can then determine to what extent our students need increased access and a deeper familiarity with these tools in order to meet state and federal standards in the area of technological literacy.

On the other hand, there are many young people who are chronically connected to their mobile devices (and to information) outside of the school day. Many prefer online communication as they have more user choice and access to content on demand, in dramatic contrast to having little control over their neighborhood and local community relationships. If we want our students to navigate racial, ethnic, cultural, economic, and political diversity, then face-to-face deliberation is essential to critical thinking and decision making. Face-to-face communication requires tolerance of immediacy, exposure, and vulnerability that is absent in online communication. As urban educators, we need to ask tough questions: "Can our students communicate (offline) effectively and civilly with one other? Can they speak eloquently and craft a logical argument? What is the purpose of the brick and mortar classroom?" It does not make much pedagogical sense to use face-to-face classroom time for students to sit behind a computer, other than for live technical demonstrations or a formal class presentation. Ultimately, however, it is the teacher's decision when an individual student needs more practice with the tools (technological literacy) and when the student needs to take a step back, unplug, and engage in critical reflection (media literacy). Perhaps a future purpose of our brick and mortar schools is to compensate for a decrease in face-to-face interaction among young people outside of the classroom. The classroom community can be a source of strength for student learning, as communication is immediate, transformative, and in real time.

It is purposive that the title of this chapter situates technology as a question rather than as a definitive statement. While the internet and its associated applications pose tremendous possibilities for urban educators and students, they also present numerous challenges from social, political, and economic standpoints.

How Important Is Technology in Urban Education?

Considering the highly mediated lives of young people and their increased access to technologies outside of school, urban educators might stop and reconsider the school classroom as one of the last places of refuge where our students are encouraged to unplug and reflect.

NOTES

1 . Ellul, J. (1980). *The technological system*. New York: Continuum.

Finn, J. D. (1972). Automation and education: Technology and the instructional process. In R. J. McBeath (Ed.), *Extending education through technology: Selected writings by James D. Finn on instructional technology* (pp. 141–160). Washington, DC: Association for Educational Communications and Technology.

Winner, L. (1986). *The whale and the reactor: A search for limits in an age of high technology*. Chicago: University of Chicago Press.

2. Downing, J., Mohammadi, A., & Sreberny-Mohammadi, A. (Eds.). *Questioning the media: A critical introduction*. (2nd ed.). London: Sage.

3. House panel expands probe into E-Rate program. (2003, March 13). Washington, DC: Reuters News Service.

4. Wells, J., Lewis, L., & Greene, B. (2006, November). *Internet access in U.S. public schools and classrooms: 1994–2005*. Washington, DC: National Center for Education Statistics.

5. Ibid.

6. National Science Foundation (NSF). (2006, February). *Science and Engineering Indicators 2006*. Arlington, VA: Division of Science Resources Statistics.

7. Wired less: Disconnected in urban America: A report on life without the internet in urban America. (2009). Internet for Everyone. Retrieved July 6, 2009 from http://www.internetfor-everyone.org/americaoffline/urban/intro

8. Ibid.

9. Opsahl, A. (2009, July 8). Broadband stimulus excludes urban areas, says city CIO. *Government Technology*. Retrieved July 26, 2009 from http://www.govtech.com/gt/700419

10. Wired less: disconnected in urban America: A report on life without the internet in urban America. Internet for Everyone. Retrieved July 6, 2009 from http://www.internetforeveryone.org/americaoffline/urban/intro

11. *Americans and their cell phones*. Pew Internet & American Life Project. Retrieved July 22, 2009 from http://www.pewinternet.org/Reports/2006/Americans-and-their-cell-phones/1-Data-Memo-Findings/06-This-survey-and-the-state-of-the-cell-phone-population.aspx?r=1

12. *North Carolina Department of Public Instruction and Digital Millennial Consulting Join with Qualcomm to Give 100 Smartphones to Students in North Carolina*. Public Schools of North Carolina. State Board of Education Department of Public Instruction. News Release. Retrieved August 10, 2009 from http://www.ncpublicschools.org/newsroom/news/2007–08/20080204–01

13. U.S. Census Bureau (2007, October). Computer and internet use in the United States. Retrieved July 21, 2009 from http://www.census.gov/population/www/socdemo/comput-er/2007.html

14. Demographics of internet users. Pew Internet & American Life Project. Retrieved July 21, 2009 from http://www.pewinternet.org/Trend-Data/Whos-Online.aspx

15. Ibid.

16. Means, B., Penuel, W. R., & Padilla, C. (2001). *The connected school: Technology and learning in high school.* San Francisco: Jossey-Bass.

17. Education Commission of the States (2009). Demographics: Overview. Retrieved July 29, 2009 from http://www.ecs.org/html/issueSection.asp?print=true&issueID=31&subIssueID=0&ssID=0&s=Overview

18. U.S. Department of Education. Enhancing Education Through Technology (Ed-Tech) State Program. Retrieved July 25, 2009 from http://www.ed.gov/programs/edtech/index.html

19. Sandholtz, J. H., Ringstaff, C., & Dwyer, D. C. (1997). *Teaching with technology: Creating student-centered classrooms.* New York: Teachers College Press.

20. U.S. Department of Education. Enhancing Education Through Technology (Ed-Tech) State Program. Retrieved July 25, 2009 from http://www.ed.gov/programs/edtech/index.html

21. Ibid.

22. Framework for 21st Century Learning. Partnership for 21st Century Skills. Retrieved August 10, 2009 from http://www.21stcenturyskills.org

23. Tomorrow's Jobs. *Occupational Outlook Handbook, 2008–2009 Edition.* United States Department of Labor, Bureau of Labor Statistics. Retrieved August 10, 2009 from http://www.bls.gov/oco/oco2003.htm

24. Ibid.

25. Aufterheide, P. (1992). *Proceedings from the National Leadership Conference on Media Literacy.* Washington, DC: Aspen Institute.

26. Copps, M. J., (2006, June 7). Remarks of Commissioner Michael J. Copps. *Beyond censorship: Technologies and policies to give parents control over children's media content.* Washington, DC: Kaiser Family Foundation. Retrieved November 1, 2007 from http://hraunfoss.fcc.gov/edocs_public/attachmatch/DOC-265842A1.pdf

27. Gutiérrez, K. D. (2008). Developing a sociocritical literacy in the third space. *Reading Research Quarterly, 43*(2), 148–164.

28. Wells, J., Lewis, L., & Greene, B. (2006, November). *Internet access in U.S. public schools and classrooms: 1994–2005.* Washington, DC: National Center for Education Statistics.

29. Hargittai, E. (2007). Whose space? Differences among users and non-users of social network sites. *Journal of Computer-Mediated Communication, 13*(1), article 14. Retrieved July 29, 2009 from http://jcmc.indiana.edu/vol13/issue1/hargittai.html

30. Hawkins, J., Panush, E., & Spielvogel, R. (1996). National Study Tour of District Technology Integration: Summary Report. *CCT Report No. 14.* Center for Children and Technology.

31. Bell, L. (2001). Preparing tomorrow's teachers to use technology: Perspectives of the leaders of twelve national education associations. *Contemporary Issues in Technology and Teacher Education, 1*(4), 517–534.

    Levine, A. (2006). *Educating school teachers.* Washington, DC: The Education Schools Project.

32. Kleiner, B., Thomas, N., & Lewis, L. (2007). *Educational technology in teacher education programs for initial licensure.* Washington, DC: National Center for Education Statistics.

33. U.S. Department of Education (2009). Evaluation of the Enhancing Education Through Technology program: Final report. Retrieved July 28, 2009 from http://www.ed.gov/rschstat/eval/tech/netts/finalreport.html

34. Silverblatt, A., Baker, F., Tyner, K., & Stuhlman, L. (2002). Media literacy in U.S. institutions of higher education. Retrieved August 12, 2009 from http://www.webster.edu/medialiteracy/survey/survey_Report.htm

CHAPTER ELEVEN

Winthrop R. Holder

How Can Urban Students Become Writers?

> I know it's been forever and a day since I e-mailed you, but that's mainly because I've been wrapped up in these stupid classes. Let me say class (English) [sic].

I received the above e-mail from one of my former students. Her name is Kenesha Vassell. I was then at the midpoint of this chapter. She is a freshman/sophomore in Florida. I suspected her note was a call for help. The following night I received another e-mail. It read:

> I'm . . . send[ing] you two of the essay that I had to turn in, one which was due today. I know they might sound a little bit on the stupid side, but that's only because I really don't like doing her essays. She puts too much emphasis on little things. Not to mention how uninteresting the . . . topics are. . . . Her intentions may be to teach us to write, but it is difficult to write about things that are retarded. (LOL). Well, here they are . . .

I was more than a bit shocked. Kenesha Vassell had been a prolific writer both in my sophomore global history class and in her junior year, when she graduated. Moreover, two years after graduation she was instrumental in encouraging my "current" students. They had started a journal like the one Kenesha had edited while in high school. Acting as a coach of sorts, two years after graduation, she contributed an article to the new publication. Her commentary was well received by students two or three years her junior. Her crisp and provocative writing style spawned a mini debate within the group.

I began asking myself what had gone wrong. If this student was really an effective writer in high school, why was she having such difficulty with compositions in college? If one of my more stellar students was having so much difficulty with college writing, how credible was I in writing about how to teach writing to urban students?

I thought about her predicament. She was being asked to write about things that were to her "retarded." The topics weren't personal and emotional. When topics are personal and emotional, students find meaning. They write. I reflected on my very own difficult experience with college writing. Outside of the classroom I wrote profusely. Within the classroom my English professors thrashed my writing. Rather than accept my high Cs, I would argue or challenge the professors and end up with different grades: high Ds and low Cs, except in one speech course. For most of my college friends, science was the bugbear. For me, writing, was my Achilles' heel, or so my professors would have had me believe. There was a double irony at work here. At the time, I couldn't understand how I could have been so mediocre in English (writing) but do so well in speech. It was as if my speech professor were saying to me: "Although the other English professors do not think you know how to write, you certainly know how to talk and transcribe speech."

Yet, all that is written is worthwhile. All that is written should be accepted and praised. Suggestions can be given as to how it can or should be improved. This way the teacher builds on what the student offers and encourages rather than demoralizes and silences the student.

I was the first in the family to attend college. There was no one to at least inform me of how to navigate the English department or to temper my speech. I could have gotten better grades in college writing and other courses in which critical speech or talking back, was a potential liability. Kenesha was like that also. She had an outspoken, fiery, tell-it-like-it-is disposition. I realized that I had to come up with thought experiments that could perhaps allow her to discover ways of navigating and surviving her college writing courses.

In writing this chapter (outlining a framework on how to teach writing to urban high school students), communicating with her became a part of the process. I e-mailed her. I reiterated what I had always told her, that she could write. I shared my college writing experience with her so that she could realize that while she may have problems with the professor's approach, this did not necessarily mean that there were any major problems with her writing.

My task, then, was not so much to help write her paper but to find a way to further demonstrate her writing prowess in such a way that she would disabuse herself of the notion that she couldn't write. Two weeks passed. I thought that Kenesha had reclaimed her former writing prowess. Then I was confronted by this e-mail:

> Subj: I need help
> Date: 3/6/03 10:50:32
> Mr. Holder
>
> I have a report due on Wednesday, but I can't figure out a thesis statement. I'm pretty sure, well at least I would hope that you know what that is. It's supposed to be a compare or contrast essay and I can't think of anything. Nothing political (LOL). I'll give you an

example of what someone wrote. The thesis was: Although having roommates does have advantages, when it comes to sharing a bathroom, living alone is the better choice. And then her three topic sentences were: When living alone, the chance of having to take a cold shower is much more than when living with roommates. When living alone, someone barging in on you while in the bathroom is not such a dilemma than it is when living with roommates. Running out of bathroom supplies happens more often while living with roommates than while living alone.

I will be greatly appreciative if you could help me find one.

Nesha.

After rereading this e-mail, especially the last sentence, about helping her find what was already present in her writing, I became even more convinced that the key to unlocking Kenesha's predicament was hidden in plain sight before our very eyes. And it was while reflecting on an appropriate response that I recalled Freire (1997) saying:

> The pitfall of a linguist is to believe that writing words is freezing them in time. Writing fixes the force of orality in time, but the reader, in engaging with that force, is continually reinventing and redialoguing, and so the text remains alive and unfrozen (p. 31).

This realization led me to think of a way not only to concretize my assertions about her ability to conceptualize and write but also to devise a mode for her to revisit, reengage, and reclaim her words which were frozen in *Crossing Swords,* the high school publication of which she was a member of the editorial collective. So titling my email, "Much Ado about Little," I wrote:

> Nesha:
>
> There's very little that your professor is requiring of u that you did not do in high school. Reread your writings in *Crossing Swords,* especially the following essay which you wrote in your junior year and evaluate it 2 determine to what extent (if any) it conforms with your professor's desire 4 a thesis, topic sentences and development, etc.
>
> Remember what I've always said that u r an intuitive writer and that you are familiar with, and use many of the writing techniques/conventions that your professor may be introducing as something esoteric. . . . After rereading your essay I want an answer to my questions. . . . Have u been writing within or outside the convention?

In the essay, entitled "Classroom Melodies: Giving Voice to the Voiceless," which I attached to the e-mail, Kenesha Vassell had written:

> Finding a classroom where it wasn't the same routine of entering, answering the "Do Now" and for the rest of the period copying notes, came as a shock and surprise to me. I wasn't used to debating and I never enjoyed participating in class. For, I wasn't accustomed to being in a classroom where students' voices were given such respect. The "calypso classroom" is how I would describe my tenth grade Social Studies class. I use this term because calypso is a form of music where different instruments and beats are used to form one melody. Although all instruments are not always in harmony and sometimes appear to be fighting each other for dominance, the mix always provides a beautiful end product: harmonious music.

As our classroom was filled with students presenting different opinions and points of views this often led to frequent heated debates that weren't always harmonious. But in the end after debating, our ideas either enlarged those of our opponents or we were able to help each other to see and appreciate another side of an issue. This constant give and take is what made the class so different.

Learning is supposed to be enjoyable as well as informative. Even though learning does not only take place in the classroom, it begins there. So part of the responsibility lies on the teacher to make students want to learn. *In order for students to learn, the classroom cannot be conducted as a dictatorship where students' **voices are silenced and the teacher has all the say**.* If it is that way all the time and students are not able to question the teacher's "facts" or ask why or how, students may not be excited about learning. Instead, they would be forever asking themselves: "Why is my answer wrong? Why won't the teacher listen to what I have to say?" As a student, I have noticed that some teachers just don't care anymore. Part of the problem is that some teachers don't know how to get students involved. They seem not to know how to engage and excite students about learning.

Although I was lucky enough to find a good teacher who actually loves to teach, what about the other students who may not be as fortunate? Why should they be stuck with a teacher whose motto is: "I don't care if you don't want to learn because I could just sit here and get paid?" How can you expect someone to want to learn in an environment where the teacher doesn't care or where he or she doesn't know how to make the classroom interesting? Maybe if these teachers would stop worrying about getting paid and put their interest into teaching, then students would want to learn. Then classes would be more interactive as in the calypso classroom, and fewer students would cut classes because they will now have something to look forward to.

Teachers do have a greater impact on their students than many people believe. For example, before the calypso classroom I never wrote anything beyond what was required in the classroom. *It wasn't until my history teacher encouraged me to start writing, not just in the classroom but also about whatever was on my mind, that I began to pay closer attention to my environment and began writing on a daily basis. And I've been writing ever since!*

Because we are teenagers, too many adults sometimes underestimate our knowledge and interests. They think because we hang out a lot or we may be chillin' in the hallways before class that we are unconcerned youth who don't know what's going on in our surroundings. That's one of the most serious problems with some of the adults. They like to stereotype us and put us into their narrow categories when all we need is someone to tell us that we're good and encourage us to reach for the stars. Everybody has a talent or skill! All we need is someone, even a teacher, to pull it out from us.

In the classroom I began to notice that my social studies teacher, the adviser, had a talent for pulling information from students by presenting topics in a way to involve the entire class in discussion. Even the "bad" students were interested. Everybody got a new identity from debating and writing. If you were a hall walker or a class cutter, you weren't known as that in the class, but as the person who either wrote a particular essay or made a unique point in a discussion.

The discussions and writings in the calypso classroom gave everybody a chance to be in the spotlight. It gave everyone the chance to voice his or her opinion and to appreciate the reaction of classmates. It created a sense of community because rather than condemning one another's viewpoints, we started to appreciate and learn to see the other side of an issue.

Writing gave me a new identity. As I walked through the hallways, many teachers, security officers, and even students whom I didn't know told me that they read something I wrote. Writing has also enabled me to get involved with positive activities such as The Society for Social Analysis and my school journal, *Crossing Swords*, of which I am now the senior editor.

Writing has also been a way for me to express my feelings and voice my opinions on many issues that are of concern to me. Like Garfield McNeill, my fellow classmate, once wrote, "The pen is mightier than the mouth!" and I would definitely agree. Just saying something verbally may account for very little, because as fast as you say it, that's as fast as it may be forgotten. It's when you write that you actually make and leave your mark. People start to notice and understand you and that's when the voice of the voiceless is finally heard (*Crossing Swords*, 2000, pp. 30–31).

Does this essay read as coming from someone who would be unsure of her ability to come up with a thesis and supporting data for a college composition? I well remember Kenesha's words when she submitted the essay to me: "Would you believe that I never write such a long essay in English where I get credit for writing, but here I am writing my behind off for no credit for you and your magazine?"

"Since when do you write for me?" I asked.

"A'ight, don't give me another lecture about Rosemarie. . . ."

"Yes, always remember Rosemarie Dunbar's words. 'Do we write only for our teachers and ourselves? No. We must begin thinking that we write for an audience beyond the teacher and the classroom.'"

"OK, Mr. H. I get it."

Kenesha's essay not only resonates through time but also captures the feelings and sensibilities of the generations of students before her who wrote in the journal. Why did they write so much when there was not the tangible or traditional benefit of credit and grades? Students had not only discovered a voice but also a vehicle to freeze their texts in space and time so that future generations, even themselves, could "(re)read . . . the(ir) written texts," envisioning it as "the reinvention of oral speech." It was only after reflecting further on both her essay and the March-April 2003 dialogue that I realized that far from 'teaching' students any techniques of writing, my classroom and the after school project it spawned had actually provided students with what Postman refers to as, "an inspired reason for schooling" (1996, p. 18), one that disparaged the reductionist focus on grades and preparation for passing tests. Instead, students discovered the joys and rewards of dialogue and discovery, as Kenesha so vividly underscores in her essay above. Moreover, by displaying a willingness to move along a "path where the effort of the thought was justified not by the finding but by the seeking" (Boorstin, 1999), they were displaying a commitment to not merely to "answering questions but to questioning answers" as my friend Danny Weil often says.

Hence, embedded within the writings of Kenesha and many of my students who mentored me was the notion that rather than teaching how, or even motivating them, to write, what we were in fact doing, intuitively, unknowingly, was fomenting an urge within them to write. Indeed, it was as if we had stumbled upon Freire's view that "technique is always secondary and is only important when it is in the service of something larger. To make technique primary is to lose the purpose of education" (Freire, 1997, p. 304).

However, to better understand the dialectic and drama as it evolves, we must turn to students' very own words, especially since, as Kincheloe et al. (1999) note, "often missing in the literature written for teacher education are student[s'] thoughtful discussions of teacher [mis]education" (p. 242). As a corrective, then, we must reinscribe students' distinctive voices where they can be most helpful: in discussions of the theatre of urban education. What better way to create reflective teachers than by facilitating interactive settings wherein we become students of our own students and classrooms? Indeed, it was a rereading of Kenesha's high school essay and her explanation of how I encouraged her to celebrate the poetry of everyday life in her writings that led me to refocus this chapter from teaching writing to fostering a community of writers. Key to this reconceptualization is our ongoing dialogue, serving as it has as the source text for this exegesis/contribution.

Perhaps no better resource fosters this sense of self-reflection more effectively than students' reflections or confessions on educational issues. Fortunately for us, between 1988 and 2000, each new generation of students and I collectively published more than 1,700 pages of student commentary on almost every facet of the human experience: war and peace, poverty and profligacy, communism and its demise, teen sex and its consequences, sense and nonsense, effective teaching and its antithesis, apartheid, truth commissions and reconciliation, military interventions and resistance movements, racism and its palliatives, shock and awe, and on and on.

How, then, did we get students to write so insightfully and profusely? Did we infuse the classroom with writing techniques or was there a simpler narrative at work, creating communicative communities across space and time, akin to Chaucer's *Canterbury Tales?* Can there be many dissenting voices to the proposition that students compose more freely, creatively, and profusely when they envision writing simply as tale telling—as practiced uninhibitedly in their natural environments in the lunchroom, ballpark, or when chillin' with friends? In these theatres of resistance no one dares censor their rap as they venture, sometimes unwittingly, on a literary pilgrimage to self-knowledge.

However, before we interrogate the writing of a few more students, perhaps it may be best to isolate from Kenesha's essay some of the key ingredients that, in her view, foster a community of writers:

- respect of students and their ideas (unsilencing of student voices)

- questioning that engages, excites, and involves the entire class in discussion (a reason or purpose to look forward to being in class)
- discovery of new self (from debating and writing)
- sense of community in which robust dialogue is encouraged and welcomed
- joy of movement away from routine or ritualized work to transforming, self-affirming engagements

Kenesha's 2000 essay may well have been the most extensive treatment of the nature and drama of the engagements in our classroom. But when, in the fall of 1998, she was first placed on my roster as a sophomore, she entered not merely into a classroom but, like her contemporaries, into a living tradition by participating in "the ongoing conversations that incorporate our past and shape our future" (Applebee, 1996, p. 3).

How was this conversation fashioned? From the start, were the students and I aware of what we were getting into? Perhaps the adult reflections of one of the very first students who set the tradition in motion may provide some insight into how a community of writers evolved, perhaps unwittingly. In the very last journal that was published before the school was unceremoniously closed in 2001 due—in a high-powered New York State review team's verdict[1]—to its consistent failure in all aspects of education and the fact that there was no redeeming qualities to the school, Ann M. Green in her essay "Moving Shadows: Retrospective and Prospective," wrote:

> One day I found myself in a strange and large place called high school. Over the years this large place became a comfortable and familiar place I now refer to as Hale (Sarah J. Hale High School). Even more familiar and equally memorable is the Society for Social Analysis and the journal that arose from it, *Crossing Swords*. The history of the Society and the Journal is intriguing.
>
> It all started with a small group of students in pursuit of a medium to express their creativity. Under the guidance of a persistent social studies teacher, affectionately known as Mr. Holder, even to those of us now in our late twenties, the group bonded together to form the Society for Social Analysis. During the first few weeks, the group experienced great turbulence as we tried to organize our inexperience into a corporate-like organization. We did not know at that time that our mentor had no idea where the collaboration of such terrific energies would lead, as he later admitted. However, like the intellectual development of young people, we each contributed something different and combined our contributions to create another step on our way to the pinnacle of our potential.
>
> We were given the opportunity to do something that would endure for years and we took it. Fortunately, yes fortunately, we did not know that it was an opportunity to train us for the future. Like most teens, I was simply hoping to finish the year of class that I had to endure with a teacher who wanted me to read, analyze, and react to some form of literary piece. Could anything be more frustrating than to have to write a few paragraphs or an essay five days a week for two semesters? *I was being forced to be my own teacher, teacher to my teacher, and to my fellow students as they were to me. Could it get worse—developing my thinking skills?*

So it continued week after week. *We wrote, read the writings of others, edited their works, and typed them.* The developments that came later were incredible. Not only were we thinking and acting like journalists and researchers, we had to go public with our work. Time went by quickly, we had a journal ready for the public to read, and we were organizing a small gathering of fellow students, parents, and teachers to introduce our creativity, ability, and potential. *This was our moment to affirm ourselves as productive people.*

We never had a public speaking class on our high school schedule, and so Mr. Holder must have thought it necessary that we be 'thrown' into one. We were out front introducing people, singing, and reading our works. Even more inconceivable, on a few occasions we were radio personalities on WLIB (1190 AM) and WBAI (99.5 FM). There we were telling a listening audience about our views on a wide variety of topics and how we came to be an "organization." What was happening to our quiet public school?

It seems like it was a good thing, because over twelve years later I am still speaking in front of people and The Society and the Journal are still going strong. I still marvel at some of the ideas and the way we formulated them into words. Recently [June 11, 1999], the Society had its Twelfth Annual Celebration and I was honored to be present.

Have you ever walked in on a speaker after the introduction was made and felt captivated by the ideas that were unfolding? Or, perhaps you've picked up a magazine with the cover missing and started to read something, anything. You might not know who the speaker is or what publication you're reading, but still you are deeply caught up in the depth of thought, imagination, and passion that went into the piece. This is what I got from the meeting and from the Journal. These young people are writing what they live, what they want, and they are speaking it, and more impressively they are doing it professionally. Professionally enough to use any cover on our unknown magazine. It could be *Time Magazine* or *Jet* and we could certainly introduce [students] as Langston Hughes or Maya Angelou. But for the good of posterity we'll call the journal *Crossing Swords* and we will call each author by (his/her) own name.

Roll call! Please stand up when you hear your name or when I say achiever or winner. Rosemarie Dunbar (my opposing sword), Vernette Olive, Mauricia O'Kieffe, Rabyaah Althaibani, Lakeshia Hudson, Shilue Johnson, Kenesha Vassell, Garfield McNeil, Natalie Aime Bien, Anicia Dalhouse, Ade Nicholson, Anicia Dalhouse, Ade Nicholson . . . , ACHIEVER, ACHIEVER, WINNER, WINNER, and I will keep calling until all of the children (young and old) stand up. I hope that you will echo the call for me. I hear one reply so far. Yes! That's my own voice (*Crossing Swords*, 2000, pp. x–xi).

Like the teenage Kenesha, Green, no mere Generation X materialistic conformist, Ann provides an up close view of the writing community as it took shape.

Engendering a Classroom That Matters

In more ways than one, 1991 was a watershed year. It marked the end of an era for the founders of the journal. The first generation of students graduated. After four years with the project did students and I have a sense—even an appreciation—of the nature of the writing community, flowing as it did from our classroom without borders that was evolving almost imperceptibly? Let's revisit two impressions from 1991. With graduation around the corner, Rosemarie Dunbar seized the opportunity to say "Adios!" She wrote:

Act I: *Freshman*

Everything new and different. Life had practically changed. No! Life had changed. Imagine my being in Sarah J. Hale for four years. Well, my four years are now winding down. **My long jail term is almost over**. For, what was four years of my life went by real quick.

Act II: *The Advisor*

A short persistent man who for me continued the interest Mr. Boles, my eight-grade social studies teacher in Junior High School, started. The Advisor, . . . a man you can speak with the human thing present in the beginning of the conversation. A man, unlike many others, who will say: "Yes, you have a point." Yet, not saying you're wrong or even right. But just saying, "You have a point Ms. Dunbar." But, the Advisor, a man who, if you listen to him, puts education in a 'nutshell' and pushes you to develop, sharpen, and even to reject your point.

Act III: *Social Studies*

I liked it in Junior High School and still do. For me, social studies has been my dream and fairy tale. It is my favorite subject and what I hope will be part of my adult life. I have experienced fairytales, drama and mystery in the classroom.

Social Studies, a love I started with Mr. Boles, has intensified. It's the well-rounded part of my curriculum. I can travel from English to math through Science and long to come right back to social studies.

Act IV: *Crossing Swords*

Crossing Swords—especially the first issue—is a combination of the three persistent parts of my whole as a student, friends being a part of my whole. For me, *Crossing Swords* has been my commander, my critic and my complaining and sounding board. This journal is the first solid piece of granite cast in what some may call my young life and serves as a release and a vehicle for my voice, my anger, my joy, and my all.

As a graduating senior, looking back on four years at this school, I am proud of our creation—a unique journal. Topics in each issue capture the joy and magic of the debates and events that have occupied me while I was imprisoned here.

Epilogue: *Thanks*

I thank . . . Vernette Olive, The Advisor and the library, across the street from the school, for providing the setting that helped in the development of a path-breaking journal and allowed me to walk away a young Black female with a hell of a lot to be proud of. Adios!" (*Crossing Swords*, 1991, pp. 12–13).

Education is more circular than linear. Though students' confessional narratives often reveal deep appreciation for teachers, we are as much beneficiaries as students. If as Kenesha Vassell says, "I never wrote anything beyond what was required in the classroom," I too must note that before immersing myself in the writing community I never wrote anything that was interesting. True, I wrote numerous graduate papers, which a few professors suggested that I could easily have, with a bit of revising, submitted to scholarly journals. And I even had a few articles published in newspapers and in the odd monograph or two, but the more I read students' works, the more I realized how much of my earlier forays into writing lacked flair, pungency and edge. So with 1991 being such a pivotal year, and after reading Rosemarie's and a few other students' reflections, I realized that theirs was a tough act to follow. Still, the resiliency flowing from our arena pushed me to, as students had, rise to the challenge of writing something, anything:

The summer of '87 had ended. When they came to the school, the leaves had begun to turn brown. Their faces were bright, but hesitant. In the classroom, they would produce bright moments.

Every class produces gems. Sometimes, it's the creative use of a word or phrase hidden in a mass of sentences. Or, a student's unique view may spark a heated exchange spawning flashes of brilliance.

Too many moments of brilliance are lost. Lost from our collective memory. Should these impassioned classroom voices be treasured? Can creative minds be nurtured? For four years students, with no hesitancy in their faces, have answered with a resounding "Yes!"

"Write! Write! You never know where your writings may end up!" . . . A student's rhetorical question lingers: "How can we write ten paragraphs of facts when we are provided with inaccurate and inadequate 'facts'?" Discovery of the rewards of going beyond classroom-texts inspired these scholars-in-formation to ponder complex issues.

If the premiere issue of *Crossing Swords* encapsulated the language of a student "uprising" against lethargic and inappropriate education, and the second volume served as the springboard from which students—at different points on the achievement-spectrum launched a "search for meaning," then in 1990, through "dialogue and discovery," they transformed classrooms from an area of darkness and silence into an enlightened arena of clashing viewpoints. This legacy is sure to inform and instruct the future.

In this issue, writers explore continuity in their thoughts and discover discontinuities. The range of topics is wide, yet the discerning reader will detect a single underlying theme: human creativity and the search for truth and social justice. Captured in this publication, then, are not mere words and phrases from discursive pens, but the essence of contributors' concerns and aspirations. By engaging parents and others—beyond the school—in discourse, students continue to break down the partitions insulating grade-levels, subjects, teachers and the community at large.

And now, as spring turns into summer, the pioneering contributors become the class of 1995. Undoubtedly, many would look back and view their high school accomplishments as inconsequential when compared with future achievements. Still, present and future contributors, standing on the shoulders of giants—the ninth-graders of 1987/88—will continually discover and develop latent talents while crystallizing the tradition of robust dialogue.

To be sure, this repository, "that we . . . creat[ed] from scratch and not in the image of any other magazine in existence" facilitated the birth of ideas and movement away from partial truths and allowed participants to blaze their own trail while collectively making an individual mark (Holder, 2007).

Today, it is fashionable for the educated elite—those who ru(i)n our schools—to speak about creating parent centers and encouraging community participation as if they are introducing a revolutionary concept to classrooms which, rather than teach to the test, value and affirm students' lived realities as part of the learning circle. Yet, within the first four years of our writing community, more than twenty parents had participated in a variety of tangible ways in the classroom by typing students' work, proofreading, providing critical feedback on student writings, chaperoning students to weekend civic activities, accompanying students to a live radio interview, and attending and addressing after school functions of the Society for Social Analysis. In short, by the publication of our 1991 journal, more than 180 pages long, our improvisational classroom was well on the way to constructing an indelible bridge, or a triad of hope and renewal among students, teachers, and parents/community. Indeed within the first four years of publishing the journal, more than 25 educational officials—including teachers, the principal, the superintendent, and college professors—in addition to fourteen parents and friends from the community, published critical, though supportive, evaluations of students' writings.

Two adult views suffice as a snapshot of the dynamic between our writing community and the wider community, which not only provided a protective shield for our battleground but also nurtured students' writing skills. Kester Alves, then a Hubert H. Humphrey Fellow at Boston University, opined:

> Crossing Swords marks a relevant, constructive and timely contribution to the evolution of a genuinely participatory approach to education, which should be popularized and emulated throughout the system. . . . The ultimate result will be the development of a self-confident, intellectually aware and expressive citizenry so essential to the maintenance of a dynamic and, indeed, a truly democratic society (1991, cover).

Reader, are you still there? Can you imagine the sense of fulfillment that students felt once they realized that their words were not, as Shilue Johnson observed, "squandered and tossed like pennies in the air" (*Crossing Swords,* 1997, p. 159), but were read with gusto, in corridors way beyond the school? This may well have been belated confirmation of ninth grader Rosemarie Dunbar's dictum: "If you think what you have to say is important enough to be said, then someone will think that your writing is important enough to be read." (*Crossing Swords,* 1988, p. 58). As such, by creating a lively writing and reading classroom community, students' work, after circulation within the school, was then critically appreciated by a burgeoning community of adults committed to facilitating, encouraging, and engaging students' distinctive voices while emoting concern for their developing social consciousness. In that sense we were, in fact, discovering that our classroom no longer had borders. It was against this backdrop that community activist Jane Califf, then chair of Brooklyn Clean Air Committee, noted: "It's terrific that students critique each other's essays. I haven't seen that before in collections of students' writings. That's surely a way to make students think" (1991, back cover).

The preceding two views were based strictly on a reading of students' works. One can only wonder what readers' reactions would have been if they had actually met some of the students, or even if they had had the chance to visit the classroom or the after-school meeting of the group, as Clara Williams repeatedly did over the 1989-1991 period. Reflecting on her interactions with the group and in a piece in which she challenged students to "Carry the Torch" she wrote:

> The last of the student founders of The Society for Social Analysis will graduate this June (1991). Will the journal, *Crossing Swords,* continue? Recently I attended an after-school meeting of the Society for Social Analysis and was struck by similarities of meetings of the past. Some of the founders/seniors were offering input but Opal Bablington, a ninth grader, chaired the meeting. I saw this as the passing of the baton of leadership and felt proud.

> But, I couldn't help but wonder if the new guards at the journal would have the same zeal as the founders? Would the Friday after-school meetings of the Society be the priority of the new members? Would they—if need be—do as I saw Ann Marie Green do many times . . . hobble to school at the end of the week on crutches to attend the society's meetings?

> You see Ann Marie was injured in school and this led to a leg cast and in-home tutoring. She did not have to attend school, but because of her commitment to the Society and its work, she came to meetings on crutches. Once, a snowstorm canceled a Friday meeting—but no one told Ann Marie—can you believe she came? That's commitment!

> . . . No longer can S. J. Hale students say "No one cares about what we have to say," or "No one even listens." *Crossing Swords* is yours. Use it; to fight back (against) the "adults," small minded enough to think of you as "failures." Use it! If you don't, who else outside of your teachers will hear you? (*Crossing Swords,* 1991, p. 150).

What was particularly moving about Ms. Williams' contributions and interactions with the group was that although her niece had transferred from the school in 1990, she continued arranging her work schedule to attend meetings of the group and for two years served as its de facto co-advisor. No condescending educational bureaucrat had to tell her and the many parents who continuously supported the group what real education looks like or train them about how to facilitate and nurture intellectual stimulation in their children. And in spite of all the claims from on high about how it takes a village to educate a child, few of the proponents of this view could recognize the interlocking layers of the village if the layers were in their face. Ms. Williams, an ordinary citizen, made extraordinary contributions to sustain our literal village, which was visible to all but the elite who utter nothing but vague platitudes while many urban teens wither away as the system atrophies.

Being a central link between community and school, Ms. Williams was in more than a unique position to chart the evolution of the writing community. In the 1989 journal she observed:

> Our future is safe! There is an abundance of future leaders. Our children are receiving what Dr. Carter Woodson described as a "real education . . . to inspire people to live more abundantly, to learn to begin with life as they find it and make it better." How do I know? I have seen the student contributors to the journal, *Crossing Swords,* in action.

> My first visit to the after school meeting of the Society for Social Analysis was a result of my niece having attended one of the Society's sessions and saying that she did not intend to attend another. It didn't make sense. I had read the first volume of *Crossing Swords* and thought it to be phenomenal. Several of my niece's essays were included and Social Studies was her favorite subject.

Where was the logic? To find it, I thought I would visit just once—drop in and drop out as parents/guardians are supposed to show a little concern—and see for myself what went on during meetings. I was in for a pleasant surprise. I didn't expect to see students governing themselves and Mr. Holder, the advisor, doing just that—being overruled when offering advice the students did not agree with. Strange? I thought so, too.

I experienced the joy of students voicing their opinions without being intimidated by sharp disagreements. I was impressed with the level and intensity of discussion: Students holding fast to their views and sometimes changing their opinions when confronted with their colleagues' more forcefully reasoned positions. I was also fascinated by their ability to criticize each other's writing and concerning themselves with the message and not the messenger.

The rotation of leadership roles was another pleasant surprise. Although there is a president, all members got the chance to chair meetings. Democracy in action? Was I dreaming? Since conducting meetings is a skill which needs developing, some meetings went smoother that others. Should they discard the practice of rotational leadership in the interest of "perfect" meetings? One member (Mauricia O'Kieffe) rationalized the situation: "Just because something is difficult to perfect, that doesn't mean we should stop trying."

My first visit was so fascinating that I had to return. Since then I have attended meeting frequently. I feel certain that the members and the contributors to this journal are making our society better, now and in the future (*Crossing Swords,* 1989, 60).

Ping. Ping. . . .
Subj: My essay due 2morrow
Date: 4/8/03 11:40:30 PM Eastern Daylight Time

This is the essay that I am turning in tomorrow. I just wanted you to tell me if i could write the intro the way i did, with the convo. I've been working on it all day, so I'm almost done.

Just from the tone and heading of Kenesha's e-mail I sensed that she had recaptured her old self. So without even a bit of trepidation I downloaded the essay and began reading:

"So what did you do last night?" says Kelly

"Nothing much. Just talked on the phone to Kevin," replies Jan.

"You're always on the phone with that loser. What you need to do is drop that zero and get with a hero," John interjects from way across the room.

"O.K. class, quiet down!" a booming voice shouts from the front of the classroom.

"So you going to the club this weekend? Kevin's friend will be there," says Jan.

Kelly replies, "O' word, I'll be there of course."

"Did anyone finish reading the chapter I assigned?" the same voice echoes.

John interrupts once again, "Man, that club is going to be crazy, I'll see you there, right, Jan."

This is a typical conversation that may take place in a classroom. The voice that veers from the front of the room is a teacher trying to take control of her class. Many students would have probably figured that out, because this is nothing out of the norm.

All I could say to her after reading this far in her essay was: "Way to go sis! Rage on!" I could feel the vibes oozing from her pen and the space from which she composed her narrative. If art mimics life, then, how many white swans must a skeptic see before conceding that swans are white? What, then, is the likelihood that at the very same time Kenesha was composing her introduction, I too was struggling with a similar construction?

Vignettes: Promoting Reading/Listening, Speaking, Writing, or Class Conflict?

You . . . broke the rules. You started that store, made room for black men and women, and didn't take no collection, and didn't tell 'em what to think. You . . . opened your heart. That's revolution, brother, rebellion against the rule."
—(*Walter Mosley,* Always Outnumbered, Always Outgunned)

Mr. Holder pushed us to talk. That's what we are doing; we are talking in the journal.
—(*Rosemarie Dunbar, WLIB 1988 radio interview,* Crossing Swords, *1989, 104))*

A specter is haunting American education—the specter of indigenous knowledge. All the prowess of the miseducated elite has entered into an unholy alliance to exorcise this specter: educational czars and their charlatans, administra(i)tors and sycophants alike.

It is high time those autochthonous educational change agents openly, in the glare of the shock and awe of the establishment, published their views, their intuitions, their inclinations, and met this nursery tale of the specter of indigenous knowledge with the banter and cantos of the dialectics of the oppressed.

To this end, disempowered students of all learning dispositions and disinclinations, in collaboration with recalcitrant teachers, have sampled pages from their rhyme books and produced this critical dialogue, encapsulating at times the spectacular vernacular of Ebonics, the language of resistance. . . . The educational system, misguided by its philosophy of poverty that stunts students' intellectual, creative, and emotional growth, is rearing its own gravediggers.

The history of all hitherto authoritarian classrooms is the history of class struggles. Serenity and impatience, fluidity and rigidity, stasis and mobility, in a word autonomy and dependence stood in constant opposition to one another, carrying on an uninterrupted didactic monologue in the theatres of discourse, discord, and dystopia . . .

It was against this backdrop that one afternoon during the 1989–90 school year, as students ambled into the room and took their seats, I went to the chalkboard and began writing:

How Can Urban Students Become Writers?

Do Now: Explain each viewpoint and state to what extent you agree or disagree with each:

Viewpoint #1: "'And there would come a time when nations would beat their swords into plowshares.' (Isaiah) Finally we are at that time!"

What are plowshares? Did you see the Grammies last night? Isaiah tore up the place! Nah. You mean . . . Which Isaiah? Isaiah Thomas, the Celtics guard? Be serious, don't you know your Bible? And, what u know 'bout the Bible? Wait up, I'm no nonbeliever. What are plowshares? Ignoring the voices behind my back I continued writing . . .

Viewpoint #2: "A great democratic revolution is taking place in our midst; everybody sees it, but by no means everybody judges it in the same way."
De Tocqueville

Talking intensified. So I said: "I hope you know how to copy and talk and think and listen at the same time and . . ." *What's wrong with him, springing names and words on us just like that? If we never heard of Toc . . . whatever, how can we know what he means? It was the bomb! What? The Grammies. I don't have time for this!* His "Do Nows" is a simple statement, *just read it and even you might understand. Don't try to play me or else it's on. Every day is the same thing. You hold me back when I want to absorb info like a sponge. Can I hold the pass? Hi cutie, can I have your digits?* That's enough! Settle down and consider the statements and give it your best shot. That's all I ask. *But how can we when we never heard of them. I have one more. Are we supposed to answer all? Yes! You Odin or what? Why not give us a break?*

Viewpoint #3: "You never judge a system by its adherents; you don't even judge a religion by its believers. You shouldn't judge socialism by its adherents, judge it by its principles."
Kwame Toure (Stokely Carmichael)

We work everyday, why not lighten up? OK. Rows 1 and 2 respond to View #1; rows 3 and 4 do Viewpoint #2, and Row 5 do Viewpoint #3 and #2. *Why two for us and we have the least people?* Because you can bear the burden.[2]

No way am I doing two for the same credit as everybody. Don't you know he doesn't give credit for busy work? Later for him then! Who is Kwame what? That doesn't even sound like a real name. And on and on . . . Until from the back of the room I heard a student who rarely attended classes shout out, *What kind of history teacher are you and your students don't know 'bout Stokely Carmichael's Black Power?*

I responded, "Why not tell us more about Stokely Carmichael?" The student obliged us for a minute or two. I asked the class, "What then do you think Toure means by the statement?" Discussion ensued until someone said, "If a priest does wrong that does not mean one should give up on religion."

I interjected, so if there are problems in socialist states, what does that mean?

A near unanimous response: "Communism is bad!" "But . . ."

Next we moved on to a discussion of Isaiah's statement. After a few questions someone was able to ask, "Is the statement saying that nations would, instead of preparing for war, prepare for peace?" *Make food, not war.* Someone from Row 5 retorted, *You mean make love, not war?*

Then I asked, "Which New York building do you think would be the most appropriate to place Isaiah's statement on?" *The Empire State Building.* Why? *It's the tallest building so everybody would be able to see Isaiah's graffiti. Be serious, it should be on the Twin Towers. That's the tallest building. Why not on the library or the Pentagon?* A student from Row 5 quickly retorted, *When did it move to New York?*

Again the student at the back of the room put up his hand and said, "It should be on the United Nations building."

I asked, "Why?"

"Duh. Isn't that what the U.N. is about, making peace?"

Writing her skillfully titled "Classroom Hysteria" and reflecting on her 1997–2000 classroom experience, Anicia Dalhouse may well have captured the timbre and flare of the intellectual battleground that was the classroom. Dalhouse noted:

> The environment in that classroom was different from all of my other history classes. All the teachers seemed to be so uptight in the classrooms, to the point that it contributed to kids not wanting to learn. But my sophomore teacher left room for hysteria in the classroom. He truly realized what was necessary in order to teach teenagers. There had to be times for hysteria, but he knew when enough was enough.
>
> Throughout the term my friends and I who sat in the back of the classroom used to complain about the room being too cold [whether or not it actually was], just to cause a distraction from doing the work, but the teacher outsmarted us by telling us that we had an air conditioner in the back of the classroom. That was one of our everyday laughs…
>
> After being in the classroom for a while I began to realize that the teacher wanted to see kids achieve in school and he complimented us all the time about our good answers or the good essay and even the good point that was made in class yesterday. I think that was one of the teacher's key characteristics in motivating me to do well in his class. I was a talkative child in school—the one with the smart remarks who pointed out every joke. So it was a miracle that my social studies teacher caught my attention. Everybody knew that I hated school and hated work, especially writing essays, because they required too many paragraphs.
>
> My friends and I used to often joke that Mr. Holder only gave us essays because he wanted writings to put in *Crossing Swords*. But the more I wrote, the more the teacher complimented me about my ideas and writing. [H]is ability to listen to students, no matter how small their deeds may be, and make that child feel motivated to learn is what makes him so unique. His keenness to encourage children's ability to express their thoughts on paper and to motivate them to learn history is what makes the teacher so special. It was my history class that motivated me to excel in school (*Crossing Swords*, 2000, p. 32).

Suddenly, the hand of a student whose head had been on the desk as if sleeping since the beginning of the period shot up; without even waiting for me to acknowledge her hand and pronouncing Tocqueville flawlessly, she said, "I get it he was talking about the revolutions in the Soviet bloc against communism." After placing Tocqueville in historical context and making a mental note to present them with an excerpt of his writing, we considered the breaches in the Soviet Union's former Iron Curtain. But, before we consider the responses that were written stemming from the classroom discussion, let me present the introduction to the section of the journal in which many classroom essays were preserved.

> It's ironic to think that what took decades to build could have been easily destroyed in a matter of seconds. This just proves how effective organized masses of people can be.
>
> As you may know, the world has been going through tremendous changes; South Africa, Eastern Europe, Panama and that's just to name a few countries [sic] where important changes have taken place within the last year. The people in these countries with the moral support of the world fought the injustices they were experiencing [from] their governments.
>
> Right now I believe the world is just watching and listening as if it were a sleeping giant. People are forging bonds and this is most essential to provide a better future for future generations.
>
> In this section you will find various controversies as students discuss the changes in today's world. These students decided to share their views on the world with the world (*Crossing Swords*, 1990, p. 95).

This was the way that Nikki Burton, a senior, introduced the section, "As the World Turns and Warms up, Walls Crumble!" in the 1990 journal, which dealt with world issues. Writing in that section, Judy Forbin, then a sophomore, offered "What's LEFT? Communism's Sinking Ship?"

> It is . . . two and a half times the size of the U.S.A. Located on the . . . Eurasia landmass, most of it has mid-latitude wet and dry cold winter climate. If geography serves us well, we are talking about The Soviet Union.
>
> Russia's geographic factors have had a large impact on its history. Because it had few natural barriers it was easily invaded. In earlier times the Moguls invaded. This kept Russia out of the Renaissance and pushed it further behind culturally than the other European nations.
>
> At the beginning of the twentieth century Russia was ripe for revolution. The wide gap in living conditions led people to fight for land reform, food, and social justice. By 1917 the Russian Revolution was successful and communism was introduced. After the revolution there was civil war (1917–1921).
>
> In 1917 Vladimir Lenin became the leader of the . . . world's first proclaimed communist state. Lenin decided to adapt the ideas of Karl Marx, the father of communism. Ever since that time the U.S.S.R. has pursued the goal of establishing a workable communist state. . . .
>
> In 1985 Mikhail Gorbachev became the leader. He was from a younger generation and apparently had a more liberal outlook. He espoused a policy of glasnost, which means a new openness in Soviet society. He took small but meaningful steps to increase citizens' individual freedom. He also freed political prisoners.
>
> As a result of this openness, the people of Lithuania and other republics are fighting for their freedom from the jaws of communism. Even in the Soviet Union as all over the

world, especially in Eastern Europe, people are realizing that the 'great' communist Empire is failing around the ears of its fathers; the Brezhnev's, Khrushchev's, Gorbachev's, and all the other 'chevs.'

Gorbachev championed the idea of 'perestroika' to deal with economic problems. By this policy he intend(ed) to lessen the role of central planning, or total government control of the economy. Certain capitalist economic policies will now be allowed.

In foreign policy issues Gorbachev has taken a hands-off policy in internal events in Eastern Europe. No longer is the Soviet Union willing to 'preserve communism' at all costs. This 'democratization' of Russia's foreign policy is the greatest change of all.

In the past, countries of Eastern Europe were forced to live under very oppressive governments and conditions. This relaxation of power allowed the people to rise up and change their governments. The falling of the Berlin Wall in August 1989 was "the straw that finally broke the camel's back." Then the domino effect took place. Countries like Hungary, Rumania and others began demonstrating for a democratic government. The people of Eastern Europe want freedom; freedom of speech and religion and the ability to trade and travel as freely as other peoples of the world.

I hope that the march to democracy continues and just maybe it will be the end of communism. Many people now realize that communism does not work! (*Crossing Swords*, 1990, pp. 96–97).

From today's standpoint, where can we find students' impressions of some of the earth-shattering events of the last 15 years of the twentieth century? It is this sense, we were creating not only a writing community but also a repository— a time capsule, if you will—of students' developing internationalism and civic consciousness. Not to be outdone, junior Tricia Parris, spoke about the "Triumph of Democracy or Collapse of Communism":

COMMUNISM! What is it and what did it do to people? Can we do without it? Why has it faded?

In *Webster's New World Dictionary of the American Language* communism is defined as "any theory or system of common ownership of property." It is socialism as formulated by Karl Marx and Lenin as well as many other individuals. . . .

In August 1989, the Berlin Wall, which separated communist East Germany from West Germany, was opened after 26 years. Today some people refer to it as a gate of peace. The gate became a symbol of peace and hope as East and West Germany came closer together. This celebration of happiness showed that there was indeed an end to communism in Eastern Europe. Now people are concerned about the power of a unified Germany. Can Germany bury its past? . . .

In the 1940's the communists came to power in Rumania. The government was able to quickly establish total control over the society. Despite an orderly society, the people faced numerous hardships; food shortages, denial of basic rights and the ability to practice one's religion and freedom of speech. These were a few of the many hardships which citizens faced for almost a half century.

In December 1989, Rumanian citizens got rid of their leader, or, should I say dictator? At first the leader was able to get away. . . . However, they later captured and executed the dictator. Some people who were fighting to overthrow communism said that if they lose the war then they would lose their lives. The people won. You could see the joy on their faces. A sad era had ended. They were cheerful and hopeful for a better life. . . .

As I look at the global village I see people breaking away from communism in Poland, East Germany, Hungary, and now Rumania. Is the U.S.S.R. next? (*Crossing Swords,* 1990, pp. 98–99).

As can be seen, students demonstrated intense interest in worldwide struggles for freedom, going beyond a mere concern with grades and passing tests. They, therefore, were not merely recording history as filtered through their collective eyes, but also making history. The intensity, passion, and insightfulness with which they were following and recording their interpretations of world events reminds me of Friedrich Engels's reactions to Marx's *The 18th Brumaire of Louis Bonaparte:* "This eminent understanding of the living history of the day, this clear-sighted appreciation of events at the moment happening, is indeed without parallel."

To be sure, given the symmetry of students' impressions of communism, one can easily dismiss these views as merely a knee-jerk reaction to press coverage of the time. How then should we view their views on the invasion of Panama, apartheid, and later the Gulf War that sometimes run counter to the popular, official view? By demonstrating such clarity of expression and prescience, were they not turning history on its head?

The students were writing at a time, during the waning years of the Cold War, when many felt that peace between East and West was on the horizon. This led to the coining of a new term to capture the hope of the post-Cold War era; in the media and wherever issues were discussed there was talk of the 'peace dividend.' It was within this setting that I circulated news articles, in addition to many of the writings from the 1988 journal, to serve as source texts for the 1990 discussion. Chsauna Jenkins's "Dividends of Peace? Watching and Waiting!" (in which she engaged in metacognition, thinking about her thinking) was framed with a note from the editors that reads,

"In the spring 1988 issue of Crossing Swords *Chsauna Jenkins, Ann Marie Green and Cindy Holley opined: 'Poverty is a very sad situation. [It] is far more important than a few nuclear threats! . . . Governments and citizens of the world should put forth a greater effort to aid those in need.' In the following essay Chsauna reflects on the original article in light of the lightning world changes."*

Over the years we have watched as AIDS and the homeless plagued the cities in our great country. We have also watched as the bridges began to wear and crumble down. At the same time we have watched as the country spent billions of dollars on instruments of war and on such 'urgencies' as sending men to the moon while poverty encircled the inner cities.

It's about time that the government started worrying about helping the people in our country so that when we do need defense, the country will have people to defend it. It's also about time we started being more concerned about life on earth instead of what's not on Mars.

Now that the tension between the U.S.A. and the U.S.S.R. has been eased both governments are beginning to cut back on military and defense spending. Now that there is less chance of war between the superpowers each has realized that [it doesn't] need to spend as much money on weapons of mass destruction.

If the changes—movement away from communism—were not taking place in Eastern Europe and The Soviet Union, I wonder if cuts in the military budget would have been possible. For, it is the money which normally would have been spent on weapons of war, which is referred to as the 'peace dividend.' Everybody proclaims that we are a step closer to peace. Are we really?

If we weren't a step closer to 'peace' would people and the government have been calling for increased funds for social programs to help the people of our country better themselves, and the country? How much longer would we have had to wait? More important, how much longer will we have to wait before we see some real progress in the inner cities? The government, the media and everybody can talk and talk about dividends of peace and the desire to make changes, but when will we actually see changes?

The government has some nerve. For years they have been spending billions of dollars on so-called military defense, and it is only when relations are improving with the Soviet Union that the leaders think about solving the wars, which have been going on for years, within their own country. I am still waiting to see the rewards of peace. (*Crossing Swords*, 1990, pp. 101–102).

Chsauna, demonstrating remarkable forethought and reading of the tenor and trajectory of world history, dismissed the notion of the peace dividend even before it caught on. And how on point she was.

Students' interest in world affairs knew no boundaries. As citizens developing with a deep sense of civic virtue and a commitment to preparing themselves to become knowledgeable and committed members of society, they debated the issues that were engaging the public.

Writing in opposition to the 1989 U.S. invasion of Panama, senior Natalie Bowen, opined:

It is not surprising, then, that there is a lot of anger, tension and resentment towards the United States government by Panamanians, especially amongst those who live overseas. . . . In 1983 the USA also invaded Grenada, dismantling its government and crippling the island. By these acts the United States successfully proved itself to be lawless and is thus looked upon as such by the majority of Latin American nations (*Crossing Swords*, 1990, p. 107).

The nature of the forum that we had created was such that the writing field was equalized, in that students in lower grades felt able to contest the views of seniors. Sophomore Andrea Fennicks challenged Natalie's views:

In the essay "Removing The Mask" Natalie Bowen argues that the U.S.A. had no right to intervene in Panama . . . I disagree with her views. . . .

If President Bush didn't defend our country and its citizens, people would have criticized him. Yet when the president acted, some people are still not satisfied! How else could the president have acted? He acted the best way he saw fit (*Crossing Swords*, 1990, p. 108).

How Can Urban Students Become Writers?

The debates continued, from year to year and topic to topic. Through it all, it was the students' desire not to remain passive receptacles of teachers' or the media's predigested truths that kept the dynamic of the discourse afloat, thus contributing to a robust writing community.

The Gulf War was a defining moment of the early 1990s, and, as was to be expected, students followed it assiduously. Within the classroom, I often shared different viewpoints on the issue as the springboard for classroom discussions and students' own developing civic consciousness. Indeed, we used two opposing views to frame the section of the 1991 journal, which presented views on the Gulf War. The section was presented thus:

"I object to those who would say that we lack patriotism. [N]o body in this House [of Representatives] or in this country is going to browbeat me about disagreeing with the President."

Charles Rangel (D-NY)

"If opposing injustice anywhere obliges [the United States] to become involved every-where, then only a fool would not prefer involvement nowhere."
—Charles Krauthammer, *Time Magazine*, March 4, 1991

These then were the epigrams that cast a distinctive glow on Patricia McGlashan's "*After The War: What Happens?*"

Why does America stick its nose all over the world? To this day the American govern-ment is yet to give a valid reason for rushing into war without thinking fully of the consequences at home and abroad.

At first the government claimed that economic reasons justified its presence in the Arabian Gulf; then our presence was said to be needed in order to safeguard American values. Later still we learned that the real reason was to safeguard Saudi Arabia; then it was to defeat a dangerous Hitlerite dictator. And, now we are learning that the real reason is really for the preservation of economic stability and "our way of life."

Since [Saddam] Hussein did not pull out of Kuwait on January 15, "mother hen" decided to protect her chick although many of her [other] chicks could have been roasted alive in the war fields of the Middle East.

The thousands of soldiers in Kuwait, named the crisis the "mom's war." Taking pictures, memories and lots of fear of not returning home, many female soldiers, some who are also moms, went to do their patriotic duties and left behind children and families. By law, women can't serve on the frontline, but who's to say where the frontline is?

The frontline is everywhere! These soldiers are not only filled with fear of not returning home, but afraid of a poison gas attack. Before the attack on Iraq, soldiers were depend-ing on George Bush to keep the peace in the Middle East.

America has yet to lay down that image it has as a superpower. America has to be on top of everything. Whether at home or a million miles away the government is always will-ing to risk the lives of innocent people to keep this image alive. No matter what the cost, the government wants to continue this image as world policeman.

Having passed through so many wars, one would think the U.S. would know better than to rush into another one. According to Mr. Bush, he went "The Extra Mile" to prevent war. I did not see "The Extra Mile." What I did see, however, was five months of war preparations rather than peace preparations.

Completing this section in mid-March 2003 as the United States administration silences and marginalizes the United Nations, it seems with very minor adjustments Patricia's essay can be read as if written today.

It would also appear that our patience with Hussein ran out before we got to the bargaining table. I never saw the United States running to defend the same freedom that millions of Africans seek, year after year, in South Africa. Neither did they declare war on the racist South African regime five months after declaring sanction on them that did not work. So, why the rush to war with Iraq? Is oil more valuable than blood?

I thought this was a democratic society in which people had freedom of speech and the right to dissent. Did this change while I was asleep? If not, why are attempts made to silence opponents of the war, who are also dismissed as unpatriotic? If citizens cannot express their dissatisfaction with the war in the Gulf, pardon my lack of patriotism.

Opponents of the war are just facing reality. There are serious problems on the home front for which the government says there is no money. Needed programs have been cut; teachers are being fired, class sizes are increasing, there was no money to save Freedom National Bank and major cities are going bankrupt. Yet, within a five-month period we had enough money to afford a billon-dollar-a-day war.

If you had been reading this essay, with the cover of the magazine missing as Ann M. Green suggests we sometimes do, wouldn't you have been hard pressed to date it, much less correctly identify its source?

The U.S. needs to get its priorities straight because when the war with Iraq is over the government will be faced with the same problems it tried to avoid, only the problems would have increased.

If our society thinks we have problems now, just wait until our troops come home to find limited opportunities, if any. It's possible that when many soldiers return home they will discover that the government that sent them to war does not care whether or not they are homeless and destitute. They will be like veterans of wars past; sitting and wondering why the country, they love and fought for turned its back on them (*Crossing Swords*, 1991, pp. 47–48).

Patricia's essay sparked heated discussion in the classroom and in the meetings of the Society For Social Analysis. As always, whenever I was on the brink of thinking that there was unanimity of views on any issue, there were contrary voices compelling the class to continually rethink assumptions and positions.

Sophomore Maria Ayala challenged the senior. In her essay, "The Reality of Fear," she wrote:

Patricia McGlashan argues that the American government "does not mind its business." I disagree with Patricia because all America is trying to do is to protect Kuwait from Iraq.

At first I didn't agree with what the president was doing. However, since the war has started I agree with him and support the troops one hundred percent (p. 50).

How Can Urban Students Become Writers?

Diana Garcia, a junior, employed poetry to fashion her statement on the war. She wrote:

> Serve your country
> > Dressed in green
> > Die fighting for peace
> Buried with the flag
> > Triumph in enemy's eyes
> > Swords raised in honor
> > Today you're remembered
> > Tomorrow enlists another (*Crossing Swords,* 1991, p. 50).

Still responding to Patricia's essay, sophomore Kerri Thompson wondered about "Names on a Wall, Again."

> The president keeps saying that the war against Iraq will not be another Vietnam. Does he know that for sure? Further, America had no right in Vietnam either. . . .

> Are we going to have to build another wall with all the casualties written on it again? I don't think that authorities are thinking about the many people who may die. They are just concerned with maintaining America's [image] of strength (*Crossing Swords,* 1991, p. 49).

Even after the war was over, discussion still raged in the classroom and in the pages of the journal. Responding to the preceding student commentary and writing as if she were composing a political pamphlet for mass distribution, NurJahan Simmons, a junior, asserted in her provocatively titled "Freedom and Its Denial":

> I believe that "black gold" was the real reason for the war. Thousands of African-American[s] were put under tremendous life-threatening situations because of OIL. While we, in America, lived and breathed, this outrageous action took place.

> Some people stated, "We (Americans) are fighting for the freedom of Kuwait and for our own freedom." My question is: When they say "our" freedom, who are they talking about?

> Today African-Americans are not treated equally. For anyone to believe otherwise, in my opinion, the person must have a selective perception of reality. In many inner cities, African American youth cannot walk the streets in a group without the police slowing down as they pass by and harassing us. Many times when we enter stores in our own neighborhoods, we are followed . . .

> Often we are not only accused of crimes we did not commit but are often stopped in the streets and accused of stealing cars we drive, and own. Furthermore police brutality is a frequent occurrence throughout the ghettoes of North America. In addition, there is always an undercurrent of racism to the point that you can't go into certain neighborhoods to look at a used car (Yuseff Hawkins).

> The undercurrent grows stronger as powerful forces continue to condone this type of biased attitude. The media is a good example: How they beamed to play a big role in the "Central Park Jogger Case," "The Bensonhurst Trial" and the "Teaneck Case." The irony of these examples is that they were not all given the same amount of press coverage or the same type of "viewpoints" (donated by the press). Instead, these viewpoints were fashioned to fit the needs of a predominantly "white press."

With all these facts one wonders: How can African-Americans, in good conscience, fight for a country that denies us so much? (*Crossing Swords,* 1991, pp. 53–54).</EXT>

Do vignettes, adages, counterfactual statements and the like really facilitate robust dialogue? Maybe not. Nevertheless, enlarge Augustus Caesar's adage "MAKE HASTE SLOWLY!" into a poster. Remove all posters and decorations from the room. Hang the adage above the chalkboard. Wait for the discord.

Zeitgeist: Engaging the Spirits of the Times

"[W]e were creating [Crossing Swords] *from scratch and not in the image of any other magazine in existence."*

—*Mauricia O'Kieffe, editor-in-chief,* Crossing Swords, *1989*

Reflecting on her involvement in the writing community, Vernette Olive-Carboin wrote "Therefore I Think":

It has been approximately ten years since the birth of the Society for Social Analysis and *Crossing Swords,* of which I am proud to have been one of the founding members. This journal is one that played a major role in my life. It . . . taught me nonconformity to the norm, to doubt, question, reason, research, think independently, respond positively to any issue in our society and voice my substantive opinions. These variables are critical to the formula of success.

Sometimes we limit our self-expression and are ashamed of the ideas that are within us because we see the false security of conformity. Most people believe that conformity to the norm is virtue while non-conformity is consequential. It is very difficult for anyone to bring new, creative, ideas to the majority because it usually upsets that which has already been established.

In other words, man is usually fearful about going against what the majority believes. He would rather quote something ancient or repeat what has been said for centuries rather than speak those powerful words, "I doubt, I question, so therefore, I think." For thousands of years man has been doing certain things, and when new thought emerges, coming in the form of an individual, it uproots, it confuses, and it shakes all that was thought to be significant.

I pray that the Society for Social Analysis will exist for many years to come and I hope that more students would take *Crossing Swords* seriously. This journal has certainly enabled me to think beyond the norm. . . .

In order to break the bonds of the mass mind, you must begin to doubt, to inquire, to question and to think independently and positively. The Society for Social Analysis was one motivational tool that inspired me to do these things. Therefore, I can truly look in the mirror and admire the one looking back at me (*Crossing Swords,* 1997, p. ix).

In *The Tipping Point,* an extremely fascinating book with profound implications for education, Malcolm Gladwell considers, among other things, the indispensable role that "Connectors . . . people with a special gift for bringing the world together" (2000, p. 38) play in social epidemics or spreading an idea or information. It is within this context that we can envision students' very own self-created journal, *Crossing Swords*—really writing—as their connector or "agent of infection" (Gladwell, 2000, p. 88) and writing communities was the virus we were spreading. Moreover, in celebrating the writing community reflected in their journal weren't Kenesha, Ann, and Vernette really alluding to its value as a connector in spreading a writing epidemic?

"Where are the boys? Why are there no boys with you?" asked Kay Thompson, of radio station 1190 AM WLIB, on June 23, 1988. Facing her on our first live radio interview were ninth graders Rosemarie Dunbar, Ann Marie Green, Vernette Olive-Caboin, Nikkitria Roberts, and Senyal Walton, sophomore Mauricia O'Kieffe, and Senyal's mother, Ms. Walton. Though I was taken aback (especially since I had intended to defer all questions to students) by an issue so transparent to everyone but me, I nevertheless replied, "Quite a few guys wrote but none volunteered to come."

On reflecting after the interview I realized that the reality was a bit more complex. Of the 140 students who passed through my classes over the 1987–1988 school year—the period over which the first journal was completed—42 students contributed to it, of which only six were males. And there was no male in the editorial collective of eight students. Clearly, then, though the school and my classroom could have been about 70 to 75 percent female, males were demonstrably unrepresented in the developing writing community.

This was the case in spite of my having made continuous outreach to all students, even calling parents to encourage their children to get involved in the journal or other extracurricular activities. This was the sentiment behind the student-crafted opening statement of the journal, which was signed by the editorial collective. It read:

> We of the Society for Social Analysis would like to welcome you to our journal. This journal is made up of essays and stories written by students you may know as classmates.
>
> The object of the journal and organization is to open the eyes of the 'blind' to show them how much students are willing to do.
>
> We would like to encourage all students to become actively involved in any one of the numerous clubs in our school or in the community where you live. Involvement in a club can be rewarding (*Crossing Swords*, 1988, p. iii).

Reading this statement today I still marvel at students' prescience, enhanced sense of civic consciousness, and of inclusiveness. To be sure, it was a hard sell convincing many of the merits of creating a community of independent thinkers and writers. Many balked at the possibilities and challenges inherent in such a venture. Still, we persisted in trying to "break the bonds of the mass mind." Little wonder then that Ann Marie, building on Vernette's vision of a sustainable writing community, skillfully recreated the turbulence, intensity, and uncertainty of that critical period. Miriam Sauda Perez also touched on the drama of the early days of the project. Her remarks from the *Crossing Swords* Annual Symposium, of Friday, June 11, 1999, are quoted at length:

Good afternoon. I graduated from Hale in 1988. I want to thank Mr. Holder for inviting me to speak to you . . . I applaud all the students who read. It was really inspirational. I want to say a bit before I read two of my poems.

Mr. Holder was the first person to encourage me to write. I never had a teacher who encouraged me to pursue anything before Mr. Holder. So he is very important to me, even though I really haven't kept in contact the way I should have. He's real important to me. Anyway, I'll read then maybe I'll have more to say.

The first poem I'm going to read is "Rumba for My Children." (Applause). Thank you.... And the next poem I'd like to read is called "Sweet Jazz, Bitter Blues."

> Bitter blues play
> In the streets below
> 'Black on Black'
> Suicide
> Becomes our sour
> Tune
> Man—caught up in a
> Master plan
> Women—barter vile soul
> For a five dollar vial
> Children—soldiers
> In a chaotic self-righteous street
> Corner harmony
> Of gunshots
> And voices wailing into the night
> Coltrane blows
> Jericho walls crumble . . .

As I was saying, Mr. Holder inspired me to continue writing. I was in his history class and I wrote an essay for an exam that he really liked:

> I arrived in the Thirteen Colonies and was greeted with the stroke of a whip and the shout of the word "nigger." I was quite disappointed. Things weren't like in 1988 from which I had just been transported. Here in the eighteenth century my ancestors were still in bondage.
>
> I went to praise my Allah and they called me a devil. I went to the local shop and they asked me whom my owner was. By this time I was really fed up. I began to preach to my people and to organize them against the prevalent injustices. The wicked authorities locked me up and told me I had no right to speak the Truth.
>
> They had just violated three of my 20th century constitutional rights: Freedom of speech, freedom of religion and citizenship rights for Blacks, at least on paper. I was naïve. I was shocked. Even though I had read about the wickedness of these times in my social studies textbook, I was not prepared.
>
> I was happy, when, at my trial, they found me guilty and transported me back to 1988 (*Crossing Swords*, 1988, p. 25).

. . . And [Mr. Holder] tried to convince me to write for the journal. And I was like—you know how some teenagers are—not that there is anything wrong with being a teenager, but I was like 'I don't have time for this!' . . . He called my house, and I never had a teacher in high school call my house. So I said to myself, 'This man is crazy! He's calling my house to get me to write!'

And upon my graduation he gave me some books, one of (which) was Gil Noble's auto-biography. I still have the book today. I read it and it inspired me. . . . It talked about people I didn't know. I didn't have people inspire me that way.

Anyway, I decided a year after I graduated to go to college and I have been working as a writer while attending college on and off for the last ten years. I don't really like going to school. I like learning but I don't like sitting in class, but it is something I have to do. So I went and finally I graduated this June [1999 from Brooklyn College]. I'm not going to hold up the mic any longer but I thank you for having me. And to all you young writers, keep writing. [Sustained applause.] Thank you (*Imprints,* 2000, p. 304).

And sophomore Kenisha Minott, who co-hosted the event, underlined Miriam's comments by telling the audience of 70 people (including her grandmother who had just arrived from Jamaica) packed into the vestibule of the school's library, "As you can see the book is really legendary" (*Imprints,* 2000, p. 4).

During the 1988–1989 school year, as discussion raged in the classroom, I kept hearing, like a stuck record, Kay Thompson's question in my mind, "Where are the boys?" Though convinced at that time that growth, emotional and intellectual, can't be compelled or legislated, I nevertheless toyed with the idea of viewing boys' receptivity to writing, and even learning, within the popular framework. Being unschooled in psychology and unfazed by the fads of the day (e.g., different learning styles between Blacks and Whites, girls and boys), the very theater of the classroom convinced me to continue viewing writing as an organic outgrowth flowing from the inner soul. As such, even before stumbling upon Alfie Kohn in Janice Hale's *Learning While Black,* I was operating from the frame that all students can write and will write when

intrinsic motivation is developed in learners by paying attention to the notion of . . . artistic teaching, in which children are motivated by the interesting manner in which content is presented, are given opportunities to explore ideas and content in meaning collaboration with their teachers and peers, and are presented with choices in curriculum (Hale, 2001, p. 123).

If intrinsic motivation isn't what both students and adults quoted throughout this chapter outlined, then a few more voices may clinch the issue. However, throughout students' entry into the tradition of a supportive, non-judgmental environment in which active listening is central, as organic intellectuals in formation they have been documenting their own transformations and transfigurations. As such, entry into the conversations allows them to discover and record facets of their world for themselves and the world.

Are students keen observers and critical listeners of the worlds they inhabit? Can we create settings in which they respectfully consider contradictory viewpoints while discovering the power of critical listening as a precursor to synthesis and self-growth? Can students teach teachers about what works for new, developing and seasoned writers and why it works? As teachers, are we humble enough to listen to the dialects and dialectics of youth as they tell tales of how they navigate and try to master their classrooms and world? Let's listen in on Garfield McNeil's reflections as he talks about a "Soul Saver":

Because of *Crossing Swords,* I know that true boundaries are not set until they are broken. When I first came to *Crossing Swords* I was a new poet with a lot of hidden talent, but because of my past I did not realize my true potential.

I can still remember my first poem. It was entitled "Who Shall Govern the Governors?" To this day I don't know what took hold of me the first time I wrote for the journal. The Society for Social Analysis brought peace into my life. It brought a sense of love with every meeting we held.

Although, compared to the Society (as a whole), my contribution is small, the group taught me that no matter how big or small the body of one's work is, what is important is the effort that was made. Sometimes I used to say to the advisor, Mr. Holder, "This kid only wrote six lines" to which he would reply, "At least it is six more lines than he wrote before."

It took me two years to grasp the concept. I now realize that before many of us came to *Crossing Swords* we had no idea of our gift. I think that the Society was an ignition for some and a hope for others.

If I had to describe *Crossing Swords* in two words, the words would be: soul saver. When we met on Fridays the group sustained itself because the advisor constantly challenged us. Our burning desires to realize what the skeptics say can't be done by teens is what kept us coming back for more (as some may put it).

Personally, the Society has given me a sense of pride and acceptance. I think I would have just remained complacent and careless if it were not for the Society. When I first saw the words "Associate Editor" next to my name, all the years of pain seemed to just freeze and a sense of elation filled my spirit.

Despite my environment, writing slowly became a positive addiction for me. I remember how I used to bring in pages of poetry, and even though I am an individual, when I read my work I read it as part of a collection. I saw kids my own age actually looking and listening to me. The trust that was developed in the group gave me a sense of security.

Indeed, the journal has been an outlet for creative thoughts and heated debates. I remember at the beginning of the 1999 school year that we used to have debates in the classroom. Perhaps our heated debates would have seemed peculiar to an outsider especially since we got along very well with each other without even the notion of violence (*Crossing Swords,* 2000, p. 26).

Are we really serious about encouraging writing as an essential, sustainable, life-affirming and transforming activity in urban centers of learning? How else can students memorialize classroom lore, their very being, and yes, according to Ann Marie, provide avenues for affirmation of self if not through an exciting writing circle which was unwittingly forged in the classroom? Are the powers that be really concerned about leaving no child behind, when classroom budgets are cut while expert consultancy thrives, some even from as far as Australia? What about the home-grown experts or warrior intellectuals whose expertise was forged in the crucible of urban classrooms, away from the glitter and glare of the media and the professional educators?

Isn't the latest mantra merely the fad of the day, allowing aristocrats of knowledge to crisscross and engulf the inner cities, dazzling audiences with their doublespeak while leaving victims no different than they were? Do these educational experts ever really rub shoulders with the masses and try to connect with their space? Why have urban centers witnessed so many studies, reports, and initiatives but so very little transformation? Will more talk shops and think tanks pacify the masses, or shouldn't committed educators adopt and try to infuse intellectual courage as the key to individual, social, community and ultimately national transformation?

How essential is it to create a space where student writers can publicly share their views? Would the elitist community even care about what our youth have to say? Do those who ru(i)n the system care enough about the boats stuck on the bottom? What about the media and their frequent exposes on education? Do they ever get it right? Why should we even bother?

These are excerpts from the *Crossing Swords* Annual Symposium held on June 11, 1999, which was co-hosted by sophomore Kenisha Minott and ninth grader Shana Bryce.

Kenisha Minott: I'd now like to call upon Mr. George [former Assistant Principal of Security] to present the next award.

Mr. George: Good afternoon. It's a pleasure to be back here. I left but I never really left this place. (Applause). This place will always be in my heart, and it's a pleasure to see that Mr. Holder has, for twelve years, maintained *Crossing Swords*.

He has put a lot of time and many long nights into the journal. Many times Mr. Holder would call me at four o'clock in the morning to ask advice about a poem or to review a poem and other aspects of the journal. . . .

The award that I'm going to present is to a young poet, a very promising poet. When I read his poems, the depth, the passion, and the intensity of the writings of this young man moved me. So I told Mr. Holder that the poems express such deep emotions and intelligence that I felt that I had to present this award.

Garfield McNeil is that rare young poet who comes along and dazzles us with the depth, passion, and intensity of his poetry. He handles very diverse and challenging themes in a very original and unique way. For example, in the poem "Who Shall Govern the Governor?" he raises some serious and troubling questions about morality, authority, and religion.

Ultimately he forces us to think about the question of who do our elected officials have to answer to if they do not, as he feels, answer to the people. If it is a higher authority or morality, then as he says: "Now the question at hand is: / Who shall govern the gods?" In these lines we hear echoes of the perennial question posed by the Greek dramatist[s], Euripides and Aeschylus, as they confronted the capricious gods of their religion.

This poet's range is wide. His grasp of the nuances of language is evident in the poem, "Imagine" in which we hear echoes of Lennon [and] McCartney's classic song "Imagine" as well as the Dub poet, Mutabaruka's poem "Dis Poem" with its similarly ending refrain: "Dis poem will live in your mind/you shall never forget dis poem."

McNeil is an intelligent and insightful poet who tackles such universal themes as justice and death with clarity and vision.

Based on his originality of thought and his brilliant poetic achievements, Garfield McNeil is hereby honored with the "Langston Hughes Award for Outstanding Poetic Contributions to *Crossing Swords* 1999" (sustained applause).

Garfield McNeil: In my life there are a few people who'll stand out in my mind. Even when I pass high school, you pass college, when I'm 117 years old, with your kids and grandkids, Mr. Holder will be one of those people, for he inspired me to write. . . . There are just not enough words for what Mr. Holder has done for me. He's brilliant. He motivates you, he makes you think, he captivates your mind. And I would also like to thank Hadassah Neepaul. Throughout the school year she has been a friend to me. [Applause]. Thank you. (*Imprints,* 2000, p. 11).

Do events like these help forge communities of writers? How are connections established and sustained by these interactions? Do public readings before an appreciative audience of classmates, teachers, parents, friends, and even enemies deepen the urge to be heard and to write? Let's consider two reactions to this series of genuine questions.

In the featured address at the Annual Symposium, Dr. J. A. George Irish, Director of the Caribbean Research Center at Medgar Evers College, receives a copy of *Crossing Swords:* Note the structure and flow of the spontaneous and unrehearsed student-run function:

(Host) Shana Bryce: Thank you Mr. Molofsky. Before I introduce this next person. I'd like to read [one of my] poem[s] that the adviser insisted that I read.

"Life's Necessities"
>It has always been said that your necessities
>for life are food, clothing and air. What about
>an education? Is it a necessity in my future?
>Education . . .
>Is the sweet air I breath,
>The food that
>Satisfies my soul.
>It is my shelter from ignorance.
>It is the eternal river
>That forever flows
>From the mountain of knowledge.
>Knowledge is the never-ending story! (*Crossing Swords,* 1999, p. 56)

(Sustained applause.) Now I would like to introduce Ade Nicholson, our editor-at-large.

Ade Nicholson: Good afternoon. . . . I would like to call on Dr. George Irish to come forward. . . . Dr. Irish, on behalf of the Society for Social Analysis I would like to present you with a copy of our journal *Crossing Swords.* (Applause.) Would you be kind enough to say a few words?

Dr. George Irish: Thank you. Greetings, sisters and brothers. On occasions like this I'm dumbfounded. I say that because sometimes when we get invited to functions, we don't know how to prepare. One of the things I have learnt to do in life is to come with an open mind—an open spirit—and to respond to the environment, the ambience, and the mood of the occasion. And that's the way I'm going to respond today.

Even though I've had the privilege of reading many of these poems before coming here today, *there is nothing as rich or, as touching, as hearing an author recite or read his or her own writing, because there is something that you cannot capture on the written page as opposed to when it is presented directly from the soul of the person from whom the art work originates.* (Applause.) There is something that touches you in a very sensitive way. And this afternoon I can't swear for the rest of you in the audience, but I've certainly been touched. Touched to the point where I found that I was getting a little emotional, and I've been trained not to let my emotions come out around people. I should let my intellect control my behavior and my responses.

But that's one of the sad things about the way we teach when we make students believe that the only way to respond to the realities of life is through some objective lens. And you distance yourselves and come up with some objective analysis. But *I've found that for the realities of life, the true response is one that has been touched and tinged with your personal sensibility.* And so this afternoon as I listened to the poems, particularly of those who graduated and, interestingly, those who are in the process of development right here in the school, I feel moved as a father, as a teacher, as a preacher, politician and all the numerous hats I've had to wear, to say to you young people that what you have committed to paper here is more than words. (Applause.) It's more than just ideas. It's a vision: *A vision that very often people don't associate with the people of your age, your neighborhood, your school, your race and your color.* But it's a vision, a message for the world, the universe. (Sustained applause.)

You are not speaking to Sarah J. Hale High School. You're not speaking just to your classmates; you are speaking to the universe. You are saying to the world that there is something bottled up inside. There is something I feel so profoundly about that you share it with someone. And, it takes courage to do that, specifically the sentiments you share with us today—so deep, so moving, delicate sometimes. Your hurts, your fears, your anxieties, your ambitions, and your aspirations you share them and it takes a lot of courage. Because very often we prefer to hide our true feelings, and we give the teacher the version of what we think they would like to hear. And we give to our parents some of the statements we think they'll like to hear.

But when you start committing yourselves in literary form, in poetic form, you are saying to the world, this is who I am. This is where I am. This is the real me and I am leaving it for generations to read—for generations to hear, for other students to understand; somebody passed through this world that went through certain challenges that had certain agonies, certain discomforts in life. But out of all of this, there is a message. And I thank you for the message. (Sustained applause.) And the message that I would like to share with you is wrapped up in five words.

As you go forward into life, as you face the millennium I hope that you continue to pursue excellence in all things. But there are five "A's" in particular that I want you to cherish, hold on to, and pursue.

The first of them is *aptitude.* Find out what your personal ability is, what your strength is because many other people are going to want to tell what your strengths and weaknesses are. Many people are going to want to tell you what direction you should go towards in life, and what you should avoid in life. But you personally have got to know what your true aptitude is, what the skills are that you are blessed with, the talents that God has endowed you with. Know them, understand them and try to discover how you can develop them. You have that first "A" on you transcript and you're on your way to success.

The second "A" that I want you to pursue is not in geography or history or political science or mathematics. It's an "A" that speaks to cultivating the right *attitude.* Because you may have the aptitude, you may have the ability, you may have the skills but you must have the right attitude to your parents and other humans. If your attitude stinks, no matter how many skills you have, how much money you have, no matter how much brain you have, you are a non-starter. So let's cultivate productive, constructive attitudes.

The third "A" I want you to pursue in life is related to *aspirations*. If you discover the right aptitude and cultivate the right attitude and you have learned to dream and understand that it is okay to dream, then you are on to something great. I've been to too many schools where children think to be a 'nerd' is a crime—to aspire to high achievement and excellence is something to be shameful of. I get the impression that from this group, the *Crossing Swords* group, the Society for Social Analysis, that you're not in that group, that you understand in order to succeed in life, you've got to set yourself your own goals and aspire to achieve them. Without that element of aspiration in your life, your soul will dry up. These dreams make our goals come alive, and that makes us practice the things that will make our dreams become reality.

The fourth "A" is *application*. You can dream as much as you like, but if you don't have the discipline to apply yourself to the task that can make these dreams become real, you are a loser. So get the aptitude, cultivate the attitude, pursue the application, practice the application, and the end result is the highest level of *achievement*. That's the fifth "A." (Applause.)

May God bless you as you go forward in life. I wish to compliment you, compliment your adviser, your principal, and all those who have inspired you in life. Never get trapped in the circumstances around you, but let your vision transcend the superficial realities so that you can discover the deeper realities, which are going to be the alternative measure of your stature as a person. (Sustained applause.)

Shana Bryce: Thank you Dr. Irish for your powerful words of inspiration.

In terms of envisioning a structure and orientation to facilitating writing, I need not underscore the saliency of emotion in educational theatre. What then do we have here if not a journal which connects students of different grade levels and eras, all through the construction of a writing community that continuously reinvents itself to face the challenges of each new era? Further along in the transcript we find:

Kenisha Minott: I'd now like to call upon Lakeisha Hudson, a 1997 graduate and former editor-at-large of *Crossing Swords,* 1995–1997, to present the next award.

Lakeisha Hudson: Good afternoon. Before I introduce this next award, I would like to say that I was only introduced to [this recipient's] writings a short time ago and what struck me about one piece of her writing was that it inspired an entire section in this issue of *Crossing Swords*. And the title of this section is "Witness to History." One thing that stood out was that she spoke about the changes and the challenges that the students are going through with the number of principals that they have had in a very short period.

I think that history is repeating itself. I graduated in 1997, but when I started in 1993 we went through the same thing, such as the walkouts and the changing of principals. We were fed up with what was going on, but we overcame it. We made it with the help of teachers, fellow students and [others]. We overcame the changes and the challenges, and you can do it as well. As someone said, students now have to play a major part in the rebuilding process of the school. (Applause.)

I started writing for the journal during that time of the school crisis in 1993 and Mr. Holder constantly called upon me to write articles, so I continued. I'll be starting my third year of college, and all the writing has really helped. When you are up all night writing papers, sometimes till three in the morning, sometimes three or four papers a week, you would really check back and say, "I'm glad that I let someone help me improve my writing." It's going to really pay off, and you'll say over and over "Thank you Mr. Holder. Thank you for inspiring me." So I'm just here to say to you, "Just keep writing, just keep doing it." I know you're going to say it's hot, and you don't feel like sitting here writing, but just keep doing it. The last day of school when I was graduating and everybody was getting ready for the prom, getting their nails done, I was sitting in a classroom writing this final essay for Mr. Holder. All my friends left me and went to the nail place, but I stayed. And it will always be in my memory that I stayed and completed the essay.

Like I said, the one essay of the student whom I am to present this award to inspired all these students to write about the changes and the challenges that are taking place in the school. Personally, I know her. She is a great student. Mr. Holder constantly tells me how much she reminds him so much of me. And I am honored to present the Paulo Freire Award for Exemplary Analytical Skills to MONIQUE SCOTT. (Applause.)

The education system is renowned for providing manuals for this and that. This mandate is another ruse the educated thought police, who run the system, use to impress themselves that they are doing something tangible. Most manuals end up in the dustbin of history. In this chapter it would have been quite easy to prepare free flowcharts featuring graphic designers, T-charts, Venn diagrams, and even borrow a few ideas from the workshop model and present findings that promote differentiated instruction.

Just as I was about to ambulate down that road, I was struck by two sayings: "Students get amazingly excited when they produce knowledge that has an audience in the school and community" (Kincheloe, 2001, p. 37) and "If we do not have some knowledge of children's lives outside the realms of paper-and-pencil work, and even outside their classroom, then we cannot know their strengths" (Delpit, 1996). Both statements instruct us to seek out alternative, even nontraditional and unscripted ways of engaging the texts, students, the classroom, and the lunchroom, that site of teeming creative conflict. What are the implications for the teaching of writing, rather, for fostering the urge to write within students? Throughout this chapter, by unfreezing tales from a journal, I have attempted to allow students, and their adult members of their borderless classroom, to tell the story behind their writing. One may argue that it was luck and chance that sustained the writing community. If that's the case, why are we so unlucky in other desired areas, such as clean and uncrowded classrooms, adequate supplies, and on and on?

Looking back on all that students wrote over a relatively short period of time I can't help but marvel at the serendipitous discoveries that we were fortunate enough to recognize. If each vignette tells about a different piece of the puzzle of how to, knowingly or unwittingly, foster a setting for the release of ideas on paper, then could my story fill in a small piece. At the 1999 function I was introduced thus:

Kenisha: I call upon Mr. Holder to present the next award:

Mr. Holder: This is a very special award. I don't remember who it was, but I think it was Keisha who said that like most ninth graders when she came into my class, I gave her a magazine to read.... But a strange thing happened last term. This group of ninth graders came in and I gave everybody a copy of *Crossing Swords,* and the following morning a ninth grader came to me and said, "Mr. Holder, may I have another issue?" I was a bit perplexed so I asked, "What do you mean?" And the student replied, "I read all of it [210 pages]." Not wanting to question her further, I gave her the 1994 edition of the journal which was about two hundred and twenty pages. The next day, she came to me and requested another issue and for that entire week the student read five issues of the journal. More than one thousand pages! (Applause.)

That isn't all. She immediately knocked her way into the group. I mean she would come and volunteer to type early in the morning before school began. Sometimes when I got to school at 7:45 she would be waiting by the classroom. And whenever I arrived at eight o'clock she'd inform me, "Mr. H., you are late." But the thing that really, really touched me about this student is once she said, "Mr. H. the writing in the journal is brilliant but there is one piece that really, really moved me." "Which article?" I asked and she replied, "The piece about 'The Will to Survive.'" Once she mentioned that article, it brought back memories, for it is a stunning piece of writing indeed. And she went on and told me that she would like to meet the student who wrote it. So may I call on Mr. Shilue Johnson to present this award? (Applause.)

Shilue Johnson: It's good to be back. On behalf of The Society for Social Analysis and *Crossing Swords* I present the "Mary McLeod Bethune Award For Exemplary Analytical Skills" to Sasha Pringle. (Applause.) It's a pleasure to meet you.

Sasha Pringle: . . . I am delighted that I finally got the chance to meet you. Thank you.

Shilue Johnson: Mr. Holder would like me to say a few words. What can I say? I graduated in 1997 and this year I'll be starting my junior year at Plattsburg University in upstate New York, about twenty minutes from Canada. And to tell you the truth it is one of the best Universities in upstate New York, although you may never have heard of it . . .

Writing for *Crossing Swords* has been absolutely the best thing I ever did in high school. I'd personally like to thank Mr. Holder because without all the writing he encouraged me to do, I may not have survived in college for the last two years. [T]o tell you the truth, those of you who are about to graduate, college is no joke. It's not like high school, where you have to wait for teachers to put notes down. To tell you the truth it's not easy. It's good to be back. Thank you.

NOTES

1. For a critique of the State Report that was used as the justification to close the school, see Nathalis Wamba's "Unleashing Grassroots Knowledge," a review of Winthrop R. Holder's *Classroom calypso: Giving voice to the voiceless,* at http://www.pan-jumbie.com/index.php?m act=News,cntnt01,detail,0&cntnt01articleid=506&cntnt01returnid=55.

2. Throughout the term I had observed that students in Row 5 often refrained from participating in class discussions. The "strategy" employed here was one of many spontaneous ways of continuously challenging and inciting students to talk and then write. After all, isn't any talk better than disengagement?

REFERENCES

Applebee, Arthur, N. (1996). *Curriculum as conversation: Transforming traditions of teaching and learning.* Chicago: University of Chicago Press.

How Can Urban Students Become Writers?

Boorstin, Daniel, J. (1999). *The seekers: The study of man's continuing quest to understand his world.* New York: Vintage.

Crossing Swords: Journal of the Society for Social Analysis 1988–2000. Brooklyn, NY: Sarah J. Hale High School.

Delpit, Lisa (1996). *Other people's children: Cultural conflict in the classroom.* New York: New Press.

Freire, Paulo (1997). A response. In P. Freire with J. W. Fraser et al. (Eds.), *Mentoring the mentor: A critical dialogue with Paulo Freire* (pp. 303–330). New York: Peter Lang.

Gladwell, Malcolm (2000). *The tipping point: How little things can make a big difference.* Boston: Little, Brown and Company.

Hale, Janice E. (2001). *Learning while black: Creating educational excellence for African American children.* Baltimore: Johns Hopkins University Press.

Holder, Winthrop. (2007). *Classroom calypso: Giving voice to the voiceless.* New York: Peter Lang.

Imprints: Documents of the Society for Social Analysis. 1988–2000. Brooklyn, NY: Sarah J. Hale High School.

Kincheloe, Joe (2001). *Getting beyond the facts: Teaching social studies/social sciences in the twenty-first century.* New York: Peter Lang.

Kincheloe, Joe, Slattery, Patrick, & Steinberg, Shirley (1999). *Contextualizing teaching: Introduction to education and educational foundations.* New York: Allyn & Bacon.

Postman, Neil (1996). *The end of education: Redefining the value of school.* New York: Vintage.

CHAPTER TWELVE

Roymieco A. Carter

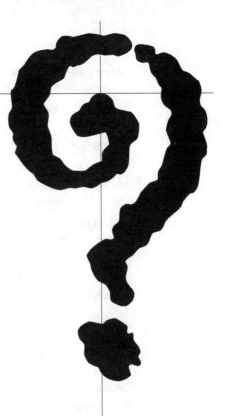

Can Aesthetics Be Taught in Urban Education?

 The answer is not as simple as the question might imply. The word *aesthetics* is loaded with history and meaning, which for some may stand diametrically opposed to "urban education." In this chapter, I examine tradition, time, and social practice in order to contextualize our understanding of aesthetics. The chapter also discusses the myriad of new ways in which aesthetics is understood and taught in urban education.

Aesthetics and the Traditional Voice

How do we understand the nature and value of everyday objects and experiences? How do we go about distinguishing the relevant from the irrelevant? Can we understand the purposes and meanings of experiences within objects? Are we able to place value judgments on the perceptions of these objects and experiences? From where do we draw the resources to defend our judgments? Should the same standards that were constructed to mystify heroic painting, classical theater performance, and traditional literature serve as the mold for creativity, expression, and beauty for the contemporary urban student? The student in the current urban educational setting is accustomed to viewing the urban public space as a visual battleground. The urban public space houses modes of expression and representation that would have been far from imaginable by the "fathers" of the traditional standards of aesthetics. The urban student is assaulted by imagery utilized for activism, propaganda, and advertising. These representations become the filters for the lived experience in the urban public space. The cultural attitudes and selected tolerances for language, expression, and literacy administered by the ambiguous social administration provide the urban student with the need to find alternate expressions of language and image. The new forms of expression are able to communicate the connected thoughts and emotions of the student in the urban public space. The barrage of visual messages forced on the urban student is complex, mixing manipulation and desire. The pressure from the outside inward on the individual is different from the traditional position of observation and disconnectedness. This change in direction makes it difficult to pass a blanket judgment on the quality of vision and aesthetic value of the urban student. When teachers in the urban setting are faced with the challenge of teaching aesthetics, rarely is it understood and presented from the outside inward. Urban education must rethink the principles of aesthetics and its purpose before teaching the value system to the urban student. The eighteenth-century bourgeois aesthete has transformed into our savvy, grounded urban student. Where once the site for viewing the transcendent image was the salon, now there are billboards on gritty subway trains. Along the route to school, the student is repeatedly confronted with overlapping social and corporate visual messages. The urban student is not expected to have the aesthetic "ascension into the divine." The new aesthetic messages through billboards warn of the dangers of AIDS alongside the horror stories of teen pregnancy. These messages are using the history of visual art to strengthen the encoded social messages for the urban student. On the opposite end of the spectrum, in the urban neighborhoods, the elaborate use of text and image is intended to deliver a different type of message. This urban gallery is the street. It becomes the canvas for the urban student to see resonating images of his or her life. The graffiti become the record of important individuals, borders, practices, and events that make up the urban space. Graffiti also serve as a backdrop for the expressions of individual style. These styles change rapidly in order to avoid absorption into mainstream culture. The urban atmosphere thrives off the energy and aesthetic vision of the urban youth culture.

There are complex historical and contemporary philosophical debates about aesthetics. One of the most famous historical debates between teacher and student was that of the teacher Plato's lack of interest in the art object as the ideal of beauty and truth versus the student Aristotle's belief that the art object can improve upon nature because it possesses the ability to reveal the essence of nature. These same philosophical debates have continued through the halls of the academies and caused the fragmentation of artistic practice in museums and galleries throughout the world. However, the basis of this inquiry is to address the aesthetic as a key that connects fundamental knowledge production to the lived experience.

In order to use this key, we will need to ease or release our grip on the reins that control the historical standards of aesthetics. It is important to note that this is not an abandonment of the traditional debate but rather a reconceptualization.

Aesthetics, as with any production of knowledge, needs contextualization, in this case through the urban space. The challenge is to allow it to collapse underneath its own weight and history. Let's begin by entertaining the idea that the study of aesthetics, as a tool of critical inquiry, can provide a nontraditional framework for teaching concepts of beauty and value to the urban student.

There are two main approaches to the study of aesthetics: the conceptual and the formal. Conceptual study of aesthetics concerns itself with the nature of beauty, truth, value, and taste. These concepts are constructions of social interactions and exchanges. They are subject to change over time and become reflections of the cultures and classes that define them. Where in history, the concern for "truth" in representation is fueled by ongoing popular debate, the marginalized embodiments of "truth" for urban students are reflected in their names, clothing, relationships, responsibilities, and experiences of pleasure found in the urban lifestyle. On the other hand, the formal approach focuses on the rules of composition and the visual principles and elements that operate as the composition's building blocks. The formal aesthetic critique places judgment on the arrangement of line, shape, color, light, balance, proportion, order, rhythm, and patterns within the composition of the art object. Urban students are well aware of the principles that build a quality hip hop track. They have no problems identifying a quality wall of graffiti. The urban student finds it easy to comprehend and respond in the appropriate style, whether it is visual or behavioral. The urban stage has already provided the student with tools to build a critique of aesthetic quality. This view must be recognized and respected. The urban student is expected to adapt to the aesthetic standards as historically defined by the institution of school. But does the school look to adapt and learn the new aesthetic qualities and values embodied by the urban student?

If we accept the statement that any activity pertaining to the nature of art and its experiences is rationalized through the philosophy of aesthetics, then the teaching of aesthetics will have to reference the traditional forms of art but also the new forms that are specific to the digital age. Students of the digital age have seen paintings move, dancers defy time and gravity by using computers and digital sensors, buildings being walked through and experienced before they have even been built, and music made without the use of voice or instruments. Urban students might find themselves in disagreement with the traditional aesthetic view. How is the urban student able to apply the traditional qualities of popular cultural aesthetics to the subcultures of hip hop, trance, or industrial music when the rules that govern the limits of quality never realized the transformations of music over time? We are all too aware that contemporary jazz is still fighting for its place at the aesthetic table. These connections can be portals to understanding new art forms. Urban students construct bridges that illuminate the pathways from the door of the academy to life in the streets. They freely interpret and manipulate the traditional art forms. The path between expression and the experience becomes the new "truth" that is beauty. Maxine Greene (1995) illustrates connections students can have through the aesthetic experience:

They can be enabled to realize that one way of finding out what they are singing, feeling, and imagining is to transmute it into some kind of content and give that content form. Doing so they may experience all sorts of sensuous openings. They may unexpectedly perceive patterns and structures they never knew existed in the surrounding world. (p. 137)

Such aesthetic experiences present the urban student with the privileged information necessary to form an academically useful value structure. The critique is established in the context relevant to the urban student, and then it is applied to the external practice or experience. An aesthetic critique operates with a purpose of identifying, appreciating, and evaluating the sense of beauty. Kant defines the 'beautiful' as that which, apart from a concept, pleases universally (Kant, 1928). This statement carries two fundamental conditions just beneath its surface. The first condition is that the urban student needs to make his or her judgment of taste as a product of subjectivity. The other is the condition of universality, which requires consensus and mainstream agreement. Based on Kant's criteria for beauty, the urban student's subjectivity must reflect the ability to experience pleasure/displeasure when faced with the work of art. The student will also need to experience pleasure/displeasure without desire in order to be an aesthetic critic of taste and judgment. Kant's definition, void of sensory perception, is an alien concept for the urban student. To see/gain pleasure in beauty is not problematic, yet making it conditional to being free of "desire" goes against the social messages of the urban environment. This understanding of pleasure in a Kantian framework of beauty places the observer (in our case, the urban student) in a position of being "disinterested." This means that a student viewing the work of art cannot experience pleasure in viewing the work of art, nor can the act of looking at or creating a work of art produce in itself the experience of pleasure.

Many urban students will find it difficult to see their life experiences and personal interests reflected in this definition of beauty and with good reason. Kant positions beauty in the safekeeping of the exceptional individuals who meet his criteria for possessing taste. These traditional restrictions need to be understood but also challenged. We need to be aware of the risks involved in subverting the use of the traditional view of aesthetics in order to know how best to maximize the uncharted territories of aesthetics, pleasure, and the urban space. In addition we also need to understand this traditional/historical critique, which usually alienates urban students from the aesthetic and convinces them that their artwork or experiences are devoid of beauty or value. However, teaching an expanded view of aesthetics provides students with the ability to realize the nature of the urban space and how it is unique to them as a reflection of the personal, social, and experiential.

Urban students are often asked to observe and analyze the representations of concepts, themes, and interpretations present in their everyday experiences. These events in the students' social interactions can be understood as works of art. Asking them to reflect upon their immediate surroundings in order to make judgments based on social values is a common practice that relates directly to the nature of aesthetics. The reflection of these events is shaped by the comparison of the lived experience and the social standards identified by the lesson plan or curriculum unit. These social standards or privileged analyses regulate the potential educational benefits. The observed work of art through the canonized aesthetic standards is valued for an alleged intrinsic beauty/meaning, not an interpretative or experiential one. The significance of a work of art is considered fixed and innate, not something that shifts from viewer to viewer. It is this limited perspective of teaching aesthetics that shortchanges the use of aesthetic understanding for urban youth. The lack of flexibility and depth in this type of lesson plan or unit truly truncates the urban student's use and discernment of aesthetics.

Educators can transform students' relationship to aesthetics by reconstructing the curriculum. A prime focus of this reconstructed curriculum is the students' environment, their assessment of it, and discussion/outline of the value structures of that environment. Without pushing students to evaluate their environment, they are left to judge objects and interactions of their lives against a value structure that is not relevant to the way they move through the world of popular culture. Beauty/aesthetics becomes a relative condition based primarily in the urban student's decision-making process. If urban students are targeted with social messages by the academy, businesses, or activists, they should have the ability to see them with clarity and inquiry. In a traditional classroom, urban students are asked to evaluate the aesthetic in an experience or object. They are usually given only the standard definitions of beauty, trust, value, and logic, which further alienates the urban student from understanding and benefiting from aesthetic experiences. Curricular spaces must be constructed in the classroom to contest, debunk, and re-create aesthetic pedagogy. Understanding can be achieved through conversations among the student, the event or object, and the many variations of aesthetic theory. In teaching aesthetics in urban education, urban students should be exposed to the traditional tools and discourse while asked to critically question these constructions. The teacher must encourage the urban student to create new tools and languages for the understanding of aesthetics. The major objective is to use students' reflection on the imagery of the urban space and its aesthetic value while developing critical insights to better prepare the urban student to negotiate the complexity of the urban environment.

Urban students' ability to connect aesthetic value to lived experience increases their learning of social attitudes, personal knowledge, and critical thinking skills. Encouraging students to discover connections among objects, theory, and lived experience uses aesthetics to transform rather than inscribe knowledge for the urban student. Having students create dialogues between themselves and art objects and using their dialogues to challenge the popular academic definitions result in the students discovering new senses of possibility. If we are to believe the canonizing statement which declares that the quality of a civilization is judged by its art, then we also have to know that the driving bass lines of hip hop, the synthetic repetition of trance and techno, the athletic contortions of street dance, the juxtaposition of styles in apparel and visual imagery, the emotion-filled voices of the slam poets all come together as parts of the new definition for quality of the current urban civilization. Transformative teaching practices place an importance on encouraging students to create aesthetic debates that peel away stale fabrications of reason that no longer reflect the current urban social attitudes.

Many of the traditional art forms (music, painting, literature, architecture, theater, and dance) have experienced shifts in meaning and use. Why hasn't aesthetics changed as well? Teaching students to "see" the art object and also to "see" the shifting of associated meanings of the art object informs them that reproducing the objects and arguments of privileged debates does little to move knowledge production forward. In a traditional context, students are asked to focus on their sense reaction to artwork. This aesthetic employs reason as a way to encourage students to reproduce but not to take responsibility for the application of the defined value system. This also implies that the students need to maintain the aesthetic perspective by creating a distance to objectify the judgment in order to inscribe the appropriate value onto the art object. This aesthetic distance places students outside of the subject/object and asks them to critique the representation against the traditional aesthetic standards in determining its value. The privileged aesthetic position for viewing art objects and experiences stunts personal discovery and produces disinterest. A nontraditional use (a shortening) of aesthetic distance would invite students to be engaged in the deconstruction of the subject. The challenge is in helping urban students see their reflection in the representation to solidify their connection to the art object. The student's connection to aesthetics is placed in jeopardy by focusing strictly on constructions of the formal composition, without also addressing the relations that the objects and experiences have to the individual or his/her meaningful relation to the intrinsic purpose or origin of the objects/experiences. Personal involvement is not a part of the traditional aesthetic perspective. The conflict of aesthetic distance versus engagement in the current urban setting does not allow for the necessary connections of utility, socioeconomic value, and personal emotion. Locating urban students within the work of art will reduce their disinterest and apathy in discussing aesthetics in the urban environment. Aesthetic distance can be shortened if we engage the urban student in the critical inquiry of the

- purpose of the transmission
- object or experience as "engaged moment"
- position of the receiver
- realization of the author (intent)
- technique of delivery
- conditions of the object/experience

- relationship of the object/experience to the local, regional, and world community.

The current teaching of aesthetics must work very hard to extend beyond the purely sensory-based, empirical, and logical approaches. Teaching the urban student to observe the created image, object, or experience only through the formal use of visual elements removes the art object from its communicative value. Students are discouraged from identifying the purpose, origin, subject matter, appeal, character, style, or expression associated with representation of the humanistic qualities embedded within any work of art. All of these questions are necessary to experience the work of art as an engagement of social knowledge production, not as a site of exclusion and alienation. The basis of engaged critical inquiry for an aesthetic critique should ask students to:

1 Identify how the author has presented an interpretation of an object, event, or concept. What are the point of view and communicated meanings presented by the author?

2 Understand the shift of meanings based on the location of the art object and how different viewers of the same art object will create variations of the interpretation. What evidence can students identify in order to substantiate their interpretation of the art object?

3 Identify a major thread of thought or theme within the art object. Is the art object part of a larger collection? What other art objects reflect common techniques or ideas that aid the viewer in the understanding of this piece of work?

4 Ask whether the art object can be connected to other nonaesthetic fields of study in order to advance the pluralistic dialogues of the art object and the transformative production of knowledge.

Does Time Shorten the Aesthetic Distance?

The cornerstone of teaching aesthetics in urban education exists within understanding the communicative components of representation. So, what is representation? Is representation the tacit concept of the art object that illuminates its aesthetic value, or is it the explicit perception of the object that gives the work of art its value? Rudolf Arnheim asks a similar question; he outlines the differences between "thing-oriented" (motoric) and "idea-oriented" (conceptual) styles of expression. In his description, he uncovers that the two styles do not operate independently of one another. Motoric acts will also resonate conceptual meanings, since in order to engage in or to act upon the world (making art objects), a student must be aware of the situation (understanding the use of representation) to respond to it (Arnheim, 1965). At its core, representation is the embodiment of codes utilized for communication. Urban students use slang as an in-group marker. It identifies the social borders between the urban student and the academy. The academy has a preoccupation with the identification and promotion of all that is quantifiable and formal. The student is well aware that the use of slang is informal and rejected by the educational system. The students empower themselves by deciding the levels of engagement by code switching. The rules for popular aesthetics and the vibrant urban student subculture reflect this same dynamic. Code is the language shared by the transmitting object (artwork) and the observer, that is, the understanding and interpretation made by the observer (urban student) of the artwork. The sophistication of visual languages is tempered only by the ability of the observer to understand these languages. The urban student will freely be able to decode the graffiti of Futura 2000, Phase 2, or Vandal, but the encoded messages of Gabriella Munter, Franz Marc, or Wassily Kandinsky appear alien and unapproachable. All art forms utilize and recognize constructions of pattern, and we refer to these representations as *expressions* or *styles*. Both the graffiti artists and the artists of the Blue Rider use color, shape, texture, and an expressive style to convey complex, thoughtful, and humanistic ideas. The observer of the work of art attaches the object to observations, ideas, and experiences that are outside of the experience of observing the art object.

The new aesthetic pedagogy must forge these connections and not perpetuate the traditional required distance between observer and observed:

> This distanced view of things is not, and cannot be, our normal outlook. As a rule, experiences constantly turn the same side towards us, namely, that which has the strongest practical force of appeal. We are not ordinarily aware of those aspects of things, which do not touch us immediately and practically, nor are we generally conscious of impressions apart from our own self, which is impressed. The sudden view of things from their reverse, usually unnoticed, side comes upon us as a revelation, and such revelations are precisely those of Art. In this most general sense, Distance is a factor in all Art. (Bullough, 1912)

Suppose an urban student, who accepts that he or she is incapable of creating a work of art that measures up to the aesthetic "greatness" privileged in the classroom, is exposed to the work of Diego Rivera. After researching Rivera's work he/she realizes that Rivera chose to describe his history and his observation of everyday life. The student realizes that to appreciate Diego Rivera as an artist, he or she needs to understand Rivera's creative attitude and originality constructed through the ways he chose to "see" the world. His murals, his use of color, light, shape, and pattern become dialogues between the personal and the social. The connections of the feelings, the messages, and the experiences of Rivera resonate with those of the student. This reduction of aesthetic distance is essential to students' learning. A pluralistic approach to aesthetic judgment is needed if we expect students in an urban environment to be able to utilize aesthetics as a component of knowledge production. The new approach is multidirectional; it will need to abandon fears that are associated with misinterpretation and complexity. "The consummatory function of the aesthetic," as explained by Eisner (1998), "provides delight in the inquiry itself. The durable outcomes of schooling are not to be found in short-term instrumental tasks. Such outcomes must penetrate more deeply" (p. 43). If students are expected to engage the art object for the purpose of understanding, creating, and/or defining its value, it becomes more important to understand the familiar, reflect upon it, then move on to the unfamiliar. Why take this approach, and what is its relation to time?

Observing a work of art from a familiar point of reference is intended to center the student in the area of inquiry, bringing him/her closer to it. The issue of aesthetic distance has a dual reality. We find a deep satisfaction when the art object is centered within our reflection. In order to get optimal clarity in what we are attempting to understand, the process of inquiry needs to develop under supportive conditions, allowing time for incubation between exposure and critique. To illustrate this point, we need only to observe Maya Lin's public monument, the Vietnam Veterans Memorial. We can see the names inscribed on the wall within our reach. The wall's span, color, and texture are all immediately accessible to the viewer. In order to get the peripheral information from our field of vision, we need to scan, shifting our focus along the way. We make connections to the event, catalog the names, and contemplate the conceptual meaning of the composition during the observation of the monument. We are left to contemplate the event of Vietnam. The communicative use of the grave black granite patterned with thousands of soldiers' names becomes fundamentally important to our perception of the wall. When we are asked, what did you see? the answer will be much richer and with greater clarity because the act of observation encompassed the reflection, the time, and the raised awareness due to the representation. If we are predisposed to a packaged "objective" definition of the monument, asked to look at the monument, then with very little time for inquiry or engagement probed for the answer, the connection and insight will most likely be superficial. The response will not be a deep reflection of thoughtful critique. It will be a recording of the formal objects that we were able to observe. Bullough refers to this as a case of "underdistancing"; it results in what he labels a response that is "crudely naturalistic," "harrowing," and "repulsive in its realism" (Bullough, 1912). Aesthetics helps the urban student to observe connections and respond with a clear view of responsibility and understanding to the environment. The reflection of the student in relation to the work of art will raise the student's awareness of the subject matter. The aesthetic distance is short and the reflection is clear.

The next step is to allow enough time for students to ask the necessary questions to gain satisfaction, understanding, and closure. The connections are made and the preliminary answers are more insightful while new and more challenging questions are being constructed. Confronting aesthetics this way becomes a motivating practice for students. It facilitates defining the purpose of inquiry while assisting students in a shift of vision to comprehend the aesthetic value of art. The ambiguity and disinterest usually accompanying aesthetics begin to fade for the student. The urban student's questions and engagement with art uncover the "aesthetic modes of knowing" that are often the purpose of works of art and reveals the intended message built into their construction. The conversation between art object and observer becomes a plan for action. The student is placed in a position of responsibility for the newly uncovered information. They become owner and catalyst for the activity of knowledge production not only in art but also in life.

It is no mistake that the context set for aesthetic judgment is heavily dependent on the types of representation put to use in the art object. The mode of representation is as important to the students' understanding as the subject matter of the representation. The way in which artists choose to use materials and techniques to express their character and mood has a direct relationship to the way observers conceptualize their comprehension of the message. The representation of an idea can take any of three basic structures:

1   *Representational* (realism, imitation, mimesis). This type of work characteristically utilizes a visually accurate portrayal of the world. The objects within the composition will appear in the work of art just as they appear in nature (Rader, 1938).

2   *Abstract* (expressionism, impressionism, cubism). This type of art object uses symbolic references in order to communicate concepts and ideas to the observer. The key to abstraction is that while it does not reflect nature, the visual components in the work of art can be connected back to their references in the world.

3   *Nonobjective* (field painting, texture painting). In this type of art object, the subject matter and technique do not represent or imitate visual reality or objects that are recognizable in nature (Hammacher, 1964).

Critical aesthetic analysis is highly but not solely dependent on the observer's ability to decode the expression of the artist in the art object. As an inescapable component of art making, expression is the artist's constructed attempt to alter, reflect, or intensify the internal feeling and emotions of the observer. Students asked to assess the aesthetic value of a work of art will need to reference the use of expression in the art object. This practice exposes the contextual nature of the subject matter. The artwork communicates the concept, object, or event central to its purpose as its subject. Alone, the subject matter operates as a notation or recording of a particular point of view. The expressive form in the artwork frames the point of view of the subject matter. This is often a challenging and uncomfortable component of the aesthetic judgment. In a traditional aesthetic structure, students would have to demonstrate a privileged ability to decode, then pass on their discovery to the waiting masses who lack such gifts. This model does not take into account how the world has changed and the possibility of multiple interpretations.

The technology that mediates nearly all of our current visual information is transparent and often taken for granted. We enter our homes and turn on our televisions, DVD players, CD players/stereos, and computers without a conscious thought to how these devices affect the ways in which we see. Our aesthetic responses to these are seen as natural and ordinary. Students surf the Web on the subway train or on their way to school. They are able to send symbolic messages to their friends without any forethought or assumed trade-offs. They have an idea; they pick up their cell phone and share the idea instantaneously. Never before has it been this easy to communicate ideas. Each of these devices alters the ways in which we see and construct aesthetic critique. The immediacy of these experiences affords all sorts of possibilities for aesthetic reflections. Though we are able to use these devices immediately, the understanding of how they change our ways of seeing comes through time, use, and application of traditional aesthetic principles in new spaces. At least three modes of communication are still relevant as channels for aesthetic experience through technology:

1   *Narrative.* If an idea is dependent on structuring a series of related events, the viewer of the structure will see the pattern rather than the individual events. In most narrative structures, the sequences will reflect a social, moral, or cultural logic.

2   *Image.* Any attempt to record, capture, mediate, or imitate reality can be understood as an image. Images are the most widely used mode of representation.

3   *Language.* The structuring of the world through a socially agreed-upon set of smaller components for the desire of communication.

Representation of an art object through one of the new technology-driven art forms is still subject to aesthetic judgment. Students can apply aesthetic values to the new forms and decode transmitted messages, subsequently redefining and discovering the aesthetic experience in the everyday urban environment instead of the museum, gallery, or public monument. Students can see the opportunities and challenges of decoding expression on a daily basis.

Why do we sit in movie theaters or in front of the television mesmerized and meditating on acts of romance, danger, kindness, heroism, violence, pleasure, and happiness if the art object is able to reveal itself only to the privileged objective observer? How do we recognize the difference between digital media art objects and the electronically transmitted data intended to sell a concept, product, or service? How are we supposed to teach students to know when the digital art object is presented for appreciation or is a reflection of a biased political, social, or moral agenda, given the extreme commercialism pervasive in the urban environment? These tensions are the very reason for aesthetics to be taught in the urban environment. Students need to be exposed to the political, social, and moral agendas. They need to critically analyze how pleasure and desire are mobilized through the new media aesthetic. The urban environment is the landscape for the reconceptualized aesthetic curriculum.

The media aesthetic, as part of the urban landscape, is a new form of aesthetic critique. New technologies become familiar parts of the lived experience, so they become easily overlooked as a delivery system for the art object. Due to the transparent nature and familiarity of the technology driving the recognition of the art object, urban students will not distance themselves from the technology. They focus on the art object and do not take into account how the representation is affected by artificial lighting, the digital properties related to the screen, and the limited amount of colors available for screen display. All of these screen properties and the transparent inundation of these devices in our everyday lives affect what we see, where we see it, and how we value the objects themselves. Urban students face a new challenge: The art objects of everyday life are requesting them to alter their moods, and their points of view are constructed by authors who are not immediately identifiable. The constructions of reality are easily recognized, but the meanings and purposes are becoming dangerously vague representations of a false logic, precisely in need of pedagogical utility.

The builders of these art objects may find it to their benefit to maintain viewers' ignorance of the practice as long as they are responding appropriately. The problem is that although the recognition and response to expression are a part of the everyday, the urban student is not consciously aware of or focused on the motivations for the work of art or the results of the contextualizing elements of the subject matter. The elements of expression are complex but discernible. The student willing to uncover the motivations that state how the subject matter intends to be seen needs to realize only a few simple concepts:

1   The art object is a product of a constructed message.
2   It is encoded with meaning and purpose by an author.
3   It uses common languages such as color and light.
4   The symbolic imagery is often an edited exaggeration of reality.
5   It is directed at "me" as a potential observer, and "I" am intended (by the author) to place how "I" feel above "my" observation of an analysis of the construction.

Recognition of and reflection on these concepts give the urban student a critical shield against the art objects that aim strictly to convince the observer that the author's intentions and moods are exact representations of the popular.

How Can Aesthetic Judgment Be Taught?

Aesthetic judgment relates mutually to the ability to think critically about the artwork and to place value on it. The challenge to teaching aesthetic judgment is not that of drawing conclusions about subjective likes or dislikes of the urban student. It is not the rationalizing of formal visual properties as they pertain to the work of art. Teaching students to place aesthetic judgments on art objects in an educational system that privileges the stance of collective agreement and correctness is counterproductive in locating the interpretative voice of the student. The balance and juxtaposition between the subjective judgment and a judgment derived strictly from reason will culminate in the production of new knowledge. This new knowledge/insight is a bridge to the institution from the social and personal location of the urban student.

In addition to exposing urban students to aesthetic critique, the educator needs to engage them in their own art making. Imagine the following scenario: The teacher has just finished a formal explanation of how to create a work of art. There is a bold statement just about to bubble forth from one of the corners of the room. A student proudly states, "I am going to change all that. I will make people change the way they think about this work. My work will be something new, something never seen before." The teacher smiles while standing in silence, waiting for the student to realize how difficult this task will be. The teacher, so as not to extinguish the burning enthusiasm of the student, then responds, "How do you plan to begin this redefining of art?" The student stumbles to find an answer worthy of his/her previously announced statement. This one statement has brought the urban student face to face with everyone who creates, judges, and values beauty. At this point the real learning of the aesthetic begins. There are a multitude of possible responses the teacher can issue that will stimulate the urban student to pick up the self-proclaimed challenge and move forward in her aesthetic sensitivity and production of knowledge. The teacher has the benefit of knowing what challenges lay ahead for the inexperience and youthful enthusiasm of the student.

Students may challenge definitions and rules because they are understood as limitations being issued by structures of authority. Teaching students to conduct aesthetic judgments means placing them in situations that challenge what is important about the definitions of taste, beauty, and pleasure. Urban students live within a commercial landscape. External pressures are constantly being applied to the image they carry of themselves through the world. In the practice of building filters for these pressures, these students are encouraged to use aesthetic judgments. The negotiation of subjectivity and universality is the condition of popular taste that enables students to decide the value of the art or other forms of expression that they encounter in their everyday experiences. This new analytical skill allows them to become critical of political, commercial, and activist imagery that attempts to inscribe new values upon them. Teachers and students may approach the act of expression and representation with differing views of subjectivity and universality. Students experience art making and the recognition of expression with the ability to appreciate its beauty, although their response may not be formed on the grounds of logic, reason, or authority. The teacher, however, has been trained to reason and to therefore identify and communicate the formal expressive properties structured within the work of art in order to have it seen as a proponent of beauty. The teacher has already answered to definitions set out by the structures of authority. They have worked through many of the complexities that the urban student has yet to encounter. Another great benefit the teacher can offer urban students is that the teacher operates as a guide through the institutional universality that accompanies the formation of aesthetic judgment. Kant illustrates the complexity of negotiation that is needed for subjectivity and universality in aesthetic judgment:

But when he puts a thing on a pedestal and calls it beautiful, he demands the same delight from others. He judges not merely for himself, but for all men, and then speaks of beauty as if it were a property of things. Thus he says the thing is beautiful; and it is not as if he counted on others agreeing in his judgment of liking owing to his having found them in such agreement on a number of occasions, but he demands this agreement of them. He blames them if they judge differently, and denies them taste, which he still requires of them as something they ought to have; and to this extent it is not open to men to say: "Everyone has his own taste." This would be equivalent to saying that there is no such thing at all as taste, i.e., no aesthetic judgment capable of making a rightful claim upon the assent of all men. (Kant, 1928)

Through dialogue, teachers can provide vocabulary and definitions to situate a foundation for a student's attitude, judgment, and values regarding art. This is a strategic positioning of subjective reasoning. The challenge is not to settle into the staunch position of institutionalized authority illustrated in Kant's example. Urban students need to be supported and assisted but not forced to have the judgment of authority overshadow the ways they have learned to appreciate music, language, dance, architecture, theater, painting, and sculpture found in their lived space. An inclusive view of aesthetic judgment will meet the desired goals for producing knowledge that transforms traditional constructions of value, taste, and beauty. The new understandings/interpretations make it possible for urban students to value and create new ways of seeing.

When asked to confront the principles of aesthetic judgment and knowledge production, urban students are asked to replace what they understand about art objects in their everyday life with popular definitions from sources unfamiliar to their reality. The definitions of aesthetic judgment are only a starting point of inquiry, not the end of knowledge production. The dialogue and inquiry that follow static definitions become the new assessment of value for the art object. For example, when urban students are shown a representation of their city, they are likely to see more than the regional borders, markings for neighborhoods, transit patterns, or population scales. Imagine what other issues can be uncovered if the students are encouraged to discuss the aesthetic judgment they place on the city as a work of art. Given motivation and guidance, they will make use of personal, economic, cognitive, moral, religious, and political experiences to express their aesthetic connections to the city as a work of art. These areas of value directly shape the urban student's aesthetic judgment. The teacher may place aesthetic value on the logical, defining it as the solution to avoid misinterpretation by the observing students. The map (as information) may not have any relevant aesthetic value to the student. Urban environments are rich with experiences that students are aware of but not able to address because of determined solutions instead of free association of the art object to lived experience. Aesthetic judgment can be formed only if urban students are allowed to recognize its aesthetic value.

The art object, as the focal point of aesthetic judgment, arguably has no intrinsic value if we take the stance that value is the way an object is used in the world. The art object takes a renewed position of importance in the way we understand our social and personal selves. The usefulness of the art object is in the dialogue of the observer and the work of art. Underscoring why students will need to work from the teaching definition outward into the lived experience makes the work of art useful in helping urban students understand and link themselves to complex life experiences. The human condition does not exist in isolation. We label our heroes based on our desires. We celebrate and admire acts of devotion and trust. We also fear events and experiences we do not understand. There is no lack of these themes and many others in the art objects throughout history and into the far-reaching future. Allowing urban students to find the aesthetic value and determine the aesthetic judgment for a work of art in their everyday lives repositions the value of the work. The new aesthetic refocuses the gaze from the traditional objects to experiences that are contextual, meaningful and relative and highlights art and expression as the products of human interaction in the material and immaterial world.

Art and Social Practice: A Way of Understanding

The teaching of aesthetics in urban education is better understood if tied to lived experiences within the urban environment—its people, languages, homes, neighborhoods, families, authorities, actions, and exchanges that take place between these and other facets that illustrate experience as the reflection of understanding for the urban student. The various of experiences brought to the institution of education become valuable tools in the teaching of aesthetics in the urban space. The aesthetic is approachable as a lens for the observance of social practices such as ritual, work, habit, and pleasure in everyday life. It is also a formal practice for the discussion of morality and value within the social atmosphere. The new aesthetic engages a social consciousness and awareness.

The urban environment is flooded with varying social practices that are prime for aesthetic investigations and insights. Urban students are oftentimes deprived of traditional aesthetic experiences and discussions. This reconceptualization of aesthetics places them in the center of the new media aesthetic. Traditional aesthetic standards are studied and challenged as they are applied and discovered within new urban public spaces. Urban students become the new aesthetes. The people, spaces, and objects in their everyday experiences become treasured embodiments of beauty. While learning to value these experiences, students also learn the freedom and responsibility of understanding.

REFERENCES

Arnheim, Rudolf (1965). *Visual thinking*. Los Angeles: University of California Press, p. 204.

Bullough, Edward (1912). 'Psychical distance' as a factor in art and as an aesthetic principle. *British Journal of Psychology, 5*, 87-117.

Eisner, Elliot W. (1998). *The kind of schools we need: Personal essays*. Portsmouth, NH: Heinemann.

Greene, Maxine (1995). *Releasing the imagination: Essays on education, the arts, and social change.* San Francisco: Jossey-Bass.

Hammacher, Abraham M. (1964). *Mondrian, De Stijl, and Their Impact.* [Art exhibition catalog.] New York: Marlborough Gallery.

Kant, Immanuel (1928). *Critique of judgment.* Trans. J. C. Meredith, Oxford: Oxford University Press. http://etext.library.adelaide.edu.au/k/k16j/part3.html. Accessed November 18, 2003.

Rader, Melvin (1938). *A modern book of esthetics.* New York: Henry Holt.

CHAPTER THIRTEEN

Luis F. Mirón

How Do We Locate Resistance in Urban Schools?

 Like most institutions funded with taxpayer monies, public schools must honor the laws of the country. Beginning with passage of the Civil Rights Act of 1964, discrimination because of race, ethnicity, gender, sexuality, or religion has become forbidden. For example, it is against the law for any public school or university to deny admission to immigrants (legal or illegal) because of their noncitizen status. However, many building administrators and classroom teachers believe that if they follow the guidelines of federal laws, their schools will be protected from discrimination, racism, and prejudice. Educators assume that by following the letter of the law, the spirit of the law will be honored and respected. Research and knowledge of professional practice tell us differently. More precisely dejure desegregation is equated with educational equality.

Desegregation of Little Rock, Arkansas, public schools after the passage of the historic *Brown v. Board of Education* decision unleashed nearly a half century of externally generated reforms of urban public schools. Today public schools are situated differently as the global political economy, and the worldwide concentration of capital in particular, has caused a host of demographic and other pressures on urban schools (see Lipman, 2002). Urban schools are now resegregated and notoriously underfunded in comparison with their more affluent suburban counterparts. Furthermore, they are perhaps somewhat academically weakened owing in part to the influx of immigrant populations who arrive with limited English, low family incomes, and a lack of cultural support for learning. This context is similar to the historical circumstances of inner-city schools serving poor students of color; however, I want to argue that the pressures are exacerbated with waves of immigration from Mexico and Latin America as well as the heavy-handed role of the state in exacting academic standards.

Between 1993 and 1998, I conducted a qualitative study of four public inner-city high schools enrolling large percentages of students from ethnic and language minority groups in New Orleans. The study consisted of approximately 50 interviews with students lasting between 30 and 90 minutes (Mirón, 1996; Lauria & Mirón, 2004). In these interviews I sought to ascertain the extent to which students from similar socioeconomic backgrounds and varying school cultures (magnet vs. neighborhood) and with different levels of academic success (A's and B's vs. C's and D's) expressed widespread "resistance" to both the formal and the hidden curriculum and to pedagogical practices.

Drawing upon this research, I will attempt to answer the question of how students resist in urban schools. In addition I summarize important demographic data on educational inequality in Chicago to provide a comparative glimpse of substantial contextual issues found in the majority of urban schools and districts nationwide. I begin by addressing the uniqueness of the urban school "problem."

Are Urban Schools Different?

Inner-city schools are different. Lipman (2002, pp. 385–389) paints a rich picture of public education in Chicago, the "dual city." As Chicago strives to become a "global city" like Los Angeles and New York, academic and social inequalities have deepened. Lipman cites the often-noted economic shift in the United States from a manufacturing to a service and knowledge base. As a result the country has a "highly segmented and increasingly polarized labor force." Lipman states that service jobs, for instance, are highly segmented by wage/salary levels, education, and benefits. Growth in highly skilled technical, professional, and managerial jobs at the high end are dominated by white males, while an abundance of low-end, low-skilled jobs are held mostly by women and people of color.

In addition, Lipman notes the widespread expansion of contingent, provisional labor: multitask, part-time, and temporary work performed mainly by women, workers of color, and immigrants who often hold down two, three, and even four jobs to make ends meet. A quickly growing informal economy employs primarily immigrant and women workers who provide specialized consumer goods and services for the well-to-do (designer clothing and live-in child care) and cheap goods and services for poor or lower-income households (e.g., unlicensed day care). He claims that there is little opportunity for gainful employment in the formal economy for large sectors of the population, specifically African American and Latino youth.

Paradoxically, as the global economy grows and capitalism intensifies, economic and social inequalities widen. For instance, the overwhelming majority of new jobs pay lower wages and offer less protection (heath insurance, pensions).

How Do We Locate Resistance in Urban Schools?

Between 1973 and 1995 real average weekly wages for production and nonsupervisory workers decreased from approximately $480 to $395. More dramatically, the wealthiest 1 percent of households increased their wealth by 28 percent from 1983 to 1992, while the bottom 40 percent saw their income decrease by nearly 50 percent.

Like most "global cities," Chicago has experienced widening inequalities that are mirrored in geography. These social and economic inequalities, moreover, are vividly illustrated in the move to gentrify old neighborhoods with expensive upscale housing and restaurants, high-tech employment, and (central to our goals here) academically achieving public schools. (Although the site of my research [see Lauria & Mirón, 2004] is not a "global city," it too is not immune to the processes and effects of globalization.) These escalating inequalities linked to the worldwide consolidation of capital have been well documented. I argue that it is the intensification of educational inequality, on a meta level, that inner-city high school students most resist and resent. The processes of globalization deny them access to a quality education and thus the possibility of social mobility.

How does the global economy produce educational inequality?

Using secondary sources, Lipman (2002) documents the economic shift in Chicago from manufacturing to service/information employment. From 1967 to 1990, the number of jobs in manufacturing fell an astounding 41 percent, from a total of 546,500 to 216,190. In comparison, nonmanufacturing jobs rose by an equally impressive 59 percent, from 797,867 to 983,580. Most significantly, as the *Chicago Tribune* reported in 1999, the trend saw manufacturing employment with average salaries of $37,000 being replaced by service jobs whose wages paid only $26,000. Because 23 percent of workers in the city belong to a union, the impact on the working class has been even more severe, often resulting in the loss of health insurance and retirement benefits. This economic transformation led to what Lipman refers to as the "production of educational inequality."

In brief, the efforts of two generations of rule by the Daleys (Richard Daley Jr. was recently reelected to a third term) have resulted in the marketing of Chicago as a "world class" city that attracts businesses in the new knowledge economy. In order to "sell" the city to affluent and well-educated professionals who will staff the kinds of firms the city covets, Chicago has embarked on the most ambitious urban school reform agenda in the nation. This reform agenda, moreover, has created a system of high-stakes testing and accountability, college preparatory "magnet schools" as well as remedial high schools, and a pedagogical culture that rewards achievement on standardized tests. For example, in some of the schools in Lipman's study, nearly two months of the academic year were spent in preparation for tests, complete with cheerleading and pep (or prep?) rallies. These everyday practices are being reproduced in urban school districts besieged by underachievement all over the country.

The New Orleans Experience:
From Political Resistance to Political Agency

Unlike previous scholarly notions of resistance, the concept demonstrated in my work extends beyond mere moments in time or simple expressions of acting out. Resistance involves a discourse practice that is an expression of human agency. This expression may take the form of political agency. The question that ensues is, How can human agency become transformed into political agency? In this section I would like to outline a new conception of how a return to the political may develop. But first I need to sketch in broad strokes the conceptual (sociological) underpinnings of this move.

Social Structures

Sociologists have long indicated that social structures serve a dual function. At their heart is an understanding that they exist interactively with human agents. Social structures both (1) constrain the actions that agents can perform and (2) provide the space to act. This includes political (collective) actions. For example, social structures are neither organic, self-regulating systems nor freewheeling spaces where agents can roam without rules. The point is that structures are products of history—people acting in behalf of their beliefs—and, once constructed, tend to re-create themselves time and time again. So where do resistance and political agency come into play within this conception?

More likely to employ passive resistance, inner-city students in particular seem to lack the capacity to exercise political agency. Subjected in many instances to a prescripted curriculum and pedagogy, they lack cultural and historical knowledge of their social situation, their "situatedness." For example, many students I interviewed in the neighborhood high schools in New Orleans were unaware of how construction of interstate highways through the city in the 1950s devastated local communities and residential neighborhoods. People and families were displaced. On the other hand, inner-city students from approximately the same socioeconomic backgrounds enrolled in magnet schools were treated to a rich curriculum emphasizing cultural diversity, oral history, and writing programs that placed students at the center of pedagogy. Therefore, given a curriculum and instructional practices that ignore students' lived cultural experiences and history, political agency is almost nil. Social reproduction happens. Students do, however, resist these structures. I argue that this form of resistance largely results in high school students disengaging from school, often dropping out or, as the data indicate below, accommodating to teachers' busywork. Though these forms of resistance may seem similar on the surface, we should bear in mind that a strategy of accommodation leading to leaving school versus remaining in school—and choosing to graduate—obviously has different outcomes and should be kept analytically separate.

How Do We Locate Resistance in Urban Schools?

Inner-city students armed with culturally relevant knowledge and coming out of a school culture that places a premium on racial/ethnic pride are more free to act. They possess the capacity to exercise political agency, which means that in cities like Chicago and New Orleans, they can petition local school boards to establish schools such as Roberto Clemente High School, serving Puerto Rican students in Chicago, and programs like "Students at the Center" at McDonough #35 magnet high school in New Orleans, a writing program built on oral history and creative arts. Such students learn to view inner-city high schools as vehicles for local community development and lobby the school board to enact these curricular models in other high schools as antidotes to dropping out of school or, worse, incarceration.

It was not unreasonable to predict such intense student resistance, because the setting of our study—an urban center beset by economic restructuring and a sagging tourist economy—left high school graduates few prospects for employment besides working in fast-food restaurants or busing tables in one of the area's numerous upscale eateries. In short, high school students had few viable career options and thus little incentive to do well in school. Surprisingly, what my colleagues and I found was that all the students we interviewed were highly motivated to graduate from high school—many of them aspired to attend college. There was, indeed, student resistance; however, the forms of student resistance varied to a certain degree by the form of school organization and culture. At times, forms of resistance converged. In general, student resistance in this urban center characterized at the time by widespread poverty, illiteracy, and violent crime was directly tied to students' perceptions of their teachers' academic expectations and everyday practices of racial stereotyping.

For instance, African American high school students in particular often complained that teachers believed that all Asian American students (e.g., upperclass Vietnamese) were intelligent and highly motivated and enjoyed strong family support for learning. By contrast, African Americans (especially males) were seen as mostly hoodlums and disinterested in learning. Moreover, some of these students complained that the principals shut down student assemblies and cultural activities. In hopes of curbing actual and perceived student violence, school administrators disbanded clubs and organizations. On the other hand, students enrolled in college preparatory magnet schools (see Lauria & Mirón, 2004; Mirón, 1996) took pride in the caring school atmosphere, the challenging curriculum, and rich extracurricular opportunities. I call this pedagogical phenomenon *academic discrimination*. Furthermore, the kinds of student resistance I will disclose below are based on high school students' relationship to this form of discrimination and institutional racism, especially their perceived capacity for human agency, expressions of student voice, and their own representations of racial/ethnic identities.

Prototypes of Student Resistance

Based on the student interview data, students manifested two broad strategies of resistance: accommodation and mobilization. These strategies of resistance, moreover, were direct responses to students' relationship to the formal and hidden curricula. As we gleaned from the ethnographic interviews, their overall goal in both of these kinds of strategies of resistance was to secure their right to a quality education (Mirón & Lauria, 1998, p. 191).

What is most striking is that, like the Chicago school reform summarized above, school cultures matter. In magnet schools in New Orleans, generally characterized by an emphasis on "diversity," the curriculum differed sharply from that of the neighborhood public schools. In the magnet schools, we found a culturally relevant curriculum and a sense of racial/ethnic pride. On the other hand, students in neighborhood schools were seemingly denied a quality education owing primarily to a curriculum that emphasized busywork and a lack of student voice. The intensity of student resistance, moreover, as will be disclosed below, largely depended on the type of school organization and corresponding everyday lived culture. Urban students' capacity for agency—the ability to act on perceived alternatives—closely paralled the form of resistance.

Accommodation

For students at the magnet schools, accommodation meant being fully engaged in the rich formal curriculum, a sense of racial/ethnic pride, and a broad array of student activities. These students perceived the school-based activities as connecting them to the wider society by providing them with practical social skills as well as instruction in global affairs. In other words, their teachers made explicit connections between local context and the processes of globalization. Furthermore, teachers, administrators, and counselors fostered student voice, in the process "authorizing" students to have a role in curriculum policy and engaging them in the mission and cultural traditions of magnet schools. Students perceived that these connections protected them from the callousness of the outside world, a societal attitude that reduced African American males in particular to a nameless statistic.

By contrast, the widespread curtailment of student assemblies, organizations, and clubs obviously hindered student voice at the neighborhood secondary schools. There, a school climate existed that systematically disengaged students from the curriculum and from the broader school culture more generally. Some of these students enrolled in neighborhood schools employed a form of passive resistance, telling the interviewers that they "did what they had to do to get by." These students were not "silenced" and they were obviously not pushed out of school, as they maintained passing averages by the end of the year. Following Anthony Giddens' theory of structuration, I want to argue that these students were not merely passive victims. Just the reverse was true: They made the decision to remain in school and graduate, thus at least securing the possibility, however limited, that they could improve their life chances.

Mobilization

All of the students we interviewed made an important strategic decision: to remain in high school. I say that this was a *decision* because, at least in the neighborhood schools, there were keen pressures to disengage stemming from the low expectations of teachers, peers, and administrators. As I stated earlier, as researchers we tacitly bought into lowered expectations when we believed students would show evidence of giving up on school for economic reasons. Just the reverse turned out to be true. I argue that this decision represents a kind of human agency. At times this converts into political agency.

Deciding to remain in inner-city public high schools, despite a weak economy, constitutes a discourse practice. Most of the neighborhood students would voice this discourse as an "antagonism" expressed to the researchers. There was little opportunity to organize collectively, as leadership practices astutely separated students from one another, in effect enacting an extreme psychological paradigm of learning. Other students, however, mobilized on behalf of their civil rights, which they perceived entitled them to access to a quality education. In other words, they formed strategic alliances with parents, school board members, and community leaders to make their demands heard on behalf of educational justice. Many of these students told us again and again: "The teacher can't take away my grades. If she does, I will tell my mama. And if my mama can't change my teacher's mind, she will take it all the way to the school board if she has to." This mobilization was grounded in a collective ideology among African Americans in New Orleans in particular that their parents' and community's struggles for civil and human rights during the Civil Rights movement of the 1950s and 60s left them with a near moral obligation to succeed academically and give something back to their local communities. At one of the magnet schools, students frequently told us, "You must remember where you came from," and, "Our teachers remind us to stand on the shoulders of those who came before us." Resistance here was clearly tied to a sense of racial/ethnic pride, respect for elders, and a collective recognition that white society was a common "enemy."

The following narratives of student resistance illustrate the prototypical forms of resistance, which at once support the capacity for political agency and vividly demonstrate how the structures of inner-city schools constrain agency. The narratives are organized by actual interview questions posed to high school students in New Orleans.

1. What is everyday life like as a student in your school?

The first question in the interview protocol of this five-year ethnographic case study asked inner-city secondary students to describe what it was like to be a student in their school. Stark differences existed between the organizational cultures of magnet vs. neighborhood high schools. Yet these differences blurred a bit as we documented how students resisted. At the neighborhood public schools, students often complained of boredom with class activities. Furthermore, the administrative practice of curtailing student assemblies ("shutdown") exacerbated boredom and isolation.

The research uncovered an unexpected finding. When we coded the interview transcripts of nearly 1,000 pages, these emotions, coupled with an apparent distrust of students by their teachers in regard to completion of homework assignments, related to the conditions of violent crime, both at school and in the local community. This is ironic given the strong regulation of student behavior. Naturally students resisted these practices and social conditions, yet the form of this resistance was voiced in accommodationist terms. As the administration in the neighborhood schools moved to shut down student assemblies and therefore preempted student voice, the students seemed to get angrier. This may have exacerbated the conditions for violent crime, an ironic unintended consequence.

> The curriculum and everything else here is way below. I used to have a 3.9 average and [at my old school] they used to motivate us better than back here. Like the teachers here really don't teach. If you get it, you get it. If you don't, you don't. Well you didn't bring up anything about violence. One week we had four fights in one day.

> I think the African American students are treated fairly by the administration. I mean that if they do something wrong, then they will just have to suffer the consequences. African American students treat Asian American students very differently. I mean they would make fun of them because of the language that they use. I say there is no need to do that because if you came from another country and you couldn't speak fluent English either, you wouldn't want anybody doing that to you.

There were stark contrasts at the magnet high schools. The interviewers recorded few negative comments about what it was like to be a student in this kind of urban high school. More typical was this statement:

> It's fun, exciting. You get involved with a lot of community activities.... Especially being a black male like myself, you get a lot of prestige and a lot of pushing from your teachers and the principal. And I really enjoy that, especially from the principal. It's just a sort of love here—and it really helps a lot of children.

2. What is schoolwork like?

Since we found the curriculum to be much richer at the magnet schools and the pedagogy more tuned in to community concerns as well as global affairs, I will underscore this type of school:

> To be a student here, it's a lot of hard work, but after you get the hang of it, you know it's fairly easy if you do all of your work. You have to study, and once you study and catch up and you know the work, then you can go ahead of the rest of the students. Then it would be easier for you. The teacher explains it, and then you already know it.

How Do We Locate Resistance in Urban Schools?

I try very hard because at my school there are a lot of people who make very good grades—and you want to be just like those people. I find myself up some nights until 3 or 4 in the morning just studying, you know, working the material in my head.

At the magnet schools, academic work implied an application of the competitive work ethic to students' studies in order to become successful. Students appeared to learn collaboratively from and to model themselves after other students (some of whom attended the same school) and to compete with students in their ethnic group for top honors.

By contrast, students at the neighborhood high schools tended not to push themselves as much. They often told us that they "did what they had to do to get by" and to graduate. Apparently they strategically chose not to do more. Some of the students actually blamed the teachers for holding low expectations, which did not require them to work harder or learn anything of substance. They frequently complained of busywork. We gleaned from these admonishments that students at these schools do in fact desire to compete academically.

On the one hand, students at the neighborhood high schools resisted: In our interviews with them, they expressed antagonism because they perceived that they were unjustly denied a quality education. But their resistance took the form of an accommodation to the wishes of their classroom teachers, who appeared to engage in an implicit (hidden) social contract of controlling students by holding out the carrot of a passing grade and eventually a high school diploma. More precisely, this form of student resistance was tied to students' notion of agency by accepting the quid pro quo of paying attention, completing seat assignments, and especially not challenging the teacher's authority in order to just get out of there. This strategy guaranteed them, in their minds, the prerequisite of completing high school as the first step in the long pursuit of a middle-class life.

3. With whom do you identify?

In trying to understand students' behaviors and relationships at school, at home, and in their neighborhoods, we asked them if they changed behavior in each of these social environments. We wanted to know whether they were able to move comfortably among "multiple identities" that were located in different discourses, for example, between studiousness and sustained focus in school and clowning around and hanging out at home and in the neighborhood. Could students from the magnet schools, for instance, keep discursively separate who they were at school from the peer pressures of the street? The most interesting finding was that 38 percent of all students—from both types of school—felt alienated from their neighborhood (had no friends, were fearful), whereas another 38 percent felt comfortable.

These results varied inversely between the two types of school organization. Among students at the magnet schools, 58 percent felt alienated in their neighborhoods and 25 percent felt comfortable. At the neighborhood schools, 16 percent felt alienated, while 58 percent felt comfortable. Furthermore we generally expected that the dynamics of students' identity politics would play out among their friends in the neighborhood. Therefore, students of similar academic performance (A's/B's vs. C's/D's) or similar social class background would express similar degrees of affiliation and identification with the home vis-à-vis the high school. This turned out to be false. The only students we found at the neighborhood schools who felt alienated from their neighborhoods were females. Inversely the only students from the magnet schools who felt comfortable in their neighborhoods were males. Secondly, when these students enrolled in the magnet schools, they had the feeling of escaping to a safer, less chaotic social environment. This was coupled with the prevailing ideology of the magnet school, i.e., that it provides a ticket to college admission. Paradoxically the magnet schools reproduced this dominant ideology, and there too the students willingly accommodated with apparent ease.

Students in the magnet schools seemed to experience greater difficulties separating their academic identities from their personal identities. Their peers who did not attend magnet schools, which offered academically rich and culturally relevant curricula, apparently could not understand why their friends changed. This caused conflicts. On the other hand, students in neighborhood schools felt less conflicted, as their friends generally attended less challenging schools as well. Of course, these are generalizations, as there is not space in this chapter to closely examine the nuances.

The interviews disclosed that at the magnet schools, students generally felt that teachers were there to help them academically, socially, and emotionally. Teachers cared. In sharp contrast, students in the neighborhood high schools generally perceived that their teachers treated segments of the student population differently. For example, black males widely perceived that their (mostly white) teachers discriminated against them by holding lower expectations for them and stereotyping most of them as hoodlums:

> Some teachers have their favorite student, but it isn't [necessarily] racism. My teacher thinks that I'm a hoodlum or a gang member. A lot of other teachers say that, though. I hear the other teachers say that.

> The teachers expect more from the Vietnamese students, that they are always smarter and stuff. It's like the Vietnamese student is always smarter, and my teachers never expect a black [male] student to be smarter than a Vietnamese student, you know. They always automatically think that we're dumb.

> From what I know, some teachers may think that, well, if a person is white, well, they are better than the rest, you know. If another [black] student makes a higher grade, then the teacher will say, well, the white student must have had a bad day. The teachers won't put them down or announce their grade in class, or anything like that. They will just keep it to themselves and come talk with the student privately.

These interview narratives disclose the perceptions among the students in the neighborhood high schools of the authoritarian school climate. Democratic practices, to say nothing of deep racial/ethnic democracy, are apparently void. Students felt stuck "back here" in their neighborhood schools, seemingly isolated from the wider society and even from each other. "Shutdown" was the norm. However, by accommodating, going along with, their teachers, students resisted. They specifically exercised their "situated" agency and made the one strategic choice available. They chose to pass their grade level and go on to graduate. This kind of student resistance obviously differs from that characterized by Robert Everhart (1983) and others as an escape from anxieties. I argue that this form of student resistance is inherently political and, perhaps more evocatively, "collective." It begins the pedagogical move from human to more political agency.

Toward a New Urban Pedagogy

Classroom teachers in inner-city public schools, whether they are white or teachers of color, find themselves in an unenviable position. They are daily besieged by the demands of the state to lift student achievement and struggle with the social realities of widespread inequality. Despite this contradictory location, teachers must strive to become transformative intellectuals.

Their first pedagogical imperative is to foster their students' racial/ethnic identity and pride. So as not to become mired in factionalism, however, classroom teachers must demand greater awareness of the identity of "the other." During these uncertain times, knowledge of the plight of Muslims, Middle Eastern women, and oppressed populations around the world is indispensable. Why is this important?

On ethical grounds alone, classroom teachers in urban centers must find the means to resist the increasing surveillance of schooling, and perhaps more perniciously the trend toward standardization of teaching and learning. These trends are clearly linked to processes of globalization and in particular the overwhelming propensity of the nation-state to converge upon neoliberal market ideologies. On pragmatic grounds, however, teachers coalescing around broader concerns, and linking these issues to global processes and events, make their political positioning stronger. They are less vulnerable. Students and teachers are thus partners in the struggle for democracy in urban schools—sites where the appeal of the "global city," like Chicago or Los Angeles, makes imperative the regulation of student bodies and teacher pedagogy through high-stakes testing and accountability.

In this regard Henry Giroux (1983) has argued that curricula that lay bare the colonizing legacies of western Europe enable classroom teachers to transform their roles. They become cultural workers who, together with their students, "take seriously the identities of subordinate cultures" (p. 154). Public schooling for racial/ethnic minorities in inner cities, therefore, can potentially assume a counterhegemonic purpose by becoming a site for cultural politics. Though institutionally rare, there are countless examples of these transformations, such as the Roberto Clemente School and other schools serving Puerto Rican students in Chicago. These schools have implemented a critical pedagogy based on the principles of Paulo Freire. Here I want to extend Giroux's argument and assert that procedurally, only by understanding how students construct their racial/ethnic identity—and finding pedagogical space to accomplish this task—is the transformation of teachers from bankers of knowledge to cultural workers institutionally possible. Schools are sites of both meaning and morality.

A Vision of Urban Student Resistance

The resources that urban students possess, as shown in our study, are uniquely situated sociocultural perspectives from their shared experiences relating to violence and the material hardships of poverty. Whether they are conscious of this or not, they share collective struggles for quality public schooling.

Educators should form coalitions with students to design interventions, forged at the national, state, or local levels, that confront (and, one hopes, interrupt) the perceived moral transgressions articulated in the student narratives. Specifically, principals and classroom teachers must deliberately foster a school climate or school/community partnerships whereby students may occupy safe pedagogical spaces and places to construct the production of meaning and morality.

This issue of creating safe spaces for student dialogues and collaborative learning environments may be more complicated than first imagined. Our data show that even when presented with transactional opportunities for information sharing with teachers, the students in our study remained skeptical. Students' collective attitude, especially in the neighborhood schools, was, "What's in it for the teacher?" Building trust takes time, but it is our contention that teachers need to constantly remind themselves that sensitive issues such as teenage pregnancy, home difficulties, and ordinary adolescent angst are everyday concerns for students. Secondly, students should lead discussions of private issues and their relationships to the formal and informal curriculum. This will help prevent the perception that teachers gossip about personal concerns. Students would feel more comfortable. Classroom practices that facilitate the articulation of student voice, for example, those at Roberto Clemente High School, should be replicated.

In general, what the student interviews revealed as necessary, but perhaps insufficient, was a school climate that increased self-discipline and provided caring in a nonpaternalistic manner along with a more culturally relevant curriculum. Pedagogically, what seemed to distinguish the magnet schools most centrally was their relevant and engaging curriculum. Students at these two public schools, above all, were connected to the world. A common complaint voiced by students at the neighborhood schools was: "[The adults there] are ignorant on the subject, so therefore how can you teach somebody something you don't know?" Globalization was a process that meant something in the everyday world of student learning. Urban school curriculum architects need to keep foremost in mind the processes of globalization and issues that can potentially unite high school students with their teachers, for example, against global economic oppression.

Public schools are not institutional isomorphs. Classroom leaders and administrators understandably often function as if schools had no connections to the broader community and political economy. They do. Moreover, many of the high school students we interviewed voiced a desire to make these relational interconnections explicit in the curriculum. They wanted help in overcoming their class backgrounds and cultural biases. One student from a neighborhood school told us, "I don't live in the best neighborhood. I don't think society really cares about me."

What is crucial, I believe, from a pedagogical perspective is to authorize student voices as "learning subjects." Despite denied access to quality public schooling and high-paying jobs owing to the disappearance of work in the inner city, demonstrated income inequality, and persistent low wages for many racial minority groups, inner-city students nonetheless choose to remain in school. Nationwide, approximately 50 percent of students in urban centers do so. High school students in our study perceive that they have few material options other than to stay in school and graduate. Moreover, those students who do graduate and eventually enroll in college often must learn to navigate separate personal and cultural identities and set spatial distances from their everyday life in their residential neighborhoods. High school students in urban centers, especially those enrolled in neighborhood schools, often have to develop new academic self-images to succeed and gain admission to college. Potentially, these students could experience an inexorable estrangement from their nonacademically oriented peers, who may get pushed out of school as a result of policy structures and school practices. They must negotiate between, on the one hand, new identities located in academic discourses and spaces embedded in their "moral strategy" to obtain quality public schooling, and, on the other, broader social and economic connections to the world.

REFERENCES

Everhart, Robert (1983). *Reading, Writing, and Resistance: Adolescence and Labor in a Junior High School.* Boston: Routledge and Kegan Paul.

Giroux, H. (1983). *Theory and resistance in education: A pedagogy for the opposition.* South Hadley, MA: Bergin and Garvey.

Lauria, Mickey, & Mirón, Luis F. (2004). *Urban schools: The new social spaces of resistance.* New York: Peter Lang.

Lipman, Pauline (2002). Making the global city, making inequality: The political economy and cultural politics of Chicago school policy. *American Educational Research Journal*, 39, 379-423.

Mirón, Luis F. (1996). *The social construction of urban schooling: Situating the crisis.* Cresskill, NJ: Hampton Press.

——— (1997). *Resisting discrimination: Affirmative strategies for principals and teachers*. Thousand Oaks, CA: Corwin Press.

Mirón, Luis F., & Lauria, Mickey (1998). Student voice as agency: Resistance and accommodation in inner city schools. *Anthropology and Education Quarterly*, 29, 189-213.

Mirón, Luis F., Bogotch, Ira E., & Biesta, Gert (2001). In pursuit of the good life: High school students' constructions of morality and the implications for educational leadership. *Cultural Studies—Critical Methodologies*, 1, 490-517.

CHAPTER FOURTEEN

David Forbes

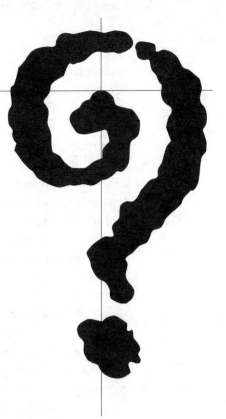

What Is the Role of Counseling in Urban Schools?

 The role of the urban school counselor today is to promote the whole development of all school community members as well as that of the school community itself. By *whole development* I mean not only the advancement of cognitive, intellectual, and academic abilities but also emotional, moral, social, spiritual, physical, and aesthetic ones. *All community members* means teachers, administrators, parents, and staff as well as every student. And by *school community* I mean the entire school culture as a living organism, including the quality of its relationships.

This holistic, compassionate counseling replaces the kind whereby counselors' primary function was to process students as raw material for future economic competition and bureaucratic efficiency, accommodating the employment needs of the market or the government. Schools too often have served to reproduce existing class relations. Given that calculus, with the loss of manufacturing jobs and the need for fewer and highly skilled workers, millions of urban working-class and poor students become relegated to the trash heap. Devalued and neglected, they are left with poor-quality public education that contributes to illiteracy, attrition, and despair. Today, however, it is no longer acceptable, if it ever was, to treat education and students as commodities instead of intrinsically valuable ends (see Miller, 1997). Counselors in urban schools no longer can afford to play the role of functionaries in an indifferent education bureaucracy that shortchanges the people it is supposed to educate. It is wisdom that enables the counselor to see the greater needs of the members of the school community and compassion that drives the counselor to help each and every one of them to become a whole person.

The emerging counselor role also does away with the old battle between two opposing counseling camps—those who would promote academic success while minimizing affective and interpersonal issues, and those who emphasize personal counseling at the expense of academic concerns. In this tired schema, politicians and bureaucrats narrowly define academic success through standardized tests, while emotional health becomes consigned to a privatized realm characterized by adjustment to the status quo. Both split off aspects of the whole person. Instead, holistic urban school counselors address multiple intelligences and the unique capacities of each individual. They advocate for quality education, social justice, and full citizenship based on everyone's interconnection with others everywhere. Unlike a teacher, administrator, or other specialized support professional, the counselor's unique position and responsibilities enable him or her to engage in the everyday tasks of the urban school as well as to step back and see the entire school as a system in need of care.

In a globalized, post–9/11 world, nothing less will do. This radical role requirement calls for the counselor to act as a "wizard" in a world of "muggles" (i.e., the rest of us, according to Harry Potter): a higher-order visionary with the wisdom and presence of mind to understand and respect the different levels of consciousness of both the parts and the whole and the compassion to help everyone evolve toward higher, more integrated levels. It means thinking globally and acting locally, and even thinking locally while acting globally (Beck & Cowan, 2002). It means being fully aware of an urban school's material and social limitations and of the varying levels of consciousness within it and succumbing to neither utopian idealism nor cynical despair. The counselor can do this because she or he knows that the world is of one piece and is constantly changing and evolving. Over and above the thinking of the standards bureaucrats and those who would commodify knowledge as a means toward material success, a mindful, compassionate counselor is attuned to this dynamic of change and growth toward wholeness, which is the very nature of learning and education itself.

An urban school is situated within an elaborate, multilayered nexus of values, goals, and behavioral patterns, with its own life conditions. This urban matrix both throbs with tensions and bursts with hopeful opportunities. Stress arises as cultural sensibilities and belief systems of groups from different parts of society and from the entire world come together in one place, rub against each other, and create friction; sometimes they ignite. Anxiety is heightened by the threat of terrorism as well as by a current presidential administration hell-bent on world military and economic domination. These compound the already existing stresses in everyday urban life: bare-bones essential services and maintenance-deferred infrastructures; competition for scarce resources such as housing, a decent wage, quality education, and cultural and recreational space; clogged streets, dangerous traffic, and inadequate mass transit; violent crime, gangs, drugs, and homelessness; public health epidemics both actual (HIV, asthma, obesity, infant mortality, lead poisoning) and possible (anthrax, smallpox, radiation from terror-targeted nuclear power plants) and noise and air pollution.

As a consequence, many urban students and family members live with low to moderate levels of posttraumatic stress on a day-to-day basis. They feel anxious and insecure, squeezed between the constraints of limited and uncertain economic resources and the relentless pull of pervasive media messages and images that glorify materialist consumption. A significant number suffer from unaddressed depression, grief, or sense of helplessness as a result of immigrant family dislocation, loss of a family member due to crime or illness, or being a witness to or victim of violence. Others exhibit self-destructive, aggressive, and impulsive behaviors, having been raised in chaotic, emotionally troubled families marked by authoritarian relations, overwhelmed caregivers, substance abuse, or domestic violence. Beneath the workaday bustle and cool pose of many students, urban school counselors often discern these kinds of problems.

At the same time, the potential for healthy growth here and now is enormous. With the ability to access instant information and establish worldwide networks through the Internet and advanced telecommunications, old, rigid systems of domination and ideology are being challenged and transformed. There is a growing planetary concern for the health of the entire biosphere. Human rights has advanced as an international political issue. More scientists recognize that the mind affects the body in terms of improving health, emotional awareness, and stress reduction (Goleman, 2003). Cross-cultural research on optimal human development shows that all children everywhere need the same things in order to thrive: healthy attachments, emotional literacy, a deep sense of meaning and purpose, the time to grow at their own pace, and caring, safe communities. Networks of educators and peacemakers who work on local and international levels are raising people's consciousness everywhere: More folks are realizing that real safety and security cannot come from the aggressive deployment of guns or bombs but only from genuine compassion for and understanding of one's self and of others.

This knowledge and its corresponding level of awareness are at the vanguard of social progress and have concrete implications for policy development and everyday practice. They stand over and above the retrograde educational policies that treat knowledge as a scarce resource for the privileged few and that seek to impose restrictive, dominant-defined standards on children without respect to their emotional and social developmental needs. This universal perspective also trumps the consciousness of those in government who assume that force, greed, and competition are the best and only means to motivate people and to ensure their safety.

In short, a higher-order global consciousness is out of the bottle. On a local scale this means that urban school counselors can draw from a worldwide knowledge base to help them assess what members of the school community need in order to maximize their health and happiness. Counselors then share the relevant knowledge and skills and make them more accessible to everyone. Some of the ways they do this are by: helping young men become more emotionally literate (for example, identifying feelings and learning to better recognize situational cues); encouraging African Americans, Latinos, and students from other under-represented groups to get on the college preparatory track; teaching schoolwide conflict resolution and peacemaking skills; leading workshops with parents on communication with their children and on participating in the school power structure; and running student discussion groups on relationships that promote higher moral reasoning and media literacy.

Armed with the proper education and support, the urban school counselor carries out these professional skills. What is most valuable, however, is the counselor's mindful awareness, the ability to hold a variety of contradictory thoughts and feelings at the same time, and to continue to act on what is right. He or she can be sensitive to the despair of people's lives and bothered by the social injustice that shortchanges students' access to quality education, all the while working with a calm, centered presence of mind and striving to create a realm of safety and compassion. Mindful counselors give from a full cup and also know how to replenish themselves.

Counselors choose not to operate from a deficit model that emphasizes people's limitations or focuses on mental pathology. Rather, counselors today help school communities and their members evaluate their strengths and resources. They encourage them to put forth a more evolved, positive vision of creativity, health, and happiness and to make it happen (Kessler, 2000). Despite many obstacles, most urban citizens the world over understand the value of quality education and desire it for their children.

For urban citizens to survive within and evolve from their complex urban matrix, a new order of school counselor is called for, one who embodies a more advanced, comprehensive consciousness and way of being. Gone is the image of the counselor who sits in the guidance office waiting for the principal to refer students for individual counseling or whose main task was to track students into vocational slots or perform class scheduling. In today's world, simple chores have given way to multitasking. Linear, print-media learning is being challenged by instant information that is targeted to whole-body, affective, and sensory processing. Those who can see the larger picture and can be flexible and creative in situations characterized by considerable uncertainty are replacing narrow, technical specialists. Proper education and support are required to bring these counselors into being.

Urban school counselors then must be encouraged to develop the capacity for higher-order, whole-brain thought and action. Rather than be captives of authority's agenda, they become the inventors of their work and creatively initiate and collaborate with members of the school community to create a common vision (Kegan, 1994). This requires that they embody a well-developed synthesis of conceptual, emotional, and interpersonal skills.

Counselors must be knowledgeable about the demands and limitations of academic standards and accountability issues, have insight into and facility with contemporary youth culture and the wider popular culture, have a working knowledge of parents' traditional cultural and class values, know how to read a student's body language as well as a report card, work with others to advocate for quality education for all, and have the capacity to listen to and help people learn to deal with feelings of anger, pain, and sorrow. In most cases they must do these things within a school that is poorly staffed, underfunded, lacking in essential supplies and equipment, and situated within a community where parents unfamiliar with school collaboration struggle on a day-to-day basis to survive.

With proper education in mindful urban counseling, counselors can best do all this in a conscious way. They move from one level of awareness to the next without getting stuck at any one place, all the while maintaining a vision of the whole. The counselor commits to being aware of his or her own experience at each moment. This means being open to the present and being fully present with each task and with the person before them. A contemplative educator, Judith Simmer-Brown (1999), suggests that in this approach one tolerates ambiguity and sets aside conceptual presuppositions about the other person. Such a stance, she says, relies on "the willingness to drop theory in order to experience more fully the actual flow of what one knows" (p. 105). With this presence of mind the counselor can be open to what is needed for all. He or she can avoid overidentification with one way of thinking or acting and maximize his or her capacity for compassion without burning out.

A mindful, open approach to experience is necessary in order for the counselor, or any educator, to be fully responsive and proactive. Without this openness to the living, changing nature of a school culture, everyday rituals and interactions become empty, deadened, and rigidified. Schools lapse into stupefied patterns. Individuals are not perceived as developing and changing beings but are cast in unbreakable molds: This child is the bright, successful student; this one is the loser and troublemaker. Learning, instead of being a vibrant process of wonderment, creativity, and exploration, is transformed into rote memorization and facts divorced from living relationships and nature.

Even reforms and innovative programs, if a spirit of presence does not embody them, become old and tired and lead to further despair. They become externalized fixes that reinforce the thinking that a new commodity or method is the answer, rather than cultivation of the courage to be aware of what is going on now. Without a mindful presence, purported solutions embodied by new curricular packages and programs, and even practice itself, become meaningless responses to the emptiness that much of urban education fosters in the first place. Unmindful program reform, by ignoring the living moment, prevents examining how people experience the meaning of what they are doing.

For example, Glickman (2003) suggests that successful schools are ones that regard themselves as sacred ground:

> These schools are not simply composites of classrooms, kind teachers, expansive hallways, and organized schedules. Instead, each school's attitude, purpose, activities, rituals, and demonstrations of student achievement have created an intergenerational institution of

sacredness founded on democratic ideals. And within each of these schools, powerful symbols of progressive education live on in those who have participated in it. (p. 2)

Glickman describes some of these schools' rituals, stories, symbols, and ceremonies. For example, students in one school gather in a morning circle in which they share their work or provide support. Another school created a quilt that shows the history of its community. In a small, wealthy school at the end of the year, everyone participates in a ritual in which they place notes expressing feelings such as sadness, anger, and regret on a boat that then floats away down a river.

However, it would be a mistake for an educator to assume that one can pick and choose from this list and apply one or more of the examples to one's own school. The point is, as Glickman says (but does not emphasize), these activities connect with the heart and soul of the school's students over generations. They are alive because they continue to speak to the inner meaning of the members of the school community. Glickman, however, does not mention the need to be mindful of how these rituals are done, whether they are performed with a full heart, and he leads the reader to assume that practicing such rituals by themselves can contribute to educational improvement. But what happens when rituals are practiced in a mechanical way and when the participants experience them as empty and meaningless rather than sacred? How does the school address this issue and connect everyday rituals with the inner lives of the participants?

The inner life is a realm with which the urban school counselor is most familiar and for which he or she is most qualified to serve as guide. In this inner space the counselor promotes the quality of everyday learning and guards and nurtures the intrinsic meaning of education, which is nothing less than full human transformation. It is also here, in schools with paint-peeling halls, broken water fountains, and shabby libraries—schools surrounded by abandoned buildings and junk-filled lots, whose yards serve as recruiting stations for gang members—that the sacred act of learning and growing with others, for now, must occur.

Transforming Everyday School Life

Imagine that we have been following around an urban middle school counselor, Ms. Smith, for a day with a video camera, then freeze-frame a certain moment. Here is what we might see:

> Ms. Smith is down the hall from her office talking with a new teacher, Ms. Brown, just outside Ms. Brown's classroom.
>
> A student, Jason, walking past Ms. Smith and Ms. Brown in the hall, is calling another student a "faggot."
>
> A student, Olga, thirteen, is waiting outside Ms. Smith's office to speak with her.

What Is the Role of Counseling in Urban Schools?

Inside Ms. Smith's office, the phone has lit up; it's the assistant principal, Mr. Jones.

A sign behind Ms. Smith and Ms. Brown announces a peer mediation group run by Ms. Smith, which is to start in a few minutes.

What follows is a deconstruction of these scenes, what the camera doesn't show us. It is the inner meaning of what the counselor does, which is both context dependent and illuminated by the mindful presence of Ms. Smith:

Ms. Smith is talking with a new teacher, Ms. Brown.

Counselors consult with teachers. They help them with classroom management issues and with individual students, some of whom the teacher refers to the counselor for assistance. In urban schools, there are a number of rigid, cynical, exhausted teachers waiting to retire. Some are also skeptical that children of color or those who need English language skills can learn much. Counselors can provide these teachers with empathy regarding their feelings of frustration and unhappiness. They then need to challenge them: If such teachers first feel heard and understood, they are more likely to be open to considering how their thinking and actions are not only toxic to themselves but harmful to the children. Counselors can try to get the teachers to consider other ways of thinking about the students and to offer them practical alternatives that work for both the teacher and the students.

There are also many new, idealistic teachers faced with scarce resources and overcrowded classrooms who are in danger of falling into despair and quitting. Their initial enthusiasm, creativity, and concern for children need to be rekindled. A counselor also would work with these teachers to provide them with support, encouragement, and a compassionate ear along with useful suggestions.

In this case Ms. Brown, a new teacher, has been seeking advice from Ms. Smith about classroom management. She has lessons to teach and test scores to improve and has been struggling with feeling frustrated and demoralized. In the beginning of the year the students' behavior ranged from sullen, bored, and alienated to angry, aggressive, and hyperactive.

Ms. Smith has been working with Ms. Brown on setting up a more responsive classroom. If the teacher can create a climate that addresses and meets more of the students' developmental and emotional needs, they are more likely to settle in and learn better. Ms. Smith has suggested that Ms. Brown adopt some group counseling skills within her classroom. As a result the students and Ms. Brown meet for a few minutes at the beginning of each class. They have established some rituals for greeting each other and for checking in on how they are feeling and sharing some news. Ms. Brown is open to Ms. Smith's suggestion that she create a time to make the classroom a sacred space, where even for a short time the children can know what it's like to feel safe and practice being at peace. Ms.

Brown is experimenting with setting up an agreement about how the class will conduct itself with input from the students.

The students have begun to feel that they are being taken more seriously and that Ms. Brown cares about them. There have been fewer fights and disruptions. Ms. Brown has been able to lighten up and share in some of the students' humor. Ms. Smith cautions Ms. Brown, however, to go only as far as she and the students feel comfortable and safe with going. Not all students are at the same emotional level. Some cannot handle a certain level of disclosure and require highly structured, limited activities. Ms. Smith also encourages Ms. Brown to seek support from other colleagues as well.

Ms. Smith is also helping Ms. Brown find ways of connecting the course material with the students' lives: using the content of relevant rap songs for lessons related to social studies and writing, doing oral history projects with students' family members and neighbors, having the students keep a journal. Ms. Brown is considering Ms. Smith's suggestion that the students do more small-group work in which they are given a problem and are required to solve it with others.

Ms. Brown is puzzled by these early adolescents' self-consciousness and self-centeredness as well as their slavish conformity to peers. Ms. Smith encourages Ms. Brown to reflect back on her own early adolescence and reconnect with some of her own feelings of uncertainty, insecurity, and need for approval. More than just promoting different pedagogical techniques, she hopes that Ms. Brown can maintain her own sense of compassion. Doing so would allow her to reach out to her students and create a more meaningful and effective learning experience for everyone.

A student, Jason, walking past calls another student a "faggot."

Ms. Smith overhears the comment and stops talking with Ms. Brown. Ms. Brown has also heard it and rolls her eyes. "They're at that all the time," Ms. Brown says. "I've gotten to the point where I ignore it. It's like, what can you do? That's just what they say."

Ms. Smith, however, stops Jason and asks to speak with him. Because she has previously established an informal relationship with him by visiting his classrooms and engaging him and his classmates in discussions, it is easier for Ms. Smith to ask him to please come over. She walks a few feet down the hall with Jason away from Ms. Brown in order not to embarrass him.

"I'm not happy about hearing you call another student a hurtful name," Ms. Smith says. "What does the word mean to you?"

Jason says it's no big deal, all the students say it all the time. "It doesn't even means the kid's gay, it's just a word we use," he tells her.

"That's part of the problem," Ms. Smith says. "It is a harmful word. It hurts kids who are gay and have a right to be who they are. It also hurts straight guys because then they don't dare act in any way that might invite the name: no crying, no showing you feel hurt by anything, no hugging…" Ms. Smith stops herself and realizes she doesn't want to give a moral lecture, especially in the hall, to a captive audience of one squirming to escape.

"Think about it," she tells Jason.

Ms. Smith is concerned about not letting the school lapse into an unsafe, uncaring place, where people are unconscious of and indifferent to the thousand daily taunts, humiliations, and injustices that happen in the blink of an eye but that over time can generate incremental wounds. Unlike Ms. Brown, she is trying to not let the little hurtful acts go unnoticed, but neither does she wish to be repressive, judgmental, and hurtful in turn. Ms. Smith realizes at that moment that she cannot do this by herself and would be foolish to try. The problem also needs to be tackled at an earlier phase by leading discussions on this issue in the classrooms and possibly even in assemblies and workshops. The entire school needs to think about how everyone treats each other but in a safe, compassionate, respectful format, not in a harsh, punitive, moralistic one. Administrators, teachers, and staff as well need to be mindful of what kinds of messages they send when they speak and act in certain ways.

It is not a matter of repressing language or of being politically correct; that kind of rigid, zero-tolerance policy tends to backfire and create further acting out. A repressive approach relies on external fixes: Certain words are forbidden; punishment must be meted out and policies enforced regardless of the circumstances as if that solves the problem of consciousness. For some, strong rules and policies are necessary and do provide a measure of safety and security for the school community. Still, Ms. Smith knows, there is a need to place the issue within a larger discussion, one that speaks to the heart of children's concerns and anxieties about gender identity, sexuality, acceptance from one's peers and oneself, and the need to feel safe. She promises herself that she will gather a task force of other school staff members, students, and parents to address the issue in a mindful way.

A student, Olga, thirteen, is waiting to speak with Ms. Smith.

Olga's English teacher referred her to Ms. Smith last week. Olga was acting aggressively toward other girls, and for an assigned composition she had written a story about a girl who self-destructs. The teacher has told Ms. Smith that Olga is very bright and speaks up in class. Ms. Smith has seen Olga once and scheduled her for a session tomorrow but told Olga to contact her if she needed to speak with her before then. Olga is hoping to catch Ms. Smith for a few minutes between periods.

Ms. Smith brings Olga inside her office and shuts the door. She tells her she has a few minutes now and gives Olga her undivided attention.

Olga is upset. This morning she had a fight with her mother, an immigrant from the Dominican Republic. Her mother has become mean and strict, she says. She won't let her stay with her friends after school. The mother is dating a man who deals drugs and whom Olga dislikes. Olga's father is in the Dominican

Republic and she misses him, but her mother makes it difficult for her to contact him, she says. She begins to cry.

Ms. Smith directs her entire presence toward Olga. She turns her body toward her and listens with an open heart and a full intent to understand her. Ms. Smith knows that very few children, or even adults, receive the luxury of this kind of nonjudgmental attentiveness, if even for a short time. Children in particular are sensitive to adults' cycles of attentiveness. Children require quality attention in order to thrive. Many adults are themselves distracted and unable to be with themselves in the present, let alone share this kind of presence with another. To make matters worse, many adults maintain their power over children by manipulating their attention, by focusing and then withdrawing their interest, and children are at their mercy in this regard. The Buddhist peace activist Thich Nhat Hanh encourages the practice of mindful listening in everyday life. He says that we often unintentionally harm those whom we love when we pay them only half a mind when they are speaking to us. Every time we tune out those we love, we destroy a piece of our relationship. We can understand that it is altogether easy to lapse into this habit amidst the infinite distractions of our complex lives; it is harder to set things aside and be in the present with someone. Yet it is a true way to establish and maintain genuine connections with others.

Olga senses that Ms. Smith is there for her. She relaxes somewhat and her breathing begins to slow. When Olga begins to cry, Ms. Smith hands her a tissue. She sees that Olga has a lot of things with which to contend in her life, involving her family, peers, school, and her sense of self.

"It hurts that you miss your *papi*," Ms. Smith says. "I wonder if you also miss your *mami* too."

Olga looks puzzled and says she doesn't know what Ms. Smith means; she's with her mother every day.

Ms. Smith suggests that Olga and her mother were probably once a lot closer. Now that Olga is growing up, she spends less time with her mother, who also has a new boyfriend.

Olga thinks about it. "That's true," she says. "It's different now."

Ms. Smith ventures to say that it's possible that her mother also misses Olga, her little girl, and still wants to keep her the way she was when she was younger. But she doesn't know how to act toward this young woman anymore. Her mother has already gone through some loss by moving here from her country.

Olga thinks about this too. Ms. Smith is cultivating Olga's sense of empathy and compassion, her ability to see others' points of view. But by the same token, she also encourages her to develop her own perspective, something that many girls begin to lose in favor of pleasing others. Ms. Smith tells Olga that she would like to invite her mother to come in for a family counseling session. Olga agrees to this. Ms. Smith tells her that she will see her tomorrow when they can talk more about her family situation. She also wants to speak with Olga about her work in school; she wants Olga to begin thinking about a good high school next year so she can prepare to go to college. She tells Olga about a group she is setting

What Is the Role of Counseling in Urban Schools?

up for other girls and invites her to join it. Ms. Smith has seen a number of young women in the school act harshly toward their own self-image and toward others and has heard them say that they are too fat and worry that they are not good enough to have a boyfriend. Ms. Smith also has seen many children of immigrant families struggle with establishing their autonomy and rebelling against the traditional values their families hold. She wants to address this issue in her groups as well.

When it is time for Olga to go, Ms. Smith says to her, "You have a right to be happy." Olga smiles for the first time. Personal joy is not a luxury, Ms. Smith believes; it is a basic entitlement, no less for these children.

The phone is lit up in Ms. Smith's office; the assistant principal, Mr. Jones, is calling.

Mr. Jones oversees the school counselors. Because Ms. Smith is with a client, Olga, she does not pick up the phone and lets it take a message. She will call Mr. Jones back as soon as possible.

Over the course of her own development Ms. Smith has had to work hard to set limits on her time and efforts. She is better at it now, but it is still not a simple matter. There are many needy people in the school, and they each have good need of Ms. Smith's skills. If Ms. Smith were not mindful, she would run around all day, drop everything, and try to accommodate everyone. When she was younger, Ms. Smith had the tendency to do just that. At an earlier job, she had trouble saying no and maintaining boundaries. She soon became resentful of many of her colleagues and her clients. She often would come down with colds; her body was telling her she needed to do something to take care of herself but she didn't listen. Each time she returned to work, she was unable to change her pattern and soon found herself falling even more behind in her work; she was on the verge of burning out. Soon after, Ms. Smith went back to school and studied mindful urban school counseling.

From her counseling education program, Ms. Smith has learned to set appropriate limits with Mr. Jones and others. At times Mr. Jones has entered her office when the door was closed and she was meeting with a student, teacher, or even a family. She has spoken to him about this. She makes sure she closes the door and places a sign out front. She takes time for lunch as well; even the pop psychology books, she reminds herself, tell you that you're no good to others if you're no good to yourself. Mr. Jones has many crises; if he is short-staffed at times, he has felt that Ms. Smith needs to drop everything and substitute for the person who is absent. Ms. Smith has told Mr. Jones that she is willing to brainstorm other ways to help him solve his staffing shortage and to do some preventive planning to minimize the administration's lurching from one crisis to the next.

Mr. Jones pushes some of Ms. Smith's (emotional) buttons. He can be disrespectful and throws his weight around. He represents some of the narrow, bureaucratic values that Ms. Smith hopes the school will move beyond: a taste for petty and rigid displays of power, a penchant for seeing students as numbers rather than people, and an insensitivity and lack of awareness of the cultural background of many of the students. Ms. Smith has worked at being mindful of her feelings of irritability toward Mr. Jones. She has noticed that he is the kind of authoritarian male with whom she grew up in her family. She has tried to become aware of any negative thoughts or feelings that arise when she interacts with him, to acknowledge them, then breathe and let them go. She realizes she is the one with the problem and decided that she did not want to live with aggravation and give anyone that kind of power over her well-being and state of mind.

Over the course of time she has noticed that Mr. Jones has less of an effect on her equanimity. She also has come to better understand his way of thinking and the values he holds and has even developed some compassion for him. After all, he is under considerable pressure from administrators to raise test scores and to improve school attendance. She sees that he is hard on himself as well as others and does not seem to be a happy person. She also has noticed that some of the boys respond positively to his style and approach. They appreciate the clear structure and no-nonsense version of right and wrong he provides, his emphasis on a work ethic with its promise of rewards to come, and his gruff but at times playful demeanor.

Ms. Smith calls Mr. Jones back. He is tense over the phone. Mr. Jones has an upcoming deadline for a report, and he needs input from Ms. Smith. He needs numbers, research-backed data that show that the school is improving. The principal is on him, he tells her; he feels like the principal, the district superintendent, the city chancellor, the state commissioner all want a piece of his hide.

"I'm sorry to hear that," Ms. Smith says. "I know you're working hard, and it sounds like these folks don't appreciate your efforts."

Mr. Jones thanks her. He slows down a bit and asks her when she can get in her part of the report. Ms. Smith tells him, "You'll have it on your desk by the end of the week, before Monday's deadline." Mr. Jones is happy about that, and the way Ms. Smith put it somehow makes him feel more reassured. Ms. Smith has been working on ways she can help the school improve test scores and decrease truancy. She did some action research projects in which she collected data before and after implementing some counseling programs. She was able to show that involving the students and parents in certain school projects contributed to better test scores and higher attendance. In this case Ms. Smith had worked to ensure that her own motives dovetailed with those of the administration: By generating data she was establishing her own successful track record in order to justify funding and support for more counseling programs.

Ms. Smith asks about Mr. Jones's family. Mr. Jones waxes effusive about his son's first year at college and his daughter's grades in high school. Before hanging up, Ms. Smith asks Mr. Jones if he would consider following up on a concern of hers. She has been getting reports from some of the younger students that some of the eighth graders are fondling each other and possibly engaging in sexual activity in certain stairwells between classes. She asks that he follow up on this and coordinate an effort among the teachers, custodians, and guards to step up more hall monitoring. On her end Ms. Smith says she would like to identify some of the eighth graders and run a classroom workshop and a more extended group for them on sexuality, intimacy, and relationships. Mr. Jones agrees to act on her request.

Ms. Smith runs a peer mediation group.

The peer mediation group is one of Ms. Smith's favorite projects. Teachers and administrators require students who get into fights to appear before the group, which then helps decide how to resolve the conflict. Of late more students are referring themselves, a sign that students respect the group and find it helpful. A number of the boys and girls are popular leaders who were elected by their classmates to the group. They take the group seriously and already have had an impact on the overall climate of the school.

The group on occasion meets on its own without adjudicating a conflict. Ms. Smith has noticed that there are two dominant trends of thinking among the group that coexist but sometimes are in conflict. Both are of a higher-order level. One tendency emphasizes communal values. These students feel strongly that everyone is equal and has a right to be heard, that people who are different should be accepted, and that consensus and collaboration are necessary. Sometimes, however, the communally oriented students get too worked up about their principles and end up rigidly advancing them: No one can be better than anyone in anything; all differences are good and equal; everyone must participate; we must share everything; we must agree on everything; no one can be confronted, because it hurts their feelings.

The second tendency is more individualistic. These students feel that there are standards for success and that some individuals deserve more than others due to their hard work and mastery. They feel that a person's knowledge and abilities rather than consensus should determine who gets what. There are winners and losers, and people should be willing to compete; the winners get the goods, and the losers take their lumps if necessary. The individualists, in turn, sometimes adopt a greedy and selfish take on things. At times they insist on individual self-interest, calculation, and domination at the expense of moral obligation to others.

Today, two boys are appearing before the group. Both are on the basketball team and keep getting into fights. A teacher who is their head coach sent them to the peer mediation group. They both are egocentric and have limited ability to see another's viewpoint. They take every slight personally and can think only in terms of revenge and retaliation.

After hearing the two boys' sides of the story, those peer mediators who value a more communal approach suggest that the two continue to talk it out until they reach a mutual agreement about how to get along. The young men do not know how to do this; the strategy fails and gets them nowhere. The more individualistically inclined mediators encourage the two boys to make their best argument about why each one is right and let the best one win. This serves to rekindle their animosity and power struggle.

Ms. Smith intervenes. She realizes that the young men's level of development is such that they cannot yet do what either of the mediator positions suggests. They are in need of a more structured arbitration. Ms. Smith summons the group privately and tells them that they will have to serve as the external authority for these young men. She asks them by what social order or rule these two would best comply and why. After some discussion the group concludes that the two would feel guilty if they let their basketball teammates down; they are to be ordered to stop fighting for the sake of the team and even the entire school, which is rooting for them. The young men appear relieved. It is out of their hands, and they accept the decision.

In this case Ms. Smith is attuned both to what the young men and the group are able to understand and to what is needed. She realizes that the boys do not have enough autonomous ego strength or internalized social constraints to resolve their conflicts. They require a more structured social order to keep them in line. The factions within her mediation group, while operating at higher levels, still tend to think that their way is the only right one. From her perch atop the whole developmental spiral, Ms. Smith maintains an overview of everyone involved. She is flexible enough to move up and down through the various levels of awareness as required in order to maximize the students' growth.

Conclusion

Urban school communities and their members face difficult conditions and are in need of care. They require a new kind of counselor who is wise and compassionate, one who can visualize the entire multidimensional interplay of the system and creatively work within it for the full benefit of all its citizens. Such counselors themselves need support and specialized education in the complexities of an urban system, in understanding and working with all developmental levels of consciousness, and in mindfulness-based counseling. As higher-order "wizards," mindful urban school counselors can then help promote individual and communal development, academic and personal growth, and order and creativity all together. Such counselors bring about true knowledge because they understand and speak to the heart of what matters and are attuned to the wonder of the present moment. Ms. Smith is out there in the schools; we need others to join her.

REFERENCES

Beck, Don E., & Cowan, Christopher C. (2002). *Spiral dynamics: Mastering values, leadership, and change.* Malden, MA: Blackwell.

Educational Leadership, 60, 34-39. Website: http://www.ascd.org/publications/ed_lead/200303/glickman.html. Accessed November 7, 2003.

Glickman, Carl D. (2003). Symbols and celebrations that sustain education.

Goleman, Daniel (2003). *Destructive emotions: How can we overcome them? A scientific dialogue with the Dalai Lama*. New York: Bantam.

Kegan, Robert (1994). *In over our heads: The mental demands of modern life*. Cambridge, MA: Harvard University Press.

Kessler, Rachael (2000). *The soul of education: Helping students find connection, compassion, and character at school*. Alexandria, VA: Association for Supervision and Curriculum Development.

Miller, Ron (1997). *What are schools for? Holistic education in American culture*. Brandon, VT: Holistic Education.

Simmer-Brown, Judith (1999). Commitment and openness: A contemplative approach to pluralism. In S. Glazer (Ed.), *The heart of learning: Spirituality in education* (pp. 97-112). New York: Tarcher/Putnam.

CHAPTER FIFTEEN

Haroon Kharem

What Does It Mean to Be in a Gang?

It became clear that school labeling practices and the exercise of rules operated as part of a hidden curriculum to marginalize and isolate Black male youth in disciplinary spaces and brand them as criminally inclined.

(Ann Arnett Ferguson, 2001)

True nerve exposes a lack of fear of dying...the clear risk of violent death may be preferable to being "dissed" by another.... Not to be afraid...has made the concept of manhood a part of his very identity, he has difficulty manipulating it—it often controls him.

(Elijah Anderson, 1995)

For many teachers, gang life is a remote and terribly frightening concept. For many Americans, in general, few things scare them as much as the possibility of running into gangs. Many of us have watched the movie *Grand Canyon* and can relate to the fear that Kevin Kline's character experienced when his car broke down in Los Angeles on his way home from a Lakers game. He faces the scariest group in the United States—a group of young black men. He is saved from death only by the intervention of a "good" black man, portrayed by Danny Glover. Black men must always bear the consequences of such white fear. Indeed, one cannot understand American history without insight into the role that white fear of black men has played in shaping the nation's institutions and its consciousness.

Too infrequently do teachers and students in urban teacher education gain insight into what it means to be a black, Latino, or Asian gang member. Many of the programs purporting to educate teachers and other citizens about gangs have little to say about why young people feel the need to join them. Feelings of powerlessness, a lack of respect from others, and low self-esteem experienced by young black men and women and the relationship between these feelings and gang membership are not common insights among educators. So often the ostensibly "random acts of violence" committed by gang members are directly related to efforts to assert their self-worth, to demand respect, and to defend their dignity. In the twenty-first century the only solution to the problems presented by gangs in the cities involves building more prisons, installing metal detectors in schools, and treating children as adult offenders. Such policies, however, have not worked, as the number of black males in prison continues to increase. Incarceration rates for black males in the United States are five times higher than they were in South Africa at the height of apartheid.

From my vantage point as a black male who grew up as a gang member in Brooklyn, New York, I watch with amazement the ways that such policies are justified and implemented. Political and educational leaders often promote such policies with little effort to study and understand the experiences and perspectives of young people who grow up in urban poverty, with its attendant racism and class bias. Many of these policymakers have no experience working with or even talking to young people who face these realities on a daily basis. Without this knowledge, such policymakers make a career of responding to only the symptoms of urban social problems—not their causes. Urban schools spend millions of dollars developing more rules, hiring security personnel, buying metal detectors, constructing schools for at-risk children, and contracting anti-gang consultants. In these responses, students from gangs are viewed from outside the context of their lives and everyday experiences. Many of the answers provided to principals and teachers by anti-gang consultants never mention racism and poverty as factors that move young people to join gangs. They never ask what it might mean to be in a gang.

Such questions might produce information that could help political and educational leaders develop social and educational policies that actually work to solve the causes of gang-related problems. Students who are gang members many times speak with great insight about why gangs exist and often present very powerful suggestions about what schools can do to address the realities that create them. Such students are often far more helpful than paid consultants because they are not as concerned with telling school officials what they want to hear. Typically the only agenda such students are pursuing involves their struggle to be treated respectfully and with dignity. The knowledge they bring to school is the view from outside, the subjugated knowledge of institutions that is too often dismissed from our understanding of what really is going on in urban schools and the communities that surround them. A thirteen-year-old boy who is attacked daily on his way to school, for example, is a prime candidate for a gang. An anti-gang program that urges students to "say no" to gangs and study hard because it's the right thing to do has no meaning for the thirteen-year-old who is getting his teeth knocked out. The high moral tone of such programs can be offensive to those students who understand the complexity of moral choices involved in joining a gang.

To know the importance of listening to the voices of our urban students caught in the quagmire of poverty and racism is essential to being and becoming an urban teacher. Every urban teacher must understand the violence, fear, and sense of indignity that students bring to the classroom. Such understanding, I argue, cannot be separated from the curriculum of urban schools. While not all students experience these problems, those who don't have much to learn from those who do. New understandings of one another will emerge in the conversations that take place in this context. Teachers, principals, and educational policymakers who listen in to these conversations may learn more than they expected about the fabric of the society in which they live. We all have a story.

Returning to East New York and Ocean Hill-Brownsville for the first time in over 20 years brought strong emotional memories as I drove to an elementary school not far from where my sister used to live on Sutter Avenue and Barby Street. I was saddened that the building she lived in no longer existed, that there was no memory of the families, the kids, and the fire that claimed the lives of my niece and nephew during the Christmas holidays of 1971. My memory of East New York and Brownsville is of vacant lots, the Pitkin Avenue shopping area, walking down Sutter Avenue hearing cuts from Curtis Mayfield's *Super Fly,* Isaac Hayes's *Theme from Shaft,* Earth Wind and Fire's "Power" from their album *Last Days and Time,* or the Dramatics' *Whatcha See Is Whatcha Get.* You could go from one end of Sutter Avenue to the other and see people you knew.

My other memories are of the street gangs that lived in the Brownsville-East New York section. One constant that has not changed is the level of poverty and the look of struggle and frustration on people's faces. The people are not mean or nasty, but as they go from childhood to adulthood in Brownsville-East New York, the daily struggles begin to etch lines in their faces. The other constant is that gangs still fight over the same turf over which those before them fought, turf that none of them ever legally owned. Yet many young black males fought and died over a cement block that they loved and at the same time hated.

Street gangs have always existed for kids from poor, working-, and middle-class families in New York City. The early 1970s were no different than the present, except for the names of the gangs that ran the streets back then: the Savage Skulls, the Savage Nomads, the Black Spades, and the Tomahawks. They owned the streets of Ocean Hill/Brownsville/East New York, as well as the South Bronx. They fought each other for control of turfs and no doubt supplied the precursors of those who fought the crack turf wars of the 1980s. There were no drive-by shootings back then, but gang battles were brutal, and anything that could maim or kill became a weapon. This was a time when a black teen had to know how to "use his hands" in close-quarter fights, because that was how you earned respect. Hollywood has created an image of gang members as karate and kickboxing experts. I never saw anyone use karate or kickboxing in a fight. The violence in gangs today differs from our lifestyle. We did not spray a rival gang member's house with automatic-weapons fire (such guns were not available on the streets yet). We did not threaten or hurt the family of a rival gang member. The killing has changed—not only is it more violent, but bystanders and family members are also injured and killed. Ocean Hill-Brownsville gang wars took a toll on black youth as the funerals mounted and prisons became full of gang members from the streets. Mike Tyson was from our neighborhood; he was a little too young to become a Tomahawk, but probably admired us as he watched us walking and sporting our colors without fear of the police.

Street gangs require only a few unspoken codes, the violation of any one of which can demand dire penalties. Allegiance/loyalty is the most important ingredient. If you grew up with most of the members, you had more than a mutual allegiance. There was a familial love that bound the members to each other—and an inner silent pledge to protect each other, your turf, and your community from all outsiders. There is this assumption (especially promoted by the movie industry) that gangs harass the community. However, I remember that many shopkeepers in black and Hispanic communities knew most gang members, from childhood. If any harassment took place, it was usually the result of the shopkeeper's treatment of community members. The majority of the neighborhood people were not afraid to walk the streets, as everyone knew each other and the community was made up of extended family members and friends; in fact, many gang members kept the streets safe for the neighborhood. While the neighborhood had its collection of pimps and prostitutes, drug dealers, and other kinds of street entrepreneurs whom we knew on a first-name basis, we were not involved in those activities. In fact, some of the hustlers on the street were once in gangs themselves and knew what lines not to cross. They were tolerated as long as their hustle did not harm any family members of gangs (mothers, fathers, brothers, sisters, even extended family).

While drugs were rampant in Brownsville and East New York, most gang members were not involved in selling drugs as they are today—one could not be a viable Savage Skull, Savage Nomad, Black Spade, or Tomahawk and be on hardcore drugs. It is not to say that we did not consume drugs, but anyone becoming addicted to hardcore drugs lost any respect he ever had within the gangs.

As a young black kid in the Fort Greene section of Brooklyn, the first street gangs I remember were the Fort Greene Chaplains and the Mau Maus from the Marcy Projects on Flushing Avenue. As a kid in the first grade, we all looked up to these older gang members with awe—they seemed to sport their gang jackets (now called colors) without fear of the police. These were our heroes, the ones we wanted to be like, and we admired their stories, battle scars, their narrow escapes from the police, and their passage through the prison system. We wanted their approval and acceptance and waited for our turn to be able to join them and share our own stories of passage. Many of the older gang members were older brothers, cousins, or neighbors.

As I teach potential public school teachers, most seem to forget or not realize that when children leave the school premises, they have to survive in neighborhoods. They have to physically and verbally defend themselves and their family members. Some potential teachers believe, whether through societal beliefs or statistical data, that black children rarely make it into honors classes and should be relegated to compensatory or special education classes (Ferguson, 2001). I remember when we first moved into the Farragut Houses in Fort Greene, our building was right across the street from the Brooklyn Navy Yard. From my tenth-floor bedroom window I could see clear across Brooklyn. I can remember many nights when the gangs would fight the sailors and white workers from the Navy Yard. A sailor or worker verbally sexually harassing a teenager or young woman in the neighborhood drew immediate retaliation. This was always a major cause of the fights. My first trip to the store for my mother was an awakening experience that prepared me, as similar errands did for other kids, to know how to handle myself when I became older. I had to walk through the entire Farragut Houses projects to get to the store. This was a nightmare, as fear would grip me and many other kids, as we were always challenged by small roving bands of kids from the project. When I would reach the store, there were always older kids waiting for me to come out with change I supposedly did not have. Parents always sent their kids to the store to buy groceries or something they themselves forgot to purchase. To a kid in elementary school, it was either fun because you got to go outside (if you were being punished) or a nightmare if you ran into older kids waiting for you on the way to or from the store. Once confronted, you had two choices: You could give up the money and get slapped around a little or you could fight, and if you lost, you still lost the money. No matter what choice you made, you better not lose the money. If you did, you would have to face the wrath of an angry parent. Some parents walked with you back to the store to confront the kids who took the money and beat you. It was common to see a mother standing there telling her child that he better get their money back. Readers may think that mothers were too harsh on the kid, but one could not grow up in the projects and have his or her self-respect questioned. (When my mother took my brother and me anywhere, we had to be on our best behavior so as not to embarrass her in front of white people.)

Young black males are perceived as behavior problems in schools because teachers and educators fail to understand their cultural norms, that self-respect is highly regarded, and for some it is the only thing they have. The idea of having "respect" has caused so much death among black males, and yet it is the least understood quality of being a black male. Growing up in the projects, this "respect" was crucial to survival and dignity. Having respect made others leave you alone. Such respect was earned by how well you could protect yourself from physical violence through the use of physical violence. While this respect may generate pride within the individual and respect from others, it is generated by a fear that emerges at an early age. Young black males are forced to make decisions while very young concerning their survival and well-being. I remember a fight I had with a bigger and older kid when I was in the second grade. All day in class and at lunch, my only concern was the fight. I did not pay attention to anything the teacher said all day. My greatest fear was what would happen if I ran away. I knew if I shied away from the fight, I would have no respect at all from my peers, and I would be labeled a punk—a designation that would spread not only around the school but also throughout the projects.

Teachers need to understand that no child wants to be associated with being a goofy milquetoast, like Urkel in the TV sitcom *Family Matters* (a cartoon of a black intellectual). I remember that by fifth grade I was trying not to carry any books to school because when I got into fights, I hated to have my books sprawled all over the sidewalk. More importantly, it was not cool or hip to carry books. While I enjoyed reading and read books voraciously—as did so many other kids—I did not want to be seen as not being cool. Gloria Ladson-Billings (2001) tells the story of a young black male who felt that his sense of respect among his peers in the community was more important than bringing his books home to do his homework. The teacher who saw that the student was clowning in class and not doing his homework could have punished him but instead struck a deal with him that allowed him to complete his homework and maintain his sense of respect with his peers in the community (pp. 77-8). Culture is more than historical heritage in this case; culture here is also defined as how young black males see themselves and the world. More importantly, the teacher was sensitive enough to see that the problem was not necessarily a behavior problem. Buoyed by this understanding, the teacher allowed the student to maintain his dignity and in the process empowered him to complete his homework.

I have observed many elementary school-aged black males struggling to holding back tears as teachers and other school administrators berate and scold them for minor infractions. Such students are attempting to maintain their sense of manhood and respect. What often happens is that tension builds up inside until something or someone causes them to become violent. They strike out sensing that they have no outlet, no alternative. Many young black males have a sense that no one cares for them, so why should they themselves care what happens? Nathan McCall (1994) makes an important observation: "For as long as I can remember, black folks have always had a serious thing about respect. I guess because white people disrespected them so blatantly for so long that blacks viciously protected what little morsels of self-respect they had left" (p. 55).

Last year I witnessed a third-grade teacher scream at one of the black males in her classroom to the point that he left his seat and walked out. The teacher continued to scream at him into the hallway. I followed the kid into the hallway and waited until he walked back down the hall toward me. When I asked him if he understood that if he maintained this path of just walking out of the classroom he would be sent to the principal's office, he replied that he knew it and did not care. I continued the dialogue and asked, "If you keep this up as you get older, you know where you are going to end up?" He replied, "Yes, prison." I was not only saddened but angered, wondering how schools became training grounds for the prison system, that this third-grade student already knew where he was headed because no one cared enough to detour him from the path he was traveling. I understood that this young black male felt that the only recourse he had was to leave the class to hold onto what little self-respect he had left.

When I entered the third grade, I did not realize that I was part of the experiment of desegregation. I was bused, without my mother's permission, to a predominantly white school in the Fort Hamilton section of Brooklyn. The policymakers who passed and implemented the desegregation never allowed us black kids to tell them what we thought about all of this busing. Why was I taken from a school just across the street from our apartment to a school all the way across Brooklyn? Why was I forced to be outside to catch the bus at 7:15 A.M. every morning until the sixth grade? (By the way, kids from the projects did not have school buses—we were required to use public transportation.) Also, why was this desegregation just a one-way street? No white kids were bused into the Fort Greene or Red Hook schools where some of the other black kids came from.

In the classes in the school to which we were bused, we were not allowed to talk because many of the teachers did not think we had any knowledge to contribute to the class. If one of us raised our hand, he/she was passed over. This made me mad and stopped me from even trying to participate in the class lessons. We were always placed in the back of the classroom and punished more harshly for behavior problems. If we got into a dispute with the white kids, it was always our fault. Many of the black kids had physical altercations with white kids over being called a "nigger," and we always ended up in the principal's office for starting the fight. Everett Dawson, a black teacher in North Carolina in the 1970s, said that he attended in-service seminars on how to deal with black students who were coming to the predominantly white schools. The "experts" on black students told a group of white teachers that the "black students weren't going to be polite [and] were not going to bring in all their homework every day, and [warned] the white teachers [about what they] were going to have to accept from the black students once the schools were integrated" (Foster, 1997, p. 7). According to the narrative, the experts continued this for three days until a black teacher raised the question: "How are black teachers to get along with the white students?" Are potential teachers to assume that because a child is black, there will be problems? Are there workshops on what images and what societal beliefs a white teacher may bring to a classroom of black children? Does the term "at risk" (which really is a racial code word for a black or Hispanic child from a poor community) bring to the mind of the teacher an image of this child as one who cannot learn like any other child?

I remember vividly a geography lesson on the continents. When the teacher asked the class what kind of things would be found in Africa, all the students, even the black students, responded by saying jungles, elephants, gorillas, lions, and giraffes. There was no mention of people or cities, no mention of any civilization, because in their minds Africa was not a civilized place; it was the Dark Continent. I can remember most of us black students getting quiet in the class because Africa was not a place we wanted to be associated with in comparison with what was discussed in class about the European and North American continents. We resisted participation in the lessons on Africa because we did not want to be people of African descent. To be called an African was an insult, even though the Black Power movement was just getting under way. Any reference to Africa throughout my school life was always that of the jungle, of wild animals or seminaked people who were in need of civilizing. As David Livingstone wrote in 1867: "We come among them as members of a superior race…that desires to elevate the more degraded portions of the human family" (Coupland, 1928, p. 107). Why would we want to associate with Africa or its cultural norms if everything we were shown about the place we came from was primitive? As I write, the words of Carter G. Woodson, written back in 1933 come to mind:

> The same educational process which inspires and stimulates the oppressor with the thought that he is everything and has accomplished everything worthwhile, depresses and crushes at the same time the spark of genius in the Negro by making him feel that his race does not amount to much and never will measure up to the standards of other peoples. (Woodson, 1990)

Our teachers never realized that our silence and resistance to their geography lessons had connections to a racist ideology that celebrated Eurocentric paradigms while it disparaged who we were as children of African descent. I can also remember a teacher telling one of the black students who had raised his hand and yelled out the answer to put his hand down, that we needed to learn how to be obedient to the rules so that we could learn "how to be taught." I never understood what she meant until years later. She was telling us that we needed to learn complete obedience to the school rules, but more importantly she was telling us that we (and our culture) were deficient and in need of correction. The cultural orientation and ideological teacher preparation she had received in college had informed her that black children were all part of a deficient culture whose language skills needed *drilling* in the rules of "proper" English. The teacher had been abstractly trained against racism but had not been trained in how to translate the abstract into actual experience. Her pedagogy was still paternalistic, and she delegitimatized our culture, history, and language.

Today, middle-class black teachers who refuse to identify with poor blacks have joined with those whites who believe that children from the projects are inadequate, pathological, and in need of civilizing. Recently, I was sitting in the office of a colleague when a former student came in to see the other professor. I asked her how teaching was and she responded with confidence, "They are animals!" I was surprised because within one year of teaching she had already come to believe that the kids in her elementary school were no better than animals that needed to be caged. When teachers can refer to young children and teenagers as animals, it is no surprise that within the course of the day there are many negative comments and few acts of encouragement. Many studies claim that the majority of the behavior problems in schools are caused by black males who need to be banished to the principal's office or expelled into the streets so that the other students can learn (Ferguson, 2001).

What Does It Mean to Be in a Gang?

As I look back, I see bitterness among the black males who were bused to the white schools. By the time most of us were in the sixth grade, many hated going to the school. We had also become aware about race, and we knew we were not welcome in the white schools. Thus, we lived in a different world five days a week from 8 to 3. We were forced to live in a world where race was foremost in our consciousness, knowing as we did that the teachers thought we were unteachable. During lunchtime, when the white kids went to the store, we were not allowed to go, as the parents told the school they did not want us walking around their neighborhood. The other world was life in the projects, with its black and Puerto Rican families. Here we could be ourselves, as we were removed from the fearful microscope of white people.

By the time I reached the seventh grade, we were all in small gangs, or as they are called today, "crews." We were still being bused to the predominantly white schools in the Bay Ridge section of Brooklyn. Thus, we were still fighting white kids in school and on the way to the bus or train. Back in the projects, we mimicked the older gangs in our neighborhood. We would fight the gangs from Fort Greene over the smallest things just about every Friday night. However, these were only fistfights that were mostly caused by a kid from either project venturing into the other's project to see a girl or an argument at a party. Most of us were still going to school, even though we were beginning to skip classes, being sent to the principal's office more often, becoming petty hustlers, and beginning to hang with the older gang members.

By the time I had reached the tenth grade, I was no longer going to school and was living with my older sister. I joined the Tomahawks, who were small when I joined in the beginning but had the reputation as being one of the toughest gangs in New York City. As our reputation spread, we grew to over 500 members with chapters all over Brooklyn. The violence was constant, as we fought rival gangs from the South Bronx and other parts of Brooklyn. We periodically fought with a Crown Heights gang called the Jolly Stompers, who were kids from lower-middle-class/working-class black families. As I look back on all that we did as young black males, whether it was how we dressed, fought, or talked to girls, it always concerned our need for respect. The emphasis of the streets and our lives was rooted in respect. Some of the most brutal fights stemmed from petty incidents that embodied some affront to a person's respect.

The first part of my life having been spent on the streets of New York City, the second part has been spent correcting the consequences of the first part. As I attended college, I came to understand that many black males received two degrees: One was earned in college; the other was earned as we studied who we were as black men, reading about African/African American history, sociology, psychology, and every other discipline to gain the knowledge we needed to appreciate who we were. Some might say I have arrived in society having received a doctorate degree. While I have crossed over the poverty line into a world of scholars and professionals, my life as a black man in American society has not changed much at all. I still get stopped by the police and questioned, I still get those looks from some whites as to why I am driving or walking through their neighborhood. I still receive looks from people that say I am intimidating to them, no matter how unaggressive and unthreatening I act without losing my "respect." It amazes me that some white people hate it when black males act aggressively on the job, but yet at the same time demand aggressive behavior on the ladder to upward mobility. They want passive young black males in the class-room but then expect us, all of a sudden, to become aggressive as long as it does not threaten their position.

Negrophobia or the fear of the black man has a long history in the United States. It affects how black children are educated and prepared to become citizens in a country that consistently views them as a societal problem. For too long this negrophobia has caused the dominant society to tell us as black males that we are good for nothing, and we have internalized this and other opinions of the oppressor (our not being "capable of learning anything," our being "unproduc-tive") to the point where we believe the lie ourselves. This negrophobia has caused a whole educational system to not expect much from black males. Instead, it has caused our society to construct and spend billions of dollars on massive prisons to house them rather than educating them.

REFERENCES

Anderson, Elijah (1995). The code of the streets. *Atlantic Monthly, 273,* 80-94.

Coupland, Reginald (1928). *Kirk on the Zambesi: A chapter of African history.* Oxford: Clarendon.

Ferguson, Ann Arnett (2001). *Bad boys: Public schools in the making of black masculinity.* Ann Arbor: University of Michigan Press.

Foster, Michele (Ed.) (1997). *Black teachers on teaching.* New York: The New Press.

Ladson-Billings, Gloria (2001). *Crossing over to Canaan: The journey of new teachers in diverse classrooms.* San Francisco: Jossey-Bass.

McCall, Nathan (1994). *Makes me wanna holler: A young black man in America.* New York: Random House.

Woodson, Carter G. (1990). *The miseducation of the Negro* [1933]. Trenton, NJ: Africa World.

CHAPTER SIXTEEN

Leah Henry-Beauchamp & Tina Siedler

Why Is Health
an Urban Issue?
Asthma: A Case in Point

We never signed up for this e-tour of duty. I knew being a parent was going to be hard. It was expected that our children would get sick, but the hospital, the medicine, the worry was never what we had in mind.... I hate asthma! Asthma makes me feel helpless in my ability to help my own son. It's terrifying when taking a simple breath becomes a chore.

Mother of a four-year-old

When students enter a teacher education program, they expect courses in curriculum, methods, and content knowledge. Colleges of education place emphasis on meeting the needs of teacher certification for individual states, preparing students for exams and assessment, and, on occasion, teaching about diversity and cultural difference. Preservice teachers do not enter a program expecting courses on or even mention of issues of health and safety. The occasional mention of urban health usually centers on problems with drugs and alcohol. In fact, images of the bad health of urban dwellers are obsessed with the consequences of addiction, crime victimization, and/or the dangers of sexual encounters. Issues like low birth weight, infant mortality, lead paint poisoning, poor diet, and the dangers of transportation are ignored. Teachers who plan to teach in urban areas must become well versed in the identification and treatment of both symptoms and diseases that are endemic to the city environment. In this chapter, I will discuss only asthma and its ramifications on young children. This chapter should serve as a model for teacher educators and teachers in what details are needed in order to educate those who are attempting to educate our urban children. I encourage readers to collect equal information on other ailments that are particularly serious in our cities.

Asthma: The Specifics

Asthma is a serious health issue that affects millions of urban children. The number of children diagnosed with asthma has steadily increased over the past ten years. Estimates from current research indicate that over one quarter of all African American children in urban areas have asthma. Despite various educational programs and efforts, there continues to be a growing number of children with asthma who are in need of services. It is crucial that parents and educators are familiar with the basics of asthma, including signs of an attack, potential promoters and triggers, and methods of treatments and prevention. With a general understanding of asthma, adults will learn to feel secure and confident in treating a child with asthma at home or in the classroom.

Asthma is a chronic lung disease which is caused by an increased reaction of a person's airways to various stimuli (ALA, 2003a). Asthma is considered a chronic condition because the lungs of a person with asthma are always inflamed. Asthma is also an episodic disease, causing attacks to occur when a person's inflamed lungs are constricted to the point where normal breathing is difficult or sometimes impossible. Attacks usually occur after a person with asthma comes in contact with a trigger and can consist of episodes of wheezing, coughing, shortness of breath, and a tightening in the chest. These attacks vary in intensity and may start suddenly or take a few days to develop (Butler, 2000). If asthma is not properly treated, it can cause death.

The statistics for pediatric asthma are alarming. It is estimated that 7.7 million children under the age of eighteen have been diagnosed with asthma; 3.8 million had an asthma episode in 1999 (ALA, 2003a). The numbers of children with asthma have contributed to its being the leading serious chronic illness among children and the leading cause of missed school days due to chronic conditions (ALA, 2003a). Most children have mild to moderate cases of asthma which can be treated by medication and monitoring. For some children the illness can be more severe and cause multiple hospitalizations and other complications. For children under the age of fifteen, asthma is the number one cause of hospitalization (ALA, 2003a). The estimated annual costs of treating asthma in children under the age of eighteen are estimated to be $3.2 billion (ALA, 2003b).

When asthma symptoms become exacerbated, children may not be able to attend school. These symptoms cause children to miss 10 million school days each year (AAAAI, 2002). Loss of a child's school day can lead to a parent or caregiver missing a day of work:

> I have missed so many days of work because of asthma. What am I supposed to do? My kid can't breathe—literally. My boss at first was sympathetic, but now that he realizes the

reality of having a kid with asthma, I get no sympathy. A cold is one thing. The chicken pox is completely understandable. Even a high temperature or vomiting. Those are the kinds of excuses my boss understands. He does not understand asthma…. A couple of times, I have to admit, my child has told me he can't breathe and I have corrected him saying, "No baby, you just can't breathe well today!" I sent my sick child to school, just to keep that job. I love my kid. I hate the job. I really need the money. Tough choice. Asthma forces me to make calls like that.

This decrease in productivity among parents and caregivers has an estimated annual value of $1 billion (Butler, 2000).

A person does not grow out of asthma: It is a chronic condition. Asthma is a hereditary disease. The odds of having a child with asthma are three times greater in families that have one parent with asthma and six times greater if both parents have it (Butler, 2000). However, as people with asthma grow older, they become more accustomed to warning signs of an attack, how to avoid triggers, and the best treatment options for them. Asthma can become a manageable condition for many. However, for young children, it can be dangerous:

The scariest moment in my whole life was March 26, 2002. Our second child was a month old. I remember parts of that day so clearly. It was such a beautiful winter morning. The whole world seemed to be blanketed in snow. My son had been coughing and wheezing for days. I had taken him to a doctor and had religiously given him the prescribed medicine. At any rate, I needed to change my daughter and I did not have a diaper downstairs. I left my son alone in the family room and quickly ran upstairs with our daughter in my arms to get the diaper. The whole thing took a total of 60 seconds. When I got back downstairs it was silent…. Time started doing that thing—you know, go real slow. My son was lying face down in a pool of clear vomit. I panicked. He was sheet white and barely conscious.

It has been a year and I still cannot tell you how I managed to get the three of us to the emergency room at the hospital…. We laugh now, but my husband wanted to know why I wasn't embarrassed being in the hospital with my pajamas and slippers on. But at the time all I was thinking about was my son. Seven days later he was released from the hospital.

Because of their age and inexperience, children in urban settings will not always be aware of triggers and how to avoid them. If they are infants or toddlers, they will not be able to communicate their symptoms to their parents. In these cases it is the responsibility of the parents to be extremely vigilant and aware of their child's health behaviors. There is also the concern that it is not "cool" to use an inhaler and that children and youth can be teased and bullied when it is apparent that they have asthma.

Promoters and Triggers of Asthma

There is no one definitive explanation for why asthma continues to affect so many children, but there is research as to why asthma and asthma attacks happen. Without promoters and triggers, a person with asthma would never experience an asthma attack. Asthma *promoters* are things such as allergies, tobacco smoke, and respiratory infections, which cause the hypersensitive lungs to become inflamed (ALA, 1997). Asthma *triggers* include tobacco smoke, exercise, weather, medications, emotions, and chemical irritants, which cause an asthma attack in the already inflamed lungs. In urban areas, air pollution from motor-vehicle exhaust, dust, dirt, and poor ventilation contribute greatly to the increase in asthma. It is important for children, parents, and educators to understand and be aware of these promoters and triggers, so that they can take the necessary precautions in preventing asthma attacks whenever possible.

Smoking is one of the most dangerous promoters and triggers for children with asthma. The American Lung Association found that wheezing attacks in children could be reduced by 20 percent if parents didn't smoke in the home (ALA, 1997). For a child, secondhand cigarette smoke can serve as a promoter and trigger. The smoke irritates the lungs, causing them to become inflamed. Once inflamed, the smoke can then cause the lungs to constrict further, resulting in an attack of wheezing. An estimated 200,000 to 1 million asthmatic children have had their asthma condition worsened by exposure to secondhand smoke (ALA, 2003a). Parents of an asthmatic child should not smoke around that child or allow visitors to their homes to do so.

The most common promoters of asthma are respiratory infections, including influenza and cold bugs common in children. Viruses invade the airways and cause inflammation. Children with asthma should avoid people with the flu or colds. Parents may want their child to receive a flu shot each season. Ironically, the difficulty of getting flu shots in the large city contributes to the increase in asthma. Health clinics are difficult to get to, are not always staffed or open, and are poorly advertised, and many caregivers have no release from work in order to get children to the clinics for shots.

Once promoters have inflamed the airways of a person with asthma, the person is primed for an attack. It is at this point that the triggers do their damage. The triggers signal the airways to constrict beyond the point at which normal breathing can occur (ALA, 1997). It is important that children with asthma, their parent(s), and educators be aware of triggers:

> I guess as a parent you worry about your child's first day of school. It seems silly to think that I spent so much time worrying about the wrong things on my son's first day. Would he make a friend? Would he like his teacher? Would the kids tease him? I never would have thought to worry about would the teacher be wearing half a bottle of perfume. I never in a thousand years thought to worry if the teacher, in her mad scramble to get her room and bulletin boards set up, would be spraying adhesive when my child was in the room. And I certainly never thought to worry that the teacher wouldn't even realize that my son's uncontrollable coughing was the beginning signal of his respiratory distress. I never thought my son's first day in pre-K would end up with a four-hour stay in the emergency room and one steroid shot later to control an asthma attack. And I was not prepared for my son telling his father "school made him sick."

Asthma has different triggers. Walking to school or taking a subway or bus can contribute to triggering attacks. Exercise is one of the most obvious triggers. During most types of exercise, about 80 percent of people with asthma may experience a tightening in the chest, coughing, wheezing, or general discomfort (ALA, 1997). When people exercise they are required to breathe hard and fast, and this is difficult for a child with asthma. However, this does not mean that children with asthma should not or cannot exercise. If they can learn to control and be aware of their asthma symptoms, exercise should not be a problem. In fact, many doctors feel that regular exercise combined with asthma control may actually result in better long-term breathing (ALA, 1997).

Many children with asthma also suffer from allergies to substances like pollen and molds. Most develop what is called allergic rhinitis, more commonly known as hay fever (ALA, 1997). Children with allergic rhinitis release histamine that can trigger an asthma attack and cause a runny nose and watery eyes. An increased amount of pollen in the air can irritate the airways. Parents and educators should be observant of pollen counts (widely available in the media and on the Net) and keep children with asthma inside when the count is high. If possible, during days of high pollen counts, windows should be closed at home and in school and air-conditioning used if an option (ALA, 2003c).

Many children with asthma are allergic to dust mites, which are common in homes and classrooms. City schools that lack adequate ventilation and good custodial services are breeding grounds for mites as well as molds. The feces of the mites are inhaled into the lungs and are irritants to the airways, triggering an attack. To take control of dust mites, parents should put their child's mattress and pillows in airtight covers, wash the covers weekly in hot (at least 130°F) water, vacuum the child's bedroom at least once a week, and store books and toys that can collect dust in another room (ALA, 2003c).

Pet dander, or tiny pieces of skin that flake off of a domestic animal, is well known as a trigger of asthma attacks. Dander of cats and dogs can be an especially potent allergen, causing wheezing attacks in children (ALA, 1997). Rodents and birds can also cause a problem. If possible, parents should remove pets from their homes, as should educators from their classrooms. If pets cannot be removed, they should not be kept in the child's bedroom or near the child at any time. If there is forced-air heating in a home with pets, air ducts in the bedroom should be closed (ALA, 2003c). In addition, parents should wash pets weekly and avoid visits to places where animals are present.

Some triggers that occur in households and buildings are not so obvious. The presence of asbestos or lead-based paints is often found in public housing projects and old buildings, and these are triggers that dangerously affect asthmatic children. Excess kitchen smoke from cooking can irritate the airways of an asthmatic. Windows should be opened or a circulation fan used during cooking to prevent the smoke from getting too thick. Household products such as hair spray, talcum powder, perfume, paint, and deodorizers also have strong odors which can irritate the airways of an asthmatic child (ALA, 2003c). Again, parents should take the necessary precautions when using these products around their children who have asthma.

Perhaps an unavoidable trigger is that of air pollution, which includes ozone (smog), nitric oxide, acid aerosols, and diesel exhaust fumes. Researchers recently found a strong correlation between smog and serious asthma attacks (ALA, 1997). The inner city in North America is a haven for the complex fumes and smokes that harm our children. These pollutants inflame the airways and leave them more sensitive to a host of other allergens. Children with asthma are reportedly hit harder by air pollution than are adults. When the level of ozone and exhaust particles is very high, some hospitals have indicated that visits and admissions of children with asthma become 20 percent to 30 percent higher than usual (ALA, 1997).

There has recently been a debate over whether asthma can be triggered by emotional episodes. During emotional crises, a child may cry, yell, or hyperventilate, thus triggering an attack because of the force of air passing through and irritating the airways. While these episodes may have this effect, it is important to remember that asthma is not a psychological disease (ALA, 1997). In addition to emotional episodes, stress may trigger an attack because of the chemicals released by a person's body in response to it, which can also cause the airways to constrict.

Treatment for Children with Asthma

Parents of children who are asthmatic need to work in partnership with their doctor to develop an asthma treatment program that meets their child's needs. Parents of very young children with asthma need to be extremely vigilant of their child's symptoms and be able to communicate them to their doctor. Because these children are so young, they will be unable to express their symptoms or recognize the signals of an asthma attack. It is the parents' responsibility to serve as the voice of their child during this critical time of early development. It is also their responsibility to intervene early in the course of an asthma attack with medication to arrest and reverse airway constriction (ALA, 1997). As children get older, they become more involved in managing their asthma and eventually are able to recognize signals of an attack and administer medications independently. It may be up to a teacher to point out to the caregiver that a child is symptomatic of asthma. It is also essential that teachers be aware of conditions, the location of inhalers, and their use in the event of an attack.

Many of the medications used to treat adults with asthma are used for children. However, the doses of asthma medication for children are often lower than those for adults. Children with asthma may require special delivery systems for their medication. Very young children may require a nebulizer or a metered-dose inhaler with a spacer and face mask. A nebulizer allows a child to receive the medication by inhaling a mist through a mouthpiece or face mask. Nebulizers are a good alternative treatment for those children who cannot master the use of a metered-dose inhaler. Metered-dose inhalers require a child to be able to coordinate their use.

Devices such as spacers and face masks were developed to eliminate some of the problems children may have in medication administration. Spacers are tubes attached to the end of a metered-dose inhaler which collect the medication mist before it is inhaled (ALA, 1997). They make it easier for children with asthma to coordinate the metered dose, and they also put children at ease during the medication process. Face masks can be attached to mouthpieces with nebulizers and metered-dose inhalers. When used with a nebulizer, a face mask allows the flow of medication to be continual. With every breath, the child is inhaling asthma medication (ALA, 1997). When used with a metered-dose inhaler, a face mask must be used with a spacer. This combination is effective in training a child to use an inhaler. Once again, the "trendy" or "coolness" index is not usually met with asthma inhalers. Rapper Snoop Dogg (Calvin Broadus) makes it clear that he has asthma and openly uses his inhaler. It is essential to reinforce images like Dogg's in order for students to feel comfortable using their inhalers.

Medications used to control asthma in children fall into one of five groups: inhaled bronchodilators, anti-inflammatory leukotriene modifiers, systemic bronchodilators, and systemic corticosteroids (ALA, 2002). Inhaled bronchodilator medications are the most effective in opening the airways, which are narrowed by asthma. They have few side effects, and administration is available by both metered-dose inhaler and nebulizer. For children with mild asthma, this may be the only type of medication needed. Because this medication is so effective, it tends to get overused, which is a great danger to the child. Recent studies suggest that overuse of these medications may actually worsen the asthma and increase the possibility of death from it (ALA, 2002).

The National Heart, Lung, and Blood Institute (NHLBI) recommends daily use of anti-inflammatory medications (such as cromolyn and nedocromil) for children with asthma classified as mild intermittent, moderate, or severe (ALA, 2002) in order to control inflammation of the airways. These medications are considered to be safe, have minimal side effects, and are available for adminstration by metered-dose inhaler or nebulizer. Anti-inflammatory medications oftentimes fail because they are not taken regularly. They do not have an immediate effect and are often mistakenly discontinued (ALA, 2002). The most recent asthma medications approved by the U.S. Food and Drug Administration are the leukotriene modifiers (ALA, 2002). These medications are taken in pill form and sold under the names of Accolate, Singulair, and Zyflo. Parents should consult with their doctor to determine whether this new class of anti-inflammatory medication will benefit their child.

Theophylline is the principal systemic bronchodilator medication, used in pill or liquid form for children (ALA, 1997). This class of medication is effective but has more reported side effects in children, such as agitation and restlessness. When taking theophylline, a child's blood levels should be monitored to reduce side effects and ensure the proper dose (ALA, 2002).

Systemic corticosteroid medications are highly effective in controlling asthma and reversing episodes (ALA, 2002). However, these medications can cause serious side effects when used for long periods of time. Because of this, their use is limited to chronic severe asthma that cannot be controlled with the first three groups of medications discussed above.

With each of these medications, parents should always consult with their doctor as to the best treatment option(s) for their child. Each child has unique and special needs and the asthma treatment should address them. The medications used for asthma treatment are safe and effective when taken correctly. If not taken properly, these medications can, in some cases, cause harm.

Back to the General

If this chapter were a general informational chapter on asthma, there would be discussions for parents or caregivers about proper medical care, learning the correct treatment, and contacting the school nurse for additional support and information. The reality in urban teaching dictates that we would be wrong to assume that there are any school facilities that deal with illness, wrong to assume that there is a school nurse, wrong to assume that all parents/caregivers are aware of what asthma is, and wrong to assume that there is a basic understanding as to the dangers of urban asthma. We cannot assume that the facilities that are expected in suburban settings are even dimly duplicated in the urban setting. In a perfect world, the parent/caregiver would be able to speak to all those who come in contact with the child and expect that they would assist. In overcrowded, understaffed public urban schools, we do not have a perfect world. However, as teacher advocates, we can be aware that there are certain basic rights that students do have. Under the Americans with Disabilities Act (ADA), the school is responsible for making any necessary accommodations the child may require to be able to participate in all school activities. The school cannot discriminate based on the child's illness. Title III of the ADA requires a place of public accommodation and that the school make reasonable modifications to its policies, practices, and procedures where necessary to ensure full and equal enjoyment of its services by individuals with disabilities (*Alvarez v. Fountainhead, Inc.*). Asthma is a manageable condition and should not prevent children from participating in all learning and social activities with their classmates. Teachers have a responsibility to make sure that accommodation is made for instruction of students with medical conditions.

There are several issues that teachers and parents should address to ensure that a child stays healthy during school. One of the first is the development of an individualized health plan (IHP). This plan should be a complete written document providing specific information on the child's condition(s), warning signs, and medication treatment, along with details of administration or monitoring of therapy (i.e., whether the child requires assistance from teachers or the school

258

Why Is Health an Urban Issue? Asthma: A Case in Point

nurse); contact information of the parents and doctors; and any other pertinent information regarding the child's medical issues. This document should be created with input from the child's doctor and reviewed at a meeting with the parents and all school staff who work with the child.

Parents and teachers should work together with their parents' doctors and the school administration to address the needs of children with asthma. It is essential that all parties have an ongoing dialogue regarding these children's condition. This ongoing communication is necessary for them to be able to manage their medical condition in school. In the case of asthma, one tool for providing communication between parties is a "Student Asthma Card" and/or "trigger sheets" which are filled out by the student's parents and doctor (SchoolAsthma Allergy.com, 2002), which should include criteria for specific asthma triggers and warning signs for each child. These forms can be used as a quick reference for teachers, and a master can be kept with the student's asthma action plan or IHP. Parents should review the information regularly with school staff and be alerted to any changes the staff observes in their child.

Make sure that you, the teacher, are aware of any and all medical conditions that your students have, and attempt to educate (if needed) and collaborate with parents in order to secure the best health for each student.

REFERENCES

(Websites accessed November 13, 2003)

AAAAI [American Academy of Allergy, Asthma, and Immunology] (2002). *Topic of the month: August 2002: Back to school with allergies and asthma.* http://www.aaaai.org/patients/topicofthemonth/ 0802/default.stm

ALA [American Lung Association] (1997). *Family guide to asthma and allergies.* Asthma Advisory Group. Boston: Little, Brown and Co.

——— (2002). *Asthma medications for kids: Five asthma medication groups.* http://www.lungusa.org/ asthma/ascastnedgr.html

——— (2003a). *Asthma in children fact sheet.* http://www.lungusa.org/asthma/ascpedfac99.html

——— (2003b). *Pediatric asthma: A growing health threat.* http://www.lungusa.org/asthma/ merck_pediatric.html

——— (2003c). *Asthma triggers in children.* http://www.lungusa.org/asthma/asctriggers.html

Alvarez v. Fountainhead, Inc., 55 F.Supp. 2d 1048, 1051 (N.D. Ca1.1999). Case No. C 99–1202 MEJ.

Butler, Rachel (Ed.) (2000). Asthma news from the American Lung Association. *Asthma Magazine* July/August, 9-13.

Immunotherapy Weekly (2001). Health tips for kids coping with asthma and allergies, 27.

SchoolAsthmaAllergy.com (2002). *Teaching toolkit: Tools for teaching students with asthma/allergies and their parents.* http://www.schoolasthmaallergy.com/2002–2003/sections/toolkit/ tools_students/index.html

CHAPTER SEVENTEEN

Katia Goldfarb

Who Is Included in the Urban Family?

 The *ideal* family conjures up an image of a mom, a dad, and two children—preferably, one boy and one girl, in that order. As we continue conjuring, we envision a stylish home surrounded by trees and, of course, enclosed in a white picket fence. The mother has a career, but she has chosen to stay home until the children grow up. Her position will be waiting when and if she decides to go back to work. The father happily leaves for the commute to his job every morning, as part of his conscious decision; the city is not the best environment in which to raise a family.

Families who have the economic resources to entertain this decision are the only ones who can fulfill the above mythical image of family living. Urban families are either wealthy enough to offer their members the necessary experiences to compensate for the suburban context, such as private schools, periodic vacations, and modern and spacious apartments, or they are stuck with life in the city as their only viable option. In this chapter, I will describe some of the most crucial contextual issues affecting urban families with children of low socioeconomic status and limited formal education.

The Pathologization of Families from Minority Groups

One of the most important of these contextual issues involves the right-wing pathologization of urban families of minority groups. Deploying the concept of "family values," right-wing operatives have argued that there is little we can do for urban students because they come from pathological families. The urban student signified in such representations is, of course, of color. This is accompanied by a concurrent deployment of the concept of "urban troubles," used to signal the existence of gargantuan unsolvable problems in contemporary cities. The causes of these insurmountable problems involve the demographic changes of the last 40 years. As nonwhites constituted a larger percentage of urban dwellers, they began to manifest their own family pathologies. Along with these domestic people of color, a rash of non-European immigrants (so proclaim right-wing leaders) have brought family pathologies with them to American cities that "threaten the historic identity of the United States as a 'European' country, thus endangering the country's 'character' and 'value structure'" (Bennett, Dilulio, Jr., and Walters, 1996). Thus, urban institutions such as schooling were pathologized by "these people."

In this right-wing world, crime is caused by this degraded family life, not by poverty. Thus, political and educational policies in this ideological construct see no reason to address poverty or formulate attempts to alleviate it. The best thing we can do is to bring pathological family members to Christ, many conservative politicos argue. Through Him we can restore family values and begin the process of improving urban family life for poor people and especially poor people of color. Until such salvation occurs, however, right-wing analysts such as William Bennett, John DiIulio Jr., and John Walters maintain that urban areas and their schools will be victimized by ultraviolent superpredators, the worst criminals any society has ever known. As Cornel West (1993) argues, the right-wing's use of terms such as *superpredator* and *feral, presocial beings* caters to the worst types of racial prejudice found in the United States. What is wrong with African American and Latino families, these critics contend, is a manifestation of moral poverty. Moral poverty causes criminal behavior—a tautology that can be neither proved nor disproved. The only thing virtuous white people can do in this circumstance is to punish perpetrators—lock 'em up and throw away the key in "three strikes and you're out" policies or execute them. Moral poverty is an excellent twenty-first-century way to say that the bad parenting of black and Latino parents causes socially irresponsible behavior (Bennett, Dilulio, Jr., and Walters, 1996).

In this explosive context, the pathologization of the family is central to the right-wing position. Morally impoverished black and Latino superpredators have never been exposed to loving parents who can teach them good from evil, to stay away from drugs, or to resist violence. This family collapse is a single-bullet theory of urban minority poverty and school failure. Bombarded by such crypto-racism, many educators have been induced to complain: "How can we teach these children when their parents don't care about them?" Unfortunately, many white middle- and upper-middle-class Americans don't know very much about their poor nonwhite fellow countrymen and countrywomen. As an example, contemporary popular wisdom fueled by right-wing talk shows and think tanks posits that poor minority women produce huge numbers of "illegitimate" babies.

Who Is Included in the Urban Family?

Actually, birth rates among single African American women, for example, over the last three decades have fallen by 13 percent. Incidentally, during the same decades, the birth rates for single white women increased 27 percent. Such data might induce right-wing spokespeople to tone down their descriptions of black mothers living in poverty as "brood mares" and "welfare queens" (Coontz, 1992).

As the rate of financial polarization grew in the last portion of the twentieth century, of course problems emerged in poor urban neighborhoods that worry all of us. Violence is of concern to all Americans, though African American and Latino poor suffer far more than anyone else. The right-wing effort to lay the cause of such problems exclusively at the doorstep of the alleged moral poverty of urban nonwhite people with their broken families, high divorce rates, unwed pregnancies, family violence, and drug and alcohol abuse is misleading. In this context, Joe Kincheloe (1999) argues:

> The same problems confront families whose members serve as police officers or in the military, yet most Americans refrain from blaming them for their dysfunctionality. Typically, we have little trouble understanding that the context in which police officers and soldiers operate is in part responsible for such pathologies. Work stress from danger and conflict can produce devastating results. With this in mind, it is not difficult to imagine the stress that accompanies living for just one week in an inner-city war zone. Now imagine living there with no hope of getting out. (p. 243)

The right-wing view of poor urban African American and Latino families as corrupt and morally bankrupt is not the only perspective on this matter. Many educators, sociologists, and urban studies scholars argue that such families are often very resilient, hard working, and self-sufficient, are in possession of loving kinship networks, and value education for their children (Hill, 2003). Many researchers have pointed to the strength of the extended African American family, for example (Wicker, 1996; Ashworth, 1997). The power of such families often succeeds in maintaining the lives of its individual members despite overwhelming problems and travails. To not understand the ways that cousins, grandparents, great-grandparents, aunts, and uncles provide support when times are bad is to miss a profound dimension of urban black family life. Thus, there is a dialectic of strength and weakness of African American and other poor urban families from minority groups in contemporary America. It would be misguided to argue that racism, class bias, and the ravages of poverty do not tear the fabric of such families and create profound problems for them. Concurrently, it is amazing how the inner strengths of urban minority families work to help their members persevere in spite of some extremely difficult situations.

Urban Families in Historical Context

As with any other family, urban families interact with their natural and human-built environments. Their lives are affected by the available emotional and material resources. They have to interrelate with their immediate context such as extended family, workplace, school, welfare system, and health system. They have to coordinate communication between these organizations. Their lives are influenced by policy and laws often endorsed by politicians far removed from their realities. And every day, they have to fight against the negative image held by mainstream society of low-income urban families.

The creation of this particular group of families can be traced to the capitalistic industrialization of the United States following the American Civil War. The Industrial Revolution brought a reorganization of work. Different social groups had access to different jobs that held extremely different statuses and earning possibilities. The national economy moved from the traditional colonial agricultural family-based system to a wage economy. An increasing number of goods and services were produced and rendered outside the family.

Rural migrants and high numbers of European immigrants settled in cities growing around mill towns, steam- and later oil- and electricity-powered factories and sweatshops. Within this process, a middle class based on ownership of business and industry and a working class based on low-pay and low-status jobs were created. These economic and social changes were lived very differently by varied groups. Slave society developed into a distinctive African American culture, and Native Americans have had numerous structures of family living. These groups did not share the same context as that of the old and new European immigration. However, the ideal image of the family, even though its origin can be found in the patriarchal structure of the New England colonies, is still regarded as the family form to be used in judging any other form of family living.

As cities grew, families who had the economic resources started to migrate out of the urban areas in search of what was called a "better standard of living." The odors, noises, crowds, limited personal space, traffic, and what was defined as low educational standards were among the issues used as reasons to leave the cities and build more homogeneous, stable, and private communities. The new immigrants and the working poor remained.

Parallel to these economic and social changes, the roles within the family were also reorganized. A clear differentiation between the private and public worlds was created in which the private/family domain belonged to the woman and the public/work domain belonged to the man. Working-class women and children from poor families did not have the privileges these developments were offering (Chavkin, 1993; Cherlin, 1988; Redding & Thomas, 2001).

In the present times, there are additional social forces influencing families and individuals. There is a growing production of new technologies that is changing the economy to a service/information-based system. The United States is rapidly pressing for a global economy. Big corporations are merging and/or relocating and/or investing outside the country. Lastly, there is a growing trend in which corporations are shifting from manufacturing to knowledge-based institutions. Within these processes, low-income urban families with children are facing bigger and more rapid social and economic changes. Their situation is aggravated by specific issues influencing their daily lives. Some of these areas are increasing and permanent poverty, medical care, overcrowding, mobility and loss of extended family network, immigration, language, diversity in family structure, work/family influences, violence, stress, environmental problems, access to cultural life and enrichment activities, the family/school relationship, and, of course, the class and race issues previously discussed (Ruiz-de-Velasco & Fix, 2000; Delgado-Gaitan, 2001).

The Wages of Poverty

The lack of economic resources greatly impacts the dynamics of urban families. There is a constant struggle for the basic necessities. Since the working adults are dependent on weekly or monthly wages, any drastic change in the economy will have immediate repercussions. These families may face fluctuating times when they will need government assistance, requiring from them the use of their time and energy to access the necessary services. By having very limited job opportunities, children and adults will have extremely low possibilities of receiving adequate and continuous medical care. Chronic illnesses as well as prompt diagnosis will be hindered. The implications of a deteriorating health status for the responsible adult(s) will create a vicious and difficult-to-break cycle in which unemployment becomes a regular part of life. As for the children, research has shown that one of the most important issues affecting readiness to learn is the nutrition and health status of the child. Families, in turn, rely on the emergency room for medical care.

Overcrowding has been a constant issue in urban settings, whether it is within the household or as part of city life. Immigrant families especially find themselves sharing small physical spaces. In the attempt to help family or members of the community, people will be willing to sacrifice their personal space on the assumption that more economic resources will open up for the family system. In situations like this, there may be growing frictions among members and increasing frustration. Outside the household, cities also feel crowded. There are fewer and smaller public spaces. There are fewer and smaller natural spaces. Buildings are tall, imposing, almost identical. The feeling as you walk through the city is that you are moving within a contingency of people.

As economic and domestic issues become increasingly problematic, family members may decide to move in search of better job opportunities. Working-class families have relied on extended-family members for child care, economic help, and emotional support. Extended family is a crucial resource for the sustainability of low-income urban families and the well-being of the children (Ruiz-de-Velasco & Fix, 2000; Trumbull, Rothstein-Fish, Greenfield, and Quiroz, 2001).

Immigration and Language in Urban Family Life

Immigration and language are becoming increasingly crucial areas in understanding urban families. Immigration is one of the most important economic and social changes. The current immigration is influencing society not only because of its numbers but also because of its diversity. As in the past, new immigrants tend to settle in established communities of people from their own national origin. This traditional trend influences issues such as access to education, availability of jobs where fluency in English is not required, and the offering of basic services (such as health care, education) in the appropriate language. The issue of immigration has been part of the antagonism between minority groups struggling for the same scarce resources. Division and hostility are also part of the problematic between immigrants and the powerful mainstream society. They challenge the exclusive ownership and access to social goods.

One hundred years ago, 90 percent of immigration to the United States was from European countries; today, 90 percent is from non-European, mainly Latin American and Asian, countries. Therefore, there are going to be drastic changes on the face of the nation. This increases the number of U.S. residents who are foreign born and also the number of their children. Currently, in major urban settings like New York, Los Angeles, and Chicago, minority groups make up the majority in numbers but not in sociopolitical power. The United States is witnessing birth rates of racial minorities increase faster than that of the majority population. In the year 2000, Latinos outnumbered African Americans. It is clear that immigration is one of the most important issues facing major metropolitan areas.

For families, immigration implies a series of social, economic, and familial adjustments. Immigrants are entering the country in a moment of economic difficulties. There are fewer jobs available, and social and economic mobility will not be as easy as it was for prior waves of immigrants. Since the current immigration is not from European countries, new arrivals will face social and institutional discrimination. Immigrants will face the options of blending in as soon as possible, rejecting the dominant culture, increasing and strengthening ethnic ties, or developing bicultural or multicultural forms of family and community living (Kincheloe & Steinberg, 1997; Dickinson & Tabors, 2001).

Different Types of Families

Currently in the United States there is an increase in the diversity of family structures. As with any other group, low-income urban families are also facing an increase in the number of family structures that do not resemble the ideal image. There are single-parent houses with different custody arrangements; homes in which the parent has remained single by choice or as the result of divorce, separation, or death; families with two cohabiting adults and children; multigenerational families; two-parent homes of same-sex couples. There may be members of the extended family or of another, unrelated family living in the house. There are families with one child and families with many children. The low-income urban family with children is not a monolith or beyond the diversity of family

Who Is Included in the Urban Family?

structure, and we find urban families from bicultural or multicultural backgrounds.

Work/family influences are also shared by any family who has at least one member in the workforce. Low-income urban families with children face the increasing need to find permanent and well-paying jobs. Some families have to resort to two jobs, which may mean leaving the children alone for longer periods of time. There are going to be increased challenges for the adults in trying to keep up with different sets of work-related expectations. The majority of the time, the jobs that adults from low-income urban families can find are not personally satisfying. They are usually labor intensive, not stimulating, and low-paying, which only aggravates an already stressful situation. The mother or father will have a stronger probability of carrying his or her frustration from one world to the other (Grigorenko & Sternberg, 2001).

Families and Violence

Violence is an endemic problem facing low-income urban families. There is violence at the institutional level. Minority groups (ethnic/racial, gender, age, sexual orientation, social class) face constant violence in our social institutions: such as the legal system, in which African Americans are disproportionately incarcerated; the schools, where children are labeled "slow learners" because they do not speak English; and government organizations whose policies exacerbate the struggles of families with small children to keep jobs and have their children in quality day care. Children are exposed to drugs, gang activity, alcohol, and homicides. These problems are not exclusive to poor neighborhoods, but when access to quality and appropriate education does not exist, when safety in these neighborhoods is not supported, and when you can make a lot more money selling drugs than going to school to get a high school diploma, the ground is fertile for the proliferation of violence.

Environmental Dimensions of Urban Family Life

As mentioned before, families are influenced by their natural environment. The access to clean water, clean air, peace and quiet, and open spaces should be a right for all human beings. As if low-income urban families with children do not have enough to contend with, their physical and natural environments add to the challenges. Usually, these families live in multistory or high-rise apartment buildings with numerous other families, with little or no recreational space. Their neighborhoods are often located close to airports, busy intersections, commercial, and/or industrial zones, or neglected areas. Their apartments are often in need of repair. Children and adults are still exposed to lead-based paint. Buildings are not fumigated. These conditions prevent healthy development.

Access to Urban Educational and Cultural Resources

Minority and low socioeconomic status also hinders access to entertainment and enrichment activities. Shows, restaurants, movies, plays, museums are often beyond the economic reach of low-income urban families, even though they may live just a few blocks from them. All the extracurricular activities that enrich the education and the cognitive, emotional, and physical development of children may be out of reach for urban families with tight budgets unless the services are provided by a community center and sponsored by local or federal funds. Children and parents from all socioeconomic backgrounds are interested in meaningful and accessible experiences offering the optimal environment for growth.

Right-Wing Subversion: Efforts to Help Urban Families Undermined by Family-Values Ideology

All of these urban family issues are colored by the right-wing ideology of family values, with its pathologization of poor families of color. Such a way of seeing maintains that all the social and educational programs in the world cannot help such families. This is the same argument made by Richard Herrnstein and Charles Murray in *The Bell Curve*—poor people of color are genetically inferior, lacking intelligence and moral fiber, and are thus beyond salvation. We do not need more money to help them, the argument goes; they need simply to acquire more family values (SOCQRL, 2003). Indeed, in the right-wing ideological universe, it is assumed that poor black and Latino parents don't want to work to provide for their families and thus don't merit help.

In addition, the conservative use of the "absence of family values" argument has served as a convenient smoke screen to obscure the public's view of the poverty caused by free-market economics over the last 25 years. Using a "politics of nostalgia," the right wing has successfully reconstructed America's view of its family history. The perspective paints a misleading picture of a past in which extended families worked together, pious mothers protected little boys and girls from exposure to adult issues, virginal newlyweds consummated their marriages after religious nuptials, and faithful husbands devoted much of their time to familial needs (Kincheloe, 1999).

The legislation that has come out of this right-wing ideology has exerted a negative effect on the efficacy of urban families of color over the last couple of decades. The welfare reform legislation of the 1990s limited aid to the poorest families to merely five years in a lifetime and required mothers to work in order to get any assistance—even mothers with babies as young as three months. Education and job training for poor mothers are discouraged in this legislation, and states have the prerogative to deny aid for a wide range of reasons. Because of these stipulations, poor women have been forced to take low-paying, dead-end jobs instead of improving their education (Stafford, Salas, Mendez, & Dews, 2003). As poor women take these jobs, they enter into a vicious circle. Child care is hard to find in poor urban communities—especially high-quality child care (Covington Cox, 2003). Mothers who choose to stay at home with their children have their benefits cut off, while those who take jobs often face the prospect of having to leave children alone at certain times. These mothers are often charged with child neglect.

Another result of the right-wing legislation has been the rise in the numbers of poor urban African American women and Latinas in prison. Right-wing drug policies have placed disproportionate numbers of poor urban African American and Latino men and women in prison—this taking place while there is no evidence of higher rates of illegal drug use by this population. In this context we are struck by statistics such as the rate of drug-related imprisonment of black and Latino males being 30 to 40 times higher than that for white males (Drucker, 2003). The effect of this mass incarceration on poor urban black and Latino families is devastating. The sponsors and supporters of the legislation responsible for these outcomes have expressed little concern for the families affected by mothers and fathers in jail. Prisoners' families must get by any way they can. Drucker (2003) concludes that the mental and physical health of families of prisoners is so damaged that the very conditions that create the tendency toward crime are exacerbated. Such legislation serves to devalue families in the name of family values. Teachers in schools in low-socioeconomic urban areas will be forced to deal with the damage caused by such social policies, as poor children of color may be the ones most victimized by such draconian measures.

Conclusion: Poor Urban Families Face Great Challenges

The above descriptions are only some of the issues that low-income urban families with children face. High levels of stress are a constant in all of these areas. Stress influences all aspects of human development. It impacts our physical and emotional health. It can serve as an impediment to self and family realization. Natural and adequate levels of stress should help us perform better. Excessive stressors tend to result in crisis, and if the appropriate material and emotional resources (existing and new) are not available, family living is disrupted.

The family/school relationship is a common experience for all families with children. In the specific case of low-income urban families, the issues presented above permeate the context of this relationship. The quantity and, most important, quality of interaction between schools and families directly influence the development of children. It has been documented that a positive communication between schools and families improves students' achievement, especially in families from minority and immigrant groups. Although there are political, ideological, theoretical, and practical differences in the ways the partnership between schools and families is carried out, this relationship is a recurrent theme in educational reform.

The issues affecting schooling, the role of the family, and the family's relation to formal education have taken many permutations. We have defined the role of the family as "the enemy," in which parents, family, and guardians are to be blamed for everything that goes wrong with the children. We have relegated their participation to fund-raising by allowing families to be involved within the schools as long as they keep their participation connected to bringing material goods. Educational and curriculum issues are viewed as the prerogative of the experts, teachers, and school administrators.

The type of family involvement is directly connected to the school's tacit and explicit policies, which are usually supported by district policies. Regardless of the rules and regulations set by the decision makers, access to information and extent of family involvement depend on the openness of the school to maintain a genuine dialogue with families for the benefit of the children. If we continue basing the need for family involvement in school on the sole concern of improving students' academic achievement, we are in danger of removing parents from helping in problems to whose solutions they can contribute the most.

Research suggests that there is nothing to lose and everything to gain from mandating and implementing school/family partnerships. It has been found that standardized test scores are higher. In terms of family outcomes, there is evidence of a more positive self-concept, acquisition of skills, and positive attitudes. Also, such a partnership affects the school and school district by showing an increase in student attendance and reductions in the rates of dropout, delinquency, and teen pregnancy. The responsibility for educating the children should be shared. None of the current social institutions can carry out alone the enormous challenge of educating the future generation. For example, if it is not demanded that businesses (particularly those offering low-paying, low-status jobs) enact flexible and family-friendly policies, society cannot blame mothers and fathers for neglecting their children. Families are not able to attend parent/teacher conferences and other school-based activities because such attendance usually involves losing a day's pay—an unacceptable outcome for poor families.

In the context of immigrant families, it has been found that language and prior experiences are the real reasons for lower levels of family involvement. The majority of our urban children are being educated by middle-class white female teachers who often do not speak the students' language(s). Such families get the hidden message that they are not important in the formal educational process of their children. A common practice in schools is to use the children as translators for their parents and in family interactions at school—by so doing, research shows, there is a potential for conflict in the role reversal between children and adults and the perception that cultural practices are not being respected by school personnel. Another barrier to immigrant families' involvement in schools is the lack of understanding of the American educational system. Immigrants are neither tutored in becoming nor expected to become active decision makers in the process of schooling their children. Another reason for the ostensible lack of involvement is that different cultural practices give to the teacher the honor of establishing communication, as the expert (Hiatt-Michael, 2001).

Most of the adult immigrants in low-income urban families were not able to go to school past the third grade. They feel that they do not have the knowledge or the language skills to engage in meaningful communication with the teachers and school administrators. It has been found that often, the school administrators and teachers view such parents' absence from the school as a lack of interest in the education of their children (Britto and Brooks-Gunn, 2001).

Educators at all levels should be trained to understand the importance of working *with* and not *on* the community and the families. Families should be seen as equal partners in the education of their children. Their voices should be heard and respected. We live in difficult times of war, economic troubles, violence, racism, class bias, and terrorism. As educators, we are not sufficiently prepared to recognize and deal with the overwhelming influence that social, cultural, and linguistic contexts have in the life of our children. We need families and communities to face the challenges of educating the next generation.

REFERENCES

(Websites accessed November 18, 2003)

Ashworth, Pam (1997). POS334-L: The race and ethnicity book review discussion list. [Book review of *Tragic failure: Racial integration in America*]. http://lilt.ilstu.edu/gmklass/pos334/archive/wicker.htm

Bennett, William J., & Dilulio, Jr., John, & Walters, John. (1996) *Body count: Moral poverty and how to win America's war against crime and drugs.* Simon and Schuster.

Britto, Pia Rebello, & Brooks-Gunn, Jeanne (Eds.) (2001). *The role of family literacy environments in promoting young children's emerging literacy skills.* San Francisco: Jossey-Bass.

Chavkin, Nancy F. (1993). *Families and schools in a pluralistic society.* Albany: State University of New York Press.

Cherlin, Andrew J. (Ed.) (1988). *The changing American family and public policy.* Washington, DC: Urban Institute.

Coontz, Stephanie (1992). *The way we never were: American families and the nostalgia trap.* New York: Basic Books.

Covington Cox, Kenya (2003). *The effect of childcare imbalance on the labor force participation of mothers residing in highly urban-poor counties.* http://www.nul.org/documents/ all_abstracts. doc

Delgado-Gaitan, Concha (2001). *The power of community: Mobilizing for family and schooling.* Lanham, MD: Rowman and Littlefield.

Dickinson, David K., & Tabors, Patton O. (Eds.) (2001). *Beginning literacy with language: Young children learning at home and school.* Baltimore: P. H. Brookes.

Drucker, Ernest M. (2003). *The impact of mass incarceration on public health in black communities.* http://www.nul.org/documents/all_abstracts.doc

Grigorenko, Elena L., & Sternberg, Robert J. (Eds.) (2001). *Family environment and intellectual functioning: A life-space perspective.* Mahwah, NJ: Erlbaum.

Hiatt-Michael, Diana B. (Ed.) (2001). *Promising practices for family involvement in school.* Greenwich, CT: Information Age.

Hill, Robert B. (2003). The strengths of black families revisited. http://www.nul.org/documents/all_abstracts.doc

Kincheloe, Joe L. (1999). *How do we tell the workers? The socioeconomic foundations of work and vocational education.* Boulder, CO: Westview.

Kincheloe, Joe L., & Steinberg, Shirley (1997). *Changing multiculturalism.* Buckingham (UK) and Philadelphia: Open University Press.

Redding, Sam, & Thomas, Lori G. (Eds.) (2001). *The community of the school.* Lincoln, IL: Academic Development Institute.

Ruiz-de-Velasco, Jorge, & Fix, Michael (2000). *Overlooked and underserved: Immigrant students in U.S. secondary schools.* Washington, DC: Urban Institute.

SOCQRL [Sociology Quantitative Research Laboratory] (2003). *Cycle of unequal opportunity.* http://www.socqrl.niu.edu/forest/SOCI270/UequalCycle.html

Stafford, Walter; Salas, Diana; Mendez, Melissa, & Dews, Angela (2003). *Race, gender and welfare reform: The need for targeted support.* http://www.nul.org/documents/all_abstracts.doc

Trumbull, Elise; Rothstein-Fish, Carrie; Greenfield, Patricia; & Quiroz, Blanca (2001). *Bridging cultures between home and school: A guide for teachers: With a special focus on immigrant Latino families.* Mahwah, NJ: Erlbaum.

West, Cornel (1993). *Race Matters.* New York: Vintage Books.

Wicker, Tom (1996). *Tragic failure: Racial integration in America.* New York: Morrow.

CHAPTER EIGHTEEN

Philip M. Anderson
& Judith P. Summerfield

Why Is Urban Education Different from Suburban and Rural Education?

The question posed as the title of this chapter suggests certain assumptions about urban education—first, that urban education is *different* from other forms of education. Second, urban schools are not the "norm" and are to be contrasted with, or measured against, suburban and rural schools rather than the other way around. Furthermore, given generally held notions about urban schools, the implication is that urban is deficient in relation to the other categories or that urban has problems the other two categories do not.

Historically, the urbanization of schooling took place after the Civil War. By 1880, the number of city high schools had surpassed that of the old rural academies, and by the turn of the century, they were the dominant institution in American education (Sizer, 1964, p. 40). The urban institution of learning *replaces* the rural: Ideologically, the rural, i.e., the normative or "natural," is replaced by the urban, the "artificial." As we will discuss below, the distinction is important for understanding both the perceptions about urban schools and many of the proposals for reforming urban education.

The suburban school did not become a force until the vast suburban development in the years following World War II. Since then, suburban high school systems have replaced both the rural and urban institutions as the "successful" model of education in the United States. Suburban schools are typically perceived to be academically sound, physically safe, and the best routes to the best colleges, which provide the best career and life opportunities. At the same time, the "burbs" and suburban schools are often vilified as white-flight, middle-class enclaves, the epitome of artificiality in Western culture. Whichever view one takes, the original ideals of suburbia represent the pervasive rural bias in American life. The suburbs signify fresh air, trees, and grass, the *natural* environment, and, more significantly, the persistent attempt to construct the urban present and future out of remnants of the rural past.

However, like any other marker in the American semiotic, whether it be Wyatt Earp or Helen Keller, the Horatio Alger hero or the American commonsense individualist, the *rural,* the *suburban,* and the *urban* aspects of our culture need to be unpacked. Fact must be separated from perception and deliberate fictions. If we are not comfortable with the fact that the Earp brothers and associates were a gang controlling gambling interests in Tombstone, Arizona, or that Helen Keller was a Socialist, we turn to the "heroic" elements of the story. If the Horatio Alger kid was always a lost member of the nobility in the first place (or married into it) and if large overseas corporate mining, trapping, and logging trusts or government land giveaways sponsored our frontierspeople, we ignore the subtext and dream of our ability to "be anything we can be."

Looking at the urban, suburban, and rural school question provides a similar set of problems for us as a culture: Narratives prefigure each of these categories of schooling. Images in our minds are called up by the myths of rural, suburban, and urban schooling, reinforced by our information and entertainment culture. In popular iconography, urban schools are coated with graffiti and are dangerous. Urban schools are successful when ex-Marines enforce "tough love" on "minority" students. Rural schools are set in meadows and are white (inside and out, place and people). Rural teachers are sad-eyed country philosophers (everyone from Ichabod Crane to Conrack) or caring, unmarried young women. Suburban schools are surrounded by cars; student problems are about relationships and getting into college (all suburban students are "college bound"), and social events crucial to the lives of the students provide the plot development. Differences in the literary form of popular books and films about schools are as distinct as the content: Urban school stories are almost always drama or tragedy, and suburban school stories are almost always comedies with happy endings. Rural school stories are usually fairy tales.

Fact and Fiction in American Education

First, we will look at the facts of the matter, based primarily on research by the National Center for Education Statistics (NCES, 1997; DeVoe et al., 2002). In the classifications and data defining urban and rural education, one finds that the myths do not hold. Is the west more rural than the east? The NCES figures for 2000 show, for example, that Nevada schools (11.5 percent rural) were more urbanized than New York State's schools (16.7 percent rural). That translates into Nevada supporting only 39,062 rural students, while New York manages 477,997 rural students. While Delaware's schools are 25 percent rural, only 14.2 percent of Arizona's students attend rural schools. In the south, interestingly, both Texas' and Tennessee's school populations are 79 percent urban/suburban. The numbers make us question our preconceptions.

And the questions about rural *versus* suburban *versus* urban suggest that the categories, constructed as dichotomies, as one or the other, are part of a larger discussion about often-competing cultural values. The categories of data collected by the NCES presuppose questions about values or systems of belief of particular constituencies. In other words, the questions are asked in the first place because they represent important interests and positionings of power, privilege, and resources. Embedded within the NCES demographic constructs are cultural tensions among urban, suburban, and rural values.

The NCES categories reflect established national trends, issues, and priorities. Within the demographic categories are implicit questions about the organization and funding of schooling. The categories, in effect, represent vested interests and deeply rooted belief systems that define the educational "problems" of American schooling. We begin with the most controversial data concerning rural, suburban, and urban schooling: crime statistics.

The latest are from 1999, measuring what are defined in the table titles as the "number of nonfatal crimes against students ages twelve through eighteen at school or on the way to or from school." The crimes are differentiated as *theft, violent,* and *serious violent* (this parameter is included as well in the violent crime column in the NCES report). *Serious violent* equates with rape, sexual assault, robbery, and aggravated assault; *violent* is simple assault added to the *serious violent* category. According to the NCES 1999 data, the largest total number of crimes in these categories was in the suburbs, with a significant increase from 1998 to 1999 in violent crime and a commensurate drop in the urban violent crime numbers. Suburban students were victims of crime 1,340,700 times in 1999, while 681,600 urban students were victims. During the same period, 467,300 rural students were victims of a crime. More interesting is the number of *serious violent* crimes as a percentage of total crime. Both urban and suburban *serious violent* crimes tally as approximately the same percentage of total crime: 63,700 out of 681,600 and 110,400 out of 1,340,700, respectively. The long-held beliefs about urban school violence and the suburban school environment would appear to be challenged by the national crime figures. And yet, who of us has not known someone who moved to the suburbs so that their child(ren) could attend safe schools?

Interested in moving to the suburbs to lower the student/teacher (S/T) ratio for your child's education? According to the NCES, the average student/teacher ratio for all schools is approximately the same. In the central city of a large metropolitan statistical area (MSA), the S/T ratio average is 17.0:1. For the urban fringe of a large MSA (i.e., the suburbs, where, by the bye, 31.5 percent of U.S. students attend school), the S/T ratio is 17.2:1, higher than that of the central city. With one exception, all other categories listed—small town, urban fringe of midsize town, et cetera—have an S/T ratio of <16:1. For rural areas outside an MSA, it is slightly lower, at 15:1. Class size, on average, cannot be meaningfully addressed by location or type of geography and demographics.

Okay, how about school size? Here the myth appears to be fact: NCES statistics for 1993 show that there were more schools in rural areas in relation to the percentage of the student population; if one looks at only the number of public schools enrolling twelfth graders, rural schools outnumbered central urban and suburban schools 11,091 to 2,949 to 3,798, respectively. While rural students outside an MSA and within an MSA equal the number of urban fringe students in an MSA nationally, the individual school populations are, on average, half the size. This, of course, is logical, based on population density. Here, at last, is a number that supports the rural expectation: the small(er) school.

The numbers reported by the NCES on small schools then become interesting. Most current reform focuses on the "small-schools movement." Smaller schools are less expensive and better, we hear, because more money is spent on instruction than administration. Yet, NCES numbers show that the percentage of expenditure on instruction is virtually identical regardless of the geography and demography of the school. Every NCES demographic category of school averages around 62 percent of expenditures on instruction.

Citizens in the MSA urban fringe, on the other hand, pay more than three times the total property tax of central city inhabitants ($39,044,000,000 vs. $12,936,000,000 in 1998–99), four times that of midsize central city citizens ($10,568,000,000) and more than five times what rural citizens pay on average to support the schools ($7,278,000,000). The suburban schools are spending the most real dollars on something other than instruction, a surprising finding to some who believe that it is urban schools that are overburdened with administrative costs. Equally surprisingly, rural schools, which generally demand the lowest property taxes, also have the highest percentage of state tax support. The schools are less expensive to the locals, more expensive to the rest of the citizens of the state, and provide the same S/T ratios.

All right. If small schools are not more efficient financially and do not provide smaller classes, they should still be a place of stability, where teachers come to stay and teach multiple generations of each family. The NCES statistics on teacher mobility provide some interesting facts, specifically from 1987–88 to 1988–89 and 1993–94 to 1994-95 (NCES, 1997). During those two periods, teachers in schools of 750 or more pupils were more likely to stay in the same school than teachers in smaller schools though the differences appear insignificant. But, in the 1993–94 to 1994-95 school year report, while 87.7 percent of the teachers in schools of 750 or more students stayed in the same schools, only 78.6 percent of those teaching in schools of under 150 students stayed. The percentage staying in other small-sized schools remained just slightly less than those in the 750-or-more-students category. In that same time period, the percentage of teachers who stayed in the same school was essentially the same for central city, urban fringe/small town, and rural/small town demographics (86 percent).

One also expects that students in rural schools would be receiving more vocational training, especially given rural economies and the lack of career opportunities in general. According to the NCES, vocational education is much more likely to be found in urban and suburban schools than in rural schools. The NCES's Survey of Vocational Programs in Secondary Schools finds that urban and suburban schools offer similar types and equal numbers of programs. Rural schools offer much less to students in vocational training, especially in areas that "were projected to be fast-growing" (NCES, 1997).

The U.S. government is not the only one interested in the distinctions between urban, suburban, and rural schools. The United States' largest teachers' union, the National Education Association (NEA), sees rural education as a major problem for teachers, according to the NEA website. After first paying homage to the necessary rural myths ("the success of rural education is linked with what makes rural and small town America unique"), the NEA cites significant problems for rural teachers, including low pay, lack of professional resources and development for teachers, and significant extracurricular work.

According to the NEA, 40 percent of America's students attend rural schools but receive only 22 percent of federal funding for education. The NEA calculated the 40 percent figure by adding small-town schools (NCES = 12.9 percent) to the two rural categories. But, remember, although there are more rural *schools* per student population, small-town and rural *students* make up only 28 percent or so of the total student population according to the NCES. But the idea that a high percentage of students in the United States attend rural schools is important to America's sense of itself, as we will discuss later.

There is something at the NEA website that is relevant to our discussion of the small-schools movement below. The NEA credits small-town and rural schools with "pioneer[ing] many successful education reform tools in widespread use today":

- Peer assistance
- Multi-grade classrooms
- Block scheduling
- Mentoring
- Site-based management
- Cooperative learning (NEA, 2009)

We do not have time to critique the NEA's attribution of all of these "pioneering" (that myth-making word in the American lexicon) changes to progressive rural education. However, the point here is that the NEA is engaging in its own myth making: The idealized, small rural school is the source of all democratic, egalitarian, humanistic, romantic, and progressive ideals in American school administration and teaching.

The picture of the rural school as the source of good pedagogy, wise administration, and community integration is a necessary fiction to balance the reality of rural schooling. What are the *interests*, and *whose* interests are they, represented in the rural myths? We need first to explore the rural myth as a part of American culture, as the essential American myth.

The Myth of Rural America

Thomas Jefferson once famously wrote that he envisioned the future of America as a nation of yeoman farmers (*yeoman:* "a person who owns and cultivates a small farm; *specifically:* one belonging to a class of English freeholders," according to *Merriam-Webster's Dictionary*). Part of Jefferson's agrarian ideal, which represents a central anachronism of our neoconservative times, includes the role and notion of the rural school, the romanticized one-room schoolhouse, or better yet, in keeping with Jefferson's notion of the self-contained farm, the home-schooled child.

The recent neoconservative movement in the United States holds many of these Jeffersonian values quite dear. Part of the neoconservative reading of the Constitution made evident in the hearings to confirm Judge Robert Bork to the U.S. Supreme Court in 1987 was Bork's argument that the Constitution should hold to the intentions of the original framers. This view symbolizes a longing for a simpler agrarian past, when "we" all lived in the country in our extended families, self-sufficient and God-fearing. At its extreme, it is an idealized world like Jefferson's Monticello. But slave labor built that idealized rural world, and the slaves, regardless of progenitor, lived out of sight so as not to spoil the views (though Jefferson's household was certainly "mixed race," i.e., multiethnic).

The other mythic view is that of the simple farmer getting his book-larnin' from the Holy Bible and the *New-England Primer,* living in the natural goodness of the New World like Daniel Boone and Davy Crockett.

Attempts to return the United States to its rural past were hallmarks of various educational reforms in the twentieth century. Henry Ford made the earliest serious attempt in the 1920s when he sponsored the republication of *McGuffey's Eclectic Readers,* those ubiquitous nineteenth-century (1836–1895) reading texts promoting morality and mental discipline, for distribution to America's classrooms. He also sponsored the development of Greenfield Village near Detroit, an open-air museum to America's past that predated Disney's idealization of that past in California.

Ford's interest in the rural ideals of America's farming and small-town past may have been piqued by conscience stemming from his own contributions to industrialization and mass production. More likely, he saw salvation from America's increasingly urban, immigrant-saturated society in its rural idealized past. After all, it was in the 1920 census that the United States was first discovered to have a larger urban than rural population, to have become an urban society. The rural was the ideal of a lost America—the industrial, urban, and immigrant present was a "problem" to be mitigated by educational ideals defined by a romanticized rural past.

"Orphans" from urban centers, frequently taken from their biological parents, were shipped to the country to be adopted by farmers and were thus "saved" from the corrupting influence of the urban centers (the Fresh Air Fund, which sends minority youth to rural centers during the summer, is a modern version). In the notorious Five Points section of lower Manhattan before and after the Civil War, the Five Points Mission sent Irish Catholic children to live with Protestant farmers out west (Anbinder, 2001). The adoption was to save them from urban influence—and from Catholicism. We make this observation to introduce the other underlying ideology of anachronistic-past pursuit in the United States: The rural ideal is *American,* i.e., Anglo-Saxon/Germanic Protestant, while the urban represents the foreign and different (the rest of the world).

The orphans and their rural neighbors were also schooled through the patriotism in the *McGuffey's Readers* and Noah Webster's *Blue-Backed Speller.* And, of course, there were Bible lessons and morality tales in American rural schools. The *New-England Primer,* the eighteenth-century antecedent to the *McGuffey's Readers* as the central reading text of American education, begins with Adam and Eve (or, according to new school publishing guidelines these days: Eve and Adam) in the Garden of Eden. Who can avoid the obvious symbolic connection between the rural and the Garden of Eden? The last great effort at romanticized schooling and social reform took place in the late 1960s. Joni Mitchell's generation-defining song "Woodstock" speaks about getting back to the *garden.* In the late 1960s we were all trying to "get back to the Garden, man." Our schools became "open," and our culture became obsessed with returning to "innocence." Where was that innocence? In the country.

The personifying movie of the time, *Easy Rider* (1969), provides a pretentious example of that hippie natural ideal when our antiheroes spend some time with the flower people at a rural commune. The "innocence" of the rural space is central to the scenes, and we see children being "free" as key to the mise-en-scène. The commune is actually a parallel with an earlier scene in which our antiheroes enjoy a simple meal with a farm family ("Not every man can make a living from the land," says one antihero in admiration). The farmer in the movie is the contemporary analog to the Jeffersonian yeoman farmer, as are the hippie commune members who are planting their own food for self-sufficiency. In the end, the moral, "We blew it," is about rejecting the natural and communal in favor of drugs, money, motorcycles, and Mardi Gras.

We are spending time on the idealization of the rural in American culture because it is important to an understanding of educational discourse around the subject of school organization and curriculum. One needs to recognize that the rural ideal is central to both neoconservative and neoliberal thinking. Both value community, common sense, self-reliance, and "the simple life." Both stances are antiestablishment; both reject the larger bureaucratic views of human society. This is not a new trend in thought: Voltaire's Candide responds to the indignities of eighteenth-century civilization by moving to a small farm in Switzerland and tending his garden.

School Reform in the United States

In the United States, one can trace the full democratic development of urban schools from the progressive reforms of the early twentieth century that resulted in the establishment of the *comprehensive* high school, i.e., with the vocational track added for the laboring classes, culminating in the Smith-Hughes Vocational Education Act of 1917. Urban schools would develop new tracks for the formerly excluded working-class students, and the cities would develop new "vocational" high schools to supplement the "academic" high schools. The next two decades saw various attempts to develop a comprehensive system of education practice for urban centers that promoted progressive views of a modern industrial society while maintaining democratic ideals. The famous Eight-Year Study of the 1930s was focused on researching the effectiveness of democratic education practices as opposed to foreign models of schooling from modernized, i.e., urbanized, Europe, which was promoting Fascism, Communism, and National Socialism to replace the monarchies recently deposed in the new European nation-states. World War II then made most of that discussion irrelevant until the 1950s.

The Second World War marked the end of a half century of war, the only respite being during the 1920s, which was followed by a decade of worldwide economic depression (what historian Robert Graves called "the long weekend"). The only way to undo the psychological and social damage of those years was to reinvent society. Besides, the world had changed. There was no going back to the farm for the returning servicemen and the displaced working women. We needed an equivalent space, a way to recapture the rural ideals of America.

In the postwar search for meaning, the attempt to reinvent the world, the United States invented the *suburb*. The suburb was the perfect compromise between the urban and the rural. The men could work in the city while the children were raised and schooled in the country. The suburb was the ideal of living in the industrial world. As for schooling, the suburban had the advantages of the urban, providing sophisticated academic high schools for the elite, while it avoided the corrupting influences of the urban school system. *Corrupting influences* is a euphemism for nonwhite, for foreigners, and worse, their ideas and morals, religions, and genetics.

Suburban high schools have remained the ideal of American education, the standard against which urban schools, constructed *ideologically* as failing, are measured. Suburban schools have the test scores; they have the football teams, and they have the Ivy League acceptances. Despite the intellectual contempt with which suburban life is held in some sophisticated urban circles, many urbanites give up the city for the "children's education."

The rural school, and rural life, has been disappearing in the twentieth century. Recent newspaper articles have contrasted the 1940 census with the 2000 census and marveled at how far America has come, with universal electricity, indoor plumbing, and telephones in American homes, in contrast to 60 years ago. But the real assault on rural life, that is, the transformation of the rural into the modern, i.e., the civilized, was the invention of the comprehensive, consolidated rural school system spurred by the reports of James Bryant Conant in the late 1950s and the development of the state university systems in the 1960s.

In Conant's case, there was a simple argument that the small rural high schools, and rural areas, could not provide adequate scientific laboratory space (to accommodate post-*Sputnik* National Defense Education Act spending), gymnasiums (sports were considered patriotic and healthy), or properly educated and supervised teachers (many rural teachers had two-year degrees) for education in the modern era. America rushed to build new, modern schools on a suburban model, bringing together children from any number of communities, and many small schools were closed.

Times have changed once again. The urban is "good," in certain neighborhoods at least, and the urban "pioneers" and "homesteaders" (always the romanticized rural imagery!) have rediscovered urban life. Most of the criticism of urban schools recently is over their *size*. Now it is Conant's vision of the comprehensive school that has become the "problem." The old leftist criticism that schools were artifacts of an industrial society in a postmodern information age was picked up in the 1980s by the neoconservatives. Large schools have been deemed artifacts of a bygone industrial era. Add to that criticism the critiques of neoliberals who see the large high school as a "shopping mall," with its implication of fragmentation and, of all things unholy, suburban values. The movement toward small schools is all the rage these days for both neoconservatives and neoliberals.

Prominent among the neoliberal thinkers is Theodore Sizer, father of the "essential school" movement. The important issue for our purposes is the ideology of the curriculum associated with the essential school: the essential or core curriculum. In all of his writings, Sizer calls for schools to strip away the nonacademic to get back to the essentials, the essentials being the academic curriculum. The pedagogy of the essential school is driven by the imperatives of the Paideia curriculum, as reinvented by Mortimer Adler, which is an attempt to go back to the roots of Western civilization in the ancient Greek ideal. Back to the symposium, back to the garden. Sizer's model is a direct reaction against the comprehensive school and the consolidation movement spearheaded by Conant.

What is most interesting about the essential school movement is its historical antecedent: the New England academy of the nineteenth century, which Sizer (1964) documented. The academies, like essential or core curriculum schools, did not have vocational education. Essential schools tend toward the size and organization of the academy model; they tend to be community based, i.e., homogeneous. The administration is minimal; the bureaucracy limited, and one finds the teacher facing his multiaged homogeneous community and teaching the essential knowledge of the world to the future small farmers that Jefferson so revered. And, in an 1885 NEA document, "The Place and the Function of the Academy," we are reminded that the original Academy was a "garden or grove near Athens" that numbered Plato among its members. This was the *original* rural school.

Except the future isn't in the rural past. How well does the rural ideal fit the needs of modern society? Sizer himself says, "The academy failed because it was primarily a rural institution" (p. 40). And the world has changed. The modern urban world is diverse, complex, and large in scale. The small-school movement appears to focus on single, simple, and small-scale answers to large issues. The solution, rural anachronism, may not fit the problem, urban futurism. The solution, a simple, basic education for all, may not fit the problems, the complex intellectual demands of the urban global world. The solution, small communities of like-minded people, may not meet the challenges of cross-cultural understanding. In any case, a longing for a simpler past is not likely to be an answer to the complex future we face in the twenty-first century.

But certainly there is something different about urban schools that distinguishes them from suburban and rural schools. Based on funding figures from the NCES, there are three areas in which the federal government puts more money into schools in central city MSAs than schools elsewhere: bilingual education, vocational education, and Title I (supplemental services for economically disadvantaged children). Children-with-disabilities funding is a significant item, but as much federal money goes to the suburbs. Nonetheless, resources are necessary for a higher proportion of nonnative speakers, children of poverty, and students with job training needs in urban schools as well as for the number of children with disabilities.

One could argue that a simple core academic approach serves none of the needs of the students who bring these preconditions to the classroom. One can see why neoconservatives are obsessed with a core curriculum of cultural literacy and immersion programs for learning English. The melting-pot myth is at work here, but one wonders how the melting pot works in a transnational world. One also wonders why bilingualism, so common in other western nations, is treated as a problem to be eradicated in U.S. schools. Looking back to a preindustrial, romanticized rural America for answers may be a form of wishful thinking or a reactionary political stance. One wonders if something more than school reform is at stake.

The schools are, inevitably, a battleground for defining the nation. Do we envision an old United States or a new United States? The proponents of the new see the United States as a complex, urban, global, multiple entity—multiethnic, multiracial, multireligious, multiclass, multigendered, multinational, multidimensional. The plurality of all constituencies needs to be accounted for in the new vision. The students in the schools, public and private, cannot just "become Americans": They live in and represent multiple cultures. Urban education *is* different because it is the emergent American culture, a complex, urban, multidimensional culture. The "problems" of urban education represent opportunities to transform the culture. How we invent the next phases of American urban schooling is how we invent the nation.

Aiken, Wilford (1942). *The story of the eight year study.* New York: Harper Brothers.

Anbinder, Tyler (2001). *Five Points: The 19th-century New York City neighborhood that invented tap dance, stole elections, and became the world's most notorious slum.* New York: Free Press.

Bryan, Ford. (2002). *Friends, families & forays: Scenes from the life of Henry Ford.* Detroit: Wayne State University Press.

Conant, James Bryant. (1962). *Slums and suburbs.* New York: McGraw-Hill.

Conroy, Pat. (1972). *The water is wide.* (2002 ed.). New York: Dial Press.

DeVoe, Jill F.; Peter, Katharin; Kaufman, Phillip; Ruddy, Sally A.; Miller, Amanda K.; Planty, Mike; et al. (2002). *Indicators of school crime and safety: 2002.* Washington, DC: U.S. Departments of Education and Justice. NCES 2003(009/NCJ 196753. http://nces.ed.gov/ pubs2003/2003009. pdf. Accessed November 14, 2003.

Ford, Paul Leicester. (1897). *The New England primer: A history of Its origin and development.* New York: Dodd, Mead and Co.

Irving, Washington. (1820). "The legend of Sleepy Hollow". (1991 ed.). New York: Tor Classics.

Jefferson, Thomas. (1785). *Notes on the state of Virginia.* (1998 ed.). New York: Penguin Classics.

NCES (1997). *Characteristics of stayers, movers, and leavers: Results from the teacher followup survey: 1994-95.* Washington, DC: U.S. Department of Education. http://nces.ed.gov/pubsearch/ pubsinfo.asp?pubid=97450. Accessed August 20, 2009.

National Education Association. (2009). www.nea.org/home/20412.htm. Accessed August 20, 2009.

Powell, Arthur, et al. (1985). *The shopping mall high school.* Boston: Houghton Mifflin.

Report of the NEA Committee on Secondary Education. (1885). The nature and function of the academy. in *The Journal of Proceedings and Addresses of the national education association.* New York: J. J. Little.

Sears, Barnas (1880). "Fifty years of educational progress." in *The lectures read before the american institute of instruction.* (Proceedings of the American Institute of Instruction, Forty-ninth Annual session). Boston: American Institute of Instruction.

Sizer, Theodore R. (Ed.) (1964). *The age of the academies.* New York: Teachers College Press.

Voltaire. (1759). *Candide: or, optimism.* Translated by Burton Raffel. (2006 ed.) New Haven: Yale University Press.

CHAPTER NINETEEN

Lourdes Diaz Soto

Educar para transformar

How Do We Teach Toward a Critical Bilingual/Bicultural Urban Pedagogy?

You must be the change you wish to see in the world.

—*Mahatma Gandhi*

Introduction

It is clear that the problems urban children face in our education system are difficult and may appear insurmountable. Freire (1970) has taught us, however, that education can be an integral part of the practice of freedom (as opposed to the practice of domination) and that this process is ultimately going to lead to humanization and *conscientization* (consciousness raising).

Paulo Freire, the Brazilian educator (1921–1997), is among the most influential thinkers of the late twentieth century. His work is one of the foundations of critical pedagogy. He maintained that he did not invent a literacy method but that his goal was to *educar para transformar* (to educate in order to transform). Pursuing a critical Freirean pedagogy that calls for reading "the word" and "the world" (Freire, 1970) may help us to garner our collective wisdom, in solidarity, to face a world that seems incomprehensible.

In his life Paulo Freire received wide recognition for his contributions to literacy. His focus was on the dialogue between teacher and pupil. He believed that the acquisition of knowledge creates social change and that politics and education are strongly linked. He asserted that the pupil is the master of his/her own learning and that education is the path to liberation. He also noted the complexities of the human condition:

> The oppressed, instead of striving for liberation, tend themselves to become the oppressors...the very structure of their thought has been conditioned by contradictions of the concrete, existential situation by which they were shaped...this phenomenon derives from the fact that the oppressed, at a certain moment in their experience, adopt an attitude of adhesion to the oppressor...the oppressed find the oppressor their model (Freire, 1970, 29–30).

We are now seeing examples of this condition, which might be compared to Gramsci's notion of hegemony in which the oppressed have learned to consent to degradation, colonization, and oppression.

In many nations of the world children are facing dehumanization and degradation. The emotional effects remind us of the importance of an education that is liberating and transforming in nature. For example, Sergio Pinheiro (2006) submitted a report to the United Nations documenting that violence against children is a global problem in homes, schools, in care and justice systems, work settings, and communities. In addition the Innocenti Research Centre (2007) notes that the United States has the highest child poverty rates as compared to 19 other industrialized nations. These are problems that we need to address in order to reach a more equitable space.

Freire's approach relies on generative words and themes. This approach, for those of us who teach younger children, can be likened to the Language Experience approach. Sylvia Ashton-Warner (1965) developed the idea of an "organic vocabulary" born from "dynamic life itself" to teach literacy to Maori children in New Zealand. The idea was to use "significant" words that have meaning in the child's life. A generative theme can lead to discussion, study, projects, and activities on a topic that is valuable to the children.

The dialogue in the project becomes a critical conversation with a focus, a purpose—it is dialogic, and it is collaborative. In this type of teaching there is reflection and action. Freire felt that it was important for the learner to be involved in dialogic action, which has two dimensions of reflection and action, with the teacher. The learners are challenged (with problem posing) to focus on their daily reality and thus gain access to transforming the world.

In addition educators need to be cognizant that there are ethical areas to consider as we are teaching "other people's children." Again, Freire highlights how we as progressive educators can engage ourselves:

> Educational activists recognize the ethical dimensions of teaching other people's children, they work to provide them with the highest quality of education they would desire for their own children, and they learn to work as an ally with the community. Educational activists share power with marginalized groups, they seek out networks, and they teach others to act politically and to advocate individually and collectively for themselves and other marginalized groups. This involves developing a "critical consciousness." It also involves organizing themselves and others "reflectively for action rather than for passivity" (Freire, 1985, p. 82).

Educar para transformar

In one of my favorite books by Freire (1988), he outlines the "indispensable qualities" that each educator needs in order to reach our optimal levels of teaching/learning and praxis. Similar to Reverend Martin Luther King Jr., who called for a bringing together of the head and the heart, Freire details qualities that are not just academic (of the head). These qualities include: humility, lovingness, tolerance, courage, tension between patience and impatience, and joy of living. For Freire (1970) the importance of the struggle for liberation means that we must view challenges and oppressive situations as limiting but yet able to be transformed. Together in solidarity we can begin to transform our daily reality in order to experience true humanization. We will experience the "act" of transformation as we deal with our own internalized oppressions. This transformation and true humanization are disciplined "acts" of agency that require constancy and a patient lifelong devotion.

The school Curriculum as Possibility

The school curriculum becomes the site for debate, mandates, and issues of power. I am seeing teachers struggle with mandates that are causing virtual burnout of our best and brightest. According to the National Commission on Teaching and America's Future (2007), one out of every three teachers leaves the profession within five years. This teacher dropout problem is costing the nation $7 billion a year by diminishing teaching quality and undermining our ability to close the achievement gap. It is clear that the current educational system is not hospitable to the needs of our young teachers.

Britzman (2002) states that "disillusionment toward knowledge persists as one of this century's great epistemological themes" (p. 96). And we note it is not just the students but also the teachers themselves who are struggling with disillusionment. For the past six years in the U.S. we have witnessed what has happened to the curriculum when the Bush administration mandated and imposed The No Child Left Behind Act of 2001 (signed into law in 2002) filled with accountability provisions (U.S. Department of Education, 2002) but without financial, educator, or local community support (Neill, 2003). The imposition of standards of knowledge as yardsticks for all learners has meant additional pressures on teachers to teach to the test (Deubel, 2008).

We have witnessed the obsession with high-stakes testing, leaving teachers feel powerless and helpless in the face of top-down mandates. Valenzuela (2002) notes how teachers, principals, students, and schools are held accountable in ways that lead to collateral effects, including the marginalization of the curriculum, children, or both. Teachers are expected to implement a sanitized curriculum lacking rigor and connections to daily realities (*Rethinking Schools*, 2003). We have seen the courage of workers for justice, and we have seen the courage of teachers (Ayers, 2004) intent on making a difference in the lives of their students (Soto, 2002). Herbert Kohl (2000–2001) notices that it appears that justice is often not worth fighting for because just having to advocate for teaching social justice is a statement about the moral sensibility of our schools and society.

For bilingual children and minority children, urban schools have become sites of oppression. The xenophobic tendencies toward bilingual and immigrant children are obvious even in the CNN newsroom where Lou Dobbs takes it upon himself to demonize immigrants. The U.S. has reached a crossroads in its immigration policies and enforcement strategies (NCLR, 2007) Gloria Anzaldúa eloquently describes the linguistic terrorism.

> Somos los del español deficiente.
> We are your linguistic nightmare, your linguistic aberration,
> your linguistic mestizaje,
> the subject of your burla.
> Because we speak with tongues of fire
> we are culturally crucified.
> Racially, culturally and linguistically somos huerfanos—
> we speak an orphan tongue (Anzaldúa, 1999) p. 80).

I remind my university students that regardless of what the political English-only winds mandate, our children will still be in the classrooms. Our concern is for the well-being of our learners. Our concern is to ensure that education becomes the practice of freedom.

As we face total disillusionment and total discouragement bell hooks' words may be encouraging. hooks reminds us that education is a hope-filled endeavor:

> My hope emerges from those places of struggle where I witness individuals positively transforming their lives and the world around them. Educating is always a vocation rooted in hopefulness. As teachers we believe that learning is possible, that nothing can keep an open mind from seeking after knowledge and finding a way to know (hooks, 2003, p. xiv).

In our classrooms in teacher education and in our daily realities we can observe how our students struggle with their own lives, how they gain *conscientization*, how they begin to critique the media and the political world around them. It is a struggle that we face if we are interested in social justice and equity in our lifetimes.

So how can we make a difference in the lives of oppressed learners? Kharem and Villaverde (2002) offer teachers the notion of forging alliances. Teacher allies become co-workers with people of color to see and understand the daily realities of the oppressed populations while "tearing down the walls of oppression which will allow the human spirit to reach its potential" (p. 5). This type of curriculum signifies that the dialogic, the critical, the anti-racist, and the political are an integral part of the classroom. How we work together as allies will determine how we create change in our society. Forging alliances is a powerful weapon as Audre Lorde's (1984) often-quoted advice reminds us "the master's tools will never dismantle the master's house." The master in this case is the western patriarchal imperialistic perspective that encourages rugged individualism while the idea of alliances seeks collaboration and working in solidarity. Anzaldúa and

Lorde announce that acting in solidarity we can challenge the imperialist notion of rugged individualism, patriarchy, and competition. Our goal of social justice and equity will require new ways of knowing and new ways of organizing ourselves.

It will only be when our alliances are built with compassion and love that the internalized wounds of our learners and our nations will be healed. The painful stories of Golden Eagle, a Native-American Latino child (Gutierrez-Gomez, 2002) entering kindergarten, of Irene Pabon (2002) growing up in Puerto Rico, and of Lynus Yamuna (2002), who saw students wearing a dunce cap and signs around their necks for speaking their Melanesian language remind us that the colonizers' imperialist eyes have gazed upon a people in other countries than America. Colonization and oppression have come at a significant cost to learners. How the privileged patriarchal ways of knowing have subjugated learners is evident when the oppressed (again as described by Freire) take on their language, their characteristics as fully assimilated yet totally disregarded beings. "Imperialism still hurts, still destroys and is reforming itself constantly" (Smith, 1999).

An anti-imperialist/counterhegemonic approach to teaching and learning is described by Moll (1996) as relying on the wisdom of "funds of knowledge." With such funds of knowledge teachers can integrate the community's ways of knowing into the literacy of the classroom. The integration of the family wisdom means that the expertise each family brings is honored and respected. This liberatory approach evokes organic *conscientization*. The integration of community/family knowledge as an integral part of the curriculum is counterhegemonic as it liberates the epistemic knowledges that surface.

Latinos can be a source of wisdom and strength in our diverse urban communities (Soto, 2007). The wisdom within our communities and our students provides our best source of strength in a historically situated dialogic struggle. We can think about the wisdom of our ancestors, our *abuelitos* and *abuelitas*. It is by standing on their shoulders that we are able to be here today. Our grandparents worked in the vineyards with humility and hope while our parents worked in factories and banded together for social justice and equity. This type of wisdom/knowledge can be a third space for the curriculum. In arguing for a critical libratory/transformative approach to teaching and learning, i.e., a critical pedagogy we can rely on Bhabha's work as we envision a third space as a possibility:

> This is a space that is somehow in between, interstitial, not fully governed by any specific recognizable set of traditions. Within this space, anything is possible. Our very identities come into question. This may not always feel safe or comfortable; on the contrary, the "third space" is in a certain sense defined by the fact that all of us, regardless of race, creed, culture or gender, feel equally open and unsafe there. This is the space where change happens. (Homi Bhabha, 1994, p. 190)

A Critical Pedagogy

Educators will need to study power and privilege within a critical multicultural perspective as Steinberg and Kincheloe (2001) have proposed. They describe the many faces of multiculturalism and how critical multiculturalism departs from a) conservative (monocultural) multiculturalism, b) liberal multiculturalism, c) pluralistic multiculturalism, and d) left-essentialist multiculturalism (Kincheloe & Steinberg, 1998).

Critical pedagogy draws upon the Frankfurt School of Critical Theory of the 1920s and focuses on issues of power and domination. This model promotes a deep understanding of the ways that power and domination influence schooling. It works to expose the schools' role in sorting students; it identifies the equity issues surrounding the education of students of diverse race, social class, and gender. It supports the elimination of human suffering, examines issues of privilege, is committed to social justice, and rejects notions of meritocracy (Steinberg and Kincheloe, 2001).

Kincheloe and Steinberg join Giroux, Kanpol, McLaren, hooks, Lorde, Darder, Moll, Anzaldúa and many others who continue to chip away at the Eurocentric hegemony in schools. I join all of these writers/thinkers/scholars in the struggle to capture the complexity of how to comprehend a critical pedagogy. In fact, I am re-imagining and maybe even re-inventing Freire via the convergence of all these scholars.

Freire's (1985) notion of reading the word and the world along with Bhabha's (1994) theory of a third space, and Anzaldua's (1987) border crossing project all denounce injustices and announce transformative acts via liberatory agency. With the addition of the voices of a critical multiculturalism we can envision decolonizing, liberating perspectives in the curriculum and in the classroom. We can no longer stand by as hypnotized beings while the world around us acts out with aggression. This model opens up a space of possibility where dialogue, democratic participation, creativity, and Freire's ongoing cycle of action/reflection/action can take place. Just as Audre Lorde reminded us of the "master's tools," Joe Kincheloe (1993) argued that a "homogenous community often is unable to criticize the injustice and exclusionary practices that afflict a social system" (67).

Critical Bilingual/Bicultural Pedagogy

I would like to suggest how we can create a critical bilingual/bicultural pedagogy keeping in mind the works of Freire, Bhabha, Anzaldua, and the scholars already cited.

First, a critical bilingual/bicultural pedagogy will ensure that our children will read the word and the world, as Freire suggested. We must design, implement, and incorporate a liberatory pedagogy where *concientization* and transformative action can take place.

Second, a critical bilingual/bicultural pedagogy will ensure home language maintenance, second language learning, biliteracy, and biculturalism. It will be academically rigorous, centered on children's daily realities, grounded in the wisdom of diversity. Remembering Anzaldúa's notion of *los deslenguados* and Luis Moll's funds of knowledge can ensure projects of respect and affirmation of languages and cultures when the white patriarchal notions of supremacy are denounced.

Third, a critical bilingual/bicultural pedagogy will ensure democratic participation with an authentic voice. The annunciation of transformative and liberatory acts with a language of critique allows for solidarity and community participation within a dialogue of respect and humility.

Fourth, a critical bilingual/bicultural pedagogy will be instrumental in ensuring that children of the world begin to experience elements of decolonization and liberation.

As we denounce the privileged patriarchal western ways of knowing we can announce decolonizing methodologies that reconceptualize issues of race, class, and gender.

Fifth, a critical bilingual/bicultural pedagogy examines critically new electronic technologies that are shaping everyday life through the media, in particular, television, and computers. The ability of learners to critique the symbolic violence disseminated by the media (Kellner, 1995) ((including the demonization of immigrants) opens a window for the examination of ethical projects and how we (the others) are portrayed.

Sixth, a critical bilingual/bicultural pedagogy will infuse the curriculum with antiracist anti-sexist projects. Our students have for too long been the victims of the colonizers' agenda with white supremacists as the norm along with racism, heterogeneity and patriarchy. With projects of social justice and equity we can begin to reach a third space of a liberatory transformative curriculum.

Seventh, a critical bilingual/bicultural pedagogy will encourage us to explore spaces of healing for our common wisdom, our common good, and our love for each other. As we implement decolonizing projects with funds of knowledge, critical multicultural projects, and focus on equity, we may reach a transformative stage where we can actually heal the pain and struggles previous generations have lived. We need to continue to dream for our future generations and ourselves.

As we continue to explore territories of social justice and equity we realize that ethical action is most crucial at this educationally challenged crossroads. These words have inspired my work as a critical bilingual/bicultural pedagogue— they may help your journey as well as we work toward *educar para transformar.*

> *We must raise the international of hope.*
> *Hope above borders, languages, colors, cultures, sexes, strategies, and thoughts,*
> *of all those who prefer humanity alive.*
> *CONSIDERING THAT WE ARE:*

For the international order of hope, for a new and just and dignified peace.
For new politics, for democracy, for political liberties.
For justice, for life, and dignified work.
For civil society, for full rights for women in every regard, for respect for elders, youth, and children,
for the defense and protection of the environment.
For intelligence, for culture, for education, for truth.
For liberty, for tolerance, for inclusion, for remembrance.
For humanity. (Zapatistas, 1998, 51–52).

REFERENCES

Anzaldua, G. (1987). *Borderlands/La Frontera: The new mestiza*. San Francisco: Aunt Lute Books.

Ayers, W. (2004). *Teaching the personal and the political. Essays on hope and justice.* New York: Teachers College Press.

Bhabha, H. (1994). *The location of culture*. New York: Routledge

Britzman, D. (2002). The death of the curriculum. In Doll, W.E. & Gough, N. (Eds). *Curriculum visions*. New York: Peter Lang.

Darder, A. (1991). *Culture and power in the classroom*. New York: Bergin and Garvey.

Deubel, P. (April, 2008). Accountability, Yes. Teaching to the test, No. *T.H.E. Journal* Retrieved April 7, 2009: http://www.ask.com/bar?q=Teachers+Teaching+to+the+Test&page=1&qsrc= 6&ab=1&u=http%3A%2F%2Fwww.thejournal.com%2Farticles%2F2241

Freire, P. (1970). *Pedagogy of the oppressed*. New York: Herder & Herder.

Freire, P. (1985). *The politics of education*. South Hadley, MA: Bergin and Garvey.

Freire, P. (1988). *Teachers as cultural workers: Letters to those who dare to teach*. Boulder, CO: Westview

Giroux, H. (1992). Resisting difference: Cultural studies and the discourse of critical pedagogy. Pp. 199—212 in *Cultural studies*, eds. Grossberg, Nelson, and Treichler, (Eds.), New York: Routledge.

Gramsci, A. (1971). *Selections from the prison notebooks of Antonio Gramsci*. Translated and edited by Q. Hoare and G. N. Smith. New York : International Publishers. (Original work written in prison 1929—1935)

Gutierrez-Gomez, C. (2002). Golden Eagle enters kindergarten. In Soto, L.D. (Ed). (2002). *Making a difference in the lives of bilingual/bicultural children*. New York: Peter Lang Publishers.

hooks, bell (2003) *Teaching community. A pedagogy of hope*. New York: Routledge.

Innocenti Research Centre (2007). *Child poverty in perspective. An overview of child well-being in rich countries*. Retrieved April 7, 2009, from www.unicef-irc.org

Kanpol, B., and McLaren, P., eds. 1995. *Critical Multiculturalism*. Westport, CT: Bergin and Garvey.

Kellner, D, (1995). *Media culture*. New York: Routledge.

Kharem, H. and Villaverde, L. (2002). Teacher allies: The problem of the color line. In Soto, L.D. (Ed). (2002). *Making a difference in the lives of bilingual/bicultural children*. New York: Peter Lang.

Kinchloe, J. (1993). *Toward a critical politics of teacher thinking: Mapping the postmodern*. Westport, CT: Bergin and Garvey.

Kincheloe, J. & Steinberg, S. (1998). *Changing multiculturalism: New times, New curriculum*. London: Open University.

Kohl, H. (winter 2000–2001). Teaching for social justice. *Rethinking Schools*, vol. 15 (no 2). Retrieved April 7, 2009: http://www.rethinkingschools.org/archive/15_02/Just152.shtml

Educar para transformar

Lorde, A. (1984). *Sister Outsider*. Trumansburg, NY: The Crossing Press.

McLaren, P. (1995). *Critical pedagogy and predatory culture: Oppositional politics in a post-modern era*. London: Routledge.

Moll, L. C. & Gonzalez, N. (1994) Lessons from research with language minority students. *Journal of Reading Behavior* 26(4): 439-461.

National Commission on Teaching and America's Future (June 2007). The high cost of teacher turnover. Retrieved April 7, 2009: http://nctaf.org.zeus.silvertech.net/resources/research_and_reports/nctaf_research_reports/documents/CTTPolicyBrief-FINAL_000.pdf

Neill, M. (Fall 2003). Don't mourn, organize! *Rethinking Schools*, vol. 18 (no. 1). Retrieved April 7, 2009: http://www.rethinkingschools.org/archive/18_01/nclb181.shtml

Pabon, I. (2002). A life span/Toda una vida: The pain and the struggle that will strike: El dolor y la lucha que embiste. In Soto, L.D. (Ed) *Making a difference in the lives of bilingual/bicultural children*. New York: Peter Lang.

Pinheiro, P.S. (2006). *Study on violence against children*. Report to the U.N. General Assembly. Sixty-first session item 62a: Promotion and protection of the rights of the child.

Rethinking Schools (Fall 2003). Rethinking our classrooms: Teaching for equity and Justice. Vol. 18 (no. 1). Retrieved April 7, 2009: http://www.rethinkingschools.org/archive/18_01/roc181.shtml

Soto, L.D. (Ed). (2002). *Making a difference in the lives of bilingual/bicultural children*. New York: Peter Lang.

Soto, L.D. (Ed). (2007). *The Praeger Handbook of Latino education in the U.S.* Westport, CT: Praeger.

Valenzuela, A. (2002). High-stakes testing and U.S.-Mexican youth in Texas: The case for multiple compensatory criteria in assessment, *Harvard Journal of Hispanic Policy*, Vol. 14, pp. 97–116.

Yamuna, L. (2002). My story and the Melanesian knowledge. In Soto, L.D. (Ed) *Making a difference in the lives of bilingual/bicultural children*. New York: Peter Lang.

Zapatistas (1998). *Zapatistas encuentro: Documents from the 1996 encounter for humanity against neoliberalism*. New York: Seven Stories Press.

ADDITIONAL RESOURCES

HYPERLINK "http://www.freechild.org/youth_activism_2.htm" Freechild Youth
Activism for Social Justice Webpage
HYPERLINK "http://www.hrw.org/reports/2001/children/"
Rethinking Schools. HYPERLINK "http://www.rethinkingschools.com"
www.rethinkingschools.com

Shirley R. Steinberg

Transformational Urban Education: Answers Bringing the Next Set of Questions

 In 2004, Joe Kincheloe and I put this book together because we felt that educators don't ask enough questions. We wanted to ask questions, specific questions which were directed to urban education, instead of staying within the traditional educational approach of giving answers. Questions should beget more questions. The first edition asked nineteen questions, and this volume has added new questions. After completing the second edition, I realized that questions doubled as fast as we attempted to answer them. To write this afterword, I asked my colleagues/ friends/partners in education to pose more questions. Some asked questions, and some elaborated on those questions. I invite you to share these additional questions with your students and peers and join us on the journey to discovering some answers. Please contact me through the freireproject.org website if you are interested in continuing the dialogue or speaking to our contributors.

Regina A. Bernard-Carreno asks:
- *What are the "off hours" life of and the "during-class instruction" role(s) of the urban teacher?*
- *Who are urban teachers? How do they connect/disconnect from their students?*
- *Do urban teachers represent the students they teach and in what ways?*
- *Could Claire Huxtable teach kids from Compton?* She's Black and most of the Compton students are Black.

Joanne Carris asks:

- *How can schools be transformed for adolescents who read below a third-grade level into a meaningful, supportive educational experience that addresses their academic, emotional, and social needs?*

Andrew Churchill asks:

- *How does one respectfully balance the tension between developing the kinds of cultural capital that are helpful in navigating the current zeitgeist of a Eurocentric patriarchial curriculum based on positivist logic enacted with high stakes testing and both respecting students' individual histories and realities as well as helping change the oppressive climate of the sociopolitical status quo?*

George J. Sefa Dei asks:

- *What is 'urban education' in the contemporary contexts of Euro-Western modernity?* Epistemologically, urban education can be situated through a particular counterinsurgent partition to the sum of Western materiality of knowledge. 'Urban education' as it resides within and beyond the reach of the Euro/Modern/American city today, must be contextualized within and beyond the reservoirs of Southern geographies. In many inner cities today, notwithstanding the creativity and innovation of a number of youth, we are faced with a disturbing degree of nihilism, hopelessness, and a sense of living a dead-end existence, as well as the pervasiveness of lost and stolen dreams for a number of youth. In part, this situation can be attributed to the 'disappointment of education' for its failure to provide a complete account of the histories of ideas and events that have shaped and continue to shape human growth and development. We call for a critical urban education to seriously engage questions of equity and social justice anchored in the understanding of power and social difference so as to allow youth to actualize their dreams and aspirations and the agency of working to transform their lives and societies. Urban education must move beyond good intentions to broach the meaning of knowledge for social transformation, the implication of self and collective complicities as well as implications of allowing knowledge to compel meaningful social action. Such education must engage a radicalized spiritual sense of self and the collective to strengthen both individuals and their communities. It must also engage the multiplicity of knowings and herald the power of marginalized and colonized bodies to assert their own agency and power, to initiate social and educational change that makes sense in everyday social practice.

Venus Evans-Winter asks:

- *To whom are are urban teachers accountable? Are they accountable to parents, students, school boards, state or federal government? Who are students accountable to in a democracy? What are the moral implications for not educating the majority of the U.S. school population? I am afraid some of the questions I* had when teaching in Brownsville lead to potentially dangerous solutions. But, for example, I wonder if school should even be mandated if it does not serve the needs of the population. But who will determine the needs? Of course, the population under ideal circumstances, but that is a long road back and unlikely in this climate.

Lee Gabay asks:

- *Why is New York City (and most large US cities) spending ten times more on incarceration than education?*

C. P. Gause asks:

- *Given the socio-cultural and political implications of "schooling" and the reification of hegemonic sorting and selecting practices enacted by standardized curricula, how can urban educators create sustainable inclusive democratic learning communities?*
- *How can these communities allow students to be engaged in creative free-flow exchanges of ideas and knowledge production?*

Rodney Handlesmann asks:

- *How do urban schools account for/create/discipline diverse abilities?* Not to discount but rather to reveal the culturally/historically located social construction of "dis/ability."
- *Are schools places where all may succeed?* I believe that the answers to this question necessarily link to questions re: the purpose of schools; the meanings of "success/failure"; and hierarchies of ability which pervade academics (as well as social theory) and which link directly to ideological, political and economic systems which define what economic/political/cultural "rights" or privileges a person has access to based upon hierarchies of value vis à vis ability (and labor for that matter).
- *What does it mean that numerous rights-based movements and arguments for inclusion, historically, are based upon ablest arguments—e.g., women are as smart as men; black people are as smart as white people, etc.? What does it mean when people of diverse abilities do not meet the requirements of conventional "smartness" in a particular context? Historically, since "ability" has been linked discursively with one's right to citizenship and participation in society (and schools), how do critical theories address "ability" meaningfully, moving beyond critiques of the socially constructed, and culturally-inscribed nature of IQ, so as to speak to the diverse "dis/abilities" we find in our schools? If one accepts that people manifest diverse abilities, what would anti-oppressive notions of ability look like? And what would their consequences be?*

Brian C. Johnson asks:

- *How might educators actively promote the positive racial identity development of all students, especially those from underrepresented racial groups?* This must include methods of defeating stereotype threat and negative self-fulfilling prophecies.

Curry Malott asks:

- *What is it about urban education that renders it pregnant with the potential to foster a real challenge to the labor/capital relationship in North America, and, ultimately, globally?* This question alludes to not only the concentration of people in urban areas, and its cultural, ethnic, and economic diversity, but also to the influence urban contexts in the United States, for example, have traditionally had on the rest of the country. In other words, there is the possibility for the emergence of a united confederation of people who rely on a wage to survive to set a radical, liberatory precedent for the rest of the nation and world. Within this context we could argue that a postformal approach to educational psychology and critical pedagogy offers a useful model for beginning to build an epistemologically inclusive education with the theoretical capacity to bring Indigenous, Eastern, Marxist, postmodern, and other philosophies under one critical roof.

Elizabeth Meyer asks:

- *How is sexuality education being presented in urban schools?*
- *Does it go beyond abstinence-only and reproductive biology?*
- *Does it include discussions of healthy relationships, diverse sexualities and gender identities?*
- *How is the sexuality curriculum shaped by other urban issues such as dropouts, gangs, poverty, and racialized student populations?*

Donale Mulcahy asks:

- *If poverty is an overriding consideration of urban schools, why don't urban schools focus their curricula on understanding the economic, systemic, etc., reasons for poverty, and the cycle of poverty, instead of avoiding it by focusing on subject matter that is irrelevant to someone living either in poverty or in the environs of poverty?* Perhaps if poor communities were encouraged and aided to understand poverty at the different levels in their schooling, it would be a beginning for a true war on poverty.

Bernardo Pohl asks:

- *What can I, as a suburban teacher, learn from urban education?* I teach in a suburban school, and yet, we are officially Title I. Our school is surrounded by two high income neighborhoods and six low income ones, and this is not counting the scores of trailer parks and low income apartment complexes. Our school is no longer a white inclusive enclave, but a school with 60% minority population. We face the same problems as any urban school: dropouts, gang activity, teacher burnout and high turn-out rate, single family students, and the list goes on.

Transformational Urban Education: Answers Bringing the Next Set of Questions

- *Does a moral debate have a place in urban education?* Education is in crisis. The standardization movement has stifled the profession. Schools are places that students learn to dread. On one hand, the American society vests so much faith and puts so much currency in education, and yet, our faith in education is not matched with similar actions. On the contrary, we, as a nation, have to deal with a lack of funding and resources, an increasing turn-out rate for teachers, a constant attack from media and politicians, and an increasing number of disgruntled taxpayers demanding better results. We expect our schools to be places in which our children become model citizens and productive members of society. However, our students attend a rigid bell-to-bell schedule, which resembles an assembly factory line. Teachers are expected to teach 32 hours of instruction a week with very little time for planning and curriculum development. More and more, districts and schools are facing deeper and tighter budget cuts. *As a society, why do we not question these appallingly low standards?*

Kathalene Razzano asks:

- *In what ways might urban spaces be used to further promote and facilitate innovative, location-based, self-reflexive modes of knowledge production from both students and teachers?* Urban spaces (i.e., as geographic spaces, as commercial spaces, as geographical spaces, as community) are littered with sites of knowledge production and dissemination. I'd like to see us develop a pedagogy which interrogates these spaces in ways which increase students' awareness about urban spaces and their relationship to these spaces.

Mary Weems asks:

- One of main complaints I hear from classroom teachers, and administrators is about the lack of parental involvement in the schools. While the reasons for this are complex, the majority of the people I encounter in this setting assume that it's because the parents don't care and this has a negative effect on the education of our children. *How can we educate the parents of children who attend urban schools about the socio-economic, and political purpose of public education?*
- *Is it feasible to envision a time when teachers and others in urban schoools will organize to rebel against the classroom, curriculum and creativity–crippling impact of proficiency testing?*
- Other than sorting, and ensuring (at least temporarily) that students have consumed and supposedly comprehend content about particular subjects, testing does not contribute to the development of critical thinking, socially-conscious young people. The problems with testing and over-testing have been talked about, written about, and challenged in public and private settings for years "yet" layers of testing continue to be added to younger and younger grade levels. *When will this counterproductive, teacher-student spirit-damaging madness end?*

- *When will the languages and/or dialects our children in urban schools speak be honored rather ridiculed as being inferior to so-called standard English?*

Shirley R. Steinberg

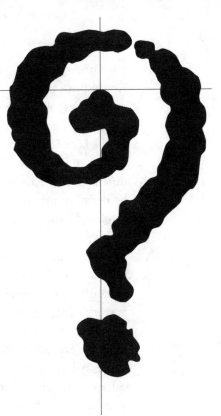

What Didn't We Ask?
Keepin' It Real

 The number 19 is my metaphor for the city. It is an arbitrary marker for urban movement. Walking down the stairs to the subway in downtown Manhattan, travelers go under the 1 and the 9 . . . the red line, the train that runs north and south on the west side of the island. The red number 1 + 9 (19) is indelible in my mind as the label that signals the cavernous expanse traveled every day by thousands, tens of thousands. Nineteen is the hurried glimpse of straphangers, school kids in uniform, subway sleepers, musicians, beggars, and buskers. Nineteen is the urban—continually moving, dirty, smelly, dark and dank, yet energetic, strong, and unyielding. The dichotomies of the urban landscape fill our every sense. And we have 19 questions . . .

Can we stop at 19? Have we answered all the questions? Of course not, there are 19 and 19 more . . . 190, 1900 more urban questions to ask. This book only scratches the grimy surface of those questions. We wrote this book and asked these questions because we love the urban, the raw, the sophisticated, the beautiful, and beastly part of cities. We love the pulsating beats of the trains, the people, and the huge police horses. The urban scape is the culmination of the postmodern condition: aged and new, traditional and cutting-edge. We are committed to the urban, and to urban dwellers—most importantly, to urban children and schooling. Consequently, we must ask questions and tentatively find answers and solutions to the enigmatic conditions in which we find ourselves: teachers in a love/hate struggle with the environment of the city classroom. I hope that you were able, as you read this book, to complicate the discussion and multiply both questions and answers.

Other than using the sociological and demographic definitions of *urban*, I would pose that it is indeed difficult to define exactly what the urban is. It is easier to say what the urban is not. Urban life is not gentle, yet it is not always rough. It is not spacious, yet it is not necessarily cramped; it is energetic, yet it can be lazy. Urban life is unique—urban schools and children are unique. In the context of this book, we have addressed urban existence and urban public education in its distinctly, uniquely, North American setting. We qualify our discussion by defining urban education as schooling that includes the lower and middle classes of public school children (excluding magnet schools and test-admittance schools).

I work with New York City teachers who are finishing their masters degrees in education. Several of them mentioned to me that they believed that one of the most difficult things they have had to cope with was the fact that no one in the mayor's office or district has ever asked them what they thought about urban education. Indeed, at the beginning of the school year, they were herded into Madison Square Garden for the yearly pep talk. They remarked that they were addressed by the usual politicos, union members, and supervisors—but that the voice of teachers was mute. I want to end this book with the voices of teachers. I asked a group of 30 Brooklyn teachers to write short answers to my questions:

What Does It Mean to Be an Urban Student?

- Being an urban student means that transportation is difficult and you have to use a public bus or subway and be there to catch it at just the right time—otherwise, you miss school. Sometimes it's dangerous.
- Being an urban student means you live in a rented house and have free or reduced lunches.
- Being an urban student means that parents have long days at work.
- Being an urban student means that you have little opportunity to belong to sports teams.
- Being an urban student means suffering through traffic congestion and waking to the sounds of garbage trucks and car alarms.
- Being an urban student means seeing rats crawl up the buildings on garbage cans and smelling urine.
- Being an urban student means that classrooms are overcrowded and schools are rundown.
- Being an urban student means that there is less individualized attention given to you. Suburban schools can spend more time with each child.
- Being an urban student means that classes are constantly changing and you lose and gain classmates all the time.
- Being an urban student means that school supplies are minimal, if they exist at all.
- Being an urban student means that you are neglected.

What Didn't We Ask? Keepin' It Real

- Being an urban student means no field trips. Just because we live in a city with museums and shows doesn't mean that our students go to them. Most of my students (grade 9) have hardly ever left Brooklyn.
- Being an urban student means often not being safe in school. Shouldn't schools be safe places?
- Being an urban student means that you go to the worst schools and have the least qualified teachers. Why is that?
- Being an urban student means that the odds are stacked against you.
- Being an urban student means being a guinea pig for every new school initiative and pilot program, and those programs don't work.
- Being an urban student means that you know that there are two urban school systems—for the poor and for the rich. The rich get everything and the poor get all the attention in the news.
- Being an urban student means always being depicted in the media as a criminal, a gangster, or a loser.
- Being an urban student means that you live in a high-rise building, with small or broken elevators . . . so it is a walk-up.
- Being an urban student means that you know which areas of town are for the haves and which are for the have-nots. Even though the schools are public in both areas, the middle- and upper-class schools (the white schools) have more.
- Being an urban student means living in a "bad neighborhood."
- Being an urban student means being told that you are bad because you are from the inner city.
- Being an urban student means being aware of corruption in every part of the education system. Someone is always getting paid off, someone is always getting laid off.
- Being an urban student means being overlooked.
- Being an urban student means you have to think about everything: how to get to school, will you be safe? Suburban and rural students don't think about those things.

Naturally my students are defining urban schools as they see them. However, these generalized statements are also stereotypical of media depictions of urban schools and characteristic of the assumptions made by nonurban teachers and parents.

In *Nineteen Urban Questions*, we have attempted to address some of the issues raised by these teachers. We talked about differences between urban students and nonurban students. We also talked about why we were committed to teaching in urban schools. The above statements and my tenor in this chapter are not designed to discuss urban education in a deficit model. To see it in this light is to use middle-class, white, suburban eyes. Part of understanding urban schools is to *keep it real*; the only way to enlighten and empower ourselves and our students is to tell it like it is, analyze it, understand how power works to maintain conditions—and then change it.

Because urban education means dealing with masses of children and teachers, urban politicians have a tendency to make large pronouncements, intending to solve all problems and address all issues. Instead of meeting individual needs, urban school districts are subject to quick and drastic changes. We must remember that along with large populations of students, there are large populations of voters. In their attempt to capture sizable quantities of votes, cover-up solutions are rampant. I remarked in class one day that I had noticed the large amount of scaffolding on different school buildings in town. Along with that observation, I made the comment that after several years, the scaffolding was usually still up, and I saw no apparent improvement in the buildings. A student told me that her fiancé was a vice-president of a scaffolding company. She laughed and said that the scaffold was there on a semipermanent basis. There were no plans to change or improve the building—the scaffolding was erected to make sure nothing fell from the building, and to be in constant readiness in case contract bids were sent out. The city actually spent enormous amounts of money maintaining scaffolding—not buildings.

Our school systems in urban areas are surrounded by scaffolds. These have come from different contractors: Edison Schools Inc., *Success for All*, No Child Left Behind. All of them have been erected, maintained, and seen by citizens, but none of the buildings has been touched.

We live in a co-op in the Lower East Side of New York City, in a building maintained by the residents, all of whom are shareholders. Our maintenance fee is used for improvements. We have a board of directors that decides on any of these changes. A couple of years ago we came into the lobby to see that all the walls were being prepped for tiling. The next day, it sported new marble tiles. Three or four days later, the tile had been torn down. I thought that the inspector must have found a problem with the grouting. Several days later, new tile was up. The next week, the tile was down a second time, new boxes of tile were piled up in the hallways. The tile went up, and one more time it was taken down. After three full rounds of tile, I was sure that either the tile contractors were incredibly stupid, or the inspectors amazingly inefficient. Weeks later I asked my neighbor about the tile. He laughed and replied with the usual 'you aren't from around here, are you?' look. I was informed that in order to fulfill obligations with different contractors and accept bids from several different companies, the inspectors are paid off to insist on multiple installations. Everyone was happy with this arrangement—inspectors were compensated and the three tile suppliers and contractors had all been given work. That was just how things ran in the city.

Success for All (SFA) was created through a seed grant from the American government. The highly successful program was instituted in myriads of urban schools. It is found in many cities. Practicing a rote, strictly monitored, teacher-proof program, urban administrators bought the program as the final solution for urban ills. The SFA group (which is a for-profit organization) now lists yearly profits in the hundreds of millions of dollars—but urban scores have not changed, and many teachers have left due to the lack of pedagogical stimulation of the program. In 2003, New York City ceased using SFA and began a hybrid program which drew from different models in the United States and Australia. Within ten years, all five boroughs of New York City have gone through two tile contractors. Who will be the next?

Urban curriculum is often designed to cover the most with the least. Urban assessment is designed to evaluate what was learned by all and usually results in scores that reflect the successful few. Authors in this book who wrote about curriculum were attempting to whet your appetite to create uniquely urban curricula. In order to reach students and capture their talents, we believe that it must be returned to the hands of skilled teachers. Using a Vygotskian notion of cultural contextualization, we believe that curriculum must be designed with the students, their lives, and their needs in mind. Student work and teacher content must be directly and intimately connected with the lives and cultures of urban students. Evaluation and assessment must also reflect these conditions.

Our authors addressed the domestic and physical surroundings of urban students. In this short book, we are unable to discuss in detail other issues that make urban education unique. We talked about the determined creativity of urban kids and parents, yet we didn't expand on the conditions in which urban families create. Issues like transportation, security, travel distance, building safety, and work stoppages are also unique to urban settings. We didn't mention movement—the mechanical and kinesthetic actions which govern cities: movement to and from school, work, and home. Conditions of movement, cost of movement, and the often limitless time spent in merely moving from one place to another on the urban grid must be considered. Urban movement can be exhausting. One must calculate large portions of time on either end of any appointment in order to be assured of appropriate arrival. That is a cultural context that suburban and rural children are not engaged in. Urban movement depends on the mechanical, as it is guided by the human. Along with that notion, we didn't discuss labor, the difficulties of being in an urban labor force and the complexities faced by urban laboring families. Again, these are chapters for the next book.

Issues of urban health were discussed in brief. The case of urban asthma was addressed. With every word that was spent on discussing asthma, another urban disease or malady was not discussed. Helen Epstein, writing in the *New York Times Magazine* (10/12/2003) asked, is simply living in America's urban neighborhoods "Enough to Make You Sick?" Discussing epidemic heart conditions, arthritis, asthma, infant mortality, AIDS, and many other maladies, the article correlates disadvantaged neighborhoods as a geographic determinant to poor health—to a "ghetto miasma." Lead-paint poisoning, dust and fallout from debris, rat and mouse droppings, nonworking toilets, limited facilities for the handicapped, mold, poor or no ventilation, lack of air conditioning—we didn't get to those conditions. And solutions or assistance? Without health inspectors and school nurses, these conditions will remain unchanged for years. Urban health is an essential issue, yet in most schools of education it is never even addressed, let alone investigated. When was urban health made an issue in an election campaign?

What about immigration? We discussed non–English speakers, using Spanish-speaking students and parents as our example. With the scores of different languages spoken by students in urban schools in North America, we need a discussion of the unique needs of the culture and student. When can that discussion take place? When can an IEP (individualized education plan) be designed for a student from Kiev, Jakarta, or Juarez? How are teachers to connect and communicate with caregivers who have arrived with little or no instruction in American education?

The issues continue. Like the bulging urban population, the questions bulge in our minds. Teaching in urban settings is layered with complexity and unending questions. Our authors have attempted to begin the conversation with you. We have opened the door to question the issues, the possible remedies, and most importantly, the cultural context of teaching in the urban environment. Urban teaching is not for everyone. It is for the creative, strong, committed few. I hope you are one of the few, I hope you join us.

Contributors

Philip M. Anderson is Professor of Secondary Education at Queens College and a Professor of Urban Education at The Graduate Center of The City University of New York. He previously served as chair of both programs and as Acting Dean of Education at Queens. He most recent publications include *Pedagogy Primer* (Lang, 2009), various book chapters on curriculum and culture, and co-editor of Joe Kincheloe, et al., *Urban Education: A Comprehensive Guide for Educators, Parents, and Teachers* (Rowman & Littlefield, 2007).

Rochelle Brock is the executive director of The Urban Education Teachers Program at Indiana University Northwest in Gary, Indiana. She is the author of *Sista Talk: The Personal and the Pedagogical.*

Roymieco A. Carter teaches at Wake Forest University. He is a well-known graphic arts instructor and multimedia artist.

Antonia Darder teaches at the University of Illinois, Champaign-Urbana. She is an author, poet, painter, and political activist. Her work is focused on the struggle against oppression and the annihilation of the spirit. Her works include: *The Critical Pedagogy Reader; Latinos and Education: A Critical Reader; After Race, After Multiculturalism; Reinventing Paulo Freire: A Pedagogy of Love.*

Vanessa Domine is an Associate Professor of Educational Technology at Montclair State University in New Jersey, USA. She teaches both traditional and online courses in education and technology within MSU's teacher education program. Her research and scholarship focus on media and technology literacies among young people and the pursuit of democratic practices within education. She is the author of *Rethinking Technology in Schools* (Peter Lang, 2008) and the Executive Director of Project Literacy Among Youth (PLAY) at http://www.kidsplay.org. Domine currently serves on the Board of Directors for the National Association for Media Literacy Education.

Christopher Emdin is an Assistant Professor of Science Education at Teachers College, Columbia University. His dissertation, "Exploring the Contexts of Urban Science Classrooms: Cogenerative Dialogues, Coteaching and Cosmopolitanism" was named the Outstanding Doctoral Dissertation by Phi Delta Kappa International. Emdin has taught middle school Mathematics and Physical Science, High school Physics and Chemistry. He is currently developing the Urban Science Education Center at Teachers College, Columbia University, where he works with students and teachers to develop new theoretical frameworks for studying, and practical approaches for improving, urban science education

David Forbes teaches at Brooklyn College and directs the Counseling Program in the Department of Education. He is the author of *Boyz to Buddhas: Counseling Urban High School Male Athletes in the Zone.*

Katia Goldfarb is the Chairperson of Family and Child Studies at Montclair State University. A well-known scholar in the field of education, family studies, and children, she is an accomplished teacher and speaker.

Greg S. Goodman is an assistant professor of education at Clarion University of Pennsylvania. His scholarship includes publications and research in the areas of at risk youth, alternative education, multicultural education, and outdoor education. He is the series editor for Peter Lang Publishing's Educational Psychology: Critical Pedagogical Perspectives. Greg's books include *Educational Psychology: An Application of Critical Constructivism, The Outdoor Classroom, Ubiquitous Assessment, Critical Multicultural Conversations,* and *Alternatives in Education.*

Kecia Hayes teaches at Montclair State University. She is the author and editor of several books and articles on urban education. She has worked frequently with Joe L. Kincheloe as an editor and collaborator on several books: *Teaching City Kids: Understanding and Appreciating them; The Praeger Handbook of Urban Education;* and *Metropedagogy: Power, Justice, and the Urban Classroom.*

Leah Henry-Beauchamp is an Associate Professor at Kean University in the Department of Special Education. Her research interest includes school reform, inclusive education, and health related educational issues. Her most recent publication dealt with Type 11 diabetes within urban educational settings.

Adriel A. Hilton is a public policy fellow at the Greater Baltimore Committee, where he works closely with the CEO and policy advisors to research, develop, and advocate a public policy agenda related to the organization's work. His academic and professional interests are related to public policy and higher education with particular emphasis on minorities' access to and persistence in higher education. Most recently, Hilton was a

Frederick Douglass Teaching Scholar at Clarion University of Pennsylvania in the College of Education.

Winthrop Holder is a New York City school teacher. He has worked in several SUR schools (Schools Under Review), schools deemed by the city to be "the worst." His students have worked with him in each context to establish literary magazines and "One Mic" spoken word and Hip Hop events. He is the author of *Classroom Calypso: Giving Voice to the Voiceless.*

Valerie J. Janesick is Professor of Educational Leadership and Policy Studies, University of South Florida, Tampa. She teaches classes in Qualitative Research Methods, Curriculum Theory and Inquiry, Foundations of Curriculum, Ethics and Educational Leadership and Program Evaluation. She is the author of *The Authentic Assessment Primer, "Stretching" Exercises for Qualitative Researchers,* and *The Assessment Debate: A Reference Handbook.*

aroon Kharem teaches at Brooklyn College. He is the author of *A Curriculum of Repression: A Pedagogy of Racial History in the United States.*

Joe L. Kincheloe (1950-2008) was the Canada Research Chair in Critical Pedagogy in the Department of Integrated Studies in Education at McGill University. He was the author of over 55 books and hundreds of articles. Kincheloe's most recent book was *Knowledge and Critical Pedagogy,* Springer, 2008. His research/teaching involved devising and engaging students in new, more intellectually rigorous, socially just ways of analyzing and researching education. He developed an evolving notion of criticality that constructed innovative ways to cultivate the intellect as it worked in anti-oppressive and affectively engaging ways. With Shirley Steinberg, Joe founded the Paulo and Nita Freire International Project for Critical Pedagogy (http://freireproject.org), which aims to improve the contribution that education makes to social justice and the democratic quality of people's lives.

Luis F. Miron A well known speaker and writer, Miron is the author of *Resisting Discrimination: Affirmative Strategies for Principals and Teachers,* and with Mickey Lauria, *Urban Schools: The New Social Spaces of Resistance.*

Priya Parmar is an Assistant Professor of Adolescence Education at Brooklyn College – City University of New York (CUNY). Her research interests include critical and multiple literacies, curriculum development, youth and Hip Hop culture, and other contemporary issues in the field of Cultural Studies in which economic, political, and social justice issues are addressed. Some of her published works include *Knowledge Reigns Supreme: The Critical Pedagogy of Hip Hop Activist KRS-ONE,* "Spoken Word and Hip Hop: The Power of Urban Art and Culture," (with Bryonn Bain) in *City Kids: Understanding, Appreciating, and Teaching Them,* and co-editor (with Shirley Steinberg and Birgit Richard) of *Encyclopedia of Contemporary Youth Culture, Volumes I and II.*

Elizabeth Quintero is Professor at California State University, Channel Islands. She has collaborated with Mary Kay Rummel to write two texts, *American voices: Webs of*

Diversity (Quintero, Elizabeth P. & Rummel, Mary K. 1998, Columbus, OH: Merrill Education) and *Becoming a Teacher in the New Society: Bringing Communities and Classrooms Together* (Quintero, Elizabeth P. & Rummel, Mary K., 2003. New York. Peter Lang Publishers). Both books use critical pedagogy as a frame for activist learning and research in a variety of contexts. She is the author of *Problem-posing with Multicultural Children's Literature: Developing Critical, Early Childhood Curricula* and Refugee and Immigrant Family Voices.

Tina Siedler holds an MPH in health education, and is currently completing her Master's in the Art of Teaching at Montclair State University.

Lourdes Diaz Soto holds the Goizueta Endowed Chair in the School of Education at Dalton State College. She is the author of *Making a Difference in the Lives of Bilingual/Bicultural Children; The Praeger Handbook of Latino Education in the U.S.;* and *Power and Voice in Research with Children.*

Shirley R. Steinberg is the author of numerous books and articles on cultural studies, media literacy, qualitative research, and issues of race, class, gender, and sexuality. Most recently, Steinberg teaches at McGill University, where she directed The Paulo and Nita Freire International Project of Critical Pedagogy. She is the founding editor of *Taboo: The Journal of Culture and Education,* and has established the Baeza Congress, an international collection of scholars and students engaged in issues of social justice, global networking, radical love, and indigenous knowledge. An international speaker and frequent contributor to TV, Radio, and print, Steinberg's most recent book is *Diversity and Multiculturalism: A Reader, 19 Urban Questions: Teaching in the City,* and, with Joe Kincheloe, *Christotainment: Selling Jesus Through Popular Culture.*

Judith Summerfield is Professor of English and Dean for General Education at Queens College of The City University of New York, and Professor of Urban Education at The CUNY Graduate Center. Previously she served as Acting Dean of Arts and Humanities at Queens and University Dean of Undergraduate Education for the 19-campus CUNY system (2003-2009). Recipient of major awards from The Carnegie Foundation for the Advancement of Teaching and the Modern Language Association for her teaching and pedagogical writing, her most recent work is editing *Reclaiming the Public University: Conversations on General and Liberal Education.* (Lang, 2007) and the forthcoming edited volume, *Transformative Spaces in Higher Education: Creating Community for Teaching/Learning* (Springer, 2010).

Linda Ware researches the impact of P-12 special education practices on the lives of children, families, and teachers in work that has informed her numerous publications in disability studies and education. She was formerly the program head for the undergraduate and graduate special education program at City College/CUNY and now teaches at SUNY Geneseo in education, women's studies and the interdepartmental program where she offers the writing seminar, *Disability in America.*

Jan Valle's educational experience spans three decades beginning as a special education teacher at the middle and high school level and later, work with a developmental pediatrics clinic as an educational diagnostician on an interdisciplinary evaluation team. Her experience as an educator, parent advocate, and mother inform her recent book, *What Mothers Say About Special Education* (2009). She is co-author, along with David J. Connor, of an inclusive education textbook. She is on the faculty of City College/CUNY.

NEW QUESTIONS POSED BY:

Regina A. Bernard-Carreno, Baruch College

Joanne Carris, City of New York Public Schools

Andrew H. Churchill, McGill University

George J. Sefa Dei, Ontario Institute of Studies in Educaiton

Venus Evans-Winters, Illinois State University

Lee Gabay, City of New York Public Schools

C.P. Gause, University of North Carolina, Greensboro

Rodney Handlesmann, McGill University

Brian C. Johnson, Bloomsburg University of Pennsylvania

Curry Malott, D'Youville College

Elizabeth Meyer, Concordia University

Donal E. Mulcahy, Wingate University

Bernardo Pohl, Langham Creek High School

Kathalene Razzano, George Mason University

Mary Weems, John Carroll University

Studies in the Postmodern Theory of Education

General Editors
Joe L. Kincheloe & Shirley R. Steinberg

Counterpoints publishes the most compelling and imaginative books being written in education today. Grounded on the theoretical advances in criticalism, feminism, and postmodernism in the last two decades of the twentieth century, Counterpoints engages the meaning of these innovations in various forms of educational expression. Committed to the proposition that theoretical literature should be accessible to a variety of audiences, the series insists that its authors avoid esoteric and jargonistic languages that transform educational scholarship into an elite discourse for the initiated. Scholarly work matters only to the degree it affects consciousness and practice at multiple sites. Counterpoints' editorial policy is based on these principles and the ability of scholars to break new ground, to open new conversations, to go where educators have never gone before.

For additional information about this series or for the submission of manuscripts, please contact:

Joe L. Kincheloe & Shirley R. Steinberg
c/o Peter Lang Publishing, Inc.
29 Broadway, 18th floor
New York, New York 10006

To order other books in this series, please contact our Customer Service Department:
(800) 770-LANG (within the U.S.)
(212) 647-7706 (outside the U.S.)
(212) 647-7707 FAX

Or browse online by series:
www.peterlang.com